# The American Indian Experience

A
*Profile:*
1524
*to the*
*Present*
*Edited*
*by*
*Philip*
*Weeks*

# The

# American

# Indian

# Experience

*Forum Press, Inc.*

*Arlington Heights*

*Illinois 60004*

Copyright © 1988

Forum Press, Inc.

All rights reserved

This book, or parts thereof,
must not be used or reproduced
in any manner without written permission.
For information, address the publisher,
Forum Press, Inc., 3110 North Arlington Heights Road,
Arlington Heights, Illinois 60004-1592.


Library of Congress Cataloging-in-Publication Data

The American Indian experience.

  Includes bibliographies and index.
     1. Indians of North America—History.   2. Indians
of North America—Social life and customs.   3. Indians
of North America—Government relations.   I. Weeks,
Philip.
E77.2.A463   1988        973'.0497        87-33182
ISBN 0-88273-117-3


Manufactured in the United States of America
92 91                 3 4 5 6 7 EB

To Dick and Helen Weeks, whose examples demonstrated to me the art of raising a family with care, tenderness, and devotion;

To Bill and Anne Darvas, who have shown me more love and generosity than any son-in-law has a right to expect, much less receive;

To Rich Weeks (and his family), in whose company I shared the special exhilarations only youth brings once;

And to Michael and Jeanette Weeks, who make my world a bright and happy place.

# Contents

# Foreword

**A**s Americans have become less enthocentric and increasingly pluralistic, they have been more willing to accept and understand other cultures. The increase in scholarly investigation of racial, ethnic, and minority diversity within American society suggests a growing desire for a more inclusive, deeper, and hopefully richer understanding of the national heritage. An important dimension of this heritage is that of the American Indians, whose story has been described as "among the most intriguing in history . . . ," one which has "captivated scholars for centuries."[1] American Indian history, once it became involved in the politics and economies of Europe, and later the United States, was one of overwhelming conflict within tribes, with other tribes, and in the relationship with Europeans and Americans. Not that such characteristics were unknown in Indian societies prior to contact with Europeans and Americans, for most certainly they were. However, from the point of contact onward, these characteristics were magnified and exacerbated, while the stakes of cultural and racial survival were never higher or more in jeopardy. The post–Columbian American Indian experience, "from the point of view of the Indians themselves," asserts one historian, "meant the harassing, the overwhelming, and the extinction of a set of ancient, multiform cultures by a monolithic invasion from far away."[2]

The purpose of this volume is to present a profile of relations among American Indians and Europeans, and later Americans, from the early sixteenth century onward. As with so much of American Indian history since contact with Europeans and Americans, it can best be told from the framework of white history. Indian policy was formulated from the white perspective, rather than the reverse. And it was, and largely still is, whites who so influentially and dramatically affected the American Indians, their lives, culture, and history. The volume is introductory. It does not purport to tell the entire story of the history of relations between Indians and whites. It is aimed at providing general readers and college students with an overview of significant aspects of the American Indian experience with those people who ultimately controlled the continent.

1. Arrell Morgan Gibson, *The American Indians: Prehistory to the Present* (Lexington, Mass., 1980): 2.
2. William T. Hagan, *American Indians* (Chicago, 1979): ix.

*The American Indian Experience* draws on the expertise of seventeen specialists to highlight this saga. One value of this work is that it presents a synthesis in each chapter of the most current reflections of these scholars on recent scholarship and their own area of competence. Each author has included a section of suggested readings following his or her chapter. These selections will be an aid to those readers who wish to expand their knowledge of the American Indian experience or a particular facet of this subject. While this volume follows a time line from 1524 to the present, it was not always possible to place all topics in a strict chronological pattern. Similarly, there are instances were the topic of one chapter overlaps the material of another chapter. While a conscientious attempt was made to keep this to a minimum, the drama that unfolds in this volume is not easily compartmentalized, especially the closer one draws to the present. A case in point is chapters fifteen, sixteen, and seventeen, which have in common different aspects of some similar topics. The first probes one of the pivotal federal policies in the twentieth century, the policy of termination and relocation. The second investigates one important facet of the contemporary experience for an increasing number of Indians—life in urban America, a reality shaped in no small measure by the policy of termination and relocation. The third closes the volume by comprehensively examining developments since the Second World War, including, appropriately, a discussion of termination, relocation, and urban Indians, among other topics. Efforts have also been made to maintain a rough equality in the average length of chapters. Yet, some are longer than the average, a reflection that time, geography, material, and methodology are important considerations, too, in the exposition and development of a topic.

I would like to express gratitude to the contributors for so willingly agreeing to participate in this venture and for their conscientious and first-rate work. Special thanks is also extended to Arthur S. Link of Princeton University for his interest and support of this project; to Martha Kreger for skillfully taking the manuscript the final editorial mile; to *Timeline* magazine for generously reassigning previously published material for use as the basis for chapter ten; to my attorney James F. Burke, Jr., for expert handling of a number of concluding details; and to the individuals to whom this volume is dedicated for reasons which have made each special in my life.

Philip Weeks

# The Authors

David Wallace Adams, Cleveland State University, is the author of "Education in Hues: Red and Black at Hampton Institute, 1878–1893," *South Atlantic Quarterly* (1977), "Schooling the Hopi: Federal Indian Policy Writ Small, 1887–1917," *Pacific Historical Review* (1979), and "Self-determination and Indian Education," *Journal of American Indian Education* (1974).

Donald J. Berthrong, Purdue University, is the author of *The Southern Cheyennes* (1963) and *The Cheyenne and Arapaho Ordeal: Reservation and Agency Life in the Indian Territory, 1875–1907* (1976), as well as several edited works.

Blue Clark, California State University in Long Beach, has published in many scholarly journals on the subjects of ethnic studies and American Indian history.

Thomas W. Dunlay, University of Nebraska, is the author of *Wolves for the Blue Soldiers: Indian Scouts and Auxiliaries with the U.S. Army, 1860–1890* (1982).

Donald L. Fixico, University of Wisconsin—Milwaukee, is the author of *Termination and Relocation: Federal Indian Policy, 1945–1960* (1986), "Tribal Leaders and the Demand for Natural Resources on Reservation Lands," *The Plains Indians of the Twentieth Century* (Peter Iverson, ed.) (1985), and "Twentieth Century Federal Indian Policy," *The Scholar and the Indian Experience* (William Swagerty, ed.) (1984).

Arrell Morgan Gibson, University of Oklahoma, is the author of numerous works including *The Chickasaws* (1971), *The Kickapoos* (1963), and *The American Indians: Prehistory to the Present* (1980).

William T. Hagan, State University of New York College at Fredonia, is the author of *American Indians* (1961, 1979), *Indian Police and Judges* (1966), *United States-Comanche Relations* (1976), and *The Indian Rights Association* (1985).

Robert H. Jones, University of Akron, is the author of *The Civil War in the Northwest* (1960), *The Roads to Russia* (1969), and *Disrupted Decades: The Civil War and Reconstruction Years* (1973), and he is coauthor (with Fred A. Shannon) of *The Centennial Years* (1967).

George W. Knepper, University of Akron, is the author of *Akron: City at the Summit* (1981), *An Ohio Portrait* (1976), *New Lamps for Old: One Hundred Years of Urban Higher Education at the University of Akron* (1970), and "Ohio Indians in Fact and Fancy," *Hayes Historical Journal* (1981).

Roger L. Nichols, University of Arizona, is the author of *The American Indians: Past and Present* (3rd ed., 1986), *Stephen Long and American Frontier Exploration* (1980), *Natives and Strangers: Ethnic Groups and the Building of America* (1979), and *General Henry Atkinson: A Western Military Career* (1965).

Theda Perdue, Clemson University, is the author of *Slavery and the Evolution of Cherokee Society, 1540–1866* (1979) and *Native Carolinians: The Indians of North Carolina* (1985), and the editor of *Nations Remembered: An Oral History of the Five Civilized Tribes, 1865–1907* (1980) and *Cherokee Editor: The Writings of Elias Boudinot* (1983).

James P. Ronda, Youngstown State University, is the author of *Indian Missions: A Critical Bibliography* (1978), *John Eliot's Indian Dialogues* (1980), and *Lewis and Clark Among the Indians* (1985).

Bernard W. Sheehan, Indiana University, is the author of *Seeds of Extinction: Jeffersonian Philanthropy and the American Indian* (1973), *Savagism and Civility: Indians and Englishmen in Colonial Virginia* (1980), and "The Problem of Moral Judgments in History," *South Atlantic Quarterly* (1985).

Dwight L. Smith, Miami University, is the author of *From Greene Ville to Fallen Timbers* (1952), *Indians of the United States and Canada* (2 volumes, 1974, 1983), and *The War of 1812* (1985), and is coauthor (with C. Gregory Crampton) of *The Denver, Colorado Canyon, and Pacific Railroad* (1986).

Graham D. Taylor, Dalhousie University, is the author of *The New Deal and American Indian Tribalism* (1980), "Management Relations in a Multinational Enterprise: The Case of Canadian Industries Ltd.," *Essays in Ca-*

*nadian Business History,* Tom Traves, ed., (1984), and is coauthor (with Patricia Sudnik) of *Du Pont and the International Chemical Industry* (1984).

Philip Weeks, University of Akron, is the author of "From War to Peace: Rutherford B. Hayes and the Administration of Indian Affairs, 1877–1881," *The Old Northwest* (1985), and is coauthor (with James B. Gidney) of *Subjugation and Dishonor: A Brief History of the Travail of the Native Americans* (1981) and (with James J. Rawls) of *Land of Liberty: A United States History* (1985).

Donald L. Worcester, Texas Christian University, is the author of *The Apaches: Eagles of the Southwest* (1979), *The Chisholm Trail: High Road of the Cattle Empire* (1981), *The Spanish Mustang: From the Plains of Andalusia to the Prairies of Texas* (1986), and *The Texas Longhorn: Relic of the Past, Asset of the Future* (1986).

# Part I  From Contact to Removal

James
P.
Ronda

# 1. Black Robes and Boston Men

Indian-White Relations in New France and New England, 1524–1701

**S**ometime toward the end of the fifteenth century, two worlds virtually unknown to each other began to drift into a common orbit. That common orbit would eventually become a collision course, producing changes with unimagined consequences. On the eastern side of the Atlantic were a multitude of peoples, cultures, and languages loosely united by a militant Christian ideology, growing acquisitive capitalism, mounting national rivalries, and an occasional spark of Renaissance curiosity. These were the tribes of western Europe. On the far shore of the great ocean were other peoples busy wresting a living from the land, rivers, and lakes of the northeast woodlands. In hunting camps, fishing stations, and palisaded villages these men and women shaped their days to a rhythm of weather and land. These were the tribes of eastern North America. Soon Micmac merchants, Huron diplomats, and Mohawk warriors would face French traders, Jesuit missionaries, and English farmers. It would be a confrontation that would forever change tribes on both sides of the great sea.

The long and often complex tale of relations between Europeans and native peoples in the land stretching from the Gulf of St. Lawrence to southern New England and from the Atlantic west to the eastern Great Lakes has neither a clear beginning nor a tidy cast of characters. One beginning may have come from the nameless and unlettered European cod fishers who ventured toward Newfoundland and the Grand Banks in the years before Columbus. Perhaps the two worlds inched closer when John Cabot made his 1497 voyage for the English crown from Bristol to northeastern North America. Cabot's landfalls are as uncertain as the identities of those native people he met. But whatever his misconceptions about North America as part of Asia, Cabot brought Micmacs and Beothuks into the path of venturesome and enterprising Englishmen. For

*3*

the French, latecomers to the race for American empire, a beginning came in 1524 when the Florentine navigator Giovanni da Verrazzano was employed by Francis I and a syndicate of French merchants to find the ever-elusive Northwest Passage. From his ship, the *Dauphine,* Verrazzano explored the American coast from South Carolina north to Maine. With a keen eye for land, natural resources, and people, Verrazzano produced the first European survey of the eastern edge of what was to become the United States. His experiences with native people from New York harbor to Narragansett Bay and the Maine coast are especially important for what they reveal about future relations between Europeans and coastal Algonquians.

After a brief mid-April visit to New York Bay and Delaware bands in the region, Verrazzano sailed north to Narragansett Bay. There, in present-day Rhode Island, Verrazzano and his crew spent nearly two weeks exploring the coast and enjoying the company of friendly Narragansett Indians. While the Narragansetts and their Pokanoket neighbors were perhaps seeing Europeans for the first time, they already had some European trade items among them. The "sheets of worked copper" that some Narrangansetts wore as prized ornaments were probably pounded out pots from the codfish and fur trade further north. Always the careful observer, Verrazzano noted Narrangansett techniques of house construction, canoe building, and land management. While the explorer tended to see all Indians through the haze of a classical golden age, when he did report above native ways Verrazzano was remarkably accurate. As for the Narrangansetts, they were fascinated by Europeans weapons, ironware, textiles, and mirrors. But the Indians showed no special interest in exchanging native implements for those of the tribe from across the sea. Confident of their own place on the bay, the Narrangansetts were neither threatened nor cowed by the *Dauphine* and her crew.

What Verrazzano portrayed as an almost Edenic environment of prosperity and harmony ended when the explorers headed northward along the coast of Maine. While changes in the landscape were obvious, Verrazzano was not immediately aware that he had passed from a zone of initial contact between Europeans and Indians to a zone of previous and sometimes violent encounter. That became painfully evident when the *Dauphine* entered Casco Bay and the territory of the Abenakis. It was not the first time people of that bay had seen the tall ships with their outlandish strangers. Abenakis had already engaged in a fur trade with cod fishers. More important, the Abenakis had three years earlier suffered unrecorded troubles at the hands of the Portuguese adventurer, Joao Alvarez Fagundes.

Abenakis wanted the metal goods offered by the cod fishers, but they had learned to be wary of the traders. Sudden violence, kidnappings, and sexual assaults had been part of the coastal fur trade long before Verrazzano dropped anchor in Casco Bay. In a telling passage in his report to King Francis I, the explorer described how his men were compelled to trade and how canny the Abenakis had become.

> If we wanted to trade with them for some of their things, they would come to the seashore on some rocks where the breakers were most violent, while we remained in the little boat, and they sent us what they wanted to give on a rope, continually shouting to us not to approach the land; they gave us the barter quickly, and would take in exchange only knives, hooks for fishing, and sharp metal.

Verrazzano's comments suggest some important conclusions about Indian-European contact before formal French and English ventures pushed inland from the Atlantic. Among the Delawares and Narragansetts, Verrazzano found people confident enough to offer him a warm welcome. There was interest in European goods but no special desire to possess them. So long as Verrazzano's actions were peaceful, these coastal Algonquians regarded him as a wonderous curiosity cast up by the sea. On the other hand, the Abenakis already had learned the bitter lesson that these strangers were to be approached with caution. If the cod fishers wanted fur, it would be given only on Abenaki terms. Indians would determine the trading site, the goods bartered, and the rate of exchange. And on no account would the unpredictable Europeans be allowed to occupy the land. The people of Casco Bay were not yet caught up in market forces beyond their control, nor were they dependent on outsiders for the tools of life and the weapons of war. With political power still in native hands, it was still possible to be selective in accepting pots without trading away sovereignty and identity. But how long native people in the woodlands could remain their own masters in the face of invaders seen and unseen was an open question. At the beachhead on Casco Bay at least, the war was being waged and won on native terms.

After the voyages of John Cabot in 1497 and 1498, the continuity of English exploration and Tudor expansion in the Northeast was temporarily interrupted. On the other hand, French efforts begun by unknown Breton fishermen and continued by Verrazzano were now extended in 1534 by Jacques Cartier. A master mariner from St.-Malo, Cartier had already made voyages to Newfoundland and Brazil. More important, the

Breton crews of his two ships were experienced in the cod fisheries of Newfoundland. Cartier's first journey to what would become the heart of New France was intended to locate a passage to Asian markets. Notions of a lucrative fur trade with native people and thoughts of an even semi-permanent French base were not part of the original plans.

Early in the summer of 1534, Cartier poked and probed his way through the Strait of Belle Isle between Newfoundland and Labrador and then turned south to sail along the western side of Newfoundland. Disappointed in his quest for a northwest passage, the French explorer then headed southwest toward present-day Edward Island. In July Cartier was at Chaleur Bay. It was there that he had extended contact with a large number of Micmac Indians. Like the Abenakis, Micmacs had traded with Europeans before Cartier, and they assumed that the French adventurer was yet another stranger in search of furs. With pelts fixed on sticks, the Micmacs avidly pursued Cartier to such an extent that at first the explorer believed he was under attack. Once it was plain that Indian intentions were commercial and not military, a trade in knives, hatchets, and beads flourished. Although some three hundred Micmacs crowded to see the French, Micmac women remained at a cautious distance. When Cartier later moved to Gaspé Bay and met some St. Lawrence Iroquois, the same pattern of trade and caution was repeated. European traders had often kidnapped coastal Indians, and Cartier seems to have followed the same path. Domagaya and Taiognoagny, two sons of a St. Lawrence Iroquois headman named Donnacona, were taken by the French. Cartier may have had in mind the use of these two Indians as guides for future expeditions. Donnacona may have seen the taking of his two sons as a means to establish proper relations with the Europeans. While the native people who met Cartier perhaps viewed him as another cod fisher turned trader, Cartier was not interested in gathering furs or even in encouraging such an enterprise. Determined to find the Northwest Passage, he probed the waters around Anticosti Island and became convinced that the St. Lawrence River was indeed the entrance to the famed passage to the Far East. Pleased with what seemed a successful reconnaissance, Cartier returned to France in early September to seek support for a second voyage.

Cartier's second voyage to the Gulf of St. Lawrence (1535–1536) was the most important French undertaking of the period and one that had lasting consequences for relations with native people. From his two Iroquois informants, Cartier learned about the size of the river and Gulf of St. Lawrence and the presence of a wealthy "kingdom of Saguenay." Prospects for the river being an eastern passage coupled with immediate rewards from Saguenay were enough to give Cartier financial backing from Philippe de Chabot, admiral of Brittany. Guided by Domagaya and Taiognoagny, Cartier took his three ships into the Gulf of St. Lawrence in mid-August 1535. By September, the French expedition had entered what the two Indians called Canada, the territory of the St. Lawrence Iroquois living at Stadacona. Cartier's progress up the river had not gone unnoticed, and, on September 8, the Stadacona headman, Donnacona, came to greet the French and his long-absent sons. Once Donnacona had made an especially animated speech of welcome, the whole body of Indians and French moved to Stadacona. While there was no question that Cartier and his crew were welcome visitors at Stadacona, there were mounting tensions. Those troubles were probably caused by Cartier's insistence on traveling to the rich and powerful village of Hochelaga. Donnacona surely did not want to be passed by as Cartier handed out gifts and what seemed the unique European power to both resist and cure disease.

In an especially powerful episode, Donnacona, Taiognoagny, and some village elders disguised three men in costumes of horn and feathers to represent messengers from the god Cudouagny. Taiognoagny breathlessly reported to Cartier that the god had prophesied a death in ice and snow for the French if they ventured to Hochelaga. But the effort to deter Cartier failed, and on September 19 the French pushed up the river toward Hochelaga.

As Cartier and his party made their way up the river they met increasing numbers of Indians. When the explorers encountered a welcoming party of some 1,000 Hochelagans, it seemed a sure sign that the voyage was on the brink of success. On October 3, the French tramped from the river to the main Hochelaga village. What they saw was a typical fortified Iroquoian town. The village was surrounded by a triple palisade some thirty feet high. Inside the palisade were walkways so that village defenders could rain down stones and arrows on would-be invaders. Once inside Hochelaga, Cartier found a busy, crowded town of some fifty longhouses. Laurentian Iroquois longhouses were typically 100 feet long and about 30 to 40 feet wide. Cartier estimated that at least 1,000 people lived in Hochelaga, making it the most substantial native settlement yet seen by the French.

If Cartier was impressed by the size and strength of Hochelaga, the villagers were equally taken with the strangers from the river. The French explorers became an instant tourist attraction as Indians crowded around to see and touch Cartier and his men. The Hochelaga chief, an elderly and partially paralyzed man, was brought to Cartier. The chief's long speech seemed part welcome and part fascination with whatever powers the strangers might possess. Even more revealing of Hochelagan feelings were the efforts by many Indians to touch and stroke French bodies. As Cartier explained it, "the girls and women of the village, some of whom had children in their arms, crowded about us, rubbing our faces, and other parts of the upper portions of our bodies which they could touch." Indians who assiduously plucked facial hair always found hairy Europeans a source of amazement. But there was more here than cosmetic curiosity. The village chief, or *Agouhanna,* made it clear what all the touching was about when he made signs for Cartier to touch him "as if he thereby expected to be cured and healed." The Hochelagans did not see Cartier as the Aztecs viewed the Spaniard Cortez—a returning god ready to wreak vengeance on the unbelieving and disobedient. Rather, the French were seen as mysterious beings with supernatural healing powers.

Cartier's mission at Hochelaga was neither therapy nor ethnography. The Northwest Passage and an empire of trade continued to hold the French imagination. Despite a considerable language barrier, Cartier did obtain valuable geographical information from his Hochelaga voyage. Most important, what he learned about a kingdom of Saguenay and the role of the Ottawa River would prove crucial for future French-Indian trade and diplomacy. Although Cartier did not fully understand what he was hearing, his Indian informants were telling him about the Hurons and other northern peoples and their role in a vast trade network that extended throughout the Great Lakes and stretched as far west as Lake Superior. Cartier was in no position to take advantage of this information, but his successors would make exceptionally good use of it.

When Cartier returned to Stadacona he found that those French remaining behind had felt threatened by the Stadaconas. Such threats, real or imaginary, had impelled the French to build a substantial fort at the banks of the St. Charles River. The palisades, ditches, and cannons might have kept out the Indians, but the defenses could not repel malnutrition and scurvy. For five months—from November 1535 to April 1536—Cartier and his men were prisoners of the Canadian winter. With dozens of his men dead or dying of scurvy, survival finally depended on Domagaya, who showed Cartier a vitamin-rich potion to defeat the disease.

Before he left for St.-Malo in the spring of 1536, Cartier engaged in one last piece of confused Indian diplomacy. Still fascinated by Donnacona's tales of rich and powerful empires deep in the interior, Cartier decided to kidnap the chief and make him a prize exhibit in France. In collusion with a rival Stadacona headman, Cartier lured Donnacona and his sons to the St. Charles fort. Once inside, the Indians were held under close arrest. Donnacona evidently accepted his fate.

Cartier's second voyage did not generate the interest and enthusiasm of his first. The explorer's reports were less promising, and the presence of North American natives in French courts and salons was no longer a startling event. Domestic religious and political troubles and the lack of any quick profit delayed official action until 1538. With a temporary lull in internal difficulties, Francis I could again imagine a growing French presence in America. The plans this time called for a permanent settlement on the St. Lawrence River that would serve as a base from which to invade and conquer the kingdom of Saguenay. And beyond that distant kingdom, Asia beckoned. To meet these goals a substantial expedition of ten ships and large numbers of men and women were assembled. When the recruiting slowed, planners turned to the local jails for potential settlers. Command of the expedition was given to Jean-François de la Rocque, sieur de Roberval. Roberval was an experienced soldier who seemed to have all the qualifications and energy for such an undertaking. Bypassed for command, Cartier was appointed master navigator. Despite what seemed careful planning, the Roberval-Cartier expedition of 1541–1543 failed. Defeated by scurvy, poor timing, bad luck, and the disillusionment of kingdoms just beyond reach, both Cartier and Roberval retreated from what must have seemed an intractable continent.

The failure of the Cartier-Roberval venture did not spell the end of French-Indian contacts in the Gulf of St. Lawrence. Quite the contrary. While official France was caught up in the bloody Wars of Religion, Breton and Basque fishermen continued to expand their commercial activities off Newfoundland and in the Gulf of St. Lawrence. Evidence is sketchy, but it is plain that by the end of the century at least 500 ships were summering in the region, fishing for cod and whales. At Tadoussac, where the Saguenay River joins the Gulf of St. Lawrence, Basques established an important whaling station.

What developed from these maritime enterprises was a very active but disorganized trade in furs. In the period after Cartier, fur became the principal focus for relations between the French and native peoples. The exchange of furs for metal and textile items had many attractions for both trading partners. Indians found the products of European industry useful as both luxury goods and as utensils for daily life. At this point at least, the trade did not seem to threaten either Indian political independence or economic self-sufficiency. Trading furs with French sailors seemed just one more extension of native exchange networks that had long been a part of Indian life. For the French, furs seemed an ideal substitute for illusory gold and diamonds. Although the broad-brimmed beaver felt hat had not yet become the rage of European fashion, there was a rapidly expanding market for furs. What was in place by the end of the century was an economic partnership between French traders and Indian pelt hunters and processors. At summer fairs, first around Tadoussac and later further upriver, French merchants and Indian suppliers haggled over price and supply. Indians quickly became skilled bargainers, pitting one French trader against another and never taking the first offer. Both partners enjoyed initial success—success made even more certain when European fashion eventually decreed that every gentleman wear a beaver hat. But by the beginning of the seventeenth century it was plain to many French in the maritime fur trade that wide open competition would eventually destroy all hope of profit. A monopoly grant for the trade seemed a logical solution, at least in the eyes of the French. Monopolies were cheap for the crown to grant but virtually impossible to enforce. Grants were made for posts at Île de Sable (1598) and Tadoussac (1600), but both were dismal failures. But those failures did not daunt French entrepreneurs who saw the trade as a guarantee of quick profit.

Pierre du Guast, sieur de Monts, was one of those venturesome aristocrats who imagined a controlled partnership with Indians as the easy path to riches. In 1603 de Monts obtained a ten-year trade monopoly from the crown. The grant required that de Monts established a permanent settlement with at least sixty residents. Taking a page from Cartier's bitter winter experiences, de Monts intended to construct his base south of the Gulf of St. Lawrence at Port Royal in Acadia. While the de Monts venture eventually collapsed, the entrepreneur's cartographer, Samuel de Champlain, was far more successful as an explorer and trader. In addition and more to the point, Champlain had a broad vision of his own destiny and that of France in America. In the first years of the seventeenth century, Indian-French relations, both on the St. Lawrence River and along the Atlantic coast, would be closely tied to Champlain's initiatives.

Beginning in 1604, Champlain undertook a series of successful explorations along the New England coast. In coastal New England he was able to gain valuable trading partners among the Penobscots, Abenakis, and Micmacs. Because of eventual English penetration in the region, the French were ultimately less successful in New England than at the other focal point for trade selected by Champlain. In July 1608, he established a modest trading post on the St. Lawrence River at the present-day site of Quebec.

Champlain settled on that strategic site because he believed that Indian trade canoes heading for Tadoussac would find Quebec a more convenient market.

Beyond questions of survival, the most pressing issue facing Champlain was finding native trading partners. The Laurentian Iroquois of Stadacona and Hochelaga were gone, and many of the Montagnais and Algonquians continued to frequent Tadoussac. Champlain's quest for partners began in the summer of 1609, when sixty Algonquian and Huron warriors appeared at Quebec asking for support in a raid against their traditional Iroquois enemies of present New York State. Without fully understanding the consequences of his decision, Champlain agreed. He actually had little choice. Unless he made commercial arrangements with Hurons and Algonquians, the entire Quebec project would collapse. Selecting two men to accompany him, Champlain followed the war party up the Richelieu River and into what is now Lake Champlain. Once there, the warriors came upon some two hundred Mohawks. In the fray that followed, Champlain's guns provided the decisive edge—more for their psychological effect than any immediate physical results.

It has become a historical commonplace to claim that Champlain's participation in this raid and in a subsequent one in 1615 produced the coming decades of violence between the French and the imperial Iroquois Confederation. Champlain's actions certainly did nothing to lessen already mounting tensions between northern peoples and the Iroquois. And his growing commercial ties with Hurons and Algonquians did worry and anger the Iroquois. However, the troubles and suspicions predated Champlain. The French had been trading and arming those Indians the Iroquois saw as rivals and enemies long before Champlain. As Canadian historian W. J. Eccles has recently written, "Champlain was merely an agent of existing forces; he did not create them."

Champlain's participation in raids against the Iroquois increased his stature among the Hurons and Algonquians, but fur trade profits at Quebec remained unacceptably low. In 1612 a desperate Champlain undertook a bold and innovative strategy. He sent young Étienne Brulé to live with the Hurons. Because Huron trade routes were a family privilege, Brulé's connection to a Huron family became a crucial link for the French. And what Brulé did also set a pattern for other Frenchmen as they made personal connections in native groups. While the fur trade steadily increased after 1613, those advances brought unexpected problems for the French. If anyone was the junior and dependent partner in the trade, it was Champlain. Hurons and Algonquians quickly realized the power they held and began to pressure Champlain for more active support against the Iroquois. Such a demand—one that the French trader could not ignore—was filled with danger for partner and adversary alike.

By 1615 eastern North America had become an intricate and potentially dangerous web of alliances and trade networks. There were now two rival trade centers. Dutch merchants on the Hudson River at Fort Orange (present-day Albany) had made firm commercial agreements with the Iroquois. The Dutch-Iroquois trade, which later evolved into an English-Dutch exchange, was of major economic and strategic importance since it provided Iroquois warriors with the firearms necessary to wage war against those Indians armed by the French. Even more important, the Fort Orange trade made the Iroquois dependent on European weapons technology and would eventually force natives to expand their trapping enterprise once regional supplies of fur were trapped out. The French were now established at Quebec and had made at least marginally successful agreements with the Hurons and Algonquians. Tensions between native groups were nothing new in the woodlands, but the dangers and the rewards had been changed with the arrival of the Europeans, their guns, iron pots, and diseases.

Between 1615 and 1629, relations between the French and their native partners grew closer. In 1615 Champlain had felt compelled to make a journey to the Huron country to reassure his edgy partners. That trip brought unexpected results when the Hurons forced him to join them on a raid against the Iroquois at Lake Ontario. In a sharp engagement on October 10, 1615, Champlain was wounded. Because Huron and Algonquian warriors did not press the advantage to "defeat" the Iroquois, Champlain believed that battle a loss. But Hurons and Algonquians had achieved more than Champlain realized. There was a temporary halt to damaging Iroquois raids. For the Iroquois, 1615 was a genuine turning point. Survival required access to furs, and, with local supplies dwindling, the Iroquois felt compelled to look north to richer grounds. But so long as northern Indians boasted French guns and French allies, the conflict would be one for survival itself.

As uncertain as all this was, the fur trade at Quebec did continue to grow. But French planners like Cardinal Richelieu expected more from America than an isolated cluster of trade houses huddled along the St. Lawrence River. The absence of a permanent settlement with a stable agricultural base worried the cardinal. It seemed unthinkable that French power could ever be built on anything as insubstantial as fur. To strengthen and diversify the French presence, in 1627 Richelieu created the Company of New France. The company was intended to make Quebec a genuine settlement colony. With substantial funds and the support of influential governmental officials, the company seemed a certain success. But in the following year, England and France were at war, and Quebec was an early victim in the conflict. In 1629 English privateers led by the Kirke brothers laid siege to and finally captured Quebec. With the St. Lawrence lost, Champlain was forced to return to France, and, when the nation itself plunged into a long war, all seemed lost for France in America.

By the time Champlain returned to France, the international situation had changed dramatically. France and England had signed the Treaty of St.-Germain-en-Laye, which gave back to the French their North American claims. The revitalized Company of New France was reorganized with new capital, and Champlain was commissioned lieutenant of New France. At the end of May 1633, Champlain and three ships loaded with supplies, a few soldiers, and even some women and children arrived at Quebec. When a great fleet of Huron canoes loaded with pelts came at the end of July, French profits and survival seemed assured.

The same ships that brought Champlain and the trade goods also carried Frenchmen whose lives would become bound up with the Indian future. Father Paul Le Jeune and other Jesuits were the first missionaries of that order in New France. In the years to come, the Jesuits would prove to be the single most important force for change—often unwelcome and unpredictable change—in the lives of native people. Jesuits like Le Jeune came to New France with a long tradition of missionary work among non-European peoples. That approach insisted that each culture did have some incidental values and customs that might be preserved in the new Christian order. However, throughout the early years in New France, Jesuits pursued a cultural revolution that called upon potential converts to abandon traditional ways to become European in life-style and Christian in belief. There were few mission groups better equipped to tackle what amounted to the creation of an Indian new world. Jesuits were personally committed to the course, often to the extent of openly courting martyrdom for the faith. Superb Jesuit education in languages prepared prospective evangelists to deal directly with Indians without relying on interpreters. The Jesuits also understood the role of ceremony and imagery in native religious practice. All told, the Jesuits were the most potent force for change to appear in the Northeast. What they were to demand went far beyond the requirements of the fur traders or the price extracted by disease.

Perhaps the most revealing episode in Indian-mission relations in New France focuses on the Jesuits and the Hurons in the years between 1634 and the late 1640s. In 1634 Father Jean de Brébeuf led Jesuits to work in the Huron villages. During the first year among the Hurons, the black gowns remained something of a curiosity and a tourist attraction. Objects the missionaries carried with them, including a magnet, clocks, hand tools, and meal grinders, sparked interest. Hurons were even more fascinated with writing as a form of nearly magical communication. But for all this interest the Jesuits gained no converts. Hurons tolerated Jesuit strange ways and social blunders because the missionaries were viewed as honored French guests. To anger the guests might endanger the valuable trade with Quebec.

However, Huron hospitality began to wear thin by 1637–1638. Two powerful forces were behind this shift in attitude. First, a growing number of Hurons began to resent Jesuit mission practices. Although the Jesuits could record native cultural patterns in the annual *Jesuit Relations* with admirable clarity and objectivity, daily mission techniques were not so nearly dispassionate. The Jesuits used ridicule and verbal abuse against Huron rituals and dances. These ceremonies were what the Hurons called *onderha*, the foundation on which life itself rested. To fail to perform the *onderha* and to slander those who danced in the traditional way seemed to court disaster. But Huron anger at Jesuit assaults on native ways was overshadowed by a second concern. The arrival of the Jesuits in Huronia coincided with a devastating series of epidemics. To Huron eyes the Jesuits seemed mysteriously immune from the diseases; the pestilence even appeared to follow the black gowns wherever they went. By 1638–1639 large numbers of Hurons were convinced that the missionaries were dangerous sorcerers intent on wreaking havoc with terrifying diseases. While some village councils debated whether to kill the Jesuits as an act of patriotic self-protection, at least one village gathered up all its European trade goods and cast them into a nearby river in an act of purification. Because Jesuits routinely baptized only those on the edge of death, the belief that the black gowns spread illness gained wide credence.

Stunned by their sudden rejection, Jesuits in Huronia became even more strident in their denunciations of native traditional practices. The missionaries were critical of Huron sexual mores, child-rearing practices, and the whole round of dances and festivals that gave shape to the traditional year. If the Jesuits found much to dislike in Huron life, the Hurons were equally forceful in their often perceptive comments on European faith and practice. Hurons argued that Christianity overemphasized death at the expense of enjoying life. Indians found the prohibition against labor on Sunday to be poor economics. And the European moral precepts, especially those concerning divorce and premarital sexual relations, made little sense. Finally, Hurons pointedly noted that most French persons they knew paid little or no attention to the rules so earnestly propounded by the men in black gowns.

By 1639 there were precious few Hurons willing to listen to the Jesuits, much less let them into villages and longhouses. At the same time, as the number of listeners was decreasing, the band of missionaries and lay workers was increasing. There were now some twenty-seven priests and brothers in Huronia. In order to give some focus to mission work in Huronia, a central post named Ste. Marie des Hurons was constructed.

To the casual observer of Huronia in 1640, little had changed in the years of French contact. That year was marked by general good health and a productive harvest. But a closer look would have revealed a Huron people facing serious internal problems. Those troubles were not the immediate result of the epidemics. The epidemics of the late 1630s had struck with awesome severity, killing nearly one-half of the Huron population. Chiefs, clan leaders, elders, and craftsmen were among those lost. The measure of the loss was not in numbers but in the social impact. At a crucial time in Huron history, the Hurons had lost many important leaders. That crucial time was the result of increased troubles with the Iroquois. By 1640 the Iroquois had nearly exhausted local supplies of beaver. If the Iroquois could not find and control new sources of supply, their vital connection to traders on the Hudson would vanish. Fueled by economic pressures, tensions between Iroquois and Hurons began to grow in intensity and violence.

Bruce Trigger, the most prominent student of Huron life and culture, has characterized the years between 1640 and 1647 as "the storm within." Indeed, the Hurons were buffeted by winds both inside and outside their villages. Faced with a mounting Iroquois threat and a loss of leadership, the Hurons became increasingly dependent on the French for security and leadership. That dependence benefited French merchants who were able to exploit the trade as never before. But that dependency was most evident in the Christian mission. As disruption aided the traders, so it suddenly brought the mission a flood of converts. These newly minted Huron Christians accepted the gospel for a number of complex reasons. It is important to understand those reasons since they illuminate not only the Huron situation but the larger arena of Indian-white relations. There is no doubt that some of the converts made the decision for purely secular reasons. Christian Indians obtained preferential treatment in the fur trade, and the French would arm only those who were converts. Conversion meant protection in stormy times. But there was more here than Indians trading belief for guns and pots. Many Hurons were genuinely impressed with Jesuit piety. More important, Huron confidence in traditional ways was shaken when the shamans failed to protect the villages against disease. Since healing was at the center of so much native belief, Hurons looked at Christianity as a more certain way to survive. In the same way, Jesuit priests presented themselves as substitute shamans.

Those converts, so eagerly welcomed and counted by the Jesuits, sparked an immediate response from surviving Huron shamans. In 1645–1646 there appeared in several Huron villages what might aptly be termed revitalization movements. Such movements were an attempt to regain lost power by reemphasizing and returning to traditional ways. Huron revitalization focused on visions of native prophets and a renewed zeal for the ceremonies that were the *onderha*. But despite these efforts, the revitalization movement failed. It could not blunt the pain of constant Iroquois raids nor could it restore confidence in ancient patterns of life. The Hurons were now living in an Indian new world—a world over which they had little control.

That new world was marked by danger and dependence. But it was equally characterized by division. For the first time Hurons were pitted against each other in an ideological conflict. Traditionalists insisted that the old ways were sufficient and that abandoning them was the cause for disease and suffering. Huron Christians were just as militant in their claims. At the very time when the villages needed to be united to face the Iroquois onslaught, Huronia was weakened by deep divisions.

What Trigger has called "the bitter harvest" came in the years between 1647 and 1650. Those were years of tragedy and destruction. They marked the virtual end of Huronia as a sovereign political entity. Having failed to intimidate the Hurons, the Iroquois developed a new and effective strategy. Mohawk and Seneca warriors engaged in constant attacks on villages and often drove deep into the heart of Huronia. While Hurons put up a spirited defense, guns from Dutch traders gave the Iroquois a distinct edge. A Huron attempt to find allies among the Onondagas failed when Huron diplomats were ambushed and killed in January 1648. And throughout the period the Jesuits counted many new converts, all seeking refuge in a dying world.

The deathwatch formally began in the spring of 1649 when the Iroquois mounted an extraordinary assault on the Huron settlements. Some one thousand warriors were involved in the attacks. The villages of St. Ignace and St. Louis were destroyed, and soon afterward fifteen other villages were abandoned. Huronia was choked with refugees as most fled to Jesuit protection. Unsure of what course to follow, the missionaries resettled some 300 families on Christian Island in the Georgian Bay. By the coming of winter, nearly 6,000 people were on the island. With little food and inadequate shelter, thousands died. Fewer than 300 people survived the winter. What had once seemed so prosperous and secure had vanished in the bitter snows of Christian Island.

Because the destruction of Huronia is such a crucial event in the history of the colonial Northeast, it is worth taking a moment to explore causes and consequences. Jesuit explanations—the wrath of God on unbelievers—and Huron answers—a lack of faithfulness to the *onderha*—seems less than satisfying to modern minds. What happened in the last generation of Huronia is a classic case of cultures, both native and European, in collision.

It is possible to isolate three central forces that led to the collapse of Huronia. The fur trade has often been pointed to in Indian-white relations as a culprit producing dependency and weakness. There is no doubt that Hurons welcomed the chance to participate in a trade system that brought many material rewards. But as skilled traders long before the advent of the French, the Hurons knew how to manage commerce without losing cultural identity. The fur business did make Hurons dependent on the French for firearms. However, the fur trade by itself did not plant the seeds of the bitter harvest.

We come closer to the root problem by looking at disease. Throughout the northeastern woodlands, disease was one of the central forces for change in native life. As Francis Jennings so aptly put it, the European invaders of America found not a virgin land but a widowed one. The shattering epidemics in Huronia destroyed more than thousands of lives. The waves of disease engulfed Huron culture, severed links with the past, and effectively killed much of the future. And of course the epidemics prompted a crisis of confidence in faith that allowed Jesuit missionaries to gain converts.

The Jesuits themselves were unwitting agents of chaos in Huronia. The mission dream was to produce a Huron society purified of its cultural sins and united by Christianity. What the dream became was a nightmarishly divided society, half Christian and half traditionalists, and fully at war with itself. The Jesuits believed that they could remove the *onderha* and replace it with Christian belief and practice, without doing any damage in the process. But the Jesuits succeeded in promoting the very conflicts and divisions they sought to avoid. All of this was done in villages under attack by disease and implacable foes.

Had the Hurons not been facing a massive Iroquois invasion during the 1640s there might have been time to cope with the changes wrought by disease and the missions. But Iroquois raiders did not give that respite. The spring offensive of 1649 could only be slowed by valiant Huron efforts.

The demolition of Huronia was not only a shattering blow to native people, it also had immediate consequences for the French. The fur trade, the life-support system for New France, had been severely hurt by the Iroquois blockade. Jesuit missions were destroyed and missionaries were killed, forcing what amounted to a thorough reappraisal of conversion tactics. Throughout the 1650s, Iroquois warriors continued to threaten the very existence of New France.

By 1663 it was plain that New France was on the edge of collapse. Such a collapse would not endanger the French national economy but it would be a blow to the growing prestige of the Sun King, Louis XIV. If New France was to survive, aid and direction had to come from the crown. With empire in mind, Jean Baptiste Colbert, minister of marine, began to develop a grand strategy for the colony and all its peoples. That strategy was to create an overseas empire founded on a diversified economy. Colbert sought to encourage agriculture and light manufacturing along the St. Lawrence River. The minister believed that the fur trade diverted men and capital away from the central colony and also invited further Iroquois conflict. Colbert understood the imperial value of trade as a means to secure Indian allies but he feared that the trade by itself could never provide a reliable foundation for French power in North America.

But none of those grand plans could ever come to pass so long as New France lacked competent leadership and sufficient military force to break the Iroquois stranglehold. To that end, Colbert and the king sent Jean Baptiste Talon as intendant (civil administrator) and Alexandre de Prouville, seigneur de Tracy, to take charge of military affairs. De Tracy was given substantial numbers of troops, including the experienced Carignan-Salières regiment. In 1666 the French were able to inflict sufficient pain on the Mohawks that the Iroquois fur trade blockade was temporarily lifted. The essential problem for New France—its geographical location in relation to that of the Iroquois—could not be altered, but at least the situation had been eased.

Colbert imagined that a lessening of tensions with the Iroquois might allow the St. Lawrence colony to develop as he had planned. The irony was that once there was a measure of security from the Mohawk and Seneca raids, the fur trade sprang back to life. Even though a glut of fur from northern Indians depressed market prices some 50 percent, the profits were still handsome. By the 1670s Montreal merchants and Jesuit missionaries were extending French influence into the western Great Lakes. It was an expansion filled with danger for both the French and native peoples.

The central figure in that expansion was the governor general of New France, Louis de Buade, compte de Frontenac. Frontenac's vision of New France was every bit as vast as Colbert's, but it was fundamentally different in character. While Colbert thought in terms of a balanced economy focused on the St. Lawrence settlements, Frontenac sought an extensive fur trade empire that would dominate the Great Lakes and outflank the English by finding water routes south from the Great Lakes. Frontenac's commercial empire was built on fur trade posts and Jesuit mission stations. The explorations of Marquette and Joliet and La Salle, for all their drama and romance, were designed to extend the trade system and bring more Indians into it.

Frontenac's success was not without a price. At the very time when the French were bidding to monopolize the western trade, the Iroquois were thinking of doing the same thing. Having blasted the Hurons but with a temporary check to their designs by de Tracy, the Iroquois were now intent on expanding their power into the Ohio Valley and the Illinois country. Once the Five Nations made peace with their neighbors in 1676, they were free to surge westward toward the lakes.

The storm broke in September 1680 when a flotilla of Iroquois war canoes invaded the Illinois country. Frontenac had been warned of the invasion by the Jesuits, but he ignored the warnings. Although most French traders and missionaries managed to escape, one large Illinois Indian village was destroyed. The next twenty years were some of the most troubled in the long history of French-Indian relations. In the summer of 1684 a French force under Governor General Joseph-Antoine le Febvre de La Barre was humiliated in an abortive invasion of Iroquoia. Despite the best efforts of skilled soldiers like the Marquis de Denonville, New France seemed ever closer to disaster at the hands of the Iroquois. In August 1689, when a force of some 1,500 warriors attacked Lachine, a settlement just outside Montreal, the end seemed very near.

What lay ahead was a ten-year round of bloody raid and counterraid. In those years, the French-Iroquois conflict spilled over into English territories, both in New York and in New England. The common brutalities of the conflict had a sobering effect on both the French and the Iroquois. For their part, the people of the longhouse gradually realized that in an effort to achieve Great Lakes hegemony they had overextended their forces. The French undertook a similar reevaluation of their role in North America and reached a very different conclusion. If the Iroquois after 1701 would pursue a policy of militant neutrality, the French were determined to challenge English rivals and win the race for empire. In August 1701 a throng of Indian diplomats met with French officials at Montreal to negotiate a lasting peace. The Iroquois gained security and the French were free to exploit the western fur trade. Only the English seemed the losers, having depended on the Iroquois to shield them from French attack. The treaty of 1701 marked the end of a century of conflict. It also heralded the coming age of imperial wars between France and England and their respective colonies.

It has become historical wisdom to insist that the French had better relations with native peoples than the English. The argument usually runs that the Gallic temper was better suited to native ways and even found intermarriage attractive. Such an interpretation would have surprised the French and their longtime foes the Iroquois. The French were as ethnocentric as their English rivals. But certain accidents of geography and history did give French traders, soldiers, and missionaries a distinct edge in the struggle to win Indian hearts and bodies.

First, the French central colony along the St. Lawrence River was built on lands not currently occupied by any Indian group. The French, unlike the English, did not have to begin the colony with an act of dispossession.

Second, the nature of the fur trade required active Indian cooperation. Whatever Frenchmen thought of Indians and native ways, the traders needed Indians as partners.

Third, unlike the English, the French economic strategy did not require occupation of the land.

Fourth, Jesuit mission Christianity after the fall of Huronia tended to downplay the disruptive "civilization" program pursued by earlier missionaries. Jesuits sought converts but did not demand cultural suicide.

Fifth, the fur trade created a large number of men with personal and family ties to native groups. Such links worked against overt violence toward Indians.

There are few more enduring images in American history than Pilgrims and Indians enjoying a peaceful first Thanksgiving together. That event has become part of national mythology perhaps because we all have the uneasy feeling that the peace will all too soon be shattered by violent conflicts, death, and dispossession. Few parts of the history of Indian-white relations in North America have produced more passion and passionate writing than the troubled dealings of Puritans and coastal Algonquians. Puritan apologists have described the New English as evenhanded dispensers of justice while critics have characterized the same people as backwoods thugs and murderers. In the process of defining heroes and villians, historical truth—rarely a clear-cut commodity—has been a casualty. The concluding portion of this chapter will examine the lives of Indians and English New Englanders as they groped toward an uncertain future.

English interest in what became known as New England began long before there was any thought of permanent settlement in the region. In the 1580s English adventurer and Renaissance man Sir Humphrey Gilbert turned his attention to the region he called Norumbega. Interested in the economic possibilities around what is now Narrangansett Bay, Gilbert sent a ship to the bay in 1580. When Gilbert himself journeyed across the Atlantic in 1583, he turned away from coastal New England toward Newfoundland. Gilbert's death at sea the same year put an effective damper on English efforts to do any more than fish in New England's bountiful waters.

English activities along the coast began to change in both frequency and character in the years after 1602. A series of important but often ignored expeditions established an English presence on the coast and had far-reaching consequences for Indian-English relations. The first of those probes came in the spring of 1602 when the enterprising earl of Southhampton hired Captain Bartholomew Gosnold and the ship *Concord* for a trading venture to the coast. The Southhampton plan was to have at least some of the crew winter on the coast as the seeds of a future settlement. When the *Concord* reached Cape Neddick on the coast of southern Maine, the ship's company was astounded to meet Indians sailing a Basque shallop and dressed in European clothing. The Indians' dress and their words spoken in broken English were plain evidence for long contact with Europeans. Gosnold decided to sail south toward what he eventually named Cape Cod. While the journey was an economic success—something proudly announced in an important pamphlet written by John Brereton—relations with the Pokanoket Indians were less than tranquil. When *Concord* sailors built a fortified camp on Cuttyhunk Island and refused to trade, Indians took those actions as a sign of hostility. While the English saw trade in purely economic terms, native people viewed the same exchange as a means to establish friendship and balance between strangers. In early June relations were tense enough to produce an attack on an English party foraging for food. One English sailor was wounded. That affair was sufficient to convince Gosnold to abandon any plan to winter on the coast. With his stores of sassafras (believed to be an effective remedy for syphilis), fur, and cod, Gosnold could claim success and downplay any native troubles.

The *Concord* expedition, with its promise of economic reward, prompted a syndicate of Bristol merchants in 1603 to organize a follow-up voyage. Led by Captain Martin Pring, two trading vessels made the Atlantic crossing and landed at Provincetown harbor. Pring was prudent enough to know that images in promotional pamphlets might not square with New England realities. His first move was to build a fortified camp. Pring intended the fortress to serve as a base for gathering sassafras. Early contacts between Pring's men and Nauset Indians were friendly despite English worries about sudden attack. In one particularly charming encounter, Indians and English gathered around a blazing fire to sing and dance while a cabin boy played his guitar. But for reasons that are no longer clear, initial friendship dissolved into mutual suspicion and hostility. As the Pring party was ready to leave, large numbers of armed Nausets surrounded the English camp and seemed ready to attack. Pring was able to escape, leaving behind yet another piece of English-Indian misunderstanding.

Once again the profits produced by the Pring enterprise spoke louder than any troublesome relations with native people. In 1605 George Weymouth was hired by an odd assortment of Plymouth fish merchants and English Catholics to take the ship *Archangel* on a voyage to northern New England. For some two weeks, there was an active trade between the English and Kennebec and Abenaki Indians. This sort of trade—tobacco and furs—was nothing new to coastal people who had already enjoyed a brisk exchange with French traders. The powerful Penobscot sachem went so far as to invite Weymouth to visit his Penobscot River settlement. But Weymouth feared ambush and rejected what might have become a diplomatic triumph. Instead, the English kidnapped five Indians for use as informants on future voyages.

In the period immediately following the Gosnold-Pring-Weymouth voyages, English merchants and colonial promoters continued to focus on the New England coast. The ill-fated Sagadahoc colony and the trading voyages to the south sponsored by Sir Ferdinando Gorges pointed to steady English interest. Despite that interest, by 1614 there was still no permanent English presence in New England. More important, the English image current among many coastal peoples was a decidedly negative one. The English were viewed as dangerous, unpredictable men who might suddenly kidnap unsuspecting Indians. Even more significant for native people, the English did not seem to understand the noneconomic aspects of trade. English merchants seemed obsessed with profit margins while Indians frequently saw trade as a diplomatic means to establish friendship and equality between strangers.

The pace of English activity in New England quickened in 1614 with the arrival of John Smith. So often identified with the history of early Virginia, Smith played a crucial role in bringing native and English worlds into contact. In 1614 Smith was engaged by merchant Marmaduke Rawdon to direct a New England voyage searching for whales and precious metals. If whales and gold proved elusive, Smith's instructions allowed him to search for fur and fish. Smith did not find whales, and, while most of his crew traded for furs, Smith took a small detachment on an exploring jaunt. That reconnaissance produced a detailed map of the southern New England coast and a full description of the native peoples of the region. That Smith named the region "New England" is a clue to the shape of the future. While he was certain that hordes of gold and mountains of copper were to be found in North America, Smith had a very different vision for New England. Attracted by the obvious prosperity of Indian villages and the richness of the land, Smith proposed the extension of an English landed domain, a "new" England, to challenge native occupation. Smith's map of New England illustrated that vision by replacing Indian towns with settlements bearing English names.

Smith knew that his agrarian New England would be a frontal assault on native people. Drawing on his Virginia experience and his self-image as an English Hernando Cortés, Smith proposed strong means for dealing with native reactions to an English invasion. Historian Neal Salisbury has summed up Smith's New England Indian policy as "the proper combination of deception, intimidation, and brute force." Smith believed that a stoutly armed force would be necessary for not only the protection of any future colony but also as a means to extort corn from native neighbors. Smith's dream of an agricultural, heavily armed New England ready to use force against its neighbors did not come to pass under his leadership. But Smith's prescription did not go unnoticed by those English folk who would soon venture to a distant Plymouth.

In the typical telling of the growth of English New England, there is hardly a missed step between John Smith's landed vision and the Pilgrim landing in 1620. But the years between John Smith and William Bradford were ones of terrifying change for native people. In the years between 1616 and 1618 parts of the New England coast were devastated by epidemic diseases. The nature of that disease has always been a source of controvery. Neal Salisbury has argued that the killer was a "variety of plague," while ecological historian William Cronon maintains that the disease was chicken pox since native New England lacked the rats and human population densities required for the plague. Whatever the precise nature of the epidemics, the consequences were plain. The coastal Abenakis lost most of their population. But the region that suffered the most dramatic population lost was the southern coast from Massachusetts Bay to Plymouth Bay. Whole villages recorded by Champlain and Smith simply vanished. Entire tribes like the Patuxets were annihilated. The diseases not only visited horror on one generation but gravely weakened subsequent ones. The epidemics continued after 1618, and each wave of sickness made Indians less able to resist the growing power of English settlers intent on engrossing the land.

The potent vision of the first Thanksgiving tends to obscure the tension and violence between the English and coastal Indians from the moment of landing in 1620. That the Pilgrims expected trouble was plain in their hiring of Miles Standish as military adviser. Like his contemporary John Smith, Standish believed that Indians would respond only to massive shows of force and firepower. Standish molded Pilgrim Indian policy to suit his perceptions of natives as hostile savages. Standish made Plymouth an armed camp and from that Separatist fortress militiamen sallied forth to rob graves and extort corn.

To the Pokanoket sachem Massasoit, the English must have seemed bewildering neighbors. Some sort of balance had to be achieved with the bearded strangers. Because the Pokanokets had suffered severely in the recent epidemics, Massasoit may well have seen the troublesome English as protectors against the always dangerous Narragansetts. In March 1621, Squanto and Samoset arranged a meeting between Plymouth officials and Pokanoket representatives. The treaty that emerged from the gathering is worthy of notice since it reveals the unequal measure of power already present in New England Indian-white relations. Both parties promised to aid each other in case of attack and agreed to attend meetings unarmed. Reflecting the constant fear that they were about to be overwhelmed by Indian warriors, Pilgrim diplomats drafted the first treaty provision declaring that natives were not to "injure or do hurt" to the English. Significantly, nothing substantive was said about possible English assaults on Indians. The treaty's next stipulation made it even more plain that Plymouth was to be the fountainhead of all law and justice. Revealing the powerful ethnocentrism that was to dominate virtually all Indian-white relations, the 1621 treaty required Indians guilty of crimes against the English to be sent to Plymouth for punishment. It would have been unthinkable for Pilgrim lawmakers to suggest that those who wronged Indians be punished by native justice. It was only at the conclusion of the treaty that some provision was made for the punishment of those English who took Indian goods. After making clear native responsibility for theft, the treaty added that English settlers would be punished by the colony for infractions against Indians. As Neal Salisbury has aptly put it, the English "regarded the treaty as one not of alliance and friendship between equals but of submission by one party to the domination of the other."

In the years that followed the 1621 treaty, relations between the New English and native peoples grew in tension, complexity, and potential for violence. Weakened by disease and threatened with constant demands for more land, New England Indians faced an uncertain future. While they had not yet fully lost political sovereignty and cultural integrity, both were under steady attack. That assault was a three-pronged invasion, pressing Indians on the flanks of land, law, and cultural values.

In so many ways the English invasion of North America was a contest for natural resources waged by two agricultural peoples. Steady pressure on the native land base became one of the major sources of friction between English and native farmers. That tension exploded into violence in 1637 in the Pequot War. Intent on extending both political sovereignty and land claims into the Connecticut River valley, colonial forces from Connecticut and Massachusetts Bay engaged in a virtual slaughter of Pequots at their Mystic River village. The treaty of Hartford (1638) proclaimed both English victory and the dissolution of the Pequot nation. It was a measure that other native people could not ignore. Land hungry English settlers would make war on any who stood in their path and would with no hesitation proclaim such violence as the will of a righteous God. Faced with increased English population and the threat of violence, many New England sachems made land cessions that could only spell economic ruin. The New English conveniently saw themselves as productive workers of the land while denying the same description to Indian farmers.

Closely linked to land troubles were heightened tensions resulting from different perceptions of law. The treaty of 1621 had lasting legal influence in Plymouth Indian-white relations. It established legal practices and fixed attitudes which would be fleshed out by subsequent legislation and court action. More important, the Plymouth treaty makers assumed that the English colony would be the center of justice and that native deeds would have to conform to English standards. The treaty assured Indians that they could gain equal justice but assumed that such justice would be English in both form and substance to say nothing of execution. All told, the treaty implied that native custom law, one of the central bonds of traditional society, was no longer valid.

The first test of legal arrangements between Pilgrims and Indians came in 1638. Late in the summer a band of runaway Plymouth servants led by Arthur Peach, "a lusty and desperate young man," murdered a Narragansett Indian boy who had been trading at the Massachusetts Bay Colony. After robbing the lad, Peach and his gang attempted to escape to New Netherland. Their flight was thwarted when the dying boy found aid among other Indians who in turn apprehended the killers. After some debate that involved Indian leaders, Roger Williams, and representatives of the Bay Colony, it was decided to try Peach and the others in Plymouth.

On September 4, 1638, the General Court of the Colony of New Plymouth was the stage for one of the most important legal actions in the history of the colony. Governor Thomas Prence and his assistants closely questioned Peach, Thomas Jackson, and Richard Stinnings. Testimony was also taken from several Narragansetts. The evidence left little doubt that Peach and his cohorts were guilty. The government knew that such a murder, if unpunished, might encourage future assaults and would surely provoke strong native response. However, the trial and its obvious verdict raised a troubling question in the minds of many colonists. Should an Englishman be tried and executed for the murder of an Indian? Driven by expediency and a genuine concern for justice, the jury sentenced all three men to death. The decision was not without its critics. Colony historian William Bradford reported that "some of the rude and ignorant sort murmured that any English should be put to death for the Indians." In spite of adverse public feelings, the executions were carried out.

The Peach case had significance far beyond its sordid details and potent outcome. The case suggests that even at this early date there were two contradictory trends present within Indian-white legal relations. The government did act quickly and forcefully to bring Peach and his men to justice. On the other hand, and perhaps more important for the future, there were many voices in the colony questioning equal legal treatment for native people. As the English colony expanded in population and geography, those voices would become louder and would eventually gain the force of both law and court practice. When some thirty-seven years later Plymouth was again the scene of another important Indian trial, the decision would not be so just.

In the years between the Peach case (1638) and King Philip's War (1675), legal affairs continued to be a source of friction between Indians and their neighbors. The Plymouth government did struggle to use law to protect native interests, as in the case of trespass by English animals on native corn-fields. The surviving evidence suggests that until the decade of the 1660s legal relations between the two peoples was characterized by almost equal measures of protection and subjugation. But as the troubles that would finally spark war grew, the scales of justice began to tip toward law as a means to intimidate. As in racial slavery, law gradually became a means for social control.

In the five years before King Philip's war, Plymouth authorities acted to broaden legal jurisdiction over Indian life. As the colony expanded toward Indian settlements and fields, the number of cases involving land and tres-pass increased. To deal with this caseload the General Court of Plymouth developed special procedures for handling these suits. In 1670 the Court ordered that all matters between Indians and English not touching capital offenses be brought first to local selectmen for a decision. This regulation did not, however, dissuade Indians from coming to Plymouth on court days to press their claims. Faced with throngs of natives on court days, the government decided in 1673 to ban Indians from the town of Plymouth during regular court sessions. Indians were permitted to attend only the July and October meetings. The 1673 act was one more step in creating a separate legal system for Indians.

Joining troubles promoted by geographical expansion and legal distinc-tions was the tension generated by Puritan missions to the Indians. While missionaries like John Eliot would have vehemently denied it, Puritan and Jesuit missions shared similar approaches to conversion. Jesuits seeking Huron converts and Puritans preaching to Bay Indians assumed that cul-tural transformation—"civilization" as they termed it—was a necessary precondition to salvation. In southern New England the civilization pro-gram fashioned by Eliot and Bay Colony Indian superintendent Daniel Gookin focused on the praying towns. These towns were to be model Christian Indian communities where converts and their own pacified lead-ers could pursue the arts of agriculture and faith without interruption from those natives yet unwashed by the gospel. By the end of the eighteenth century at least ninety-one praying towns had flourished at one time or another. More important, some 133 Indian preachers and lay leaders had given natives directions to convert to Christianity.

The praying towns and their native residents do not necessarily mean that massive numbers of New England Indians quickly saw the Puritan light and abandoned traditional beliefs for what one native woman called "the new wise sayings." In fact, Indian responses to the Christian mission reveal the full complexity of native-English relations in early New England. Praying towns attracted followers from those villages and bands that suffered the most substantial population losses. Epidemics produced not only weakened leadership but a crisis of spiritual confidence. Much of native religious belief and practice centered on healing. Powwows or priests saw their principal function as maintaining a healthy balance between individuals and supernatural forces. When the shamans could not restore health to those striken by smallpox or other unfamiliar scourges, many Indians turned to Christianity for what seemed the sovereign remedy. Christianity became a survival ideology, protective coloration in an increasingly hostile world. The praying towns were, in James Axtell's apt phrase, an Indian Marshall Plan. This is not to imply that Indians who became Christians were somehow insincere in their professions of faith. Native believers on Martha's Vineyard adapted Christianity to their own needs, creating vigorous towns and churches. For many New England Indians, Christianity was a means to preserve cultural identity.

While some New England natives found Christianity attractive, many others firmly rejected it. That rejection, voiced by shamans, sachems, and ordinary Indian folk, amounted to a thorough critique of Christian belief and English Puritan practice. In a series of forceful exchanges, Indian shamans challenged many of the theological notions proposed by Puritan divines. One Indian asked, "May a good man sin sometimes?" while another wanted to know "If a man be almost a good man and dyeth; whither goeth his soule?" Indian theologians questioned Christian notions of heaven and hell, punishment after death, and the concept of sin. Native political leaders were also critical of the mission. Sachems and village elders saw the missionaries as the advance guard of English political domination. One sachem pointedly explained what conversion would mean to his own power. "If I be a praying Sachem, I shall be a poor and weak one, and easily be trod upon by others, who are like to be more potent and numerous; and by this means my tribute will be small, and I shall be a great loser by praying to God." One Indian woman, neither shaman nor sachem, put the native critique best when she bluntly declared, "We are well as we are, and desire not to be troubled with these new wise sayings."

But the new wise sayings, the people who spread them, and the economic and political system that sustained them could not be stopped by words no matter how eloquent or pointed. The tensions produced by demands for land, legal inequities, and ideological assaults all edged native and English New Englanders closer to conflict. The Pequot War in 1637 was symptomatic of that gathering storm. Despite rivalries, arguments, and misunderstandings, a general war did not come until the 1670s. Part of the explanation for that long period of uneasy peace rests in the efforts of the Pokanoket sachem Massasoit. Unlike the Narragansett sachem Miantonomi who had early warned against English influence, Massasoit believed that some measure of peaceful coexistence with the English was possible. The sachem saw the English as valuable allies against the Narragansetts and important sources of trade goods. With those material benefits in mind, Massasoit was willing to accept troublesome English neighbors as the price for security and prosperity. Massasoit thought in terms of cooperation; the English had visions of domination in a world with no Indians to restrain expansion.

By the time Massasoit died in 1661, the Indians of New England were living in a new world not of their own making. English farmers were changing the face of the land, colonial bureaucrats were pressing for increased political control over native people, and Puritan missionaries were intent on spreading what seemed to many Indians a subversive faith. At Massasoit's death substantial political leadership in the Pokanoket bands passed to his eldest son Wamsutta or Alexander. Wamsutta found himself in a difficult position. As English fields and animals steadily encroached on native lands, the new sachem could not ignore the voices calling for some measure of resistance to the English. When Wamsutta indicated in 1662 that he would be unwilling to travel to Plymouth to assure colonial authorities of his loyalty, English officials reacted swiftly. Militia forces were dispatched, and Wamsutta was brought to Plymouth under guard. At Plymouth Wamsutta was compelled to swear loyalty to the English regime. After being released, Wamsutta, on the way back to his village, suddenly fell ill and quickly died. While his untimely death was surely the result of some disease, many Pokanokets did not find that explanation persuasive. Wamsutta's death seemed only the most recent in a string of disasters that had dogged the natives since the arrival of the English.

It was into this atmosphere of fear, anger, and distrust that Metacomet or Philip became the new sachem. Philip was now confronted with a dilemma that would become increasingly common for native leaders in the years to come. He could either acquiesce to English demands for land and claims on band sovereignty or he could risk resistance and face the Pequot fate. The alternatives seemed stark—survival under foreign domination or some kind of violent action. Those alternatives seem especially plain to us who know the outcome of what has come to be called King Philip's War. But Philip did not pursue a single policy. At various times he sought compromise while at other moments there was open talk of war. At root, Philip accepted Miantonomi's view that "for so are we all Indians as the English are, and say brother to one another; so must we be one as they are, otherwise we shall all be gone shortly."

Throughout the 1660s and into the 1670s Philip attempted to export his brand of pan-Indianism and force it into a military alliance. Despite his best efforts, Philip found his message either rejected or ignored. Tribal and band rivalries, old quarrels, and Philip's youth all worked to what can only be called a failure. When the struggle did finally erupt, native forces were unified in neither leadership or cause.

It is one of the great seductions in the study of history to assume that events of great consequence have equally grand causes. King Philip's War was surely the product of forces set in motion long before 1675. But "forces set in motion" is a phrase that tends to obscure the faces of the past and the decisions made, the alternatives chosen or rejected. The conflict was the result not of nameless forces but of human beings. The immediate spark for the war was the death of John Sassamon and the execution of three Pokanokets charged with his murder.

In December 1674, a Natick Indian named John Sassamon warned Plymouth officials of an imminent attack on the settlement by Philip and his warriors. Sassamon, who had served as a Christian preacher and secretary to Philip, was evidently bent on spreading rumors about the sachem. A recent argument between the two was behind Sassamon's falsehood. Plymouth authorities discounted Sassamon's warning and promptly forgot about his winter visit. In January 1675, a group of hunters stumbled on Sassamon's body under the ice of a local pond. Once identified as Sassamon, the body was buried without further examination.

It was not until the spring of 1675 that the full import of Sassamon's death came to Plymouth officials. They evidently recalled the Indian's claim that if Philip discovered his role as an informer, death would be certain. Plymouth governor Josiah Winslow and his assistants took this to mean that Sassamon had been murdered at Philip's order. With neither witnesses nor physical evidence, colonial officials arrested and charged three Pokano-kets. Among them was one of Philip's closest friends and advisers. It now seems plain that Governor Winslow seized on Sassamon's death as an excuse to intimidate Philip. Early in June 1675 the three men were tried at Plymouth. Mindful of the gravity of the situation, colonial officials took the unprecedented step of impaneling an Indian jury along with an English one. But the verdict was never in doubt. The Indians were found guilty and executed soon after.

The executions were a challenge that Philip could not ignore. By what right did English law extend to Indians involved in a case with no English principals? Many of Philip's warriors quickly saw the executions for what they were—judicial murder with a political motive. Those warriors began to pressure Philip for an immediate and violent response. John Easton, deputy governor of Rhode Island and an important actor in the events of the summer of 1675, caught the mounting tension after the execution. "So the English were afraid," wrote Easton, "and Philip was afraid and both increased in arms." Fearing that a general war was almost upon them, Easton and others in Rhode Island attempted to mediate Indian-English differences. The Rhode Islanders, encouraged by Philip's initial acceptance of the mediation proposal, suggested that an Indian representative meet with Governor Edmund Andros of New York. What might have proved a means to air and resolve a wide variety of troubles failed when Plymouth abruptly rejected any thought of negotiations. By the end of June the war exploded in a burst of violence that would change both Indian and Englishman.

King Philip's War was a two-summer-long fury of raid and ambush. In the first summer of the conflict, Philip's warriors waged a lightening war against outlying settlements in Plymouth and Massachusetts. Ill-equipped to fight this kind of war, the English suffered substantial casualties and were forced to abandon several towns. The campaign was going so well that Philip opened a second front in the Connecticut River Valley. But as winter approached, many of Philip's warriors left the field to support their families. As Philip's forces faded away, it was plain that his call for native unity had gone largely unheeded. Desperate for fresh warriors, Philip traveled to New York seeking Iroquois support. Mohawk elders listened patiently and then rejected Philip's pleas. The Mohawks saw no reason to become involved in a distant conflict. They also feared that involvement might endanger their crucial Albany trade connections.

While Philip's personal diplomacy failed to produce results, events on the battlefield breathed new life into the struggle. English officials were furious when they discovered that the powerful Narragansetts were openly supporting Philip. In mid-December 1675, colonial militia forces staged a daring raid on a fortified Narragansett settlement deep in the Great Swamp of Rhode Island. In the fierce fighting that followed, scores of Indians and militiamen died. The Great Swamp Fight was an English victory but it had unexpected and unwelcome consequences for the colonial cause. Stunned by the ferocity of war waged against women and children, Narragansett warriors drew even closer to Philip.

Success in war has often been the product of chance, time, and momentum. In the second summer of war those factors were increasingly slipping away form the natives and working for the English. After the initial shock of war wore off, the English began to learn to fight in the woods. Men like Benjamin Church emerged as disciplined, skilled soldiers. And the fortunes of war blessed the English in the summer of 1676. In July, Nipmuck and Narragansett forces suffered serious defeats. As the numbers of Philip's warriors dwindled and many Indians joined the English, the tide of war turned. By August 1676, Philip was a man hunted and haunted— hunted by a force led by Captain Benjamin Church and Roger Goulding and haunted by what might have been.

The end came for Philip in the cold dawn hours of August 12, 1676. Guided by an Indian informer, colonial forces under Church and Goulding trapped Philip in swampy ground at Mount Hope. In a flurry of shots Philip was killed. Church ordered the Indian's body quartered and the head taken back to Plymouth. Philip's death and the capture some time later of the influential elder Annawon effectively ended the conflict in southern New England.

The consequences of King Philip's War were shattering for both the English and the Indians. The war broke the political power of the southern New England bands. Leaders were either killed in combat or, like Annawon, were executed by the vengeful victors. Indian villages and fields were smoldering ruins. Those Indians who survived and surrendered found themselves sold into slavery in the West Indies to pay the colonial war debt. The war, with all its political and cultural devastation, made Christianity and the praying towns look even more attractive.

The price of victory for the English was very high. The war shook Puritan confidence in the righteousness of their errand into the wilderness. Many Puritan divines preached that the war was the judgment of an angry God visited on the wayward and unworthy English. Not even victory could restore a sense of special providence lost in two years of bitter forest fighting. English casualties were very high. The Plymouth colony lost in proportion to its population more men than the United States lost in the

Second World War. The war so disrupted Plymouth that the colony eventually ceased to exist as a distinct polity and became part of Massachusetts Bay. Burned villages, unmarked forest graves, and a lost sense of innocence were all part of the price.

Native people did not vanish from southern New England after 1676. But much had been lost and life was even more a struggle in a country grown hostile. With many leaders dead and land taken, New England Indians faced a bleak future.

## SUGGESTED READING

Historical writing on Indian-white relations in New France and southern New England ranges from the superb to the ridiculous, from jargon-choked monographs to well-crafted essays. The beginning student can do no better than to start with James Axtell's *The European and the Indian: Essays in Ethnohistory of Colonial America* (New York, 1981). In these graceful, challenging essays Axtell treats subjects as diverse as Indian missions, burial practices, and scalping. Some of Axtell's essays have become classics, including those on scalping and the white Indians. Because most of the examples are drawn from French and New English sources, the collection is especially appropriate. With Axtell as background, students can turn to the fine topical and chronological articles in the *Handbook of North American Indians*, vol. 15: *Northeast*, Bruce Trigger, ed., (Washington, D.C., 1978).

Students undertaking readings in the history of New France can profitably begin with three books by William J. Eccles. His short *The Ordeal of New France* (Toronto, 1967) is a good introduction to the subject. More valuable for Indian affairs is Eccles' *The Canadian Frontier, 1534–1760* (New York, 1969). Also useful is his *France in America* (New York, 1972). No two scholars have done more to illuminate Indian-white relations in New France than Trigger and Cornelius J. Jaenen. Trigger's magisterial *The Children of Aataentsic: A History of the Huron People to 1660*, 2 vols. (Montreal, 1976) is a landmark in ethnohistorical scholarship. Perhaps more accessible for students is Trigger's *The Huron: Farmers of the North* (New York, 1969). For its unique blend of ethnohistory and intellectual history, no student should miss Jaenen, *Friend and Foe: Aspects of French-Amerindian Cultural Contact in the Sixteenth and Seventeenth Centuries* (New York, 1976).

Studies of Indian-white relations in New England have often become polemics either championing the Puritans as dispensers of justice and the true faith or damning them as swindlers and thugs. Alden Vaughan, *New England Frontier: Puritans and Indians, 1620–1675,* rev. ed. (New York, 1979) attempts to exonerate Puritans of charges of oppression, imperialism, and towering hypocrisy. No historian has been more critical of that approach than Francis Jennings. His *The Invasion of America: Indians, Colonialism, and the Cant of Conquest* (Chapel Hill, 1975) is a slashing attack on Puritan Indian policy and its latter-day apologists. Jenning's book sparked a whole round of new books, articles, and sessions at professional meetings. More important, it signaled a thorough reappraisal of New England Indian-white relations. Perhaps the most important of the books in that reassessment is Neal Salisbury's *Manitou and Providence: Indians, Europeans, and the Making of New England, 1500–1643* (New York, 1982). A second volume will take events through King Philip's War.

Several recent books represent an attempt to look at New England Indian affairs outside the realm of official policy. Howard S. Russell's *Indian New England Before the Mayflower* (Hanover, N.H., 1980) is a fine introduction to the material culture and lifeways of New England coastal Algonkins. Students with more anthropological background may find Dean R. Snow's *The Archaeology of New England* (New York, 1980) more useful. The most arresting and innovative new book in the field is William Cronon's *Changes in the Land: Indians, Colonists, and the Ecology of New England* (New York, 1983). Moving away from the Jennings-Vaughan debate about Indian policy, Cronon takes a penetrating look at how native people used the Northeast's rich natural resources. He then analyzes the impact of English agricultural practices on the landscape.

Students with an eye for native American art and material culture will be interested in looking at the illustrated catalogs of several important museum exhibitions. T. J. Brasser, ed., *"Bo'jou, Neejee!" Profiles of Canadian Indian Art* (Ottawa, 1976), J. C. H. King, ed., *Thunderbird and Lightening: Indian Life of Northeastern North America, 1600–1900* (London, 1982), and Evan M. Maurer, ed., *The Native American Heritage: A Survey of North American Indian Art* (Chicago, 1977) are all of great value. While somewhat outside the geographical and chronological scope of this essay, Carolyn Gilman's *Where Two Worlds Meet: The Great Lakes Fur Trade* (St. Paul, 1982) is so splendid in its scholarship and photography that it deserves the widest possible audience.

Donald E. Worcester

# 2. Spaniards, Frenchmen, and Indians

European-Indian Relations in the Greater Southwest

$\mathbf{S}$panish and Indian relations in the Southwest were complicated by the variety of tribal ways of life, traditional enmities between tribes, inappropriate and inflexible Spanish regulations and policies, and the great distance from sources of supplies. At the end of the seventeeth century competition by the French in Louisiana and the trade in guns to the Indians created a new set of problems for Spain. It was not until late in the eighteenth century that the Spanish were able to cope with these problems. By then it was too late.

The province of New Mexico, colonized by Juan de Oñate in 1598, was in the heart of the sedentary Pueblo tribes. It was surrounded by independent bands of nomadic Apaches on the east and south, by the semisedentary Navajos on the northwest, and by Utes on the north. As the Spaniards learned, a treaty with any band of Apaches or Navajos meant nothing to other bands. Neither of these Athapascan peoples had, at the time, a tribal organization.

The Pueblo world was caught between Spain's dual but conflicting goals: converting the natives and teaching them Spanish ways by peaceful means on the one hand and securing wealth on the other. Unable to comprehend the Pueblos' leadership structure, the Spaniards imposed their own system, ordering the villagers to elect governors and other officials. The traditional religious leaders simply selected the officials and allowed them to deal with the Spaniards, but they did not surrender authority to them.

The Spaniards also established the *encomienda* system, whereby groups or villages were "commended" to the care of Spaniards who were to protect them, see to their conversion, and teach them Spaniards' ways in exchange for the tribute or head tax that Indian men paid in labor or products. The *encomienda* brought settlers into bitter conflict with missionaries for control of Indian labor and was the source of chronic church-state strife. The Pueblo Indians suffered as a result of this competition for their labor.

For Spanish governors of New Mexico, opportunities to acquire wealth were few. They forced the Pueblos to supply them with cotton cloth or skins that could be sold in New Spain. They also sold Indian captives, especially Apaches and Navajos, to the mining camps farther south, using Pueblo warriors on their slave-raiding forays. The Spaniards did not introduce the practice of selling captives as slaves, but they expanded it and made it a business. It earned the undying hatred of Spaniards by the Apaches and Navajos and their resentment toward the Pueblo men who unwillingly served the governors.

Spanish law forbade allowing Indians to ride horses, but in 1621 the missionaries and ranchers of New Mexico were granted permission to employ mounted Pueblo converts as herdsmen. Disgruntled herders fled occasionally, and through them the Apaches, Navajos, and Utes learned to ride horses. The Apaches had already developed a lingering taste for horse and mule meat.

The spread of the Spanish horse was continuous thereafter; Spanish herds and flocks in New Mexico, Texas, and south of the Rio Grande attracted raiding parties from far away throughout the seventeenth and eighteenth centuries. Tribes that acquired horses and learned to fight on horseback had a critical military advantage. The Apaches were the first southwestern Indians to enjoy this advantage.

In the 1670s, Apache and Navajo raiders stripped New Mexico of all livestock, except for a few well-guarded horse herds and flocks of sheep. A prolonged drought in that decade caused much starvation among the Pueblos, and the shortage of horses made the troops ineffective. The time was right for rebellion.

The Pueblos' resentment of the *encomienda* and of the padres who tried to destroy their religion had flared up in occasional uprisings that were local and easily suppressed. However, in 1680 Popé, a Tewa shaman, organized a major rebellion that would erupt on the same day in every village. Not all Pueblos favored the rebellion, for many converts had close ties to the Spaniards. These converts warned Governor Antonio de Otermín, but he did not consider it serious until many Spaniards had been killed. He gathered the survivors and abandoned New Mexico. Popé tried to force the Pueblos to reject everything that the Spaniards had introduced. His ambition for power was alien to Pueblo tradition; he was killed by men who resented him.

The Spanish refugees and families of Pueblo converts settled at El Paso del Norte. When the Spaniards finally returned to New Mexico in 1692, they met little organized resistance, but some Pueblo families fled to the Navajos and remained with them. From such Pueblo refugees, over the years the Navajos learned to keep flocks of sheep and goats and to weave the woolen blankets for which they are still famous. In 1696 another Pueblo revolt occurred, but it was crushed. The Spaniards did not restore the *encomienda* system, and the missionaries were less domineering than before. The Pueblos passively observed the rituals to placate the padres but secretly followed their own religious practices.

In 1684 the Sieur de La Salle located his ill-fated French colony at Matagorda Bay on the Texas coast. Rumors of Frenchmen in Texas excited Spanish officials, who sent several expeditions to search for them. In 1689 one discovered the remains of the colony, which had been destroyed by Indians.

To forestall future French intrusions, in 1690 the Spaniards established missions among the Tejas, a Caddo tribe of East Texas, and stocked them with cattle and horses. The Tejas at first welcomed the Spanish missionaries, but they were devoted to their own religious practices. When over-zealous padres scoffed at these practices, the padres alienated many of the Tejas. A smallpox epidemic aroused the Indians even more because they believed the Spanish caused it, and in 1693 they ordered the Spaniards to leave.

In 1699 the French established a post at Biloxi in Mississippi and began expanding the fur trade. The governor requested Jesuit missionaries because of their ability to learn Indian languages, but a jurisdictional dispute prevented them from coming. As a result, the French made no religious demands on the natives. The only labor they expected of the Indians was to gather furs and deerskins to trade. Unlike the Spaniards, who prohibited the sale of guns to Indians, the French liberally supplied their native allies with firearms. And because intertribal warfare disrupted the fur trade, French agents negotiated peace among the tribes friendly to France.

Another successful French practice was to send agents to live among the tribes; these men were often accompanied by a squad of soldiers to help the villagers defend themselves against enemy tribes such as the Chicka-saws, who were armed by British traders from the Carolinas. The presence of the traders and soldiers enhanced and maintained French influence among the tribes of Louisiana and along the Red River. The Spanish hoped to accomplish the same results through missions, but Texas proved an infertile field for missionary endeavors.

Soon after establishing the post at Biloxi, the French set up another at

Natchitoches in Louisiana, which was accessible to the tribes of East Texas. The Natchitoches post became an important trade center, where Texas Indians exchanged Spanish horses and mules for French guns throughout the eighteenth century.

Of all the instruments of change the Spanish and French brought to the Southwest, none were of greater impact than the horse and the gun. Those tribes which acquired horses had a great military advantage over enemies who lacked them. Horses and mules could be stolen from Spaniards or from other tribes. The horse also gave the Indians greater mobility, enabling them to follow and hunt buffalo with comparative ease.

Indians who had access to firearms had an equally great advantage over others who still relied on bows and arrows. To acquire guns it was necessary to reach French or British traders or tribes that traded regularly with them. After the gun trade began the Spaniards of Texas and New Mexico were constantly under pressure to supply guns to their native allies who were exposed to attacks by well-armed warriors such as the Osages. The Spanish ban on trading guns to Indians was inappropriate once the French and British guns were available, but Spanish policy was slow to change.

The Europeans also introduced smallpox and other contagious diseases, and the occasional epidemics reduced some powerful tribes or bands to impotency. This was especially true in Texas in the last quarter of the eighteenth century, when a number of tribes allied to Spain were decimated by deadly epidemics.

British traders from the Carolinas had reached the Mississippi by 1700 and some opened trade with tribes west of that river. They sought horses and mules as well as furs, but they also wanted captives who could be sold as slaves. When plantations developed in Louisiana, they also provided a market for Indian slaves. This traffic in Indian slaves is one important aspect of European-Indian relations that has not yet been thoroughly explored.

In 1718 the French established a settlement at New Orleans, and the Spanish founded missions and a presidio on the site of modern San Antonio. The missions were among the Coahuiltecan Indians, who accepted missionaries in part because of the military protection that came with them. The Apaches had recently driven them from their hunting grounds.

When news of the war between France and Spain reached Natchitoches in 1720, the commander of the French post there seized the Spanish mission at Los Adaes (near modern Robeline, Louisiana). Two years later the French surrendered the mission, and the Marqués de Aguayo established a presidio at Los Adaes. Because of Spanish concern over the French at

Natchitoches and their trade with Indians of East Texas, Los Adaes served as the capital of the Texas province until after France ceded Louisiana to Spain in 1762, when the governor transferred his headquarters to San Antonio.

Caddo-speaking tribes such as the Tejas and Cadohadachos were the most prosperous and powerful in East Texas. The great kingdom of the Caddos, as the Spaniards called their land, was between the Trinity River and the big bend of the Red River, where the Cadohadacho confederacy villages were located. The Caddo peoples lived in dome-shaped wooden houses with thatched roofs; they raised crops but spent part of each year on the plains hunting buffalo. They had a warrior tradition and had to defend themselves against Choctaws and Chickasaws from the east, Osages from the north, and the nomadic Apaches and Tonkawas from the west.

The coming of the horse and the gun resulted in frequent dislocations and forced migrations during the eighteenth century. Many tribes or bands were driven from their villages or hunting grounds by powerful enemies who had horses or guns, or both. Hundreds of captives were sold into slavery in Louisiana or the Carolinas.

Comanches first appeared in New Mexico in 1700 in company with the Utes, who spoke the same Shoshonean language. Through the Utes the Comanches learned to ride horses and to steal them from Spanish missions and ranches. Once their warriors were well-mounted, the numerous Comanches were the most formidable tribe on the southern plains. They turned on the Utes and drove them back into the mountains. They launched an assault on the multitude of small Apache bands that occupied much of the southern plains before the Comanche migration began. They forced the Jicarillas, Mescaleros, and others whose names have been forgotten to seek refuge in the mountains of New Mexico. They drove the Lipans and Natagés steadily southward from their ranges north of the Red River.

Within two years of the founding of the presidio and missions at San Antonio, Lipan Apaches retreating before the Comanches discovered the Spanish livestock herds there. For three decades they raided the area for horses to replace those lost to the Comanches, and they ate Spanish cattle when unable to hunt buffalo. Finally, in 1749 the hard-pressed Lipans celebrated peace with the Spaniards at San Antonio. Except for occasional thefts of livestock out of necessity, the Lipans generally refrained from hostilities against Spaniards in Texas thereafter. However, various Apache bands continued to harass Spaniards in New Mexico and below the Rio Grande.

The Apaches had no easy access to guns, while the Comanches were able to obtain a modest supply through trade with Wichitan and Caddo intermediaries. The Comanches drove the Apaches south of the Red, the Brazos, the Colorado, and ultimately the Rio Grande. In desperation the Lipans begged the Spaniards for a mission and presidio, but it was protection they wanted, not mission life. The Lipans' request was finally granted in 1756, and in the following year the mission and a presidio were built on the San Saba River near modern Menard. That location might have been suitable earlier, but, in the 1750s, Comanches were approaching the region. The Apache mission was doomed.

The Lipans had other enemies besides the Comanches, for Apache raiders harassed the Caddos, Tonkawas, and Wichitan tribes. The Taovayas, Tawakonis, Wichitas, and others of this group had been caught between the changes emanating from Spanish settlements and French trading posts in the Mississippi Valley. Their Apache and Comanche foes fought on horseback. Their Osage and other enemies to the north and east attacked them with French and British guns. When French agent Etienne V. de Bourgmont negotiated peace between the Osages and Comanches in 1724, the Wichitan peoples had no reason to rejoice. As life for the Tawakonis became increasingly unsafe in the 1730s, they moved south to the Red River, where they were temporarily out of range of the Osages. The Taovayas and others migrated south to the Arkansas River, where Comanche bands made a tenuous peace with them in order to trade for French guns.

While the Wichitan tribes depended on French traders for guns, the British kept the Osages well supplied with firearms. The French and Indian War drastically reduced the flow of French goods to New Orleans, which adversely affected the Wichitas. In 1756 or the following year the Taovayas and the other Wichitan tribes on the Arkansas gave up the struggle and withdrew to the Red River. There they were far from the Osages, but their horse herds were now exposed to Lipan raiders. When they learned that Spanish troops protected the Lipans at San Saba, they were irate.

The Spaniards were unaware of the presence of the numerous Taovayas and Wichitas in their new villages along the Red River. Later they would refer to all of the tribes of that region as "Nations of the North" or Norteños. When about two thousand well-armed warriors appeared in the hills around the San Saba mission in March 1758, the Spaniards were unpleasantly surprised. The warriors were mainly Norteños, but there were also Tonkawas and Comanches as well as other enemies of the Apaches, who were generally at peace with the Spaniards. In the face of such an overwhelming force, the fifty-nine-man garrison at the San Saba presidio across the river from the mission was powerless. The warriors killed some of the padres and burned the mission. They were searching for Apaches, but few were to be found there.

The appearance of this virtual army sent shock waves clear to Mexico City. It was one thing for leather-armored soldiers to face Indians armed only with bows and arrows; it was quite different for them to face a large force armed with guns as good or better than those of the soldiers. To Colonel Diego Ortiz Parrilla, commander of the San Saba presidio, there was only one course to pursue. He must avenge Spanish honor by thrashing the Norteños. Padres in East Texas and French officials in Natchitoches, who were acquainted with the Wichitan tribes, warned the governor not to attack the Norteños. But far away in Mexico City the viceroy agreed with Ortiz Parrilla. The padres protested that the Norteños had suffered much at the hands of the Lipans and that it was folly to appear as protectors of the Apaches. The Norteños, they said, were much more likely prospects for allies and converts than the Lipans.

Ignoring all warnings, in 1759 Ortiz Parrilla marched from San Antonio with a force of troops, militia, mission Indians, and Lipans. They struck a camp of Yojuanes and found ample evidence that this Tonkawa band had taken part in the attack on the mission. At the Red River Ortiz Parrilla came to the Taovayas village, which was surrounded by a moat and a stockade. A French flag flew over it, and the sounds of fifes and drums could be heard, indicating that a squad of French soldiers was stationed there. From time to time parties of Taovayas horsemen rode out to fight, accompanied by men on foot who reloaded their muskets. They fought with greater order and discipline than did Ortiz Parrilla's makeshift army, and the sight of them cooled the ardor for avenging Spanish honor. At dark Ortiz Parrilla ordered a retreat, but not all of his men heard him. Many of the militiamen were already well on their way to San Antonio.

When the French and Indian War ended, Spain reluctantly accepted New Orleans and all of Louisiana west of the Mississippi from France. To relieve the viceroy from assuming additional and complex responsibilities, Louisiana was attached to the captaincy general of Cuba. Spanish governors of Louisiana were obliged to continue the French practice of distributing annual gifts to friendly tribes and supplying them with guns; otherwise, British traders would lure them away. The governors also employed French traders and agents to deal with the tribes and to maintain their loyalty.

For the governors of Texas, Spanish rule in Louisiana did not simplify their relations with the Indians but rather complicated them. If Spanish officials in Louisiana made annual gifts of powder and lead to their Indian allies, it was logical to expect Spaniards in Texas to be equally generous. But the viceroy either failed to comprehend the governors' dilemma or ignored it. The governors were repeatedly warned to prevent Spaniards and Indians from trading with Louisiana, even though they could not offer the Indians the trade items they needed. When Texas governors occasionally gave in to their allies' demands for guns to defend themselves, they were accused of engaging in illicit traffic.

Because the Spaniards continued to provide a refuge and protection to Apaches, Spanish relations with the Norteños remained hostile, although the Indians asked for traders to come to their villages. In 1769 Athanase de Mézières, a French officer in the Spanish service, was named commander of the Natchitoches post. The most influential Indian agent of his day, he tried desperately to negotiate peace with the Norteños, but his efforts were blocked by Louisiana Governor Luis de Unzaga. The Norteños sent a delegation to talk peace with Mézières. Custom called for him to return the courtesy, but for several years Unzaga denied him permission to make the journey. As Mézières anticipated, the Norteños were offended.

The main reason for the deterioration of Indian affairs in Texas at this time was lack of understanding of the basic problems by the viceroy and his staff. Hugo Oconor, an Irish officer in the Spanish army, was partly responsible. In the 1760s he served as interim governor of Texas, and he had two goals that were contrary to the interests of the province. He was determined to stamp out illicit commerce between Texas and Louisiana, although both provinces needed and benefited from trade. His other goal was to thrash and humble all hostile tribes, particularly the Norteños. After his term in Texas ended, Oconor was named commander of Spanish forces on the northern frontier. Unfortunately for the Baron of Ripperdá, the new governor of Texas, Oconor opposed him in everything, and Viceroy Antonio María Bucareli y Ursúa followed Oconor's detrimental advice.

Because Spain had never been able to defend the northern settlements and missions adequately, in 1776 a unique military administration was created—the Commandancy General of the Interior Provinces. The commander general, whose main responsibility was to coordinate defenses against the Apaches and Comanches, reported directly to the king, which presumably made him independent of the viceroy. The viceroy controlled his funds, however, so he was not beyond the viceroy's influence.

The first commander general was Teodoro de Croix, a Frenchman and nephew of a former viceroy. At the same time, Bernardo de Gálvez, nephew of minister of the Indies José de Gálvez, was named interim governor of Louisiana. Croix and Gálvez were able young men with previous experience on the northern frontier and an enlightened attitude toward Indians, even Apaches. They reversed Oconor's policies toward the Norteños and urged Mézières and Ripperdá to form an alliance with them. They also encouraged similar efforts to make peace with the Comanches. The situation in Texas looked hopeful for the first time in many years.

Indian affairs in Texas received a serious setback in 1777 and 1778, however. Devastating epidemics occurred both years. The Cadohadachos alone lost three hundred men. The once numerous Tawakonis had only 150 men left. Because the Spanish carried the epidemic, the tribes friendliest with them were hardest hit and drastically weakened. Nearly every pro-Spanish chief in Texas perished.

The Karankawas, who lived among the snake-infested islands along the coast of Texas, had never been brought under Spanish influence. The mission at La Bahía (modern Goliad) was intended to attract the Karankawas, but few of them remained there for long. They killed the crews of ships that were wrecked on the coast and in the late 1770s became especially troublesome, raiding Spanish herds as far inland as San Antonio. Governor Domingo Cabello, who replaced Ripperdá, planned a war to exterminate them. To oversee the campaign, the governor transferred his headquarters to the presidio at La Bahía in December 1779. He remained there until the following August, waiting for troops from Mexico. Spain's involvement in the American Revolution as well as increased Apache hostility in Coahuila and Chihuahua made it impossible to spare troops for a campaign against the Karankawas.

Indian relations in New Mexico took a favorable turn in 1777 when veteran Indian fighter Juan Bautista de Anza became governor. Peace with the Comanches was his highest priority, for they roamed over the province at will, killing and robbing Spaniards and Pueblo Indians. There could be no peace with them, Anza knew, until he defeated them in their own country.

In August 1779 he set out on a Comanche campaign with soldiers, militia, and Pueblo Indians. On the way Utes and Jicarilla Apaches joined him, for both suffered from Comanche attacks. Marching only at night, he was able to discover a big Comanche camp near modern Pueblo, Colorado— Cuerno Verde's band. The chief, who was the most implacable foe of the Spaniards, was away on a raid against Taos with 250 warriors. Anza's men killed 18 warriors and captured 34 women and children as well as 500 horses and all of the Comanches' possessions. From the captives Anza learned of Cuerno Verde's raid, and he set out to intercept him. Apaches had warned the Spaniards at Taos, and they repulsed the Comanches. The Comanches evaded the ambush that Anza prepared, but Cuerno Verde and 50 of his leading warriors charged Anza's force. Cuerno Verde and many others were killed. His death removed the Spaniards' main Comanche enemy.

Most Comanches wanted peace and trade with New Mexico, for they were hard-pressed by the better-armed Pawnees and Osages. They sent a peace delegation to Sante Fe. Anza informed them that he was willing to discuss peace, but only when the Comanches recognized a head chief and every band agreed to uphold the peace. The Comanches had no head chief; every band was independent. An agreement binding all Comanches was outside their experience. The Comanches continued to send peace delegations to Santa Fe, but Anza's answer was always the same. In early 1786 they finally agreed to his terms, named Ecueracapa head chief, and vowed to uphold the peace. They killed one irreconcilable chief who refused to make peace with the Spaniards and drove away his followers.

The general peace with the Comanches was the most rewarding development in Spanish-Indian relations in the Southwest, for the Comanches also made peace with the Spaniards at San Antonio. Except for minor infractions by uncontrollable young men, the Comanches lived up to the treaty. The peace was not, however, a purely Spanish triumph, for the Comanches needed it and had persisted until it was achieved. The treaty was maintained by Comanche determination, not by fear of Spanish retaliation.

By threatening to cut off trade with the Navajos, Anza persuaded them to sever their alliance with the Gila Apaches and to wage war against them, even though both spoke the same Athapascan language. Aware that one Navajo chief could not represent all of the scattered groups, Anza planned to select four headmen as spokesmen for the Navajos in different areas. Before he could act, the Navajos chose two chiefs known to be friendly to the Spaniards.

Peace with the Comanches strained Spanish relations with the Lipans, who desperately needed guns. Earlier the Tonkawas had served as intermediaries between traders and the Lipans, but Spanish diplomatic and military pressure had ended the practice. After the pro-Spanish Tonkawa chief died during the epidemics of 1777–1778, El Mocho, an Apache captive raised as a Tonkawa, became head chief. An enemy of the Spaniards, El Mocho sought an alliance with the Apaches. He arranged a big trade fair for them on the Guadalupe River in November and December 1782. The

Tonkawas invited all who had guns to sell. The Apaches brought three thousand horses and mules to trade, but the Tonkawas and others had only 270 guns. When the fair ended, the Apaches still had two thousand horses left.

At the fair, El Mocho tried to persuade the Apaches to accept him as head chief for the purpose of driving the Spaniards and enemy tribes out of Texas. The Apaches listened but were not impressed. In 1784, after failing to get some Tonkawas to kill him, the Spaniards assassinated El Mocho when he visited the presidio at La Bahía. The other Tonkawas approved.

Left exposed to the Comanches in Texas, the Lipans sought peace with Anza in New Mexico. On learning of the Lipan overtures, Comanches hastened to insist that Anza reject them. If they had no enemies left to fight, they told him, their warriors would become women. The commander general may have been amused by their fears, but he suspected that peace with the Lipans might jeopardize Anza's alliances with the Comanches, Navajos, and Utes and instructed him to reject the peace proposal.

In late spring of 1785 Bernardo de Gálvez became viceroy of New Spain. Having served in the Interior Provinces as well as Louisiana, he was familiar with Indian problems in Texas and New Mexico. He encouraged efforts to make a lasting peace with the Comanches, and he introduced totally new measures for pacifying the Apaches. They were to be granted peace whenever they requested it and were to be pursued relentlessly when they waged war. When peaceful they were to be supplied with food and encouraged to live near presidios.

Gálvez believed that by giving the Apaches a taste for Spanish foods and for liquor (*aguardiente*) and by providing them with guns they could be made dependent on the Spaniards. He hoped they would abandon use of the bow and arrow and rely on Spanish guns, for these required repairs and access to a supply of powder and lead. By cutting off their supplies when they broke the peace, the Spaniards could compel them to refrain from raiding. Although Gálvez died the following year, his policy bore fruit. A number of Apache families settled near the presidios in Chihuahua and Sonora, although others continued raiding. When the European wars of the 1790s caused an interruption of supplies, the Apaches still living near the presidios resumed their raids out of necessity.

When the Comanche peace proved stable, the so-called Comanchero trade began. Small parties of New Mexicans and Pueblo Indians had made trading expeditions to the plains before, but they became annual affairs after 1786. Settlers and Pueblo Indians, with two-wheeled carts and pack animals, visited the Comanches, Kiowas, and other tribes to exchange knives, axes, bread, and other items for buffalo robes and dried meat. New Mexico buffalo hunters called Ciboleros also made yearly trips to the plains to kill buffalo and dry the meat.

Persuading nomadic tribes to settle in permanent villages was an unfulfilled Spanish goal. When a Comanche chief asked Anza for help in establishing a permanent village on the Arkansas River in 1787, Anza willingly provided tools and workmen to build the houses. By mid-September Comanches were living in nineteen houses, while others were being built. Spanish officials followed the progress of the settlement with keen interest, but their hopes were dashed. In January 1788 the promising experiment abruptly ended. A favorite wife of the chief died, and the Comanches moved far from the village out of consideration for his grief.

Apache raids in New Mexico and below the Rio Grande continued. In 1788 Captain Manuel de Echeagary marched with a force of soldiers and militiamen from the Tucson presidio for the double purpose of punishing the Apaches and of blazing a trail between Sonora and Santa Fe. His men captured several Apaches, who agreed to serve as guides. With their help the troops killed 54 Apaches and captured 125, making it an unusually successful campaign. Before it was over, Echeagary had enlisted 55 Apaches as scouts. Other Spanish officers protested the employment of Apaches as scouts and fighting men, but Commander General Jacobo Ugarte approved. A century later General George Crook would adopt the same practice with great success.

In 1788 the Spaniards began sending Apache captives to Mexico City, and many were taken from there to Veracruz or Havana. Thereafter Apaches were unable to exchange Spanish captives for their captured relatives. Spanish pressure on the Apaches' few allies soon left them isolated and harassed on all sides. In one attack the Comanches annihilated three hundred Apache families.

In the summer of 1789 Gila Apaches made peace overtures to Governor Fernando de la Concha, who had succeeded Anza. The following year Concha made peace with them. They promised to establish a village near the Rio Grande below Socorro, to plant crops, and to inform the Spaniards when other Apaches went on raids. To the surprise of many, the Apache band cultivated fields, kept herds at the village of El Sabinal, and warned the governor of impending Natagés' raids.

In the 1790s Spain was again involved in European wars, and imperial outposts in the Southwest were neglected. Because of hostilities between Spain and France, able Frenchmen serving in Texas and New Mexico were suspected of favoring France and were not fully used as Indian agents. But even though Spain's power in the Southwest deteriorated, the Comanches remained loyal to their Spanish allies.

As Americans pushed westward across the Mississippi, many tribes looked to the Spaniards for support against them. In 1795 a delegation of Panismaha and Wichitan chiefs called on Governor Manuel Muñoz at San Antonio, informing him that they represented thirty-three tribes who were opposed to the Americans. Here was an excellent opportunity to make new alliances, but Muñoz was old and infirm and he did nothing to encourage them.

Panismaha Chief Yrisac rode south to seek an alliance with the Spaniards and did not even stop at San Antonio. The captain of the garrison at Laredo sent him on to the governor of Nuevo Santander, but the response was not encouraging. Spanish officials apparently had lost their will or the ability to recognize and act on opportunities to win new allies.

As Spanish power deteriorated in the Southwest, Comanche chiefs continued to keep their young warriors in check or to make amends for occasional thefts. When the Spanish failed to provide the trade goods and gifts promised, small raiding parties increasingly stole Spanish livestock, but the Comanches did not resume open hostilities.

After the United States acquired Louisiana in 1803 the southwestern tribes soon felt pressures quite different from those faced in the past. The Americans knew little about the Comanches and even less about other tribes, and many of them were not concerned with making peaceful arrangements with those whose lands they wanted. The remnants of the Caddos and Wichitan tribes were unfortunate, for the good lands they farmed made them targets of the Anglo-Americans. For these people as well as the nomads, the coming of the Americans was a change for the worse.

## SUGGESTED READING

Two excellent general works on Indian-white relations in the Southwest are Elizabeth A. H. John, *Storms Brewed in Other Men's Worlds: The Confrontation of Indians, Spanish, and French in the Southwest, 1540–1795* (College Station, Tex., 1975) and Edward E. Spicer, *Cycles of Conquest: The Impact of Spain, Mexico, and the United States on the Indians of the Southwest, 1533–1960* (Tucson, 1962). Other works of a general nature are

L. R. Bailey, *The Indian Slave Trade in the Southwest* (Los Angeles, 1966), Leo Crane, *Desert Drums: The Pueblo Indians of New Mexico, 1540–1928* (Boston, 1928), and W. W. Newcomb, Jr., *The Indians of Texas* (Austin, 1961).

For the early Spanish period, see the works of Herbert E. Bolton, pioneer historian of the Spanish Borderlands: *Coronado: Knight of Pueblos and Plains* (Albuquerque, 1949), *Spanish Exploration in the Southwest, 1542–1706* (New York, 1916), and *Texas in the Middle Eighteenth Century* (Berkeley, 1915). Bolton's *Athanase de Mézières and the Louisiana-Texas Frontier, 1768–1780,* 2 vols. (Cleveland, 1914) concerns an able French Indian agent in the Spanish service. See also Oakah L. Jones, *Pueblo Warriors and Spanish Conquest* (Norman, 1966) and Charles W. Hackett and Charmion Shelby, *The Revolt of the Pueblo Indians of New Mexico and Otermín's Attempted Reconquest, 1680–1682,* 2 vols. (Albuquerque, 1942).

Among the available books on individual Indian tribes are Jack D. Forbes, *Apache, Navajo, and Spaniard* (Norman, 1960), Ernest Wallace and E. A. Hoebel, *The Comanches: Lords of the South Plains* (Norman, 1952), and Donald E. Worcester, *The Apaches: Eagles of the Southwest* (Norman, 1979).

| Dwight L. Smith | **3.** **Mutual** **Dependency** **and** **Mutual** **Distrust** | Indian-White Relations in British America, 1701–1763 |
|---|---|---|

At the opening of the eighteenth century, mainland British North America consisted of twelve colonies spread along the Atlantic coastline from New Hampshire to South Carolina. Georgia would be established some three decades later. About half of these—Massachusetts, Connecticut, New York, Virginia, North Carolina, South Carolina, and Georgia—had charter-defined boundaries that pushed their territorial jurisdiction on paper indefinitely westward into the North American wilderness. Some of these territories overlapped. New York also claimed present Vermont, and Maine was a part of Massachusetts. These colonies were flanked by the French in The Maritimes, the St. Lawrence Valley, the Great Lakes, and the Trans-Appalachian interior and by the Spanish in the lower Mississippi Valley and Florida.

Forces of change were already in process that would substantially redraw the political boundaries of North America. A decade earlier, in 1689, when Protestants William and Mary ascended the throne of England against the wishes of France's Catholic Louis XIV, war erupted, in which the three North American colonial powers—England, France, and Spain—and other European nations became antagonists. From then until 1763, this and other wars involved their empires in varying degrees. One war, ending in 1713, pushed the French out of the Hudson Bay country, Acadia (Nova Scotia), and Newfoundland. The final war, the most consequential to North America, was launched over Anglo-French territorial rivalry in the American wilderness. In the end, in 1763, the map was redrawn to eliminate France from the continent with Britain now having treaty title to North America from Hudson Bay to the Gulf of Mexico and from the Atlantic to the Mississippi River. Except for Russian activity in the far Northwest, the rest of the continent was Spain's.

In these momentous years, what then was the situation with respect to the Indians as the English were pushing their colonies from thirteen enclaves along the Atlantic coast into the eastern third of the continent? How were the Indians involved or used in these and other wars? What relationship existed between the colonies and the Indians? Between Britain and the Indians? Who shaped and controlled Indian policy? What was Indian action and reaction to these events? Was there Indian unity or division? Was the Indian situation improved or worsened as a consequence of these wars? What portents of the future?

As with so much of post–Columbian Indian history, it can best be told from the framework of white history. Era by era, period by period, it is not easy to make generalizations. Indian history can probably best be characterized by saying that it was, and is, in a constant state of flux, with one policy failing and another policy phasing in. It is as if continuous experimentation was going on trying to find a solution to the Indian "problem." Frequently policy was formulated and implemented with the assumption that all Indians were culturally similar. And usually policy was formulated from the white perspective rather than the other way. All too often political considerations, misguided humanitarian conceptions, avarice and greed, or other unfortunate determinants shaped policy. Then there was always the, sometimes great, discrepancy between policy and practice with very little awareness, understanding, or concern of these discrepancies.

These things make it exceedingly difficult to chronicle or assess any period of Indian-white history. The eighteenth century is no exception. At best, one can only note the confused picture and characterize in general terms what happened in those years and the consequences to the Indian and to the white.

It should be noted that the colonies were established over a span of 125 years. For much of that time it was far easier for the colonies to maintain communications with England than it was with each other. It was not until about mid-eighteenth century before intercolonial considerations began to be of much consequence. Hence, as in other matters, each colony tended to formulate its own policies concerning the Indians, with varying results in their implementation. At the same time, except for instructions in specific cases concerning Indian relations, there was no imperial or national Indian policy. With variables of perception, action, and reaction on the part of both Indians and whites, the overall picture may be likened to a vast jigsaw puzzle whose hundreds of pieces seldom fit together in part and never totally for the entire picture. Indeed, the pieces themselves often changed in configuration. Despite this apparent chaotic confusion, it is possible to chronicle some developments to the point where meaningful generalizations can be made and to trace the course of Indian-white relations to gain some perspective on trends.

Aside from the search for the Northwest Passage, an all water route across the continent to the Pacific and on to the Far East, something Christopher Columbus had failed to find and which did stimulate them to explore and to penetrate North America, Europeans were motivated by the immediate compulsion to exploit the newfound land's natural resources. Gold, silver, and precious stones at first and then other natural resources such as the soil, timber, naval stores, furs, game, and fish, either in abundance or believed promise, were prominent attractions. The natives aided and abetted, deterred and discouraged, and benefited or suffered from all of this.

Of the Europeans that came to these shores, the English, who also engaged in utilizing nature's bounty to their own commercial advantage, were different in that they came primarily to settle and to farm. While the Indians introduced the whites to basic training and wilderness survival to establish themselves on these new lands, the increasing success of the white venture soon placed the Indians in jeopardy. They were in the way of the seemingly insatiable land hunger of the whites. This was all hopelessly confused, especially in the minds of the Indians whose cultural conditioning held that land was for use as opposed to the European concept of private ownership. As whites began to gain the upper hand, their concept was imposed on the Indians, whether they understood it or not, whether they could reconcile themselves to it or not. Whites relied on Indians in survival and trade matters or used them for labor or military services whenever they could; however, whites made little effort to reconcile cultural differences or to accommodate to Indian culture or needs and otherwise considered them as obstacles to white progress into the wilderness.

In the seventeeth century English settlements had pushed westward beyond their seaboard beachheads, had occupied the coastal lowlands, and were establishing farms in the upland area beyond the fall line. By one means or another the Indians had been largely displaced, reduced in numbers, or forced into westward retreat to the extent that the English agriculturalists were in control. The Appalachian Mountains might well be considered as the approximate western border of the English colonies. Nature's boundary could be breached by human resolve and physical effort, but a more formidable obstacle had first to be reckoned with. Trans-Appalachia had become the stronghold of Indian tribes, some hostile to the tide of westward progressing English settlement and some friendly to the French who regarded the interior as their vast fur-trading domain. To a lesser extent, the Spanish factor was present in the South in the Floridas and along the Gulf Coast. Oversimplified somewhat, but this is the essential picture in the closing years of the century.

While the contest for control of North America was a European affair, directly or indirectly the Indians played roles of varying significance and consequence. They were more than interested bystanders. Often they were √ participants. They had much at stake—their survival and the future. As the Europeans moved into the interior, the tribes were forced to reassess and change their policies in response.

Besides the magnetic attraction of vast stretches of land to the westward for the voracious appetite of colonial farmers, another principal force played a considerable role in the Euro-Indian scheme of things. The fur trade was necessarily in the vanguard of settlement. The increasing demand for furs in European markets and the profits to be gained from the trade forced the Indians and the whites into a position of economic interdependency. This interdependency, however, was not strong enough in the long run to counteract the Indian displacement consequence of advancing white settlement. And the resulting decline of the fur-bearing animal population frequently made for bitter rivalry among competing Indian groups, which in turn made it ever more difficult for them to present a united front against the westward progressing white farmers.

European penetration into the continent resulted in shifting tribal locations and loyalties. Except for precise moments or dates, only generalizations will serve to designate tribal locations.

In the North, the Indian factor was composed of the Iroquois Confederacy and others who were principally loosely related Algonquian tribes. The Iroquois-Algonquian rivalry was traditional, uneven because intra-Algonquian hostility was all too common. For awhile, the Pennsylvania Indian situation was an exception.

The Iroquois Confederacy by virtue of its existence, its cohesiveness, and its location figured prominently and actively in the northern colonies. The Cayuga, Mohawk, Oneida, Onondaga, and Seneca, powerful tribes of the Mohawk and Hudson valleys, the most feasible route to the Great Lakes country, had forged their defensive alliance in the sixteenth century. Later, the Tuscarora, another linguistically related tribe, moved up from the South to join the Confederacy. Tribal representatives in council made the key decisions of peace and war for the Confederacy, but each tribe retained some autonomy. The Six Nations, as the Confederacy came to be known (see page 57), ably defended their homeland against all threats, Indian and white alike. They further tried, with remarkable success, to subjugate or destroy potential rivals, including other linguistically related tribes.

The Iroquois had become the middlemen for the New Netherland Dutch traders. Since guns were a principal trade item, the Confederacy gained a fundamental advantage over its French-backed Algonquian and Huron enemies. After the English took over New Netherland in 1664, they came to similar terms with the Iroquois.

The sporadic Iroquois Wars of the seventeeth century challenged the increasing French and their Indian allies domination of the Great Lakes country fur trade and the French penetration of the Mississippi Valley. In 1684, at the urging of the colonial governor of New York, the Iroquois again lashed out against the French and their Indian allies in the West and threatened the very French presence in the St. Lawrence Valley. When Louis XIV sought to assure French primacy in Europe and to expand his colonial empire, England countered with an alliance system to attain these ambitions. This exploded into four wars, 1689–1763, fought mainly in Europe but also between the French, English, and Spanish in North America.

The Iroquois War already going on merged into King William's War, 1689–1697. The French rebuilt their disintegrating Indian alliances and raided backwoods settlements of New England and New York, but they only served to convince the otherwise divided English colonies to cooperate somewhat in their war effort. The French employed diplomatic initiative through trade goods to counter English competition with the tribes in the Great Lakes region. A shift in felt hat styles, however, drastically depressed the European fur markets and forced the French to curtail the magnitude of their trade activities with the Indians. Indians, nevertheless, had provided the French with their main striking force. The Treaty of Ryswick terminating this war was an indecisive arrangement whereby the French and English gave up any gains of the war, reaffirming the prewar territorial status.

Although wilderness conflict was a standard feature, a fundamentally new motivation was now in place. The English had come to realize the vital connection between trade and empire, particularly with the Mississippi Valley as the prize. Whatever other considerations were involved in Europe or elsewhere, the English, French, and Spanish were now in contention for the heartland of North America.

An accident of geography had thrust the Iroquois into the midst of the European imperial rivalry. They were flanked by the English on the east and the French on the north and the west. With the fur trade as the principal economic base, the French posts stretched over great wilderness distances connecting the St. Lawrence and the Mississippi valleys. The Great Lakes and such rivers as the Wabash and Illinois were the lifeline connections between these extremities.

The Ohio country between these English and French positions was a no-man's-land of political sovereignty. The Iroquois asserted political jurisdiction over it by virtue of ancient conquest. Further, they used it as their hunting grounds, and it was the residence of other tribes who were politically dependent on them. The French and the English both recognized this status.

By the close of the King William's War the Iroquois had concluded that to continue the fur-trade wars and that to be involved in the French-English wars were exercises in futility. They adopted a policy of armed neutrality as their stance in French-English conflict, of political manipulation with neighboring tribes, and of peace with tribes removed. Surviving until after the American Revolution, this policy assured them the balance of power and it brought them commercial prosperity.

The Iroquois became rather astute in their diplomatic duplicity, playing one power against the other. At times the French believed the Iroquois were on their side, at other times on the side of the English. And the English sometimes viewed the Iroquois as pro-English, sometimes as pro-French. Consequently, both European powers proffered political and economic concessions to maintain Iroquois neutrality. When they occasionally departed from this basic policy to forge an alliance with the Iroquois, they were almost always disappointed.

European power politics, Iroquois-style, ran into trouble in the 1740s. As the English pushed their trade initiative into the Ohio Valley, the Iroquois and resident Algonquian tribes under their influence increasingly turned to the English traders. In 1744 the heretofore French-oriented Miami were won over, and an alliance was worked out with the Six Nations. The Iroquois appointed local officials and assigned certain tracts to the dependent tribes. With Iroquois sanctions, English trading posts and traders penetrated the Ohio country. Ominously, in 1749, English settlers and speculators were covetously eyeing the western country. The crown even granted a 200,000 acre tract to a company to fortify and establish a settlement of 200 families.

The French believed the Six Nations had overextended themselves and proceeded to challenge the English-Iroquois threat to their St. Lawrence to Mississippi Valley lifeline. Posting claim to the area in 1749 and warning the English traders and Indians neither frightened the merchants away nor convinced the Indians. The French response was direct and decisive. In 1752, they destroyed the principal British post in the heart of the Miami trading area and literally ate the local pro-Iroquois chief with great ceremony. Two years later they seized the abuilding Ohio Company fort at the forks of the Ohio River and replaced it with their own. Fort Duquesne, at the site of present Pittsburgh, would be the southern link in a chain of forts northward to Lake Erie, which thus would give the French control of the Ohio Valley. George Washington challenged this in the name of Virginia and the French and Indian War began.

The Iroquois tried, unsuccessfully, to regain their lost leverage between the French and the English. Neutrality did not work for them; neither did joining war parties of one side and then the other under the rationale they were trying to defend their lands against the other. The English hoped for a firm alliance but did not get it. In the end, the French were ousted and the English occupied posts within the Iroquois sphere of influence. The Iroquois position and power had now been seriously compromised. Whether the former role of Iroquois in wilderness diplomacy could ever be resumed was a question that belonged to the future.

As has been noted, much of the chronicle of the Indians in the northern colonies in the first two-thirds of the eighteenth century was dominated by the Six Nations and the Algonquian tribes they sought to incorporate into their sphere of influence. The situation in the colony of Pennsylvania presented a notable exception to this generalization, particularly in the early years.

When the Quakers moved in to establish the colony in the early 1680s, they found the Delaware, a tribe that had been subjugated by the Iroquois. The Delaware paid tribute to their conquerors and were forbidden to wage war. William Penn made a land purchase treaty with them. So long as the Quakers dominated the colony's government, sincere efforts were made to treat the Indians in the spirit of brotherhood. The Quakers were generous with money and gifts, and they acquired Indian lands by treaty and purchase rather than by conquest and diplomatic subterfuge.

By the mid-1720s as the components in this happy arrangement began to change, an erosion of Pennsylvania-Indian relations set in. The Iroquois overlords of the Delaware sought and got an increasing share of the presents and other considerations dispensed by the colonial government. The newly arrived Shawnee to the west of the Delaware objected to the stepped-up acquisitive intrusion of the Iroquois as well as the westward advance of white settlement. While the Quakers continued to practice their altruism, the non-Quaker proprietors who succeeded William Penn increasingly favored the Iroquois over the other Indian groups.

Pennsylvania's expanding involvement in the fur trade, the French competition factor, the dispute with Virginia over the ownership of the forks of the Ohio River country, the geopolitics of the French and the English made it increasingly difficult for the Quaker-controlled government to continue its peaceful policy with the Indians. It is noteworthy that prior to 1754 when the English tried to dislodge the French from their presence in the Ohio River headwaters country, thus triggering the French and Indian War, no consequential Indian raid or attack on a frontier settlement had occurred on Pennsylvania soil.

During the seventeenth century, the southern coastal tribes had also been crushed, subjected, or pushed aside. As in the North, the westward-advancing English frontier in the southern colonies now had to deal with the interior Indians. During the King William's War in the closing decade of the century, the southern colonial frontier was not the scene of Euro-Indian involvement as in the North and remained relatively calm in the conflict. The Florida-based Spanish, then an English ally, refrained from Florida and gulf-based attacks. And the French presence was still not very well established and was remote enough from the English colonial frontier so as not to cause any serious friction in the war.

Into the eighteenth century, the southern Indians found themselves in increasingly difficult positions as European rivalry for control of the interior grew in magnitude and intensity. The French established posts along the Gulf of Mexico coast, seeking to link these with their position in the St. Lawrence Valley and Great Lakes in the hope of increasing trade and influence with the lower Mississippi Valley Indians. The Iroquois Confederacy neutrality to the north and a new alliance with the Florida-based Spanish encouraged the French to pursue their goal of completely encircling the Atlantic coast based English colonies.

As English-French rivalry once more exploded into war, this one the Queen Anne's War, 1702–1713, the southern colonial frontier became a theater of the conflict. The French, seeking to stem the tide of the English commercial advance into the headwaters of the gulf-flowing streams and lower Mississippi Valley area and their westward-looking settlers, tried to forge a Franco-Indian military alliance among the four dominant southern interior tribes. In this they were only partially successful.

The Choctaw and Creek joined the French to thwart the activities of Charleston, South Carolina-based traders that took them westward into the lower Trans-Appalachian country. As on previous occasions, the Chickasaws rejected French overtures and actively supported the English efforts, thus effectively serving as a counterforce to the pro-French Choctaw and Creek. The Cherokee, the other important southern Indian tribe, declined the French overtures. The expected English westward thrust did not materialize by the close of the war, and the European presence in the area was not altered. Elsewhere, the French position in North America had suffered severely by the loss of the Hudson Bay area, Newfoundland, and Acadia, a portent of French erosion and decline in the New World.

Simultaneously another southern tribe, the Tuscarora on the Carolina-Virginia frontier, was chafing from exploitation encouraged by Charleston merchants. To make matters worse, bands of traders and friendly Indians made slave raids into Tuscarora towns. They were also losing some of their choice tribal lands to settlers. In 1711, the Tuscarora turned on the Carolina frontier with such fury that it was two years before an intercolonial militia and Indian force could defeat them. The Tuscarora lands were devastated, the tribe sustained heavy casualties, and hundreds of Indians were taken prisoner. The remnants fled northward to join with their Iroquois cousins in New York. The Iroquois Confederacy was henceforth known as the Six Nations.

Close on the heels of the Tuscarora War, which presented such a serious threat especially to North Carolina and had a devastating impact on the Tuscarora, the Yamasee War erupted against South Carolina with even more consequential results. The Yamasee, a Muskhogean dialect speaking tribe, dissatisfied with the Spanish environment and policies where they lived in northeastern Florida, had lately moved into proximity of the South Carolina frontier. It was not long before they came to feel their position there was untenable.

The Yamasee sustained shoddy treatment from traders; they were buffeted by unremitting penetration of white settlers into areas specifically designated as Yamasee by the colony. Hoping for improvement in their relations with the Carolinians, the Yamasee had given sorely needed manpower and other support to the colonists in the recent Tuscarora War. But the cumulative and continued abuse was more than they could bear. The Yamasee rose up in fury in 1715. Neighboring tribes joined them, and the very existence of the colony hung in the balance. The colony was saved when the Cherokees joined the Carolina side. The Yamasee and their allies were defeated.

The consequences of these wars on the southern colonial frontier were a recital of what had happened on previous occasions but with changing emphases. Indian tribes were shifting in location and loyalties and the English colonies had to face the reality of the inadequacy of their defense and trade policies and the strengthened Spanish and French influence with the Indians, thus increasing the threat to English ambitions westward and southward. France and Spain, nevertheless, were declining powers in the international scheme of things and England was rising. Setbacks in North America were only temporary. In addition to the role they would play on the international chessboard, not necessarily or always as pawns, the Indians, in the long run, would always have to consider the advancing Anglo-American settlement factor in their initiatives and responses to the European impact on their cultures, their locations, and their futures.

With the lower Mississippi Valley still a bone of contention between France, Spain, and England, the Indians were caught in a position of trying to maintain their own best interests by accommodating themselves to what they perceived to be the predominant power at the time. This also produced intra- and intertribal rivalry and tensions.

Initially it appeared the French were in the ascendancy. Prospering in the gulf coastal trade, they established New Orleans in 1718 and other coastal settlements. Traders and settlers moved up the coastal rivers into the interior. When they built a new post in central Alabama among the Creek, the Indians were impressed, and French influence became more pronounced. Creek villages in central Georgia relocated westward, other Creek, Choctaw, and some lesser tribes closed their villages to English traders, and the Yamasee attacked Carolina frontier settlements.

In defense the seaboard colonies ringed their frontier with fortifications and then began to rebuild their deteriorated relations with the Indians. Vacillating tribes were won over by presents, low-priced trade goods, and promised rewards for their allegiance. Even the Creek and some of the Chickasaw appreciated the advantages of becoming more friendly with the English. However, there were holdouts to the English blandishments, particularly the Yamasee, who remembered their fate in the Yamasee War a decade earlier. They barely survived in a new war with the English in 1728.

Unhappy with the administration of an inept French commander at Fort Rosalie which, along with Fort St. Peter, guarded French settlements along the Mississippi and increasingly envious of the superior goods the tribes to the east were getting from English traders, the Natchez of the Mississippi Valley and others joined with the Chickasaw in 1729 to annihilate the French garrison and settlements. This sparked the so-called bitter Natchez War of the 1730s with the French and their Choctaw allies pitted against the other tribes of the lower valley. In the end, the French had been put on the defensive.

Taking advantage of this situation the English successfully established their thirteenth colony. Georgia was soon more than a coastal beachhead. With the Choctaw busy helping the French and with the Cherokee, Creek, and Chickasaw friendly to the English, only the Yamasee joined with the Florida-based Spanish to drive out the Georgians. This was not enough. Georgia was saved.

With most of the Indians on the southern frontiers now in the English camp and with the Spanish and French threats to their colonies minimized, there was only skirmishing of no long-range consequence while the French and British empires were again locked in combat in King George's War, 1744–1748. Most of the activity concerned gaining Indian alignment. The Chickasaw helped the British by making it difficult for the French to use the lower Mississippi for communications between the St. Lawrence Valley and the Gulf. And the Cherokee sided with the English in their attacks on pro-French Creek factions and Choctaw. While the war ended with the treaty's cessation of hostilities and return of conquests, the Indians remained pragmatists in their allegiances, espousing whatever posture that seemed at the moment to be to their advantage. In this, their loyalties sometimes resulted in intratribal divisions.

The English and the French increased their efforts to enlist Indian assistance during the early 1750s. For the English, this aid was judged as critical in dislodging the French from the interior and opening up this area to increase trade opportunities for the southern colonies. For the French, who were equally as determined to contain their English rivals east of the mountains, Indian assistance became an ever more crucial factor.

While the new colony of Georgia became absorbed in the business of some political restructuring, the French began to mend their fences with the southern Indians. They made peace with the Chickasaws and established friendly relations with the Cherokee and Creek. These with the traditional Choctaw support put the French in a presumed position of strength. When the French and Indian War, 1754–1763, erupted, the preponderance of the Indian factor was either neutral or weighted on the side of the French throughout the southern interior. The notable exception to this came when the Chickasaw believed their British connection was more advantageous than their recent friendly relations with the French. They pushed westward and severed the lower Mississippi lifeline betewen French Canada and Louisiana.

The triumph of the English and the end of the French as a New World power did not signal a new era for the Indians in British North America. The English had long since learned that neither the wilderness nor the Indians could be exploited and controlled to their expectations. British Indian policy had long been neglected, confused, and contradictory, resulting in a mixture of successes and failures. The Indians were important factors in Euro-American affairs; they played roles in intercolonial rivalries; and their mere presence figured in English penetration into the North American wilderness. The English offensive-Indian defensive and the English initiative-Indian reaction roles were often reversed. Anglo-Indian relations at the close of the French and Indian War were as volatile as they had ever been.

Anglo-Cherokee relations along the southern frontier were becoming uneasy. In the early half of the eighteenth century, reasonably good relations had developed between them. This brought them under English influence, but not exclusively as the French continued to deal with them to a limited extent. Intercolonial trade rivalry helped set the stage for a serious threat to the English. Enjoying a near monopoly of trade with the western Indians, the Charleston merchants perceived an increasing challenge by mercantile interests in the other southern colonies. The price of deerskins and trade goods had become a matter of serious contention between the Cherokee hunters and the Charleston traders. When the traders tried to dictate terms, the Cherokee invited merchants from other colonies.

Anxious to enlist Cherokee fighting men against French-backed Indians in the Ohio Valley in the French and Indian War, the English agreed to build and garrison posts in Cherokee country as protection against French and Creek raiders in the absence of their warriors. This was a mistake. The English stepped-up their interference in Cherokee affairs. Aggressive traders increasingly exploited the Cherokee. And frontier settlement steadily encroached on their territory.

Homeward-bound Cherokee warriors who had completed their service in the British Army in the Ohio Valley quarreled with settlers along the Virginia and Carolina frontiers, sometimes stealing horses. Frontiersmen and Cherokee clashed, with casualties on both sides. Attempts to defuse the tension failed as mutual misunderstandings worsened the situation. In 1759 when the whites took Cherokee hostages and sent an armed force toward their villages, the Cherokee War erupted. Wearying of war as it escalated and dragged on, a truce was struck in 1760. But the next year a colonial-British-Indian force wreaked systematic havoc on Cherokee settlements and their crops. Lacking the means of continuing resistance, the Cherokee agreed to a peace pact and surrendered a large tract of their territory bordering on the white frontier. Beyond the treaty specifics, the main effect of the treaty was to solidify Cherokee hatred of the English.

While the Cherokee War was running its course along the southern frontier, the Indians to the north of the Ohio River were becoming increasingly unhappy with the English who were now presuming to be their masters and protectors. With the French now removed as a consequence of the recent French and Indian War, the Indians could no longer bargain for the best concessions from the English or from the French. With French competition for their trade and support gone, the English traders now dictated the terms for doing business with them. The Indians could no longer get supplies, particularly gunpowder for subsistence hunting, on credit from the English posts. Presumably they were denied credit as punishment for their anti-British efforts in the late war. Indian department appropriations were reduced, and the practice of gifts was suspended.

Indian discontent was fueled by rumors that the English were bent on exterminating the Indians. War-induced conditions had already reduced their ranks by serious proportions. Their fears were confirmed when the army used germ warfare and dogs against them. The logical consequences of these developments, as the Indians came to believe, was to free their lands for the advancing frontier settlements. Speculators were already spying out their lands and explaining that whites by the hundreds eagerly anticipated moving westward. White prejudice led to frontier violence and tension.

French traders who still lingered in the region whispered to the Indians that French explusion was only temporary and that they were coming back to help them overthrow their English oppressors. A Delaware mystic was proclaiming that if the Indians would renounce their cultural dependence on the whites and return to the ways of life of their ancestors they could regain control of their homelands and their own destiny.

Unrest and discontent spread through the tribes to the north of the Ohio River and especially in the vicinity of the several posts the English occupied as they gained control of the country from the French. One of the interesting debates about frontier history is whether what happened was carefully planned and masterminded by Pontiac, an Ottawa chief. What happened has often been called Pontiac's Conspiracy. Revisionists are not ready to accept such a label. What is certain is that on May 7, 1763, Pontiac led an attack on Detroit from his nearby village. The fort did not capitulate, so the Indians ravaged adjacent farms and laid siege to the stronghold.

As the news spread through the wilderness, other tribes sought convenient targets; fierce and bloody warfare engulfed the western frontier. Along with Detroit, only Fort Pitt and Fort Niagara escaped destruction in this widespread resistance movement, though even they were seriously threatened. Military expeditions relieved the besieged and crushed the movement. The northern tribes were demoralized.

The British government had been wrestling with the problem of the Indians in the western wilderness as the French and Indian War was winding down. Traders and speculators and land-hungry pioneers were anxious to move westward in full force and were pressuring for concessions. In the summer of 1763, the government received the news of the turn of events on the American frontier, and the king issued a royal proclamation which embodied features that were yet only in the discussion stage by his ministers.

A demarcation line between white settlers and Indian lands followed the crest of the Appalachian Mountains from Maine to Georgia. Any settlers beyond the line were to remove to its east, and the private purchase of Indian lands was forbidden. This, presumably, would reduce tension and Indian apprehension. Only traders with licenses issued by colonial governors or military commanders could do business with the Indians. Perhaps the Indians would appreciate the good intentions of the British and some measure of control over the traders would lessen their malpractices. Administratively, the proclamation also established colonies out of the real estate gained in the late war: Quebec, East Florida, and West Florida. These were opened in the hopes of deflecting settlement from its prevailing westward orientation, thus relieving pressure and reducing friction between whites and the western Indians.

Throughout American colonial history, Indian relations had been confused and often unsatisfactory to all parties concerned, in part simply because thirteen policies prevailed and lessened the chances of success of uncertain and unsustained efforts to establish a British or national policy. Occasional intercolonial efforts, notably the Confederation of New England in the previous century, had met with some limited success. Implementation of British royal commission reports had mixed and temporary results as well. English hopes for a unified Indian policy to emerge from the Albany Congress in 1754 did not materialize.

The most promising effort to establish a unified or national Indian policy resulted from the interests and efforts of Edmond Atkin. As a successful Charleston merchant and member of the governor's council of South Carolina, Atkin had become very knowledgeable about the Indians and was an expert in Indian-white relations. In a long report, which he presented to the Board of Trade in London in the early 1750s, Atkin outlined a plan for the management of Indian affairs. He gave high praise to the French system of Indian control through the judicious use of presents, the ready availability of gunsmiths to keep their knives and hatchets sharpened and their guns in good repair, and an administration that was centralized and would not tolerate injustice to the Indians. He severely censured British and colonial methods, especially those employed by his own South Carolina. The self interests of each faction in the colonies that had dealings with the Indians came before the general good. Whom were the Indians to believe when rival traders lied about each other? Such continued chaos and mismanagement could only reap complete alienation of the Indians to the French.

Atkin's scheme provided for a detailed administrative hierarchy under a northern and a southern superintendent, an elaborate system of uniform trade regulations, a penurious use of rum, an extensive system of factory-forts, and such other support personnel as interpreters, missionaries, and gunsmiths. Atkin was appointed as the southern superintendent and, along with Sir William Johnson as his northern counterpart, the Atkin plan saw some preliminary implementation. Atkin's ideas were beyond his abilities, however, and he did not establish a strong southern Indian department. He died and was replaced in 1761 by John Stuart. Johnson, on the other hand, was able and astute. But his success was not matched by the hoped for centralization and nationalization of policy that Atkin had envisioned.

Indian-white relations in eighteenth century colonial British America were not easy. Neither the Indians nor the whites spoke with one voice. Inter- and intratribal, inter- and intra-Indian confederation, inter- and intracolonial, private versus public white sectors, and international considerations, interests, and forces all had some bearing on Indian-white relations in the years 1701–1763. Whatever happened in those decades must take these factors into consideration.

Britain's triumph in 1763 in eastern North America would prove to be short-lived. And, no matter what the maps delineated and no matter which flag flew over them, the Indians were engulfed in an uneven struggle with a white culture that had the resources and will to predominate. Based on their troubled history, the Indians must have viewed the future with apprehension, with a mixture of dubious optimism and resigned futility.

## SUGGESTED READING

The person who wishes to flesh out the details of Indian-white relations in British America, 1701–1763, that have been surveyed in this essay will be best served by progressing from the general to the specific. If it is wanting or incomplete, the reader should first gain a survey knowledge of colonial American history to place the subject in context. I would suggest reading appropriate chapters in all three of these types of books in this consecutive order: any standard United States history textbook; a history of the American frontier, such as Ray Allen Billington and Martin Ridge, *Westward Expansion: A History of the American Frontier*, 5th ed. (New York, 1982); and a survey history of the American Indians, such as Arrell Morgan Gibson, *The American Indian: Prehistory to the Present* (Lexington, Mass., 1980). Since the international wars of these years are so much a part of the setting for Indian-white relations, the reader will find a convenient summary in Howard H. Peckham, *The Colonial Wars, 1689–1762* (Chicago, 1964).

Assuming and building on the background acquaintance of the general knowledge that such references offer, it is profitable to move into a more specialized and detailed look at the topic. Three excellent monographs are essential requirements for this: Douglas Edward Leach, *The Northern Colonial Frontier, 1607–1763* (New York, 1966); W. Stitt Robinson, *The Southern Colonial Frontier, 1607–1763* (Albuquerque, 1979); and a similar volume from another vantage point, William J. Eccles, *The Canadian Frontier, 1534–1760* (New York, 1969).

A few suggestions will suffice as illustrations of particular aspects or topics. Numerous tribal histories offer different orientations. Some of the essays in Peckham and Charles Gibson, ed., *Attitudes of Colonial Powers Toward the American Indian* (Salt Lake City, 1969) will be of interest.

In his *Dispossessing the American Indian: Indians and Whites on the Colonial Frontier* (New York, 1972), Wilbur R. Jacobs examines the mythology that encrusts our conventional knowledge. Two principals in the interpretation conflict are Francis Parkman, *The Conspiracy of Pontiac and the Indian War after the Conquest of Canada,* 2 volumes (Boston, 1902–1903) and Peckham, *Pontiac and the Indian Uprising* (Chicago, 1947). In his *Wilderness Politics and Indian Gifts: The Northern Colonial Frontier, 1748–1763* (Lincoln, 1950), Jacobs studies Indian-white diplomacy.

There are two fundamental ways whereby anyone can identify the literature that is already published. First, any one of the items in this brief list will cite the sources of information which its author has consulted. Second, a standard bibliography will identify topically much of the published literature. For this, I recommend Francis Paul Prucha, *A Bibliographical Guide to the History of Indian-White Relations in the United States* (Chicago, 1977) and its supplement, *Indian-White Relations in the United States: A Bibliography of Works Published 1975–1980* (Lincoln, 1981).

While much more than is generally believed has been published about Indian-white relations in British America in the eighteenth century, much more remains to be done, both to add to our present knowledge and to be subjected to possible revisionist interpretation.

| Bernard | **4.** | The |
| W. | **Images** | Problem |
| Sheehan | | of the |
| | | Indian |
| | | in the |
| | | Revolution |

It can be argued plausibly that the American Indians played only a minor role in the American Revolution. Early in the war they threatened the southern frontier, and after 1777 they kept the Kentucky and Ohio settlements on edge. But it cannot be said that the activities of the native warriors, as inconvenient and damaging as these might have been, in any appreciable way effected the outcome of the conflict. The war was won on the battlegrounds of the East by an army constructed and trained according to European standards and was not won in the West against the irregular soldiers of the native tribes, who employed a mode of warfare that Europeans had long identified with the "savage" condition. Yet both sides in the conflict eventually sought out the tribes as allies, and the British especially made extensive use of them during the war. It might be contended that the experience of the imperial wars, waged between 1689 and 1763 and still a vivid memory for both Englishmen and Americans, led easily to the belief that the native tribes might be valued allies in the achievement of victory as they had been assumed to be in the long hostilities between Britain and France in the New World. If so, the conviction was more likely the consequence of habit than conscious decision since the native tribes, for all of their activity in the imperial wars, had not been critical for the outcome.

But if the native people did not play an extensive or vital role in the war itself, they were an important factor in the thinking of Englishmen and Americans about the war. The symbolic Indian was nothing new in the New World experience but seldom in the past had the native carried quite the weight and significance that he was required to bear during the Revolution. From the earliest period of discovery and settlement, Europeans had incorporated the Indians into an intellectual scheme that satisfied the white man's need but bore little resemblance to the actuality of native life.

Although the phrase "noble savage" was not used until John Dryden invented it in 1664, and the term ignoble savage until much later, the word savage was employed from the very beginning. The word associated the Indians with the wilderness. They were assumed to represent the antithesis to civility and its distinguishing social elements. Montaigne formulated the classic definition in the late sixteenth century. According to his view the native people lived without society, government, economy, mental pursuits, and virtually every other characteristic of humanity or social order. As a later social commentator put it, the "savage" lived at the zero of the human condition. Of course it must be stressed that we have here an exercise in the European imagination, or better an expression of a very important mythic formulation. The idea of the "savage" in no way reflects the way any group of human beings live or have lived. All human organisms form societies, have language, govern themselves by some system of law or custom, and engage in economic activity. In European thinking and later in the American conception of native life, the condition of the savage could take either of two forms, though sometimes the images became mixed and the savage figure contained contradictory qualities. The noble savage was a benign, passive figure, utterly innocent, and reminiscent of the inhabitants of the Garden of Eden. The ignoble savage represented the summation of human vice. He was infinitely violent, inconstant, treacherous, and degraded. For Europeans and eighteenth-century Americans the noble savage represented an ideal from which they had fallen and to which they wished to return. Conversely the ignoble savage posed a threat to civil order and human decency.

As this dual figure of mythic proportions, the Indian served the propaganda purposes of both the British and the Americans. Overtly the ignoble savage was much more significant. Both sides interpreted the merits of their own position in contrast to the image of the savage. They both claimed to represent virtue and resorted easily to the accusations that their enemies betrayed the nature of their cause by behaving in a savage manner or allying themselves with savage Indians. At the same time Americans tended to couch public expressions describing the objects of their Revolution in terms plainly paralleled of the virtues long attributed to the noble savage.

The issue of the Indian arose in virtually the first moments of fighting between the Americans and the British. On April 19, 1775, at the North Bridge in Concord, one of the wounded British soldiers left behind by his retreating comrades was struck over the head with an ax by one of the young men of the town. Soon after, a contingent of British troops that had proceeded beyond the town searching for military supplies recrossed the bridge and sighted the dead soldier. They concluded from the spectacle that the Americans had fallen to scalping the wounded and spread rumors to this effect when they joined their comrades.

The charge that Americans scalped enemies appeared in the reports of the encounter turned in by British officers and in the official account sent by the commanding general, Thomas Gage, to the government in London. Descriptions of the incident varied, but there could be little doubt that the British officers and men were convinced that something terrible had occurred at the Concord Bridge. A number of popular pamphleteers in England took up the issue, adding to their broader condemnation of the American cause the accusation that "the Americans fought like the savages of the country."

The Americans were no less sensitive than the British about this supposed descent into savagery. Touched by British propaganda the Massachusetts Provincial Congress took depositions, which were duly published, from the two townsmen who had buried the British bodies. There were no signs of scalping. Thomas Gordon, a Roxbury minister, arrived in Concord within days of the battle seeking authentic information. In a short account published soon after and later in his history of the Revolution he told the true story. But the issue went beyond truth or falsity; it concerned the very nature of the Revolutionary conflict. In a contest increasingly ideological, both sides could not but think the worst of the opposition.

On the return march from Concord, the British troops, exhausted from the long hours under arms, severely mauled by farmers who seemed to break all the rules of civilized war, and perhaps provoked by the rumors of American barbarism, made free use of the bayonet and killed many Americans. The Americans reacted to this bloodletting by accusing the British of abandoning all restraint, of behaving like savage Indians who subscribed to none of the limitations that moderated civilized conflict. Thus almost instinctively in this first clash of the revolutionary conflict, both sides invoked the image of the Indian to condemn the behavior of their opponents.

The uniform disrelish of what was assumed to be the Indian mode of war did not inhibit either side from seeking native allies. The experience of the imperial wars made it likely that the Indians would join the fray, but the Americans had good reason to suspect that it would not be on their side. After some initial effort by provincial commanders to recruit the warriors, American policy was devoted to keeping the Indians neutral. Except for the Oneidas and a faction of the Cherokees, the native peoples joined the British cause. For some, indeed, the reason may have resided in their clearheaded conviction that in the long run their interests would be better served by the British than by a newly independent nation of American farmers.

In the past the imperial government had shown an inclination to protect the tribes from the hasty advance of the frontier into the Indian country. And no doubt the Indians could expect little sympathy from an American government beholden to settlers hungry for new land. But the more immediate reason for the success of the British in attracting the loyalty of the tribes was bureaucratic. In the mid-1750s the imperial government had attempted to remove Indian affairs from the jurisdiction of the separate colonies and place them in the hands of two superintendents, one north of the Potomac and one south. The new policy failed to exclude the colonial governments from dealings with the tribes, but it did succeed in establishing an effective Indian department in the colonies. Sir William Johnson in the North and John Stuart in the South attempted to draw the tribes within the British orbit. After the defeat of the French in the Seven Years' War and the decline of Spanish power, the superintendents were successful in cementing the loyalty of many of the native peoples. Hence, when the Revolution shattered imperial unity, most of the tribes remained wedded to the network of agents that had for the past twenty years heeded their interests.

British success in gaining Indian allies put them at a decided disadvantage in the propaganda war. They found themselves embattled not only by the Americans but by the political opposition in England. In the Declaration of Independence Jefferson could add a further item to the long indictment of the Crown for making alliance with "merciless Indian Savages, whose known rule of warfare, is an undistinguished destruction of all ages, sexes and conditions." In Parliament the Rockingham Whigs kept up an intermittent barrage of criticism over Britain's native allies, using similar images. Furthermore, there can be little doubt that the British were themselves uneasy about the relationship. They worried about and defended the policy too much not to have been seriously doubtful about the propriety of allowing the Indians to join the conflict.

In a sense it should not have been surprising to the Americans that the British should have brought the Indians into the war and thus transformed the conflict into what they deemed a savage assault on civil order. One historian has argued that between the end of the Thirty Years' War in 1648 and the beginnings of the wars of revolution in the 1790s Europeans made a conscious effort to moderate the ferocity of international conflict. War during these decades was carried on by professional forces for limited objects, and civilian populations, where possible, remained unaffected. For the British the exceptions to this trend had been their internecine conflict with the Scots and the interminable hostilities involving the native peoples of America. Wars in these theaters had proved unamenable to the moderating spirit of eighteenth-century humanitarianism. Instead it retained the ferocity and totality long thought to be characteristic of conflict involving savage people. For the British to have purposefully abandoned these canons of civil conflict by employing Indians, struck many Americans as entirely appropriate. Since their intention was the reduction of America under "an obsolute despotism," that is the obliteration of civil society, they had chosen the means necessary to their end. Total war had been characteristic of conflict in America and now the British, it seemed, had adopted it as a positive policy.

Most of the serious frontier conflict occurred in the North. Early in the war the Cherokees rose but the retaliation meted out by the Virginia militia was so swift and so decisive that the warriors retired to their villages and did not venture out again until late in the conflict. In the North intense fighting broke out in 1777. Supplied from Niagara and Detroit, native bands, usually led by white officers and frequently accompanied by contingents of white irregulars, repeatedly struck the settlements in Kentucky, on the upper Ohio, and in New York. They spread terror and destruction and managed in a short time to stifle the movement of white Americans to the West.

But in a war of images and propaganda the actual activities of the Indians, the near constant raiding of small bands of warriors with British or loyalist aid, meant less than a number of spectacular incidents seized on by the Americans to make their case against the British. When General John Burgoyne moved south from Canada into New York in the early summer of 1777, he was accompanied not only by an elaborate and cumbersome train of wagons but by a contingent of warriors. Burgoyne needed the Indians to ease his way in the wilderness, a point he knew well enough, but he plainly had misgivings about their mode of war. Burgoyne was a bon vivant, raconteur, and a playwright whose personal style fell easily into bombast. One would find it difficult to conceive of a character less likely to gain insight into Indian culture or less likely to succeed in changing the native way of making war. But these were precisely the ends Burgoyne had in mind. He wished to employ Indians on his own terms, which meant that the warriors were to cease being savages and to fight according to the rules of war honored in Europe. Of course he failed utterly to convince the warriors that they should change their ways. As his army advanced south the Indians played their usual havoc in the surrounding countryside. This aroused the ire of the frontier settlements and helped to gather the American militia who halted Burgoyne's advance and then forced his surrender.

In late July an incident occurred that deepened Burgoyne's dilemma (he needed the warriors but at the same time he found their behavior distasteful) and became the source of much controversy. Jane McCrea, a young woman from a loyalist family whose fiancé served with Burgoyne, had been captured by Indians in the British service and then murdered when the warriors argued over whose prisoner she would be. One Wyandot Panther appeared in camp with the scalp. News spread quickly, and Burgoyne was forced to take action. He found the act appalling, indeed not only was the victim a loyal subject of the Crown but he had given explicit instructions against taking the scalps of noncombatants. Torn between the need to uphold what he saw as the standards of civilized war and the fear of losing the Indians' aid Burgoyne closed the incident by merely reprimanding the warriors responsible.

For the Americans the incident would not be so easily forgotten. Jane McCrea's political affiliation receded behind the overwhelming fact that she had been wantonly murdered by savage Indians in alliance with the British. The American commander, Horatio Gates, chided Burgoyne for responsibility, and the instruments of American propaganda immediately made all they could of the event. Jane McCrea became a symbol of innocence and virtue much like the infant republic, the victim of a brutal and conscienceless murder. In the immediate situation the killing contributed to Burgoyne's defeat, but more significant Jane McCrea became one of those important images used by white men to explain the meaning of the Indian in relation to the Americans' struggle to preserve their liberty. Later John Vanderlyn's fanciful painting of the affair (two burly Indians, one poised with a tomahawk and the other prepared to take a scalp, stand over the kneeling, terrified Miss McCrea) impressed it on the American imagination and made it legendary.

Burgoyne's defeat in October 1777, because it precipitated open alliance with France, may have been a decisive event in the outcome of the war, but it did little to quiet the frontier. The following year the Americans suffered two notable, well-publicized defeats at the hands of British rangers and Indians. At Wyoming Valley in July and at Cherry Valley in November 1778 bands of warriors and irregulars proved more than a match for the American frontier fighters. At Cherry Valley some forty survivors were massacred after having surrendered. The villain in these two incidents was Joseph Brant, who actually had taken no part in the attack on Wyoming but had been at Cherry Valley. Brant seemed to the Americans the perfect symbol of the British complicity with savage war. In fact, he was one of those rare human beings who had managed by superior intelligence and stable personality to bridge two cultures. As a young Mohawk his family became associated with the household of Sir William Johnson. He attended a mission school in Connecticut, converted to Anglicanism, and visited England where he learned to make his way in polite society. Yet he soon returned to his people, where he assumed a position of leadership during the troubled times of the Revolution. His warriors, together with loyalist rangers led by John and Walter Butler, kept the frontier in turmoil. True to his European training he attempted to modify native practices in war, though he remained loyal to his people. The Americans could scarcely see it this way. As a consequence Brant seemed present at every battle, guilty of every atrocity, and forever the exemplar of the British policy of intermingling savagery with civilized conflict.

The American response to the border conflict was twofold. George Rogers Clark attempted to cut off the British attacks at the source by capturing Detroit and neutralizing the western tribes, and Washington dispatched a continental expedition under John Sullivan into the heart of the Iroquois country in the hope of quieting the New York and Pennsylvania frontiers.

In the summer of 1779 Sullivan moved north up the Susquehanna Valley against the Iroquois. Simultaneously columns of troops entered the Indian country from Pittsburgh and Albany. Washington's object was to break Iroquois power permanently with a formal attack that would bring the loyalists and Indians into battle. In an immediate sense the plan failed. Sullivan won the only battle, at Newtown, but it was indecisive and within the year the warriors renewed their assaults on the frontier. Yet in the long run Sullivan's raid did signal the end of Iroquois power and their ultimate expulsion from their ancient territory. Failing to entice the warriors into a decisive battle, the continental soldiers spent their time burning villages, cultivated fields, and orchards—and killing stragglers. Here was irony and a revelation. The Americans had entered the world of the Iroquois prepared for a confrontation with savagery. At the outset the officers toasted each other with the defiant challenge: "Civilization or death to all American Savages." But in the land of the Iroquois revealed few signs of persistent savagery. The native people lived in towns—many in cabins with glass windows—surrounded by well-cultivated fields and orchards. They kept domestic animals and in many ways comported themselves like people who had learned the lessons of civilized life. These facts, though observed, could be ignored; the native people could still be called savages and the soldiers could still believe that they did the work of civilization in avenging the sufferings of the frontier people. What could not be ignored was the salubrity of the country, and it was this observation that spelled the collapse of Iroquois power. The Indians lived in the midst of a fertile garden and at the conclusion of the war they could not hold it against the press of the frontier. That the Americans continued to think of them as savages made their displacement all the more likely.

Clark never succeeded in taking Detroit, but with the support of Virginia and the Kentucky settlements he did manage for a time to clear the British from the upper Mississippi Valley and to diminish the security of the western tribes. His thrust into the West, where he captured the Illinois towns and then forced the capitulation of Henry Hamilton, the British lieutenant governor from Detroit, at Vincennes, made one point certain. Many Americans, and Clark in particular, were deeply concerned about the problem of the Indian.

Whatever Clark's larger strategic intentions, his deepest personal objective was to strike a blow at savagery and at those Britons who promoted savage war. He began by attempting to introduce a new era in Indian-white diplomatic relations. No longer would the Americans make those conventional concessions to native usage in dealing with the Indians: gift giving, exchanges of wampum, prolix oratory, and the delicate balancing of forces among the tribes. Instead the Indians must be made to understand that if they did not immediately join the American cause (Clark explained to them the advantages of liberty) they would simply be annihilated. Clark was all the more high-handed in dealing with the western tribes because of what he believed about the character of native life.

As such, when he captured Vincennes and took Henry Hamilton prisoner, Clark seized the opportunity to make a point about the Indian and his savage ways. Since 1777 when Hamilton began sending Indian bands accompanied and often led by whites against the border settlements, he had gained the reputation as one of the principal promoters of savage warfare. He was called the "Hair Buyer" because rumor had it that he paid a bounty for white scalps at Detroit. No evidence exists to prove the scalp buying accusation, though there can be no doubt that Hamilton received these tokens of native triumph and that he employed Indian warriors against the frontier as an instrument of British policy. Because of these activities, Clark argued, as did his mentor Thomas Jefferson, that Hamilton had placed himself outside the ordinary arena of civilized conflict. At first Clark refused to grant terms of surrender. After doing so, he refused at first to abide by them. He ordered that captured white "partisans" (his term for rangers who led or accompanied Indian raiding parties) should be put to death. In truth Clark was more talk than action, for none of these violations of the rules of war were implemented. Yet there can be no doubt that he took the problem of the Indian seriously and entertained profound convictions on the mixing of what he saw as civilized and savage conflict.

The issue of the difference between civilized versus savage conflict in warfare became public when Clark sent Hamilton and a number of his followers to Virginia as prisoners. Jefferson, who had just assumed the governorship, refused to recognize the formal surrender, placed the captives in chains, and confined them to the common jail in Williamsburg. He justified his action by claiming that Hamilton had violated the elemental decencies of civilized life by paying for scalps and encouraging warriors to attack settlements. Hamilton's behavior, in Jefferson's interpretation, made him an ally of savages and an enemy of civilization. Hamilton could claim none of the amenities usually granted prisoners of war. The British complained vehemently and threatened retaliation against Americans in their hands. After seeking the advice of persons experienced in international usage, Washington recommended moderation in Hamilton's treatment. Ultimately Jefferson was forced to back down, but he never ceased to believe that Hamilton had placed himself beyond the boundaries of civil conduct.

Had Jefferson looked more closely at Clark's behavior he might have seen clearly what in fact he probably already knew. The native mode could be extraordinarily attractive to white men, especially to Indian fighters like Clark who entered the wilderness with the intention of sweeping aside the native way of life. Clark was not one of those white Indians of the revolutionary period, men like Louis Wetzel, Simon Girty, or even William Wells, who in the popular imagination had become Indians. On the contrary, he remained consciously on the civil side of the border. And yet he argued that the most efficient way to break Indian power was to adopt native methods of warfare. Thus he dressed in the native style and encouraged his followers to do the same. His men gave the war whoop, danced and feasted like Indians, and took Indian scalps, all practices that for white men characterized the native way of life. Furthermore Clark was himself a brutal and undisciplined man. At Vincennes he ordered the public murder of four Indians who had been captured on their return from a raid on the Kentucky settlements. In the years after this initial achievement as an Indian fighter, Clark gained a reputation as a heavy drinker and an undependable leader. It may be that in the end the wilderness proved to be Clark's undoing, but while he engaged in its battles he seemed to see instinctively, as did so many other Americans, that the Indian way was the appropriate manner in which to contest the continent with savagery. Neither Clark nor Jefferson perceived the irony of this widely held conviction. This tendency of Europeans to approrpriate what they supposed to be an Indian mode had a long history. From John Mason and Benjamin Church, who led New England forces against the Indians in the seventeenth century, to Robert Rogers, famous for the contingent of rangers he formed in the Seven Years' War, white men had proved how adept they could become in the wilderness. On the basis of these experiences, in the 1760s the British had organized detachments of light troops together with groups of rangers and scouts of which Rogers's formation was only the most noted. By the time of the Revolution light troops had fallen into disfavor, although the alliance with the tribes and the presence of loyalists eager to fight made their employment inevitable. Brant, the Butlers, Banastre Tarleton, and Patrick Ferguson led such bands. On the American side Clark, Daniel Morgan, Michael Cresap, John Sevier, and James Smith matched the British. In some measure all these fighters followed what they assumed to be the path of the native warriors.

The usefulness of these wilderness warriors became patent after the defeat of James Braddock and his army in 1755 by an irregular force of French and Indians. Braddock, so the story went, refused the advice of knowledgeable woodsmen, Washington among them, and marched blithely into an ambush; his men, familiar only with the formal confrontations of Europe, panicked. Braddock was not nearly so callow or his tactics so naive, but he was soundly trounced by a smaller, irregular force. In 1763, during the so-called Pontiac's Rebellion, one other incident conveyed a more ambiguous message. Henry Bouquet, a Swiss officer in the British service and a man of considerable marshal talent, led a conventional army to the relief of Fort Pitt. He met a native force at Bushy Run and decisively defeated it. Bouquet's success arose not from any process of indianization but rather from an intelligent adaptation of European tactics to the circumstance of forest warfare. According to Thomas Hutchins, who composed a tactical treatise drawing on the experience at Bushy Run, Bouquet's men employed, at least in part, Indian methods. They fought scattered, gave ground when pressed, and returned to the attack when pressure eased. But, of course, they remained a disciplined European force that acted under the command of its officers. Mixed though the experience of forest war had been, it seemed plain by the time of the Revolution that the warriors had lessons to teach.

One of the more memorable characters to attempt to carry these lessons of the imperial wars into the Revolution was James Smith. As a young man he had been captured by Indians and had lived with them for four years. Although deeply influenced by native culture, he retained much of the Indian-hating attitude of the frontier. Thus in the 1760s, with the aid of two other former captives, he organized a group called the "Black Boys" for the purpose of engaging the warriors on their own ground. They dressed in breechclothes, leggings, moccasins, and green shrouds. They fought with faces painted red and black, followed what Smith called the "Indian discipline," and took scalps. Early in the Revolution Smith raised a contingent to defeat the British with tactics compatible with the American experience. On this occasion Washington offered Smith a commission in the regular army. But as had already become clear, Washington fully understood the expedience of a judicious adaptation to the Indian way.

Hence one need not overdo the significance of this process of indianization to note that such practices were quite widespread during the Revolution, as they had been before and would continue to be after. Examples can be found in the most unlikely places. Although Washington fought the war according to a European design and was reluctant to jeopardize positions held against the British for a limited success on the frontier, he sanctioned Indian-like behavior. Soon after taking command of the congressional forces before Boston in 1775, he welcomed a contingent of riflemen from Virginia led by Daniel Morgan. These frontier fighters carried long rifles, wore hunting shirts and moccasins, carried scalping knives and tomahawks, and generally disported themselves in ways inimical to the discipline of a European-style army. Washington came to believe them wasteful of ammunition and to question the usefulness in battle of the long rifle, but he found their Indian-like manners a practicable addition to the army's tactics. He hoped in particular to convey a message to his British enemies. American soldiers who dressed like Indians, carried knives and tomahawks the way Indians did, and whooped like savages might also engage in the sort of atrocities that inevitably accompanied war in the wilderness. Perhaps he remembered that great fear that afflicted Braddock's soldiers in 1755 as they marched toward the debacle on the Monongahela. The troops, many of them raw, had become convinced that torture and mutilation awaited them in the forest at the hands of men who would deny them the civilities soldiers could depend on in Europe. Later Washington's tactics were, of course, calculated, but they would not have been possible if Morgan's men and others like them had not resembled Indians.

One might suppose that the incongruence between attitudes and action might have been a source of a great tension during the Revolution. The burden of opinion about the native people was so negative that any obvious process of indianization would have to be unthinking or so patently ironic as to elicit comment. For someone like Clark it was no doubt largely unthinking. Moreover the irony missed him entirely. Much the same can be said for many other rough-hewn men of the frontier. Hating and fighting Indians seemed to have little connection with behaving like Indians unless the association was so subliminal as to be susceptible to only the deepest psychological probing. For others like Burgoyne and Hamilton the discrepancy was acute and a source of great tension. It may be that the British did so badly in the propaganda contest not only because they had been more astute in gaining native allies but because they were more torn than the Americans over uniting the forces of civility with those of savagery. A mind as acute as Jefferson's saw the risk in indianization, but he was far more impressed by the advantages in berating the British for their policy than he was in preventing an American drift into the savage world.

Although the war had shifted the British and American conception of the native people toward the ignoble side of the dichotomy, the noble savage was far from dead in the revolutionary age. Some historians, especially in recent times, have attempted to interpret the Revolution and the later movement toward the establishment of a new government as a conscious attempt to imitate the native way of life. The principal problem with this explanation is that it attributes to native societies a number of traits that are plainly anachronistic—democracy and political unity, the two major characteristics. In fact what this interpretation must assume is that the American Indian was indeed a noble savage and that the Americans, perceiving the advantages of this mode of life, determined to adopt it and hence generated a revolution. One will not find this interpretation in any of the major works devoted directly to the Revolution. Here the sources of the breakup of the empire are located in a wrongheaded ministerial policy, internal social developments in the colonies, or the tradition of British oppositionist thought. The Indian hardly enters into the subject.

But if the Indian was not a noble savage and if the Americans paid little attention to real Indians as they formulated the meaning of their revolution, the symbolic Indian did play an important role. The principal question concerned the problem of self-identity. The Americans could not, after all, make a revolution or even establish their independence until they had managed to distinguish America from Europe. And many of the qualities that tended to set off the American—what Crèvecœur called "this new man"—from the European turned out to be precisely the qualities of noble savagery. The Indian in this sense possessed all the attributes that had been lost or forgotten in Europe. Thus Americans—and Indians—were pristine, simple, rustic, open, unaffected, honest, disciplined, equal, individualistic, and free. Europeans against whom the Americans made their revolution were burdened by the past, effete, devious, corrupt, sunk in luxury, and subjected to despotic authority. As this contrast became more apparent in the development of the revolutionary ideology, it was difficult for American commentators to resist an appeal to the qualities of noble savagery. Hence in the years after the Revolution one finds the increasing presence of the Indian in American public iconography. But it must be stressed that direct reference to the noble savage or explicit references to the need to imitate native societies are few during the Revolution. The image of the ignoble savage predominated during the years of conflict.

Because the noble savage functioned as an ideal that had been lost but might again be attained, the image had long served the purposes of propaganda and partisan controversy. That, after all, was how Montaigne had employed the conception in the late sixteenth century. The writer stressed the inadequacies of his own world by contrasting it invidiously with the noble world of pristine savagery. Long before the eighteenth century the method had become conventional. It did not necessarily connote any particular affection for the native people. In fact since the noble savage derived from the white man's mind and celebrated qualities singular to European modes of thought, it had little if anything to do with the Indian, though it must be admitted that many people through the ages have believed that the noble savage described the real Indian. The important point is that the image performed a propagandistic mission. That was how Benjamin Franklin invariably made use of the noble savage, and the same can be said for Jefferson. Neither of them held the real Indian in high regard, particularly during the Revolutionary War. When the time came to complete the Revolution in the formation of a new political order, very little was said directly about the Indians. Except for practical references to Indian affairs, the subject did not arise in either the Constitutional Convention or the ratifying conventions. Nor did the noble Indian appear extensively in the correspondence of the founding fathers in the critical years after the Revolution.

And yet it is difficult to conceive of the Revolution without reference to the Indians. During the war they remained an issue of immense significance. Both sides sought self-definition by reference to their conception of the native people. The Americans, in particular, could scarcely have defined the nature of their virtuous republic if they could not have pointed out that the British had fallen from virtue by allying themselves with ignoble savages. Conversely, the American conception of virtue, the meaning and intellectual substance of the Revolution, drew heavily from the noble savage convention. The Indian as symbol proved indispensable in the making of American independence.

## SUGGESTED READING

The literature dealing directly with the Indian in the Revolution remains small, though much of the writing on the Revolution touches also on the Indian. Two volumes that concern the tribesmen specifically are Barbara Graymont, *The Iroquois in the American Revolution* (Syracuse, 1972) and James H. O'Donnell, *The Southern Indians in the American Revolution* (Knoxville, 1973). Anthony F. C. Wallace, in *The Death and Rebirth of the Seneca* (New York, 1970) and *King of the Delawares: Teedyuskung* (Philadelphia, 1949), writes with insight on the decline of native society in the late eighteenth century. By all odds the most extensive treatment of any group of Indians in the period is a dissertation by Paul L. Stevens, "His Majesty's 'Savage' Allies: British Policy and the Northern Indians—The Carleton Years, 1774–1778 (1984). Jack M. Sosin, "The Use of Indians in the War of the American Revolution: A Re-Assessment of Responsibility," *Canadian Historical Review* XLVI (1965): 101–121, remains the best treatment of the subject. The most accessible of the general accounts of the Indians in the American story is Wilcomb E. Washburn, *The Indian in America* (New York, 1975).

The Indians' place in the white man's imagination has stimulated a substantial body of writing. Robert F. Berkhofer, Jr., covers the field in *The White Man's Indian: From Columbus to the Present* (New York, 1977). Examination of the more literary aspects of the Indian theme can be found in Roy Harvey Pearce, *The Savages of America: A Study of the Indian and the Idea of Civilization,* rev. ed. (Baltimore, 1965) and Richard Slotkin, *Regeneration through Violence: The Mythology of the American Frontier, 1660–1860* (Middletown, Conn., 1973). The subject is treated more specifically in Arthur K. Moore, *The Frontier Mind: A Cultural Analysis of the Kentucky Frontiersman* (Lexington, 1957) and more generally in Leo Marx, *The Machine in the Garden: Technology and the Pastoral Ideal in America* (New York, 1964). In his *A Cultural History of the American Revolution* (New York, 1976), Kenneth Silverman has much to say about the image of the Indian. The argument that the new nation was formed in imitation of native society can be found in Bruce E. Johansen, *Forgotten Founders: Benjamin*

*Franklin, the Iroquois, and the Rationale of the American Nation* (Ipswich, Mass., 1977). Bernard W. Sheehan, "Ignoble Savagism and the American Revolution," in Larry Gerlach, ed., *Legacies of the American Revolution* (Logan, Utah, 1978): 151–181 and "'The Famous Hair Buyer General': Henry Hamilton, George Rogers Clark, and the American Indian," *Indiana Magazine of History* (1983): 1–28, inquires into the conception of the Indian as savage.

Works dealing with the West in the Revolution inevitably have a great deal to say about the Indian. A basic study is Sosin, *The Revolutionary Frontier, 1763–1783* (New York, 1967). Biographies of white frontiersmen abound. Three of the more interesting are: Consul Wilshire Butterfield, *History of the Girtys* (Cincinnati, 1890), James Alton James, *The Life of George Rogers Clark* (Chicago, 1928), and Don Higginbotham, *Daniel Morgan: Revolutionary Rifleman* (Chapel Hill, 1961). Dale Van Every, *A Company of Heros: The American Frontier, 1775–1783* (New York, 1962) offers a popular and engrossing survey.

More general accounts of the revolutionary experience in the main ignore the Indian but much of the story of the Revolution, at least by implication, concerns the white man's conception of the native people: see Robert Middlekauf, *The Glorious Cause: The American Revolution, 1763–1789* (New York, 1982), Bernard Bailyn, *The Ideological Origins of the American Revolution* (Cambridge, Mass., 1967), and H. Trevor Colbourn, *The Lamp of Experience: Whig History and the Intellectual Origins of the American Revolution* (Chapel Hill, 1965).

George W. Knepper

# 5. Breaching the Ohio Boundary

The Western Tribes in Retreat

**P**ossibly no place in North America affords the historian a better vantage point for observing the complexities of eighteenth-century Indian life, and the interaction of Indians and whites, than does Ohio. Located directly in the main path of the westward movement, Ohio became an arena in which the conflicting ambitions of the Indians and the Europeans were fought out. Some of these activities took place exclusively in Ohio, but others were more broadly based, involving regions beyond the modern borders of the state.

Even an abbreviated list of the eighteenth-century Indian activity in Ohio is impressive. It was here that the once all-powerful Six Nation Iroquois finally had to surrender the hegemony which they had long claimed over many western tribes. Their traditional service as diplomatic and economic middlemen between the northern Indians and the Dutch and British authorities of the seaboard colonies was thoroughly rejected in the Revolutionary era when the Ohio tribes assumed direction of their own affairs. For many years the Six Nations had successfully played the British and French against one another to their own advantage. As the scene of border action moved toward the Ohio country, the Six Nations lost that capability. They became the manipulated rather than the manipulators.

While the Six Nations were losing influence, the tribes moving into Ohio after 1730 were assuming a more important role in Indian-white relationships. These tribes came to Ohio because it was relatively unoccupied and possessed an abundance of resources. They came from many directions and, as we shall see, for many motives. By midcentury they were playing a central role in the Anglo-French contest for control of the interior of North America. When the British won the contest and gained this great prize, the western Indians first rebelled against them but, within a dozen years, joined them in a prolonged border war against Britain's American colonials.

The Americans won the Revolutionary War and, in the peace treaty, won western lands to the Mississippi. The United States then established a public domain "north and west of the Ohio River," and, in the Ohio portion of that region, worked out its initial Indian policies and public land policies. Through additional warfare and through treaties, the United States pushed the Ohio Indians into an ever-smaller enclave in the northwestern portion of the future state. Under this pressure, some western Indians, led by the Shawnee brothers Tecumseh and Tenskwatawa, attempted to revitalize Indian life and deter further American encroachment on their Ohio lands. Despite encouragement from the British, they failed, and as a last expedient they joined the British side in the War of 1812. That decision proved costly as the British were forced from the Northwest and terminated their aid and encouragement. The scattered remnants of the Ohio tribes then settled on small reservations in the northwestern quadrant of the state until they were removed to new homes in the Trans-Mississippi West. After 1842 there were no organized Indian tribes left in Ohio.

During the middle years of the seventeenth century the New York-based Iroquois tribes which then formed the Five Nations raided far to the west against their fur-trading rivals and their political enemies. Included in their westward sweep were the Indians then occupying Ohio. Several tribes were eliminated in the north, along the Lake Erie littoral, including a powerful Iroquoian-speaking people—the Eries—who were destroyed as an organized society by 1654. To the south of them were villages of the Fort Ancient people. It is not clear what became of the Fort Ancients; however, they no longer figured as a substantial people after the Iroquois raids of the mid-seventeenth century.

Ohio was left virtually unpopulated for the next seventy-five years. The Five Nations maintained a loose claim to the territory, but they did not establish permanent villages in Ohio. Other Indians were apparently too intimidated to try. There is some evidence that the Five Nations permitted other tribes to trap in the Ohio country. In 1701, for instance, they agreed to a treaty which allowed the French to export furs from Ohio via their newly established post at Detroit (Fort Pontchartrain). By the 1730s, when other Indian tribes started to penetrate Ohio, the Six Nations (the Tuscarora had joined in 1720) reasserted their claim to the area south of Lake Erie, and the other tribes dealt with them on that basis.

Sometime about 1740 some of the New York Iroquois moved into Ohio and by 1742 had established villages at Cuyahoga, an area of indefinite size centered on the Cuyahoga Valley. Pennsylvania traders had given the name

Mingo to those Iroquois who settled in western Pennsylvania and in Ohio. (Mingo is presumably an Algonquian word meaning "stealthy.") Most Ohio Mingoes were Senecas, but one would also find among them small numbers of Cayugas, Onondagas, Oneidas, Mohawks, and Tuscaroras.

It is estimated that about 2,000 to 2,400 Mingoes and other Indians lived at Cuyahoga. By 1750, however, these Indian villages were widely dispersed, and the population of Cuyahoga never again assumed first importance.

The Mingoes came to Cuyahoga for at least two important reasons. A great famine had created prolonged hardship in their New York hunting grounds, and Ohio was still virgin territory with food enough to support many people. Another reason for the move to Cuyahoga lay in the imperial politics of France and Great Britain, each of whom was asserting rights to the interior lands of North America. In an effort to wean certain Iroquois away from British connections, the French commandant at Detroit established a trading post at Cuyahoga. This post, operated by Francois Saguin, succeeded briefly in wooing some Mingoes toward French interests, but British traders soon followed the Indians to Cuyahoga. The French tried to stir up the Indians to drive the British out. These efforts intensified during the early stages of King George's War (1744–1748), but, after British sea victories cut off supplies of French trade goods, the Indians became disgusted with France's inability to supply their needs and turned toward British suppliers. Some northern Ohio Indians became so hostile to the French that they even planned to assault Detroit, France's stronghold in the West.

By 1750 most of the Cuyahoga Mingoes had moved eastward, many of them to the Beaver Valley where they were closer to their main council fires and to British traders. Some stayed along the Ohio River and ultimately established villages at the mouth of Yellow Creek and at the site of modern Mingo Junction. Years later Mingo villages could be found in central and northeastern Ohio. Many of these villages contained a mixed Indian population.

With the permission of the Six Nations, the Wyandots moved into northern Ohio. The Wyandots were Hurons (of Iroquoian linguistic stock) who formerly lived in "Huronia" situated along the eastern shore of Lake Huron in the Ontario Peninsula. During the seventeenth century the Iroquois Confederacy had driven the Hurons and associated tribes from the Ontario Peninsula. Ultimately some surviving Hurons settled at Detroit where they were closely identified with French interests. Early in the eighteenth century the Detroit region became overpopulated as Ottawas,

Miamis, Potawatomies, and Chippewas also located there for trade and protection. Seeking "elbow room," the Wyandots started hunting south of Lake Erie in the 1730s, and, in the next decade, Orontony (Nicholas) led his Wyandot band to Sandusky Bay where he established the village of Junundat. Some writers claim Orontony's people were trying to escape indebtedness to Detroit traders and to position themselves more favorably for trade with the British.

It is known that this move was made with the permission of the Six Nations, but no one knows how extensive the new Wyandot claims were. Other tribes recognized Wyandot claims to parts of Ohio. In the 1750s, for example, Shawnees and Delawares settled in Ohio only after they were invited to do so by the Wyandots.

Late in the 1740s the Wyandot's strained relationship with the French led Orontony to plot an assault on Detroit. The plot aborted, however, and in 1748 he led most of his band eastward to join the villages at Cuyahoga. He did not stay long, apparently following other tribes eastward to the Beaver River to be closer to British traders. This restless band soon moved again. In 1750 they built Conchake (Coshocton) at the forks of the Muskingum River but soon abandoned it to the Delawares. Later, Wyandot villages were located along the Scioto River in central Ohio, but the center of Wyandot influence remained near Upper Sandusky, in the Sandusky River Valley.

As with the Mingoes and Wyandots, the Miamis, an Algonquian people, were early arrivals in Ohio. French explorers first encountered the Miamis near Green Bay, Wisconsin. The Miamis were soon forced south and east, however, by pressure from other tribes contesting for their hunting grounds. They ultimately found sanctuary in eastern Indiana and western Ohio. The Miamis had always traded with the French, but by the late 1740s they too were affected by that depletion of French trade goods that marked the later stages of King George's War. Some Miamis, disgusted with their dependency on French traders, learned that British trade goods would be available to them if they could locate villages far enough east to be within the range of British traders. Thus the Miami chief, whom the French called La Demoiselle and the British called Old Britain, established the important new village of Pickawillany on the headwaters of the Great Miami River. Pickawillany and a small village nearby on the Little Miami River welcomed British traders and ignored French warnings to expel them. To discipline La Demoiselle, French authorities permitted the half-breed, Charles Langlade, to lead a punitive expedition against the towns. In 1752 Langlade's raiders destroyed Pickawillany, killed and ate La Demoiselle, and drove out the British traders. Soon thereafter the Miamis drew back from Ohio toward their tribal center at Kekionga (modern Fort Wayne), although they continued to be a force in Ohio affairs for another half century. During the French and Indian War, they were staunch allies of the French.

The Shawnees, an Algonquian people, had early established a village at the mouth of the Scioto, but they did not move into Ohio in force until the 1750s. It is difficult to speak with certainty about the positioning of the Shawnee people at any given time because they were divided into five bands or septs which often operated independently of one another. These bands wandered over vast areas of eastern North America, but early in the eighteenth century some Shawnees were gathering at the junction of the Ohio and Scioto rivers. Late in the 1730s Lower Shawnee Town was an important village at that location. Some who settled here came from the Cumberland region of Tennessee and Kentucky. Later they were joined by Shawnees from Pennsylvania who had been living in close conjunction with Delawares.

Shawnee motives for moving into Ohio are somewhat hazy. Apparently the French had invited the southern Shawnees to move into Ohio so that they might trade more conveniently with Detroit. The Pennsylvania Shaw-nees, on the other hand, were caught in a complex situation which required them to respond to pressure from Pennsylvania authorities and also to pressure from the Iroquois Confederacy. About 1750 the Iroquois tried to coerce some Shawnees, who had drifted as far as eastern Ohio, to return to the Allegheny villages where they could more easily be controlled by the Iroquois and by the British in whose interests the Iroquois were involved. This coercion failed, and the Shawnees advanced into Ohio where they settled at the invitation of the Wyandots. By the 1760s the Shawnees were concentrated in the Scioto Valley, especially in the Pickaway Plains (near modern Circleville) and westward toward the Little Miami. Many Shaw-nees, however, remained in villages outside this area, frequently living with members of other tribes.

Among the Ohio Indians, the Delaware represent the clearest example of an Indian tribe responding to pressure from whites. When first encoun-tered by Europeans, the Delawares lived in an extended region centered on the Delaware River. They were the Lenape, an ancient people respected by other Algonquian tribes. White encroachment on their land forced them westward in Pennsylvania, and as they moved they encroached on lands in the Susquehanna Valley that the Iroquois Confederacy claimed by right of conquest. The Iroquois thus considered the Delawares as dependents and exerted dominion over them. The Delaware could no longer sell land nor make war without Iroquois consent.

As Delawares continued to be pushed westward during the mid-eighteenth century, they, like their associated tribe—the Shawnees—moved beyond effective Iroquois control and beyond the ready supervision of Pennsylvania provincial agents. And as with the Shawnees, Iroquois and provincial efforts to keep the Delawares concentrated in their Upper Ohio villages were not wholly successful. By 1751 the Delawares were accepting Wyandot invitations to settle on Ohio lands, and shortly thereafter villages were established along the Muskingum and its branches—the Tuscarawas and the Walhonding. Here in their new Ohio homes, the Delawares, supported by the French and by other Ohio tribes, regained their independence from Iroquois domination.

Delaware settlement in Ohio was complicated by the fact that many Delawares of the Turtle and Turkey groups (there is dispute as to whether Delaware tribal divisions were clans) had been converted to Christianity by Moravian missionaries who had worked among them for many years in Pennsylvania. Ultimately, separate villages of Christian Delawares were established along the Tuscarawas, starting in 1772 with the founding of Schoenbrunn. Delawares of the Wolf group were largely free from Moravian influence. There is some evidence that they resented the success of the Moravian villages, but the unconverted Delawares lived in peace with their Christian brothers until the American War of Independence created a new set of conditions that took the Wolf group into the British orbit. The Wolf group followed its leader, Hopocan (Captain Pipe), westward from the Cuyahoga-Tuscarawas portage to the Sandusky where they were closer to British supplies and support. The Christian Delawares remained in their Tuscarawas towns and attempted to remain neutral.

The Ottawas were perhaps the smallest tribal group with "permanent" Ohio locations. The Ottawas were Algonquians who once lived along the northern reaches of Lake Huron and in the northern portions of Michigan's southern peninsula. Like the Hurons and the Miamis, some Ottawa bands ultimately settled near the French post at Detroit. In 1742 some of these Ottawas joined the Mingoes and others at the Cuyahoga settlement. It would appear that they, like the Wyandots, may have been motivated by a wish to escape French creditors at Detroit. Apparently they believed they could get a new line of credit with British traders who frequented the Cuyahoga and regions to the east.

Most Ottawas, however, came to Ohio seeking new hunting grounds and new villages sites. Frequently they shared villages with members of other tribes. The greatest concentration of these people was found along the fringes of the Black Swamp, a supersaturated area of northwestern Ohio which was so forbidding that few Indians lived within it, except on the elevated river banks. The Ottawas maintained a special relationship (the "three fires") with the Chippewas and the Potawatomies, both of whom had small villages in Ohio from time to time.

Throughout their Ohio experience, the Ottawas remained faithful to the French interests, except for a brief period in the 1740s when they suffered from the shortage of French trade goods that affected all the western tribes. In 1763 the Ottawa war chief Pontiac became France's most vigorous advocate in the West. On the assumption that French armies, recently defeated by the British, would return to the interior of North America, he led Indian assaults that deprived the British of all their western posts, with the important exceptions of Forts Pitt, Niagara, and Detroit. In concert with most Ohio Indians, the Ottawas were on the British side during the border wars of the Revolutionary period. While Ohio was becoming an important tribal center for the six tribes already discussed, it provided a refuge and an opportunity for scattered bands of other Indian people. Mohicans had a small village in Ashland County. Other Mohicans could be found in that conglomerate of tribes which settled the Cuyahoga in the 1740s. A few Christian Mohicans lived with the Delawares in the Moravian settlements along the Tuscarawas.

Chippewas (Ojibwas) from the northern Great Lakes region also made their way into Ohio. Known locally as Saulteurs, they too were represented along the Cuyahoga in the 1740s. Chippewa Lake and Chippewa Creek in Medina and Wayne counties take their names from villages which these people established. Chippewa warriors fought along the Ohio frontier in support of French and later of British interests. Chippewas were involved in some of the land cession treaties following the Revolutionary War.

One finds occasional mention of other Indians in Ohio—for example, Abnakis from New England, Kickapoos from Illinois, and Piankeshaws and Weas (related to the Miami people) from Indiana. None of these tribes were closely identified with Ohio, however, and remain outside the scope of this review.

Most new Indian arrivals to Ohio came in the forty-year period just before the American War of Independence. When the war broke out, Ohio had as large an Indian population as it was ever to have. Even so, the numbers were small. A generous estimate would be 20,000 men, women, and children.

As has been noted, tribes migrated into Ohio for many reasons or combinations of reasons. Contrary to popular belief, not all displaced Indians were the victims of land grabs by rapacious whites, but clearly it was white land hunger which lay behind the westward movement of the Pennsylvania Indians. Trade considerations played a major role in the Ohio migrations as various tribes—or tribal splinters—vied for favor with French and British traders. There is even that strangely modern-sounding move of the Ottawas and Wyandots whose motives for relocating were apparently tied to their desire to escape indebtedness to Detroit traders. Clearly, however, the most pervasive reason for tribal movement into Ohio was the seeking out of new, unexploited hunting and trapping grounds which could be found in close conjunction with the rich agricultural lands favored by these semi-sedentary people.

The historic Indians of Ohio were in varying stages of acculturation to western civilization at the time they moved into Ohio. The Miamis, Wyandots, and Ottawas had lived for quite some time in conjunction with French influences—traders, small farmers, and priests—which had affected members of these tribes. They used French trade goods, arms and ammunition, blankets, and cooking utensils, and they drank French brandy. The white captive, James Smith, reported that Wyandots used sails as the French did to power their large canoes across Lake Erie.

Years of proselytizing by French priests had reaped mixed results among these tribes. Some small children, raised in the Catholic faith, were relatively orthodox in their Catholicism. Adults, however, seldom made fully committed converts. James Smith's Indian companion, Tecaughretanego, was a Caughnewaga (a tribe often referred to as "French Mohawks"). Tecaughretanego told Smith that:

> there were a great many of the Caughnewagas and Wiandots, that were a kind of half Roman Catholics; but as for himself, he said, that the priest and him could not agree; as they held notions that contradicted both sense and reason, and had the assurance to tell him, that the book of God, taught them these foolish absurdities: but he could not believe the great and good spirit ever taught them any such nonsense: and therefore he concluded that the Indians' old religion was better than this new way of worshipping God.

The tribes that came to Ohio from the east had long been in contact with whites. The Mingoes had done business with Dutch and British traders and officials. The Senecas, as the westernmost of the Iroquois tribes, were perhaps somewhat less closely identified with these contacts than were the Mohawks and other tribes located closer to the centers of Dutch and British influence along the Hudson. Nevertheless, that dependency, which characterized relationships between Indians and white traders, was well established. The Delawares had lived in reasonably close conjunction with whites for some time before their Ohio migration in the 1750s. They had suffered repeated removals, during which Pennsylvania provincial authorities were in frequent contact with them. The Christian influence of the Moravian missionaries was substantial among the Delawares. These Christian Delawares adopted not only the religion of the Moravians, but they also accepted much of the life-style of their would-be benefactors. Hence, we are told, some Christian Delawares in Ohio built frame dwellings, drank tea, sang German hymns, and read the Bible in their own language.

These, then, were the Indians of Ohio on the eve of the American Revolutionary War. Frontier fighting erupted in 1774 when Lord Dunmore's War was fought along the Ohio boundary. Indian raids across the Ohio brought an army of 1,000 frontiersmen under Colonel Andrew Lewis to Point Pleasant, Virginia. There Cornstalk, a Shawnee chief, attacked with an Indian army of about equal size. The ensuing battle was virtually a draw, but the Shawnee villages were vulnerable to attack by another American force under Lord Dunmore, colonial governor of Virginia. The Shawnees sued for peace, and for the next three years an uneasy truce prevailed. By 1777 mutual aggravations caused the Ohio Indians and their American enemies to renew bloody border warfare.

The displacement of the Ohio Indians was hastened by the American War of Independence. All of the Ohio Indians, with the exception of the Christian Delawares, were allies of the British who kept them supplied with weapons, ammunition, and other necessaries from the post at Detroit. On occasion, British officers and enlisted men accompanied Indians in attacks against American posts.

Fighting in the Ohio country followed a predictable pattern. In an effort to stop further penetration of their lands by aggressive American settlers, the Indians would raid exposed frontier cabins and settlements. Such vulnerable spots were located all along the frontier, stretching in a long arc from western Pennsylvania, southwestward through Virginia and Kentucky. Whenever a substantial Indian raid was directed at a relatively well-populated frontier region, the men of that region would organize a counterthrust across the Ohio River. Border heroes like Daniel Boone and Simon Kenton often scouted for them. They hoped to catch and destroy the Indian army. But pitched battles did not suit Indian purposes, and so the warriors and their dependents would fade into the forest. The frustrated pursuers would carry off such loot as they could find in the abandoned villages (horses being especially prized), leaving behind them burning villages and ruined crops. This tactic reduced the Indians' ability to sustain hostilities since they were faced with the need to build anew, thus limiting the time that warriors could afford to be away in the field.

In 1779, Colonel John Bowman's Kentuckians destroyed Chillicothe Old Town, an important Shawnee village on the Little Miami. George Rogers Clark's forces destroyed Old Piqua Town on the Mad River (also a Shawnee town) in 1780. Clark again raided northward in 1782, destroying Indian property as far north as Loramie's Post on the headwaters of the Miami. The Shawnees suffered most from these forays. They relocated their villages ever farther to the north and west to escape hostile action.

Further east, other American military units penetrated Ohio but caused little damage to Indian settlements. General Edward Hand moved against the Delaware villages on the Mahoning in 1778 in an abortive effort to reach the Cuyahoga. General Lachlan McIntosh built Fort Laurens along the Tuscarawas in 1778 to "protect" nearby Delawares and to provide a jumping-off point for a proposed attack on Detroit. Besieged almost from its inception, the fort was abandoned by early summer, 1779. Colonel Daniel Brodhead destroyed Delaware sites on the Muskingum in 1781. In early spring, 1782, Colonel David Williamson led an unofficial raid of murderous severity against the Christian Indians of Gnadenhutten, wantonly killing ninety of these peaceful people. Reverberations from this tragedy ultimately led to the permanent abandonment of the Tuscarawas Valley by the surviving Chrsitian Indians. Finally, Colonel William Crawford's ill-fated campaign against the Wyandots and their Delaware allies along the Sandusky closed out organized military action in 1782.

At war's end, Great Britain not only recognized the new United States of America, but she ceded to the new nation those priceless western lands stretching from the Appalachians to the Mississippi and from the Great Lakes to Spanish Florida. The American Congress assumed jurisdiction over that portion lying "north and west of the river Ohio." Quickly Congress adopted programs for developing this region. It provided for an orderly survey and sale of the land, for the establishment of territorial government, and for the ultimate creation of new states in the region. However, these lands were occupied by Indian peoples, and Congress recognized that they had valid claims on the land. Whites were not to be permitted to settle or encroach on these lands until Indian title had been removed—by treaty where possible, by coercion where necessary.

Congress' first postwar effort to remove Indian title through treaty took place at Fort McIntosh (Beaver, Pennsylvania) in 1785. After two weeks of feasting and drinking, the satiated Indian representatives signed a treaty that would open to settlement the eastern and southern two-thirds of what now constitutes the state of Ohio. The Indians were to withdraw into the northwestern third of Ohio or beyond. Congress regarded the Treaty of Fort McIntosh as valid and put its plans for developing the Northwest into motion.

The Ohio Indians perceived the treaty in a different light. Indian representatives at Fort McIntosh had no authority to alienate tribal lands. The Shawnees, whose lands would be affected, were not even represented at the conference, and they soon announced that they would not honor the treaty. The Treaty of Fort Finney, negotiated with them in 1786, did little to mollify the Shawnees, and there remained much uncertainty about just what had been agreed to by the Ohio Indians. In that same year, yet another devastating raid, led by George Rogers Clark and Benjamin Logan, destroyed more Shawnee villages.

In 1786 the Ohio Indians and their allies, led by Blue Jacket of the Shawnees, Buckongehelas of the Delaware, and other important chiefs formed a loose confederation designed to coordinate more effectively their resistance to further encroachments on their lands. Efforts by Joseph Brant and other leaders of the Six Nations to direct this confederation were rejected. It was, in effect, a final declaration by the western Indians of their independence from the hegemony of the Six Nations. In January 1789, two treaties were negotiated at Fort Harmar at the mouth of the Muskingum. In one treaty the Six Nations surrendered again their old claims to the Ohio country (they had first done so in 1768). The other treaty was with the Ohio Indians requiring them to honor the boundary lines of the Fort McIntosh and Fort Finney treaties. Although they signed, the Ohio tribes refused to honor these terms since tribal councils had not endorsed them.

In April 1788, settlers from New England established Marietta at the mouth of the Muskingum River, thus commencing authorized settlement in the Northwest. Prior to their arrival, hundreds of squatters had built cabins beyond the Ohio. As so often happened, some irresponsible squatters took advantage of the Indians and, among other offenses, despoiled them with liquor. The regular army's efforts to rout out these illegal settlers failed.

Each year new settlers, both "legal" and illegal, streamed down the Ohio bound for lands north and west of the great river. Indian resistance intensified as this flow increased. Flatboats were attacked; some isolated settlements—such as Big Bottom, located above Marietta on the Muskingum—were destroyed. Acting on the assumption that the treaties were valid and that the land in question had been properly ceded to the United States, President George Washington ordered the army to take military action against the Ohio Indians and their confederates.

In 1790, General Josiah Harmar led a poorly trained army north from Fort Washington (Cincinnati) toward the seat of Miami power at the forks of the Maumee (Fort Wayne, Indiana). Harmar divided his force, allowing Little Turtle, war chief of the Miamis, to defeat him in detail. Harmar retreated to Fort Washington where he surrendered his command to General Arthur St. Clair, a veteran of the Revolutionary War and governor of the Northwest Territory. St. Clair then led an army northward from Fort Washington. Though he had trained his forces and built support posts north toward Indian country, St. Clair was no more fortunate than Harmar. Late in 1791, the Indian confederation surprised St. Clair's army in camp at present-day Fort Recovery and inflicted upon it the worst defeat ever suffered by the United States army at the hands of Indians. Nearly 1,000 Americans were killed while the rest were captured or fled for their lives. St. Clair's personal bravery could not offset this disaster, and he was relieved of command. Washington now chose General "Mad Anthony" Wayne to establish United States authority. Wayne carefully trained his army and extended St. Clair's line of fortified posts. Moving in stages from Fort Washington, Wayne established Fort Defiance along the Maumee, down which he pushed in 1794 to meet the Indians at the Fallen Timbers (Maumee, Ohio). There Wayne defeated the Indians led by Blue Jacket.

. Wayne's victory at Fallen Timbers was decisive. The Ohio tribes were now convinced that they must evacuate the lands claimed by the United States since Fort McIntosh. In 1795, Wayne convoked a great conference at Fort Greenville. Over 1,000 Indian representatives gathered with Wayne and his people to confirm the Treaty of Greenville. A new line, closely approximating that of Fort McIntosh, would now separate Indian country from the lands being settled by whites. All but the northwestern third of what would soon become the State of Ohio would now be open to American development, secure from Indian assault.

Americans were forbidden to trespass beyond the line except for access to a few isolated strategic spots reserved to the United States. Such prohibitions on the mobility of frontiersmen had never worked in the past, and they did not work this time. Occasional squatters located north of the Greenville Line while others scouted out Indian lands in the expectation that they would soon be available for settlement. And they were correct in this assumption. In 1805 the Ohio tribes surrendered that portion of the Connecticut Western Reserve lying west of the Cuyahoga and the lands south of it extending to the Greenville Line. Immediately the survey of much of this land brought settlers to the area. The Sandusky Bay region, long favored by the Wyandots, was now in the hands of an aggressive and industrious people who would change its character forever.

The remnants of the Ohio tribes continued to relocate their villages in the first years of the nineteenth century. Most Delawares and Shawnees were situated in Indiana where the Miamis had preceded them. Their few remaining Ohio villages were small and rather out of the mainstream, but the Delawares, Shawnees, Ottawas, Senecas, and Wyandots still maintained an Ohio presence.

The old tribal leadership was determined to honor the Greenville treaty terms. Black Hoof of the Shawnees, for example, turned a deaf ear to the advice rendered by the Shawnee warrior Tecumseh and his brother Tenskwatawa, the Shawnee Prophet. They saw the white man as the implacable foe who must be resisted by force. Through the Prophet's religious revitalization movement and Tecumseh's diplomatic efforts among neighboring tribes, these brothers established a following which included representative warriors from many tribes. The village in which their activities centered was initially in southwestern Ohio, but later Tecumseh and the Prophet removed their village to Indiana, eventually focusing their followers in a large village on Tippecanoe Creek. The destruction of that village in 1811 by William Henry Harrison broke the back of the revitalization movement. The Prophet soon lost influence while Tecumseh took his remaining followers into the British orbit.

It is risky to generalize about Ohio Indian residence during this unsettled time, but it is well established in the records of the first white settlers that they frequently encountered Indians to the east and south of the Greenville Line. In the Connecticut Western Reserve, for example, the early settlers east of the Cuyahoga encountered individual Indians or small "villages." Most Indians remaining in this region appear to have been Senecas (Mingoes). They eked out a precarious existence. Their tribal culture was largely destroyed, and the whites perceived them as a degraded people, hardly threatening enough to be taken seriously. As war loomed early in 1812, the Seneca appear to have disappeared from northeastern Ohio. Their last foothold in the state was in the northwest where they occupied small reservations until their final removal in the 1830s.

The War of 1812 applied the *coup de grace* to Indian hopes for retaining

Ohio lands. Some of the Ohio tribes and their western allies rose for the last time under Tecumseh. In 1813 he led a large Indian force in support of British efforts to capture Fort Meigs on the Maumee and Fort Stephenson on the Sandusky. Frustrated in their efforts to seize control of northwestern Ohio, the British and Indian army retreated into the Ontario Peninsula north of Lake Erie. Pursued by William Henry Harrison's troops, Tecumseh's Indians and their British associates were overtaken and soundly defeated at the river Thames. Tecumseh was killed, and British influence in the American west was shattered, as were the last hopes of the Ohio Indians. Some Ohio Indians fought on the side of the Americans in this final struggle, but their new loyalties were not well rewarded. They were to suffer the same displacement and removal as those who fought with the British. The death of Tecumseh at the Thames symbolically marks the death of the Ohio tribes as a force to be reckoned with. The last organized Indian band in Ohio—the Wyandots of Upper Sandusky—left in 1842 for the Trans-Mississippi West.

The attractive and favored land which the historic Indians occupied in the eighteenth century was no longer a void. It was the young and vigorous State of Ohio. By 1850, the 20,000 Indians who had lived there until the American Revolution were replaced by 2,000,000 white people and a small number of blacks. The triumph of these newcomers was a tragedy for the previous occupants who now, once more, had to seek homes in distant places.

## SUGGESTED READING

The most orderly account and best interpretation of the Ohio Indian experience is *Indians of Ohio and Indiana Prior to 1795,* 2 volumes (New York, 1974). Volume I is by Helen Hornbeck Tanner and Erminie Wheeler-Voegelin. Volume II is by Erminie Wheeler-Voegelin. A standard reference is Frederick W. Hodge, ed., *Handbook of the American Indians North of Mexico* (Washington, 1907). Much essential documentation can be found in Charles A. Hanna, *The Wilderness Trail,* 2 volumes (New York and London, 1911) and in the many edited works of Reuben Gold Thwaites and Louise Phelps Kellogg. The only secondary work that approaches general coverage of the Ohio Indian story is Randolph C. Downes, *Council Fires on the Upper Ohio: A Narrative of Indian Affairs on the Upper Ohio Until 1795* (Pittsburgh, 1940). Important revisionist accounts by R. David

Edmunds are *The Shawnee Prophet* (Lincoln, 1983) and *Tecumseh and the Quest for Indian Leadership* (Boston, 1984). The Moravian missionaries, John Heckewelder and David Zeisberger, wrote about those Ohio Indians they knew, and their works provide an excellent contemporary view. The various publications of the Ohio Historical Society and the Western Reserve Historical Society contain pertinent materials not available elsewhere. Tribal histories are disappointing for the Ohio period. Their limited accounts must be supplemented from other sources.

| Theda | **6.** | Removal |
| Perdue | **The** | of the |
| | **Trail** | Southern |
| | **of** | Indians |
| | **Tears** | |

O ne of the great tragedies in American history is the
removal of the southern Indians. Indian efforts to
adapt to the presence of Euro-Americans and to conform to the invaders'
culture failed to protect them from an insatiable land hunger. With greed
masquerading as philanthropy, white Americans claimed that removal was
in the best interest of native peoples. When Indians lived close to whites,
the argument ran, they tended to acquire the vices rather than the virtues
of "civilization." Corrupted by alcohol and other features of the white
man's way, Indians faced certain destruction unless they moved beyond the
reach of civilization. If the Indians resisted the westward path to salvation,
whites felt legally as well as morally justified in forcing them to relinquish
their southeastern homeland. Indians, they believed, were only wandering
hunters who failed to make proper use of the land, and the European right
of discovery took precedence over the Indians' limited right to temporary
occupancy. The Frenchman Alexis de Tocqueville astutely observed that
through removal the United States succeeded in exterminating native
peoples and denying Indian rights "with wonderful ease, quietly, legally,
philanthropically, without spilling blood and without violating a single
one of the great principles of morality in the eyes of the world. It is impossible to destroy men with more respect to the laws of humanity." While
many whites congratulated themselves on their humane handling of the
"Indian problem," displaced native peoples regarded removal as a "Trail of
Tears." Individually, socially, and culturally they suffered, they changed,
and they rebuilt. But their lives would never again be quite the same as
they had been before.

When the United States government began implementing the removal
policy in the early nineteenth century, five major Indian groups lived in the
Southeast. The Chickasaws occupied territory in western Tennessee,
northern Mississippi, and northwestern Alabama. The Choctaws, who
spoke a language very similar to Chickasaw, lived to the south in central

Mississippi and Alabama. East of the Choctaws was the Creek Confederacy of Alabama and Georgia. In northern Georgia, northwestern Alabama, eastern Tennessee, and southwestern North Carolina lay the Cherokee country, and in Florida lived the Seminoles, a tribe made up of disaffected Creeks, native Florida tribes, and runaway African slaves. While each of these tribes was a separate political entity with its own cultural peculiarities, they all participated in the same broad cultural tradition, just as Europeans were a part of "western civilization." At the time of European contact, this Indian culture was known as Mississippian. Interestingly, whites understood little about Mississippian culture. Perhaps self-interest clouded their view, but, for whatever reason, they often overlooked or distorted major cultural characteristics. As a result, the cultural inferiority and inadequacy which whites later used to justify removal frequently had not existed in the first place.

The basis of southeastern Indian culture for centuries before European contact was a dependence on agriculture. Native peoples began to cultivate squash and gourds about 1000 B.C., and in approximately 200 B.C. they cultivated corn and beans. While agriculture may have developed independently in the southeast, it is likely that the concept as well as the crops originated elsewhere and that native traders or migrating tribes brought them into the region. Whatever the circumstances surrounding the introduction of farming, the broad fertile valleys of the southeast, a long growing season, and an annual rainfall averaging from 40 to 64 inches made the southeast admirably suited for an agricultural economy. By A.D. 700 this new Mississippian culture based on agriculture had begun to emerge.

Although men still went on winter hunts, agriculture made a stationary existence possible for southeastern Indians. No longer forced to migrate seasonally in search of wild food and game, people could build permanent houses and villages. Their societies could accommodate greater numbers, which in turn led to more centralized and sophisticated political systems. In their important villages, they constructed large earth mounds, the hallmark of Mississippian culture, on which they built public structures and dwellings for prominent people. Mound building ceased not long after European contact, probably because European diseases so decimated the population that such massive construction projects were impossible, but agriculture and village life continued along with ceremonies and festivals reminiscent of more complex Mississippian rituals.

The most important occasion celebrated by southeastern Indians in the century before their removal to the West was the Green Corn Ceremony, apparently an amalgam of the seasonal rituals conducted during the height of Mississippian. Held when the corn first could be eaten, the Green Corn Ceremony revealed a great deal about southeastern Indian culture. The fact that the major ceremony celebrated corn indicated that native peoples regarded agriculture as essential to their way of life. No similar ceremony was held to commemorate the winter hunt, perhaps because hunting was less significant in their economy. The ceremony was held at the square ground, a specially prepared arena in front of the council house. Bounded by brush arbors, the square ground represented many hours of labor. Villagers kept the square ground perfectly level and covered the surface annually with a fresh layer of dirt. Such care hardly would have been taken by wandering peoples. Indeed many generations of farmers had inhabited most village sites in the southeast and had carefully maintained these square grounds.

The people who gathered at the square ground in late summer believed that the best way to celebrate the new harvest was to destroy what remained of the old, and so they discarded any dried corn, beans, or other provisions from the preceding year. Because of this feature of the Green Corn Ceremony, southeastern Indians had little incentive to accumulate a surplus or to compete materially with neighbors. James Adair, an eighteenth-century trader, attributed the hospitality for which Indians were renowned to this practice of destroying old provisions: they believed that one might as well share what otherwise would be thrown away. Such a noncompetitive and nonacquisitive ethic was alien to eighteenth- and nineteenth-century Euro-Americans. Although southern Indians were not the hunters and gatherers portrayed by whites determined to remove them, they differed from Europeans in more subtle but equally profound ways. Indians did not compete ruthlessly with each other, and they produced only enough food to subsist from one Green Corn Ceremony to the next. Consequently many whites assumed that native people were lazy and incapable of making proper use of the land they occupied.

The Green Corn Ceremony, at least by the late eighteenth century, had social and spiritual as well as economic importance. On this occasion, people cleansed themselves spiritually and reconciled socially. Spiritual cleansing was necessary because, in the aboriginal world view, pollution could come about in a number of ways. These usually were related to an imbalance in the world caused by things being out of their proper places or behaving unnaturally. All people needed spiritual cleansing because normal everyday life entailed some degree of pollution. Hunting, for example, was polluting because blood from game belonged inside the animal's body and yet a hunter had to come into contact with it. The killing of game also created an imbalance in the natural world. Consequently, the hunter had to take special precautions in order to counteract this unavoidable disorder and pollution. If he failed to perform purifying rites, physical ailments could result. Many other activities involved pollution. Therefore, the ritual purging and bathing at the Green Corn Ceremony and on other occasions brought about spiritual purity and reestablished order in the world.

Similarly, the Green Corn Ceremony affirmed a commitment to social harmony. At this time, people forgave all wrongs except murder. They brought into the open offenses ranging from slander to adultery, and the parties involved reconciled. Disaffected spouses dissolved their marriages, and the divorced became free to choose new partners. By settling disputes and reordering relationships, native peoples restored social harmony. Southeastern Indians exempted murder because this crime created such a serious imbalance that only the death of the manslayer or one of his kinsmen could reestablish order. The responsibility for avenging a person's death rested with his relatives, members of his clan. The major southeastern Indian tribes were divided into matrilineal clans (that is, one belonged to the clan of his mother), which handled many of the judicial functions that Europeans entrusted to governments. Kin ties, in fact, were the most important relationship in aboriginal society because in addition to fellowship, identity, and economic support, kinsmen offered security.

In the case of disputes settled at the Green Corn Ceremony and even murder, no central authority charged and punished the offender because little coercive power existed in southeastern society at the time of extensive European contact. Instead, Indians were governed primarily by an ethic which sought to maintain harmony and balance in the community and the natural world. Because each individual accepted this responsibility and subordinated his own ambitions and desires to the welfare of all, tribes had no need for a king or other authoritarian form of government. Before the disruption of native life by European incursions, hereditary despots may have ruled some tribes, but by the late eighteenth century town councils made decisions after exhaustively discussing an issue and arriving at a consensus. There were leaders, of course, but they led only because their achievements commanded respect. Even in tribes such as the Creeks, who seem to have chosen chiefs from a particular clan, kinship was not necessarily a determinant of political power. This form of government appeared to Europeans to be fraught with uncertainty, and, in fact, some whites suggested that southern Indians had no genuine government at all.

Europeans, therefore, failed to understand a great deal about southern Indians. Over several centuries, native peoples had developed a complex culture characterized by permanent villages, an agricultural economy, political and social organizations which emphasized the community rather than the individual, a belief system aimed at preserving order and harmony in the world, and a ceremonial life which reflected the values and aspirations of the society. In the eighteenth century, however, the major southeastern tribes began to feel the pressure of European expansion. In this period they had extensive contact with three European powers—French, Spanish, and British—who were vying for control of the continent. The British triumphed, and this victory set in motion a series of events which culminated in the removal of the southern Indians from their ancient homeland.

Initial British relations resembled those of the Spanish and French: they sought military alliances and trading relationships. Southern forests sheltered large herds of deer which could supply European markets with leather. In exchange for the deerskins which Indian hunters brought to trading posts each spring, white traders provided them with a variety of European manufactured goods. Metal tools such as hoes, knives, scissors, needles, hatchets, and axes were in great demand as were guns and ammunition, copper kettles, and European textiles. As the volume of trade increased, many Indians developed a dependence on European goods. Guns and ammunition became essential not only for hunting but for protection against well-armed enemies, and other items were incorporated fully into native life. The Europeans' desire for deerskins seemed limitless, and they pressured Indian hunters to provide more and more skins. Hunters also became acquisitive, and many no longer were satisfied with mere subsistence.

As their material desires increased, Indians became embroiled in colonial rivalries. European powers on the North American continent sought Indian allies and often recruited those allies with guns, ammunition, sugar, rum, and other desirable commodities. Some warriors became more concerned about their own material well-being than about community welfare, and they sometimes jeopardized the safety of entire villages for personal gain. As a result, many southern Indians began to see advantages to centralized and coercive governments which could control individual actions. While such governments did not materialize during the colonial period, tribes moved in that direction in order to cope with the erosion of a communitarian ethic.

With the aid of Indian allies, the British ultimately won the North American contest. Unlike their European rivals on the continents, the British had a large and restless population, many of whom wanted to migrate to North America. Consequently, the British could not be content with forts, missions, trading posts, and scattered settlements; they needed vast tracts of Indian land. The South, in particular, attracted English colonists because the climate permitted cultivation of extremely profitable crops such as tobacco and rice. Reluctant simply to seize the land, the British sought to relieve the Indians of their territory through treaties in which the Indians sold or merely relinquished as war reparations their right to occupy the land. Such transactions proved difficult because Indians insisted that an individual could cede only his own right to the land. Because delegated political power did not truly exist in eighteenth-century native societies, even a respected leader could only speak for himself. Consequently, the British began to demand a reorganization of Indian politics and, in some cases, even appointed chiefs to act for villages or for the tribe as a whole. Although this practice was alien to Indian jurisprudence, the British defended the legitimacy of land cessions negotiated by these chiefs.

From the British perspective, the land did not really belong to the Indians. The British based their claim to North America on the discoveries of the Cabots and others who explored the New World under the auspices of the British Crown. People, of course, lived in this "newfound" land, but the British insisted that the natives had only the right to occupy the land temporarily. This limited right of occupancy stemmed from the perception of Indian peoples as wandering hunters and gatherers who did not cultivate the soil or permanently inhabit a particular tract of land. Discovery entailed the right of preemption, that is, the right to possess the land when the Indians no longer occupied it. The immediate problem for the British was how to remove the Indians from tracts of land so that colonists could exercise their right of preemption. The solution lay in treaties whereby the Indians surrendered their right to live on the land. When the Indians relinquished their right of occupancy, the "civilized" nation which had discovered the land could then settle, put it to proper use, and establish legitimate ownership. The British, therefore, viewed Indian titles as transitory and European titles as geuine and permanent.

The British policy of acquiring specific tracts of land led to a formal distinction between Indian and British territory. Normally natives and colonists did not share tracts of land: if the British acquired the land, the Indians left and whites moved in. In one sense, this was the beginning of Indian removal. Although Indian enclaves existed in the colonies, the British tended to push the native peoples westward and to create a frontier, a boundary, between Indians and whites. In 1763 after the British victory in the French and Indian War, George III formalized the boundary and prohibited migration of British colonists beyond the crest of the Appalachians. The Crown and its colonial governments also carefully regulated intercourse between the colonies and the Indians by appointing agents and licensing traders. Therefore, the British regarded the Indians as sovereign for the purpose of negotiating treaties but they did not view native peoples living on land "discovered" by British subjects as permanently entitled to the land. When the United States achieved its independence, the new country inherited the British right of discovery and a well-established method for dealing with the native peoples who temporarily resided within that domain.

The Articles of Confederation, under which the United States was governed from 1779 to 1789, placed Indian relations within the province of Congress. Often at odds with the state governments, Congress nevertheless established an Indian policy which reserved for the federal government the right to regulate trade and travel within the Indian nations. The architects of early Indian policy clearly considered the tribes in the Northwest Territory and the old Southwest to be residing on United States land; that is, they believed that Indians only lived on land which actually was owned by the United States. Under the Articles of Confederation, the United States also set up a procedure for disposing of land once the Indians ceased to occupy it: U.S. agents surveyed tracts and then sold them at minimal price in order to encourage rapid white settlement and ultimate statehood. Even in its infancy, the nation prepared to move westward, and the justifications and machinery for dispossessing the Indians were well in place by the meeting of the Constitutional convention.

The Constitution of 1789 also reserved the conduct of Indian affairs to the federal government. The first chief executive under the Constitution, George Washington, delegated his authority to various cabinet officials. Indian affairs was under the secretary of war because the pacification of the Indians through negotiation or, if necessary, military defeat was a major concern. Henry Knox, Washington's secretary of war, advocated the British concept of proprietorship and their practice of purchasing the Indians' occupancy claims. He also maintained that the privilege of acquiring Indian land belonged exclusively to the federal government rather than to individuals or states. Overcoming opposition from Georgia and other states, Congress concurred with Knox and passed a series of laws called the Indian Trade and Intercourse Acts. Through these laws, the federal government established Indian boundaries, regulated trade with and travel in the Indian nations, controlled the liquor traffic, restricted the purchase of Indian land to the federal government, and provided funds for the education and "civilization" of the Indians.

The Indian policy established by the new nation reflects a dichotomy in American attitudes toward the Indians. On the one hand, white Americans wanted Indian land. They believed that they could make better use of that resource than the Indians and that they were the rightful owners. On the other hand, many Americans were committed to "civilizing" the Indians. They believed that Indians could be transformed culturally and assimilated into white society. While the specter of hunting grounds that could be opened to white occupancy after civilized Indians abandoned them no doubt accounts for much of the interest in Indian civilization, genuine altruism motivated many whites. Convinced that "savage" peoples could not compete with civilized ones and consequently were doomed to destruction, these individuals sought to save American Indians by civilizing them.

The federal government sought to promote civilization in two ways. First, federal agents lived among the Indians and introduced the principles of commercial agriculture, animal husbandry, and the domestic arts. Second, the federal government provided financial assistance to missionary societies willing to send people into this particular mission field. Such aid was compatible with the government's goals because most Protestants considered civilization and Christianity to be intrinsically linked, and a good Christian life was a civilized one. Similarly, the architects of federal Indian policy believed that civilization entailed not only an agricultural economy, a republican government, and an English education but also conversion to Christianity.

While little of a religious nature was accomplished during the Federalist era (and the Creeks actually resisted the establishment of a school), agents did entrench themselves among the southern tribes. They encouraged the southern Indians to abandon their traditional towns and communal work habits and to settle on isolated homesteads in preparation for individual ownership. Contrary to the traditional division of labor in which women farmed, the agents furnished men with plows and hoes, and they relegated women to the domestic chores of spinning and weaving on newly acquired wheels and looms.

Many southern Indians readily accepted the government's civilization program, which was aided considerably by the erosion of traditional culture in the eighteenth century. The descendants of white traders and Indian women already were accustomed to the white man's ways and capitalized on the material aspects of the program. Also many men who formerly had engaged in hunting and war found an avenue for self-fulfillment and an outlet for aggression in the individualistic economic system and acquisitive values which agents introduced. These men, whose ancestry was Indian, plus others of mixed ancestry became civilized, or at least they acquired that "love for exclusive property" on which Knox believed civilization rested. In the late eighteenth and early nineteenth centuries, leadership of the southern tribes fell increasingly to individuals who were well on their way to acculturation. These were the people with whom U.S. agents and treaty commissioners interacted most easily and comfortably. In some cases, more traditional Indians deferred to these progressives and looked to them as interpreters of U.S. policies and as mediators of culture. In other cases, however, government officials grossly overestimated the power of people who supported federal policies and failed to realize that they had little internal support.

Most federal officials viewed the civilization program as a means to an end: The real objective of U.S. Indian policy was the acquisition of Indian land. The United States pressured southern Indians to relinquish "surplus" land in a variety of ways. The War Department authorized the construction of government-owned trading posts, or factories, and instructed traders to permit Indians to run up sizable accounts. Then authorities demanded payment in land. In 1802, for example, the federal government built a factory among the Chickasaws who within three years owed $12,000. They paid their debts by ceding their territory north of the Tennessee River. Treaty commissioners sent to negotiate land cessions bribed chiefs and exploited tribal factionalism. In the Cherokee removal crisis of 1806–1809, for example, the federal government took advantage of discord between the upper towns of eastern Tennessee and western North Carolina and the lower towns of Alabama and Georgia. Lower towns were more committed to civilization and ultimate assimilation into white society. Espousing the political fiction of tribal unity, federal officials negotiated land cessions and exchanges with lower town chiefs in the name of the entire tribe. They also lubricated the process by bribing lower town chiefs with the inclusion of secret treaty provisions appropriating funds to particularly cooperative chiefs. Treaty commissioners employed the same tactic in 1825 when they bribed William McIntosh and other progressive lower Creeks to cede tribal lands in Georgia. In both cases, the Indian nations executed the miscreants, but considerable damage was done. While the president of the United States set aside the treaty McIntosh signed, a subsequent treaty achieved the same cession. Furthermore, the willingness of the federal government to use bribery and factionalism demoralized southern Indians and encouraged self-serving individuals to cede tribal land.

In response to these tactics, southern tribes began to devise ways of coping with incessant demands for their land. With the hearty approval of the civilizers, agents and missionaries, southern tribes began to adopt Anglo-American political institutions. The Cherokees, Creeks, Choctaws, and Chickasaws began to centralize their tribal governments, to formalize political processes and structures, to delegate authority to clearly designated chiefs, and to hold those chiefs accountable for their actions. Between 1808 and 1810 the Cherokees established a national police force, created an executive committee to transact tribal business between council meetings, and made murder a national crime (instead of a family matter) by abolishing blood vengeance. In 1829, they committed to writing a previously unwritten but well-known law making the cession of tribal land a capital offense. The Creeks enacted such a law in 1811, and, as demands for tribal land increased, they gradually shifted responsibility for the conduct of foreign affairs to a national council which alternated its annual meetings between upper and lower Creek towns. The Choctaws and Chickasaws also renounced the practice of blood vengeance and made murder a national crime. In 1826, the Choctaws enacted a written law code and a system of elective chiefs which replaced the old informal system in which chiefs of three districts acted in concert. The Chickasaws extended their system of national laws and committed them to writing in 1829, four years after they established judicial districts.

These political changes did not have unanimous support. A large number of Creeks, in particular, disapproved of the Europeanization of political institutions and the attempt by elected officials to placate whites. This dissatisfaction contributed to the decision of some Creeks to fight against the United States and the Creek allies in the War of 1812. Following their defeat, many members of this faction migrated south and joined with the Mikasukis, remnant Florida tribes, and runaway African slaves to form the Seminoles. This hybrid tribe clung to old ways of governing, leaders derived their power from personal accomplishment and charisma, and the Seminoles became the most united in purpose of all southern tribes.

Among southern Indians, a significant number of people rejected or, perhaps more appropriately, ignored aspects of civilization. They preferred their traditional town councils to centralized governments, the lessons taught by elders and family to mission schools, and their own religion to Christianity. The persistence of traditional culture troubled missionaries and U.S. agents who mistakenly had believed that civilizing the Indians would be a fairly simple task. They feared for these recalcitrant savages whose days, they felt certain, were numbered by the onrush of civilization.

Some conditions in the Indian nations in the early nineteenth century seemed to confirm these fears. Exposure to civilization only further corrupted these savages. Equally distressing was the inability of others who acknowledged the virtue of civilization to resist the vices. Many Indians lived on credit, and their wants far exceeded their means. Some discovered a civilized way to avoid manual labor: they bought African slaves to work for them. Southern Indians also liked to gamble, and, although this had been an aboriginal practice, civilization introduced new contests such as horse racing on which they could wager. But most tragically, many Indians acquired a taste for alcohol. Faced with the weakening of cultural traditions, economic and political changes, and an uncertain future, they overindulged, and drunkenness became a serious problem.

The difficulties encountered by the civilization program soon led philanthropists to question how quickly and easily the southern Indians could be assimilated. These doubts opened the door for those who desired the Indians' land rather than their civilization. Reconciliation of these opposing positions came in the proposal to move the Indians beyond the reach of civilization where they could adjust more slowly and successfully to the problems which civilization brought. The Indians would be saved and their land could be opened for white settlement. The immediate problem, however, was where to send the Indians.

As a great advocate of assimilation, Thomas Jefferson had provided a solution: he had bought Louisiana. Jefferson apparently had not had Indian emigration in mind when he made the Louisiana Purchase in 1803, but his political opponents (and even some supporters) demanded to know exactly what he intended to do with this vast wilderness. Jefferson responded that the eastern Indians could now be moved west of the Mississippi and civilized at their own pace. The removal policy officially was born. Troubled by the constitutionality of the acquisition of Louisiana, Jefferson contemplated a constitutional amendment to validate his actions. The proposed amendment recognized only the Indians' right of occupancy, affirmed the U.S. right of preemption, and gave Congress the authority to exchange the right of occupancy of lands in the East for the same right to lands in the West. Although the provision never became a part of the Constitution, the Louisiana Territorial Act of the following year authorized the president to negotiate such an exchange of land for removal of the southern tribes. Exchanges were, of course, supposed to be entirely voluntary. Therefore, Jefferson did not persist when the Chickasaws rejected a proposal that they move west of the Mississippi in 1805, and overtures to the Choctaws three years later received an equally cool response.

Despite these early rebuffs, the Jefferson administration did develop the first technique for transferring the Indian population of the Southeast to Indian territory: officials simply offered to exchange land west of the Mississippi for tracts ceded in the Southeast. They believed that as white civilization encroached, those Indians who did not want to assimilate could move west. Some southern Indians, in fact, already had elected to go west. In the late eighteenth century, a band of Cherokees moved beyond the Mississippi after their massacre of a party of pioneers. Chickasaws hunted regularly in the Trans-Mississippi West, and one group apparently settled permanently in Louisiana about the turn of the century. During the same period, other Indians also went west to hunt or to fight the enemy Osage and then returned to their homes in the Southeast.

The Jefferson administration succeeded only, however, in convincing the lower Cherokees to exchange land, and in 1810 about 1,000 Cherokees moved to Arkansas. Subsequent administrations followed the Jeffersonian model and arranged territorial exchanges. Another Cherokee emigration took place in 1817–1819 after a group of Cherokees (who received private reservations which could be sold at considerable profit) ceded land in the Southeast to compensate the federal government for additional land the Arkansas Cherokees had settled. In 1820, the Choctaws agreed to the Treaty of Doak's Stand, under which they relinquished one-third of their eastern domain for a larger tract in Arkansas. Because of protest from white residents of Arkansas, however, the treaty had to be renegotiated in Washington in 1825, and the Choctaws received a tract of land in what is today southeastern Oklahoma. In 1826, the Creeks grudgingly acceded to an exchange of land in Georgia for a tract north of the Choctaws so that the followers of William McIntosh could emigrate.

The consequences of these exchanges were not exactly what Jefferson and other proponents of the removal policy had had in mind. Some Indians who moved west were the traditionalists for whom Jefferson originally had proposed removal. A surprisingly large number, however, were highly acculturated Indians. Some of these were escaping political enemies, but economics probably motivated most. Perhaps they hoped to capitalize on the westward movement, or they may simply have felt the same urge to go west as many white Americans. These progressives experienced little remorse in leaving their homeland, but the traditionalists who were the intended beneficiaries of removal felt a profound attachment to the land and refused to move. Those who still practiced traditional religion regarded their own territory as the center of the world and associated the West with death. In addition, their mythology incorporated familiar land forms. The Choctaws, for example, believed that they came originally from the Nanih

Waiya mound in Mississippi, and the Cherokees thought that they could see and influence the future through the crystal forelock of the Uktena, a monster which lived in the high mountain passes of their country. Sacred medicine, which southern Indians used to cure physical and spiritual ills, came from native plants that did not necessarily grow in the Trans-Mississippi West. For these traditionalists, removal meant not only physical relocation but also spiritual reorientation.

Exchanges of land and piecemeal removal had an additional unforeseen effect. Instead of the trickle of emigrants swelling to a stream, a burst of enthusiasm for removal was followed by long periods of almost total disinterest. Those inclined to go west took advantage of the opportunity afforded by exchanges and departed. Their removal siphoned off the very people who might have been inclined to negotiate further exchanges. And so with every migration west, public opinion in the southern tribes became increasingly opposed to removal. There was little that U.S. officials could do about this situation because, until 1829, presidents refused to force Indians to go west against their will.

The slow pace of removal angered many southerners. As prices for cotton rose, the white population in the South grew, and as the Cotton Kingdom expanded, the desire for additional land suitable for cultivating cotton increased. Consequently, southern states began to demand that the federal government, which controlled Indian relations, liquidate Indian title to land within their borders. Georgia, in particular, insisted on federal compliance with the Compact of 1802. In this agreement, the state relinquished claims to the western land, which became Alabama and Mississippi, and the federal government promised to extinguish Indian land titles within the state at some unspecified time. In the 1820s, Georgians thought that the federal government had delayed long enough. Indian land promptly became a political issue. Constitutional changes in 1825 which provided for the direct election of governors (who previously had been elected by the state senate) contributed to the uproar. Politicians seized on Indian land as an issue with broad popular appeal. In 1826, Georgians rejoiced when the Creeks gave up their remaining land in the state and withdrew to Alabama. Then they turned their attention to the Cherokees.

In 1827, the Cherokees established a republican government with a written constitution patterned after that of the United States. Georgia interpreted this act to be a violation of state sovereignty and renewed demands for the extinction of Indian land titles. The state legislature enacted a series of laws intended to establish state control over the Cherokee country and to make life so miserable for the Indians that they would leave. The legislature extended Georgia law over the Cherokees and created a special militia, the Georgia Guard, to enforce state law in the Cherokee country. One legislative act prohibited Indians from mining gold which had been discovered in their territory. Other laws prevented Indians from testifying against whites in court and required all whites, including missionaries, to take an oath of allegiance to the state. The Georgia legislature enjoined the Cherokee council from meeting and leaders from speaking publicly against removal. Finally, legislators formulated plans for a survey and division of Cherokee lands in preparation for their distribution by lottery to whites. Other southern states soon followed Georgia's lead and extended oppressive state laws over their Indian populations.

President John Quincy Adams had little sympathy for southerners in their struggle for Indian lands, but in 1828 he was defeated by Andrew Jackson. Jackson brought to the office long experience fighting and negotiating with southern Indians. He made clear his intention to acquire and open to white settlement all Indian land in the Southeast. In his 1829 message to Congress, Jackson offered southern Indians two alternatives—they could become subject to the discriminatory laws of the states or move west and continue their own tribal governments. The president and most southerners believed that they should move. In 1830, Congress passed the Indian Removal Act, which authorized the president to negotiate exchanges of territory and appropriated $500,000 for that purpose. Under the proposed removal treaties, the federal government would compensate emigrants for improvements (such as houses, cleared and fenced fields, barns, orchards, ferries) and assist them in their journey west.

The Choctaws were the first tribe to remove under the provisions of the Indian Removal Act. In the fall of 1830, a group of Choctaw chiefs agreed to the Treaty of Dancing Rabbit Creek. In this treaty, the Choctaws ceded their land in the Southeast, but those who wished to remain in Mississippi (or could not pay their debts to citizens of the state) would receive fee simple title to individual allotments of land and become citizens of the state. The federal government promised those who removed reimbursement for improvements, transportation to the West, subsistence for one year after removal, and an annuity for the support of education and other tribal services. There was much dissatisfaction with the treaty, particularly among Choctaw traditionalists who did not want to go west under any condition. Opponents had little opportunity to protest formally because the U.S. government refused to recognize any chief as long as the Choctaws remained in Mississippi. Consequently, the Choctaws began preparations for their westward migration.

Confusion surrounded these preparations and the journey west. After a dispute about routes, the Choctaws and the government agreed on a combination water and land route. Finally in late fall 1831, the first detachment of Choctaws left Mississippi. The War Department had divided the supervision of removal between the Indian trader George Gaines, who conducted the Indians to the Mississippi River, and the Jacksonian Democrat Francis Armstrong, who then assumed control. These men delegated their authority to supply the Indians to agents in the field. Many agents viewed removal only as an opportunity to increase their own fortunes, and so the Choctaws often failed to receive rations promised. The Indians who removed under government supervision suffered greatly as a result of winter weather, corruption, greed, and bureaucratic bungling, but so did those who received a $10.00 commutation fee from the United States and paid fellow Choctaws to conduct them west. The Choctaw removals of 1832 and 1833 were not as plagued by corruption and confusion, in part because military officials replaced civilian speculators as field agents. By the spring of 1834, between thirteen and fifteen thousand Choctaws had removed.

About seven thousand Choctaws remained in Mississippi under provisions of the Treaty of Dancing Rabbit Creek. Either they were heads of households who registered to receive an allotment or they could not leave the state because of indebtedness. Some who remained in Mississippi were highly acculturated Choctaws, such as Greenwood LeFlore, who subsequently embarked on a successful career in Mississippi politics. Others, however, were traditionalists accustomed to communal ownership of land who did not understand titles, deeds, and individual ownership. Frequently, these traditionalists understood only their native language, and, as a result, they became the unwitting victims of unscrupulous speculators. Often tricked into running up debts or signing their deeds over to these men, the traditionalists appealed to the government for help. United States officials turned a deaf ear to their pleas and insisted that fraudulent contracts be honored. No longer entitled after 1834 to emigrate at government expense, these landless Mississippi Choctaws either straggled to Indian territory on their own or remained in the state as an impoverished landless minority.

The federal government made allotment a major feature of the treaties signed with the Creeks and Chickasaws in 1832. The Creek chiefs agreed to cede much of their land in Alabama and to permit some Creeks to receive the remainder in allotments. Land speculators descended on the Indians and once again defrauded many of them of their individual allotments. Evicted from their homes and farms, many Creeks still refused to go west. Tension between white intruders and foraging Indians escalated and finally erupted into violence. In 1836, the War Department responded by forcibly removing thousands of Creeks as a military measure. Although many Creeks died during their westward trek as a result of the sinking of a steamboat, disease, hunger, and exposure, about 14,500 finally assembled in their new nation in the west.

The Chickasaws avoided some of the suffering of the Creeks, but, once again, corruption and fraud characterized their removal. Under the terms of the Treaty of Pontotoc, they ceded their eastern homeland, but the federal government delayed removal of the tribe until officials could locate a suitable tract of land in the West. In the interim, the Chickasaws received individual plots, and the federal government opened the remaining two-thirds of the Chickasaw territory to white settlement. Speculators promptly poured into the Chickasaw country, defrauding hapless Indians of their property. Finally, in desperation, the Chickasaws agreed to purchase a tract of land from the Choctaws, and in 1837–1838, about four thousand Chickasaws migrated beyond the Mississippi.

The scandal generated by allotment failed to temper Georgia's demands that the federal government extinguish Indian land titles within the state. The widespread suffering, however, did strengthen the Cherokees' resolve to resist removal negotiations. When Georgia courts sentenced two white missionaries to prison for their failure to take the oath of allegiance to the state, the Cherokees turned to the U.S. Supreme Court for redress of grievances. In *Worcester v. Georgia,* the Court enjoined Georgia from enforcing state law in the Cherokee Nation and orderd the release of the missionaries. The state refused to comply. Legal technicalities and Jackson's disinclination to interfer precluded federal enforcement of the decision. The missionaries remained in prison, and Georgians continued to harass the Cherokees.

A group of Cherokees began to consider negotiations when it became obvious that the Supreme Court decision would have little impact on the situation in the Nation. This group came to be known as the Treaty Party, and its leaders included Major Ridge, who had fought with the United States in the War of 1812 and had risen to a prominent leadership role in the Nation, his New England-educated son John, and Elias Boudinot, editor of the bilingual newspaper *The Cherokee Phoenix.* Motivated at least as much by economic and political ambitions as by concern for the Cherokee people, the Treaty Party enjoyed little popular support. The vast majority of Cherokees supported Principal Chief John Ross in his steadfast opposition to removal. Nevertheless, the U.S. treaty commissioner met with about one hundred Treaty Party members in December 1835, and they negotiated the Treaty of New Echota. This treaty provided for the exchange of Cherokee territory in the Southeast for a tract of land in what is today northeastern Oklahoma. While the original document gave acculturated Cherokees such as those who signed the treaty preemption rights (that is, the right to stay in the East and come under state law), supplemental articles eliminated this provision. Therefore, no Cherokees received individual allotments; removal encompassed the entire tribe. Although fifteen thousand Cherokees, almost the total population, signed a petition protesting the treaty, the U.S. Senate ratified the document. In summer 1838, federal troops seized thousands of Cherokees and imprisoned them in stockades in preparation for their westward trek. As the death toll mounted, the Van Buren administration, which had inherited the removal program, agreed to let the Cherokees conduct their own removal in the winter of 1838–1839. Despite this "humanitarian" gesture, four thousand Cherokees died enroute to their new home in the West.

The Cherokees had fought violation of their rights in the courts; the Seminoles resisted removal militarily. In 1832, the Seminoles signed a provisional removal treaty in which they agreed to go west if they found a suitable country. The next year, their agent conducted a delegation of Seminoles west in search of a relocation site and reportedly forced the delegation to sign a new treaty guaranteeing removal from Florida by 1837. Although the Seminoles signed under duress, the Senate ratified the treaty, and Jackson, who had fought the Seminoles in the War of 1812, ordered it enforced. Because many Seminoles once had been a part of the Creek confederacy, the U.S. government believed that the two tribes should reunite in the West. The Seminoles strenuously objected to this plan and demanded that their tribal integrity be preserved. Ignoring Seminole objections, the United States sent troops to Florida to round up the Indians for removal. In 1835, desperate Seminole warriors ambushed a company of soldiers, and the massacre sparked the Second Seminole War. Skillfully employing guerrilla tactics in the swamps of southern Florida and led by superb warriors such as Osceola, the Seminoles forced the United States to commit a total of forty thousand men, spend $30,000 to $40,000, and suffer substantial casualties over the next seven years. In attempting to defeat and remove the Indians, the government resorted to even more duplicitous means than bribing chiefs and exploiting tribal factionalism: commanders in the field, with approval from Washington, repeatedly captured Seminole warriors under flags of truce. Even after the official end of the war in 1842, soldiers continued to capture and deport bands of Indians until about three thousand resided in the West and only several hundred remained in the Florida Everglades.

Although remnants of all southern tribes continued to live in their ancient homeland, most occupied worthless land from which they barely eked out a subsistence. Because these Indians had little that whites wanted, the pressure to remove them diminished. In the 1840s and 1850s, state and federal governments turned their attention to other issues, in particular, the growing sectional conflict over slavery. Many white Americans quickly forgot about the southern Indians and their tragic removal.

The Indians who went west faced a number of problems in adjusting to their new situation. The native tribes of eastern Oklahoma resented the relocation of the southern Indians on their territory. During the initial stages of removal, warfare raged, particularly between the Cherokees and Osages. The Cherokees abandoned much of the cermonialism of aboriginal warfare. Instead of fighting primarily for vengeance, they looted and pillaged Osage villages, and their tactics came to resemble those of the U.S. army. In 1817, while Osage men were away hunting, Cherokees attacked their town, killed women and children, stole livestock and other property, took about one hundred captives, and burned the village. The southern Indians also had problems with other tribes who shared neither their aboriginal heritage nor their adoption of Anglo-American culture. The Seminoles and Chickasaws, who ultimately took up residence to the west of the Creeks and Choctaws, had considerable difficulty with raids by Kickapoos, Shawnees, Kiowas, and Comanches. Many Chickasaws even refused to move out of the Choctaw Nation and onto their own land until the U.S. government built Fort Washita in 1843 to protect them.

Disputes also existed between the southern Indian nations. The federal government tried to force the Seminoles to join the Creeks, but many Seminoles refused. Squatting on Cherokee territory, they presented a number of problems for officials. The Seminoles were afraid that the Creeks would seize their slaves, whose considerable freedom made them hardly slaves at all. They had reason to worry. In the negotiations which followed the War of 1812, the Creeks had agreed to reimburse white planters for slaves who took refuge with them or whom they captured. Most of these blacks, however, actually lived with the Seminoles, and the Seminoles refused to surrender them. Since they had paid for these bondsmen, the Creeks believed that they were entitled to their labor. Both the Creeks and Cherokees had slaves, but their peculiar institution more closely resembled plantation slavery in the white south than the system developed by the Seminoles. The

Cherokees objected to Seminole residence in their nation because they feared that the semiautonomous Seminole blacks would be a bad influence on their own bondsmen. Finally, the Creeks and the U.S. government resolved the difficulties by first permitting the Seminoles to establish their own towns in 1845 and then by severing the two nations in 1856.

Within all southern tribes, removal produced or exacerbated factionalism. Among the Cherokees, civil war erupted. In 1839, unknown Cherokees executed Major Ridge, John Ridge, and Elias Boudinot. Treaty Party members retaliated, and partisans battled intermittently until 1846 when the two sides accepted an uneasy truce. In other nations, voters turned out leaders favorable to removal, and the Creeks banned missionaries because highly acculturated Christian progressives had promoted removal. The disaffection of some Indians became so great that they proposed to move elsewhere; the Seminole warrior Coa-coo-chee (Wild Cat), for example, sought a permanent home in Mexico. Some of the factionalism of the removal reappeared during the American Civil War: the Seminoles as well as Creek and Cherokee factions who opposed removal favored the Union while proremoval factions actively supported the Confederacy.

Following removal, the division between the traditionalists or conservatives and the highly acculturated progressives became more pronounced. Progressives reestablished centralized republican governments and written law codes, built schools, encouraged missionaries, and took advantage of the economic opportunities afforded by the new land. They grew corn, raised cattle, made salt, and engaged in trade. Some amassed fortunes. After the American Civil War, progressives tended to advocate the construction of railroads and the exploitation of natural resources such as timber, asphalt, coal, and oil. They did not oppose the influx of white railroad workers, loggers, and cowboys, and at the turn of the century most supported allotment of land to individuals, dissolution of tribal governments, and Oklahoma statehood.

Conservatives, on the other hand, shunned many of the political, economic, and cultural changes of the progressives. Civilization had not saved their homeland, and now they regarded it with misgivings and even disdain. After removal, conservatives found comfort in what they could preserve of their traditional practices. Family and town continued to be the fundamental relationships of these people who were content with a mere economic subsistence. They found outlets for aggression in the ball play and other traditional games. Medicine men and women still relied on plants and sacred formulas to cure disease, cast spells, and control the natural world. Many conservative communities built square grounds, or stomp grounds, where they performed all-night dances, celebrated the Green Corn Ceremony, and took medicine to cleanse themselves physically and spiritually. The rituals of the stomp ground reinforced their traditional values of kinship, purity, and balance. Some southern Indians even formed secret societies in an attempt to revitalize the culture which embodied these values. The Cherokee Kee-too-wah society, for example, encouraged the abandonment of the white man's way and a return to traditional customs and beliefs. When faced with allotment and statehood, some traditionalists resisted violently, but most simply withdew to their families, communities, and stomp grounds. At best, however, these people held on to a remnant of a cultural tradition admirably suited to their native Southeast and dramatically transformed by a series of events which culminated in removal.

From the white perspective, removal accomplished its goals: the U.S. government "protected" thousands of Indians from the corrupting influence of civilization by moving them west and opened millions of acres of Indian land to white settlement. These successes can be charted in economic, political, and demographic terms, but the human cost is not so easily measured. Thousands died; others suffered permanent mental and physical impairment. Although some traditions survived, southern Indians experienced significant cultural modification and even transformation. All of this took place not according to the will of the Indians but by the dictates of white policymakers. Manipulated, exploited, and oppressed, the Indians did not have the power to direct their own course or to determine their own future. Perhaps the greatest tragedy of Indian removal is that white Americans used their power over Indians to inflict great suffering. They congratulated themselves on their humanitarianism and blithely sealed the fate of the southern Indians.

## SUGGESTED READING

The best source for the aboriginal culture of southern Indians is Charles Hudson, *The Southeastern Indians* (Knoxville, 1976).

The colonial period and the conflict of cultures are covered in J. Leitch Wright, Jr., *The Only Land They Knew: The Tragic Story of the American Indians in the Old South* (New York, 1981).

For the development of American Indian policy and its application, see Francis Paul Prucha, *American Indian Policy in the Formative Years: The Indian Trade and Intercourse Acts, 1790–1834* (Cambridge, Mass., 1962).

Specific aspects of that policy are dealt with in Bernard W. Sheehan, *Seeds of Extinction: Jeffersonian Philanthropy and the American Indian* (Chapel Hill, 1973) and Robert F. Berkhofer, *Salvation and the Savage: An Analysis of Protestant Missions and American Indian Response, 1787–1862* (Lexington, 1965).

Studies of the removal policy include Annie Heloise Abel, "The History of Events Resulting in Indian Consolidation West of the Mississippi." *Annual Report of the American Historical Association* 1 (1906): 233–450; Reginald Horsman, *The Origin of Indian Removal 1815–1824* (East Lansing, 1970); and Ronald N. Satz, *American Indian Policy in the Jacksonian Era* (Lincoln, 1975). A critical account of the removal policy can be found in Dale Van Every, *Disinherited: The Lost Birthright of the American Indian* (New York, 1966). For a more sympathetic view, see Prucha, "Andrew Jackson's Indian Policy: A Reassessment." *Journal of American History* 56 (1969): 527–539. The allotment of the Indian land is the subject of Mary E. Young, *Redskins, Ruffleshirts, and Rednecks: Indian Allotments in Alabama and Mississippi, 1830–1860* (Norman, 1961). Details of the removal of the southern Indians can be found in Grant Foreman, *Indian Removal: The Emigration of the Five Civilized Tribes of Indians* (Norman, 1932) and Arrell M. Gibson, ed., *America's Exiles: Indian Colonization in Oklahoma* (Oklahoma City, 1976).

There are a number of tribal histories and works that deal with the removal of a specific Indian nation. Choctaw histories include Angie Debo, *The Rise and Fall of the Choctaw Republic* (Norman, 1934) and Jesse O. McKee and Jon A. Schlenker, *The Choctaws: Cultural Evolution of a Native American Tribe* (Jackson, 1980).

Narrower in focus is Arthur H. DeRosier, Jr., *The Removal of the Choctaw Indians* (Knoxville, 1970). Gibson has written a tribal history, *The Chickasaws* (Norman, 1971). For Creek history, see Debo, *The Road to Disappearance* (Norman, 1941). Creek removal is the subject of Michael D. Green, *The Politics of Indian Removal: Creek Government and Society in Crisis* (Lincoln, 1982). Grace Steele Woodward, *The Cherokees* (Norman, 1963) provides a survey of tribal history. Two sides of the removal issue can be seen in Thurman Wilkins, *Cherokee Tragedy: The Story of the Ridge Family and the Decimation of a People* (New York, 1970) and Gary E. Moulton, *John Ross, Cherokee Chief* (Athens, 1978). For a tribal history, see Edwin C. McReynolds, *The Seminoles* (Norman, 1957). The standard work on Seminole removal is John K. Mahon, *History of the Second Seminole War, 1835–1842* (Gainesville, 1974).

The subsequent history of southern Indians west of the Mississippi can be found in Theda Perdue, *Nations Remembered: An Oral History of the Five Civilized Tribes, 1865–1907* (Westport, Conn., 1980), H. Craig Miner, *The Corporation and the Indian: Tribal Sovereignty and Industrial Civilization in Indian Territory, 1867–1907* (Columbia, 1976), and Debo, *And Still the Waters Run: The Betrayal of the Five Civilized Tribes* (Princeton, 1940). For information on the Indians who avoided removal, see Walter L. Williams, ed., *Southeastern Indians Since the Removal Era* (Athens, 1979).

# Part II The Climactic Ordeals

| Robert | **7.** | The American |
| H. | **Industrial** | Indian in the |
| Jones | **Society** | Trans-Mississippi |
| | **and the** | West and the |
| | **Opening** | Impact of the |
| | **of the** | American |
| | **West** | Civil War |

T he United States bustled with movement and change in the nineteenth century. The geographic limits of the nation spread from the Mississippi River to the Pacific Ocean before 1850, and between 1850 and 1870 nearly 5,000,000 white Americans crossed that river into lands occupied by Western and Plains Indians. Slightly more than half of the whites moved across in the decade of the 1850s alone, to join approximately 2,000,000 others who had preceded them. The vastness of the Trans-Mississippi West may have obscured this population explosion for the 250,000 to 300,000 Indians who justly resented the intrusion on their homelands and hunting grounds and the virtual destruction of their way of life that inexorably followed.

When the Mexican War concluded in 1848, vast sections of the Trans-Mississippi West fell under the jurisdiction of the young nation. A year later, discovery of gold in California brought over 92,000 whites to the area's rich and fertile valleys, overwhelmed an inadequate military government, and catapulted California into the Union by 1850. About 287,000 more whites appeared in California by 1860. In that year, San Francisco's population boomed to 56,800, Los Angeles to 45,600, and Sacramento's to nearly 14,000.

In 1854 the Kansas-Nebraska Act brought two large new territories into being from previously unorganized areas, and, by 1860, 136,000 white Americans moved into that area, mostly to Kansas. Kansas towns of Leavenworth and Atchison boasted populations of nearly 7,500 and 2,600, respectively, by 1860. Out in Colorado Territory, Denver claimed 4,700 the same year, and 260-year-old Santa Fe, New Mexico Territory, had 4,600. The Mormon settlement at Salt Lake included 8,200. Other towns mushroomed as well, on the plains, in the mountains, nearly every place white exploitation touched.

Roads and trails crisscrossed the Trans-Mississippi West. By 1860 the area had been thoroughly explored by hunters and trappers, gold seekers, government expeditions, and army surveyors. Old Spanish trails in the Southwest connected Santa Fe with Mexico and California. Hudson Bay Company trails abounded in the Pacific northwest. The Oregon Trail and the parallel Mormon Trail, with extensions to California, formed a very busy central overland route. By the 1860s other trails split off from the central overland route into the Rocky Mountain mining communities and, during the decade of the 1860s, into the Black Hills of the Dakotas. Settled farms grew quickly along the central route from the Missouri River to Fort Kearney, 200 miles west of Omaha (population of 1,883 in 1860). West from Fort Kearney to the Rocky Mountains, trading posts and ranches appeared every few miles, catering to travelers.

South of the central overland route, the Smoky Hill Road wound from the Kansas towns along the Missouri River to Denver, directly through the heart of the buffalo range, further threatening the livelihood of the plains Indians. The central overland route already had divided the huge buffalo herd into northern and southern branches. In 1859, the Leavenworth and Pike's Peak Express roads cut across northern Kansas from Leavenworth through Fort Riley to Denver, about 700 miles in length. The older Santa Fe Trail served both migrants and military posts, such as Forts Lyons, Union, and Larned; other roads extended on to Albuquerque and the military posts in New Mexico. Also, companies such as Butterfield's Overland Stagecoach and Mail Company began to build wagon roads by 1857. Butterfield's connected Memphis and St. Louis with San Francisco over a 2,700-mile route. By 1860, the government constructed a wagon road from Fort Benton on the upper Missouri River (accessible by steamboat from St. Louis some of the year) to the junction of the Snake and Columbia rivers west of the Rockies. Though little used, the Mullan Road between Fort Benton and Walla Walla had been under construction since 1855.

Overland mail service began on the Butterfield line in 1858, and in less than twenty-five days Californians heard the news those on the Missouri River already knew. Faster mail service arrived in April 1860, with the advent of the Pony Express. From St. Joseph, Missouri, to Placerville, California, William H. Russell built nearly 200 stations and hired young men and boys to gallop the route on a schedule of ten days across. The Pony Express operated for 18 months, when the electric telegraph replaced it.

As early as the 1840s government expeditions had crossed most of the West—as many as twenty-five of them before 1853—adding much to geographic knowledge and providing, along with a considerable popular literature, incentive to development. In 1853, at the direction of Congress, army exploring and survey teams began a careful study eventuating in four feasible railroad routes: one northern, one central, and two southern. The federal transcontinental railroad project immediately bogged down in sectional politics and had to await the 1860s before it came to fruition.

However, iron rails had already forged across Mississippi in the 1850s. The Hannibal and St. Joseph connected the Mississippi and Missouri rivers in 1859, and in the same year the Northern Missouri Railroad linked up with it to include St. Louis. The mighty Mississippi already had been bridged in 1856, connecting Rock Island, Illinois, with Davenport, Iowa, where the Mississippi and Missouri Railroad had built west to Iowa City. By 1860, 861 miles of railroad existed in Iowa and Missouri, reaching ever westward, and another 23 miles appeared in California's Sacramento Valley.

In the 1850s, then, literally millions of whites moved in, over, around, and through the Trans-Mississippi West. A highly mobile population of prospectors and miners left the early strikes in California for others in Colorado, Arizona, Utah, Montana, and the Dakotas. Businessmen freighted wagons, built stage stations, trading posts, roads, railroads, and carried the government's mail. Ranchers and farmers followed the roads, travelers sought protection of the military, and speculators laid out and advertised towns. Except for protection from or extermination of the Indians, most of these whites gave little thought to the original inhabitants whose land and hunting ground they carelessly and openly exploited. America's rapidly blossoming industrial society, leaping westward, came into direct conflict with an entirely different Indian culture they, for the most part, neither understood nor cared about.

In an earlier day, a portion of the Trans-Mississippi West had been called "The Great American Desert," and United States policy in the 1830s had been to establish it as permanent Indian reserve. Preoccupied with the sectional struggle and then the American Civil War for a decade and a half, just at the crucial moment of greatly accelerated activity in the West, the United States government failed to respond either promptly or adequately to the needs of its own Indian Bureau.

Not that the government was idle. Between 1853 and 1856 it executed some fifty-two treaties with the Indians and created thirteen new Indian agencies, evidence of changing conditions. The government aimed to broaden avenues of travel west as it became clear that "The Great American Desert"—the Great Plains—proved to be neither a desert nor a permanent reserve. The Office of Indian Affairs, charged with carrying out U.S. policy regarding the Indians, had been transferred in 1849 from the War Department to the Interior Department. It was woefully understaffed, underpaid, and full of political appointees who knew little of Indian society or problems. Rather than cooperate with the War Department, who took charge of particular Indian affairs during times of violence, the two departments continually bickered with each other.

The friction between the government agencies was further compounded by a lack of understanding between the societies. Anglo-Americans demonstrated attitudes of cultural superiority. They viewed Indians as "primitives" who needed to be taught civilized ways, for instance. White Americans also saw no reason to compromise their "superior civilization" by attempting to understand the perhaps 600 different Indian cultures. White Americans could adapt to the climate and geography but not to the Indians who peopled the land. The agents of American industrial society who sought to exploit the West, and who impatiently sought neutralization of the Indian "menace," were assisted by a government that responded in the decade before the Civil War by stationing most of its regular army west of the Mississippi.

Frontier politicians exercised great political power over Indian affairs, including appointments to service as Indian agents and licensed traders on reservations. These appointments were little scrutinized by the overworked and often ignored Indian Bureau and national administrations. Politicians often collaborated with agents and traders to defraud the Indians; they ignored the sale of whiskey to them and covered their tracks often by altering or destroying public records. Because of the rapidity with which the West was being overrun, even the reservation system on the plains could not safeguard Indian lands. As a result, the Indians could not expect justice, and both trust in and peace with the federal government evaporated.

In 1861, as President Abraham Lincoln's administration took the reins of government, most of the western tribes maintained an uneasy peace. By then as well, administration of Indian policy was fragmented, with some forty-five agents responsible to no less than eleven superintendents west of the Mississippi. Yet hope for peace among white Americans appeared dim as Northern industrial society elbowed its way into control of a federal government that Southern slaveholding agrarians sought to maintain, even by the extreme means of destroying the Union.

When secession resulted in the creation of a rival government and war followed, both Congress and the executive necessarily focused on that struggle, and affairs of the West assumed a very low priority, far below the primary ones of preserving a nation and subsequently destroying the institution of slavery. The outbreak of the Civil War slowed the flow of whites into the Trans-Mississippi West, but not by much. Indian affairs suffered even worse than before. Indians, who understood the United States government was in serious trouble, and who complained of many injustices that had gone uncorrected, took advantage of the recall of many regular soldiers from frontier posts to adjust matters themselves.

A missionary from the Minnesota frontier reported that tales of the Civil War "operate very powerfully upon the . . . Indians"; and another observer claimed that "the war for the Union, has been a fruitful source of trouble among the [Indians] . . . exciting inquiry, restlessness, and uneasiness. The effect . . . upon the . . . minds of the Indians can be easily imagined." The Interior Department believed the entire West to be a powder keg, based on reports received from Indian agents. The Shoshone were rumored to be organizing others for a war against whites in Utah; the postmaster general reported that overland mail carriers thought a "general war" with most of the tribes west of the Missouri was at hand; a missionary observed that Indians of the northern Missouri River area were "excited" and perhaps aided by the English in Canada; an acting commissioner of Indian affairs advertised that it was dangerous for anyone to attempt crossing the plains; and the Minnesota Sioux were supposed to be organizing the Chippewa and Winnebago for war. In addition, rumors circulated that Confederate agents fomented some of this trouble. While much of the information the Interior Department received reflected nervousness of frontier whites, and some was pure speculation and unfounded rumor, war in the West did follow.

Indians most directly affected by the Civil War included the northern plains tribes, largely Sioux, who occupied an area from the Minnesota Valley west to the Powder River Valley. The Santee Sioux inhabited Minnesota, the Yankton Sioux inhabited southern Dakota, and Teton and Oglala Sioux roamed the Montana area. Northern Cheyenne and Arapaho tribes shared the country, as did enemies of the Teton, the Crow. A second large group directly involved included the southern Cheyenne and Arapaho in the Colorado region and the central Rockies plus the Apache and Navajo in Arizona-New Mexico. In Oklahoma on the southern plains, there existed the Five Civilized Tribes and others, such as the Comanche, Kiowa, and Pawnee.

The first serious attempt to partition the plains among the Indians took place at Fort Laramie in 1851 when northern plains tribes agreed to remain north of the Platte River and in 1853 when southern Cheyenne and Arapaho consented to locate between the Platte and Arkansas rivers. In that year also, Kiowa, Comanche, and Kiowa-Apaches agreed to locate south of the Arkansas River. By 1855, all major plains Indian tribes had made location agreements with the United States. According to the terms of these, the Indians assented to free passage for whites along the major trails and to the existence of military posts in specified places. Except for isolated instances of robbery and small raids, no major incidents occurred for several years. This was the uneasy peace that existed at the time of Lincoln's election.

That fragile quiet shattered in 1862 with an uprising of the Santee Sioux. Over a period of sixty years, white pressure led to a series of treaties that compressed 6,600 Sioux by 1859 onto a reservation 10 miles wide and 160 miles long on the southern bank of the Minnesota River. Sioux resented loss of their land and resisted government attempts to "make white men of them," to turn them into farmers. Missionaries made little headway among them also. Unable to reach their hunting grounds in the Dakotas easily, they became dependent on the government and so were easy prey for white avarice. They mistrusted the whites, disliked restrictions of the reservation, and strongly disapproved of increasing white settlement in the Minnesota Valley. Virtually any excuse would have served to ignite them, and such an incident took place in August 1862.

A small hunting party quarreled with a few settlers near Acton, Minnesota, leaving the whites dead. Expecting reprisals, knowing that the frontier garrisons had been weakened by the withdrawal of regular army soldiers, and with the other grievances concerning their treatment by whites, the Santee Sioux chose war. They swept down the Minnesota Valley with the goal of clearing it of white settlement west of the Mississippi. However, stubborn white resistance at Fort Ridgely and at New Ulm, as well as their own lack of organization, thwarted Sioux hopes. Yet they desolated outlying settlements and killed a large number of white enemies: estimates varied, but the total came to somewhere between 400 and 800. The outbreak struck fear into all who inhabited the northwestern frontier from Wisconsin west to Nebraska. Whites abandoned their villages and farms, the frontier rapidly emptied, and crowds of fugitives sought safety in stockades or larger towns.

Acting quickly, Minnesota's governor sent an expedition, composed of volunteers and men who had been at Fort Snelling to be mustered into service in the Union Army, against the Sioux. They raised the siege of New

Ulm and Fort Ridgely and late in September defeated Sioux warriors in a pitched battle at Wood Lake. Many Sioux surrendered; others fled to the Dakotas to join the Yankton Sioux. One of the worst Indian uprisings in history, it occurred at a most inopportune time for the Union, following on the heels of the defeat at the second battle of Bull Run. The Union government made little response, other than to order Brigadier General John Pope, fresh from his disaster in Virginia, to head a newly created military Department of the Northwest with headquarters at St. Paul.

Except for annoying raids all along the Minnesota-Dakota frontier, Wood Lake broke the power of the Santee, and major campaigning ended in the area for 1862. Nearly 2,000 Sioux, including some who had not actively participated in the uprising, either surrendered after the Battle of Wood Lake or were rounded up by military scouting parties shortly thereafter. Some 1,600 remained in custody at Fort Snelling, and another 346 at Mankato. A military commission was formed to try 425 Sioux for crimes ranging from murder and rape to participation in the outbreak. Of the 321 sentenced, 303 were condemned to death by hanging. Though the Minnesota officers would have carried out the sentence, General Pope cautiously sent the trial transcript to President Lincoln, who ultimately approved the death sentence for 39 and orderd the remainder held until futher notice. On December 26, 1862, 38 condemned Sioux died on a mass scaffold at Mankato (one received a reprieve), and the others were removed to Camp McClellan, a military prison near Davenport, Iowa. In the spring of 1863, the 1,600 Sioux confined to Fort Snelling were placed on a new reservation at Crow Creek, along the Minnesota River above Fort Randall, Dakota Territory. The move was designed to protect them from revenge by hostile Minnesotans as well as to resettle them because Congress revoked their treaty and closed the reservation on the Minnesota River. Prime Minnesota Valley lands now were open to white settlement.

Yet the Sioux did not give up so easily. Outside of Minnesota they remained strong, and the Uncpapa, Blackfoot, Yankton, and renegade Santee proclaimed the upper Missouri Valley closed to whites. They warned that the Union should listen to them: "if you have no ears, we will give you ears," they proclaimed. Also, reports received at the headquarters of the Department of the Northwest indicated that Little Crow, Sioux leader of the Minnesota uprising, had mobilized fugitive Santee and Yankton Sioux for a campaign in the spring of 1863.

General Pope intended to pacify the northwestern frontier by sending two columns of troops into the field that same spring. One, commanded by Brigadier General Henry Hastings Sibley, the veteran Minnesota Indian trader who had defeated the Santee in 1862, would proceed up the Minnesota River into Dakota Territory north to the vicinity of Devil's Lake and then swing west to the Missouri River. The other column, led by Brigadier General Alfred Sully, would march north up the Missouri River from Fort Randall and link up with Sibley. Properly carried out, the object was to catch the Sioux between them and prevent their escape across the Missouri.

Sibley's column moved as planned, fought the Sioux at Big Mound, Dakota Territory, on July 24, but they eluded him. In pursuit, Sibley skirmished again two days later at Dead Buffalo Lake and then was attacked by large numbers of Sioux at Stony Lake on July 28. Sibley's artillery proved the difference, and the Sioux fled across the Missouri, abandoning large quantities of meat, hides, utensils, and other items for the troops to destroy. Unfortunately for Pope's plan, Sully failed to arrive as scheduled: he was a month late. Returning back downriver, a large patrol of Sully's encountered some of the Sioux who had recrossed the river after Sibley left. Surrounded, the patrol awaited a ceremonial slaughter scheduled to commence at sundown. However, at dusk the main body of Sully's army arrived on the scene at a gallop, and the Sioux fled, though skirmishing followed for another couple of days. This affair, the Battle of White Stone, allowed the soldiers to destroy tremendous amounts of Sioux supplies. The fugitive Yankton and Santee Sioux faced a hard winter without the supplies lost at Stony Lake and White Stone Hill.

Even so, rumor persisted that the Sioux intended to keep the Missouri River and the roads across Dakota Territory closed and to perhaps strike back at white settlements. Clearly, Sioux along the Powder and Yellowstone rivers were agitated as well, thus broadening the alliance to include the Tetons. In the spring of 1864, raiding parties struck along the Minnesota-Iowa border, harassed soldiers along the Missouri River, and as late as June took cavalry horses from Fort Randall. General Pope reacted by planning to build a series of forts along the Missouri River.

Late in June 1864 General Sully led an expedition up the Missouri again to locate one of the proposed new forts and perhaps to chastise Sioux. A detail from his army began construction of Fort Rice, near the mouth of the Cannonball River, while Sully's main force acted on reports of a Sioux buildup near Kildeer Mountain. He found and defeated a large body of Sioux there on June 28 and then crossed the badlands to the Yellowstone River, skirmishing along the way. Sully's steamboats met his column on the Yellowstone, carried it down that river to the Missouri, and then down to Fort Rice. Once there, he sent 900 men to raise the siege of a wagon train that had been ambushed between the Little Missouri and Cannonball rivers. Sully considered his expedition a success, and no further large movements of troops took place on the northwestern frontier in 1864.

Still the Sioux continued their harassment of the northwestern frontier, remaining determined to keep the upper Missouri Valley closed. Another expedition sought the Sioux out in 1865, but by then the Sioux wars ceased to be a part of the Union's burden during the Civil War. These wars instead became a continuing part of the prolonged sporadic wars with the Sioux that never really concluded until the Battle of Wounded Knee, two weeks after Sitting Bull's death in December 1890. The relentless white pressure on the northwestern frontier met with equally relentless, if hopeless, resistance of the Sioux.

The lands of the southern Arapaho and Cheyenne for some time lay fairly well off the beaten trails. But in 1858 gold was discovered in the Pike's Peak area, and in 1859 nearly 100,000 miners and others settled in the midst of the Arapaho and Cheyenne reserve. Though they had no right there, the United States ignored Indian claims and made no effort to observe the 1853 treaty. As Congress debated the creation of Colorado Territory in 1861, a new treaty resettled Arapaho and Cheyenne on a much smaller reserve, a triangular tract in southeastern Colorado where the Big Sandy Creek and the Arkansas River meet. The Indians retained the right to hunt over their former reserve until it should be further disposed of and settled.

The Sand Creek Reserve failed, however, because it included some of the driest and most desolate parts of the original reserve and because of a determination on the part of the tribes not to locate there. The only thing to commend the Sand Creek Reserve was its location away from the main roads. So the Arapaho and Cheyenne continued in wandering bands and became ever more uneasy as they saw traffic increase on the stage lines, bringing more whites into their country. They watched white settlements spring up across the range everyplace there was some water. For three years they put up with this encroachment, and then, in the summer of 1864, they attacked the stage line along its entire length from Fort Kearney to Denver.

Governor John Evans of Colorado Territory had received reports of occasional attacks on isolated settlements in the spring of 1864. He responded by asking friendly Indians to collect around the agencies, promising them food and protection, because he intended to destroy any Indians who remained in the field. The Arapaho and Cheyenne defied the governor and replied by attacking the stage line. They burned nearly every stage station, drove off the stock, and set haystacks ablaze. They disrupted communication with the Missouri River and caused stages to run only with miliary escort and wagons to travel only in tight groups for their own protection.

Yet by fall, Arapaho and Cheyenne bands came into Fort Lyon, near Sand Creek, declaring their friendship. On September 28, Governor Evans met with seven chiefs, including White Antelope and Black Kettle. Black Kettle told Evans that he wanted his people to "sleep in peace." The governor claimed he had heard that since the whites were "at war among themselves" the Indians thought they could drive the whites away. But, Evans said, it was a false hope. Soon the war would end, and the "Great Father" wouldn't know what to do with his army, "except to send [it] . . . after the Indians." Evans advised the chiefs to make the best terms they could with the military.

Colonel John M. Chivington, also at the council, told the chiefs that Colorado's soldiers were under his command and that his rule was to fight until the enemy submitted. His statement ended the meeting. No promise of the peace that Black Kettle desired came from the meeting.

That evening, Brigadier General Samuel R. Curtis, commanding the military department, wired that he wanted no peace until the Indians suffered more, and certainly no peace without his direction. The Indians, camped now at Sand Creek a few miles from Fort Lyon, had meanwhile convinced their agent of their good intentions. The agent acted as a go-between, and with his assistance the authorities at Fort Lyon gave those Cheyenne and Arapaho at Sand Creek permission to remain there in peace. Though some of the younger braves remained in the field at war, the majority of the tribes and their chiefs seemed determined to end the fighting, at least for that winter.

However, Colorado authorities, including the governor, and the Union military commander, Curtis, believed that a winter campaign against the tribes was the only certain way to peace. Evans earlier had raised a regiment for an Indian campaign and wondered what he would do with it if he made peace instead. They had been raised "to kill Indians," he said, "and they must kill Indians." Colonel Chivington agreed. In November Chivington marched the governor's Third Colorado and some First Colorado Cavalry to Fort Lyon. After dark on November 28, he led the force to Sand Creek, surrounded the camp, and ordered an attack at dawn.

Black Kettle, White Antelope, and about 500 others believed they had made their peace. They had no guarantees, but similar situations had taken place before, and they were confident. Yet when dawn broke on November 29, the troops attacked. White Antelope died early; Black Kettle raised both an American and a white flag to stop the slaughter, but in vain. Colorado soldiers destroyed the camp and mercilessly killed men, women, and children. This massacre of Indians by whites, Colorado authorities attempted to excuse by calling it a punitive campaign. The commissioner of Indian Affairs lamented it as a massacre "in cold blood by troops in the service of the United States."

After Sand Creek, Arapaho and Cheyenne bands remained on the plains, keeping on the move until October 1865 when a peace conference (attended not only by Arapaho and Cheyenne but also by some Apache, Kiowa, and Comanche) quieted the southern plains for nearly a decade. The Arapaho and Cheyenne gave up the worthless Sand Creek Reserve with the promise of a new and more hospitable one along the Cimarron River. Yet that promise too was broken as the Senate failed to confirm the treaty. The Arapaho and Cheyenne remained homeless until 1869, when by executive order they received land in Indian Territory—present Oklahoma—taken from the Five Civilized Tribes.

The Five Civilized Tribes—the Cherokee, Chickasaw, Choctaw, Creek, and Seminole—living in Indian Territory found themselves caught between the aspirations of the Union and Confederacy. In 1861, Albert Pike became the Confederate Indian commissioner and traveled through Indian territory to conclude treaties with the Chickasaw, Choctaw, Creek, and Seminole tribes. Chief John Ross of the Cherokees resisted and attempted to remain neutral, with little success. Union control collapsed as the U.S. forts in the area—Arbuckle, Cobb, Gibson, and Washita—fell into Confederate hands, and Union Indian agents turned their agencies over to Confederates.

Not all Indians chose to remain with the Confederacy, and a large number, perhaps 6,000, relocated along the Verdigris River in southeastern Kansas, dependent on a Union Indian commissioner for sustenance. The Union also promised to relocate them on their own lands again after the war. Some returned to Indian Territory from time to time to help convince their fellow Indians to support the Union, and John Ross remained a firm Unionist. But the Cherokee were divided, and another leader, Stand Watie, served as a colonel in Confederate service. The Choctaw and Chickasaw were slaveholders, primarily sympathetic to the Confederacy, while, along with the Cherokee, the Creek and Seminole remained divided. Their position was not unlike that of whites in the border states. Cherokee troops fought with Union soldiers at the Battle of Pea Ridge, Arkansas, and others served with Confederate arms. The beginning of the end of Confederate-allied Indians came with Brigadier General James G. Blunt's victory at Honey Springs, in July 1863, and his subsequent pursuit of Stand Watie.

Following the Civil War, the United States claimed that by disloyalty the Five Civilized Tribes forfeited their reservation claims and that previous treaties were void. The United States forced the tribes to give up about half their land in Indian Territory and proceeded to settle displaced plains Indians, including southern Arapaho and Cheyenne, upon them. Within twenty years, over 75,000 Indians and 6,500 freed blacks, formerly Chickasaw and Choctaw slaves, lived on twenty-two reservations in Indian Territory.

The Civil War affected other Indians besides those who inhabited the plains. In the spring of 1862, following the campaign between the Confederate "Army of New Mexico" under General Henry Hopkins Sibley and Union forces led by Colonels Edward R. S. Canby and John P. Slough that resulted in the expulsion of the Confederates, Colonel James H. Carleton arrived in New Mexico Territory with a strong Union column from California. Carleton found few Confederates to confront and so turned to ending the 250-year-old struggle with the Apache and Navajo. Carleton intended to kill Indians until the survivors felt compelled to surrender and then to put them on reservations.

Carleton ordered Colonel Christopher "Kit" Carson and his New Mexico volunteers to act against the Mescelaro Apache, while other elements operated against the Gila Apache. By 1863, after being roughly treated by Carleton's command, survivors of both Apache tribes arrived at Fort Sumner asking for peace and were confined to stockades there. Carleton then took on the Navajo. He built Fort Wingate in the heart of their territory and directed Carson to subdue them. After a highly successful winter campaign, a war without quarter, Carson drove Navajo survivors to Fort Wingate. Carleton moved them to a new reservation they would share with the Apache at Bosque Redondo near Fort Sumner on the Pecos River, about 9,000 Indians all told. Peace came to New Mexico; Carleton emerged a hero; and New Mexico became safe for white exploitation.

Carleton's Apache and Navajo policy failed to provide a permanent solution to the area's Indian problem as the whites saw it, but Indian power was broken and the tribes were much reduced in numbers by fighting and disease. By 1868 whites easily outnumbered them in New Mexico, and future outbreaks proved to be local rather than general.

In the western part of New Mexico Territory—which became Arizona Territory in 1863—relations between the Apaches and their neighbors broke down in 1861. That year the army tried to arrest Cochise, and in the next couple of years soldiers killed several chiefs, including Mangas Coloradas in 1863. The Apache lashed out in a fury not only at whites but against the agricultural Pima, Sonora, Papago, and other Indians as well. Although Carleton successfully pacified the Apache and Navajo in New Mexico, in Arizona Apache resistance continued for nearly a decade until General George Crook doggedly pursued the more powerful bands, by 1873 finally confining them to reservations.

As U.S. troops withdrew from Salt Lake City in 1861, Indian difficulties erupted in that area. Increased travel on the central overland route to California acted as a magnet for Indian raiders, and there existed real danger the road might be closed. Also, the Mormons spread out into neighboring valleys, displacing native Indians; the gold rush to Pike's Peak disturbed mountain Utes as well as it had Plains Indians. Overland stage stations in Utah and Nevada proved unsafe. In 1862, General Patrick E. Connor led California troops to Utah with the purpose of both pacifying the Indians and keeping the Mormons loyal to the Union. Like Carleton in New Mexico, Connor conducted hard-fought winter campaigns and by 1863 subdued the Shoshone Utes. And like Carleton, Connor emerged as a hero who kept the California trail open and who opened additional land in southern Utah for white settlement.

By 1860, pressure on the Indians of the Trans-Mississippi West had built almost to the bursting point. It seemed that whites threatened Indians everywhere, moving into and through their reservations and hunting grounds, driving off or killing their game, and ignoring solemnly made treaties. Shot through with corruption, inefficient, understaffed, underpaid, the Indian Bureau proved incapable of protecting their charges and administering government policy evenly and honestly. And in 1860, a sectional Republican party, representing many Northern interests, captured the White House. Powerful Northern business leaders stood among the backers of the new party, eager to cast aside restrictions they felt the old agrarian forces placed on them.

By 1860, the total value of industrial production in the United State exceeded that of agricultural products, and the minions of the industrial world sought control of the government. With secession, and the exodus of Southern agrarian Democrats from Congress, Republicans controlled that body as well. Under cover of the Civil War, they responded to industrialism with new and advantageous tariff and banking legislation, massive land grants to railroad corporations, and homestead laws.

With the nation's attention focused on the Civil War, western agents of the North's industrial society used the opportunity to open up the Trans-Mississippi West for exploitation and settlement, and they proved very successful at it. They subdued those large segments of the Indian population that stood in their way, guaranteeing white access through much of the area on the major roads; opened great acreage for white use; and cleared the way for the rapid disappearance of the frontier.

Just as east of the Mississippi Grant and Sherman emerged as heroes, west of the river Sibley in Minnesota, Chivington in Colorado, Carleton in New Mexico, and Connor in Utah came in for local praise. East of the Mississippi, industrial society remained in firm control of the government; west of the river that same society also took command. The Civil War proved as much a turning point for the Trans-Mississippi West—and its Indian population—as it had for the nation as a whole.

For the Indian in 1865, it remained only a question of time before the rest of the tribes were forced to accept the new order in their lives. Whites poured into the Trans-Mississippi West in increasing numbers; railroads spanned the region; new territories and states arose; and by 1890 not only did the frontier disappear but, for the Indians, their last sad battle had been fought.

## SUGGESTED READING

Many different sources can provide the information from which this chapter was compiled, and a good bit of additional searching and reading will flesh out the story here hinted at in outline. For the white population figures, see the *Fifteenth Census of the United States: 1930,* volume I, *Population: Number and Distribution of Inhabitants* (Washington, D.C., 1931) or the similar volume in other census reports. On roads and railroads, consult Oscar Osburn Winther, *The Transportation Frontier: Trans-Mississippi West, 1865–1890* (New York, ca. 1964) and John F. Stover, *Iron Road to the West: American Railroads in the 1850s* (New York, 1978). Edmund J. Danziger, Jr., *Indians and Bureaucrats: Administering the Reservation Policy during the Civil War* (Urbana, Ill., ca. 1974) is important on that subject. Circumstances surrounding the Sioux are dealt with in Robert Huhn Jones, *The Civil War in the Northwest: Nebraska, Wisconsin, Iowa, Minnesota, and the Dakotas* (Norman, Okla., 1960), and a larger view by the same author is found in the chapter, "The War in the Trans-Mississippi West," *Disrupted Decades: The Civil War and Reconstruction Years* (Huntington, N.Y., 1979).

| Thomas | **8.** | Ambiguity |
| W. | **Fire** | and the |
| Dunlay | **and** | Plains |
| | **Sword** | War |

Anglo-Americans and Plains Indians first came into serious conflict in Texas, where, by the 1830s, white settlement had reached areas within the raiding range of the Comanches and Kiowas. The belligerence and mutual incomprehension of the two sides insured the growth of mutual hatred and conflict. Elsewhere the American settlement frontier remained east of the Great Plains, and only fur traders, trappers, and Santa Fe traders had any considerable contact with the Plains tribes through the 1840s. The Plains people were certainly aware of the white presence; it brought them a variety of material goods on which they became increasingly dependent and diseases which devastated some tribes, especially the sedentary Missouri River folk. Plains Indians were impressed by the tools and luxuries and often ethnocentrically contemptuous of white behavior. But at midcentury they had little conception of the numbers of the whites or the power embodied in their technology and social organizations.

The westward expansion of the United States in the 1840s, and the California gold rush, changed the situation. Large numbers of whites began to cross the Plains by the Platte River route, and lesser numbers further south. Comanche leaders informed U.S. authorities that they did not object to whites crossing their territory, providing the travelers were "orderly," a requirement that casts a curious light on the Comanches' fearsome reputation. They made a distinction between "Americans" and Texans, not yet realizing the implications of U.S. annexation of the Lone Star Republic.

It was only in 1848 and 1849 that the U.S. Army first established military posts beyond the eastern periphery of the Great Plains. In 1851, at Fort Laramie, the civil authorities held the first great council with the Northern Plains tribes, attempting to insure peaceful passage for travelers and to insure intertribal peace among the Indians themselves. The Plains tribes had for decades been accustomed to refer to the President as the "Great Father" or "Grandfather," but they had no idea of the sort of authority the term implied for the Great Father's representatives. Nor could they imagine the sort of control the federal government expected ultimately to exercise over them, or the way they would be dispossessed when it suited the whites.

They could not imagine, in addition, that the white authorities regarded them as children, whose way of life deserved no respect and whose thoughts and wishes need be consulted only as a short-term expedient. David Mitchell and Thomas Fitzpatrick, the experienced fur traders who negotiated the 1851 treaty, must have realized that the Plains tribes considered themselves lords of the soil, allowing white presence chiefly for their own convenience and economic advantage; most whites, however, would never grasp this attitude or regard it as anything but foolish arrogance.

The Teton Sioux, by virtue of numbers, had by midcentury acquired a dominant position on the Northern Plains, as far south as the Platte Valley. With their Cheyenne and Arapaho allies, they were asserting control over the Powder River country to the west and the Republican Valley to the south. Only in the 1850s did they begin to encounter a power greater than theirs—the United States—and only gradually did they realize how great the disparity was or that their interests, as they perceived them, were incompatible with the purposes of the newcomers.

The first violent encounters were the product of failure of understanding and the irresponsibility or bad judgment of persons on both sides, and the pattern would be repeated many times in the future. In the famous "Mormon cow" incident of 1854, the army attempted to follow a policy of punishing individual Indians for acts defined as offenses, in this case the shooting of an emigrant's cow near Fort Laramie. In theory this was preferable to punishing whole groups for individual acts; in practice it proved unworkable. Lieutenant Grattan's attempt to arrest the particular Sioux who killed the cow led to the deaths of himself, his whole detachment, and a number of Sioux, thanks apparently to a drunken interpreter, the inflexibility of Grattan, and the intransigence of the Sioux. The army then switched to massive retaliation, and the following year General William Harney attacked the first Sioux he could find at Blue Water Creek in Nebraska.

The next few decades would see many repetitions of these events, with variations. Neither side could see the other's viewpoint, and the actions of a few men on the spot often committed large numbers of people to increasing violence. The army suffered a defeat because bad judgment placed a small number of troops at the mercy of greater numbers of Indians whose fighting prowess had been greatly underestimated. In turn, the Indians suffered defeat and serious losses, by their standards, because they allowed the soldiers, also underestimated, to surprise their vulnerable camp. The Sioux were surprised partly because their leaders assumed that they were on good terms with the whites or could settle any differences by talking. However, the whites had defined a certain group of people as hostile and then attacked those belonging to the enemy group as defined, without considering whether the Indians concerned defined themselves as enemies of the whites. On both sides, persons innocent of any direct participation in violent acts suffered as aroused fighters took vengeance. All these phenomena would be frequently repeated over the Great Plains for the next generation.

In spite of such spectacular episodes, Indian-white conflict on the central and northern Plains remained desultory in the 1850s. Settlement did not really come within the range of the Sioux and the Cheyennes, and the army, for reasons of government policy and logistics, waged only a few intermittent campaigns against the natives. On the southern Plains, on the other hand, the white settlement frontier confronted the Comanches and the Kiowas directly, and the army faced the problem of frontier defense, hampered by its own shortage of troops, inferior mobility, and tactical methods ill-suited to the problem. For several years the military tried to protect the settlers with a cordon of posts, manned largely by infantry, and a small mounted force. This passive, linear defense proved inadequate since the mounted raiders could move freely between the posts and generally be on their way home with their booty—chiefly livestock and prisoners—before pursuit could be mounted.

By the late 1850s, prompted in part by the example of the Texas Rangers, the regulars began to pursue a more aggressive strategy, with an expanded cavalry force and members of the friendly tribes of the Texas frontier acting as both scouts and fighting auxiliaries. They pursued and attacked Comanches and Kiowas in Indian Territory and even further north. This effective combination was disrupted when Texas forced the federal government to remove the friendly tribes—in the opinion of some officers the most effective defenders of the frontier—from Texas to the Indian Territory in 1859. Soon after, secession and civil war broke down all frontier defenses across the Plains.

It would be wrong, however, to imagine that Indian-white conflict on the Plains increased in the 1860s simply because the regular army was withdrawn to the East to fight another war. The real cause of "Indian trouble" was white movement westward, and the Civil War did not end or even greatly impede that. Six new territories were organized during the war years, and major gold discoveries in the Rockies created new pockets of settlement whose lines of communication ran across the Plains. The Santee Sioux outbreak in Minnesota in 1862 was the beginning of the bloodiest years of Indian-white confrontation in the region.

By 1864, Plains travel had become exceedingly hazardous, and large numbers of Civil War volunteer troops were serving in the West, especially on the Platte River road. These volunteer organizations took an especially punitive approach to Indians defined as hostile. There was a widespread belief that the outbreaks were the result of a Confederate conspiracy, which aggravated the already existing racial and cultural prejudices against Indians. The famous massacre of Southern Cheyennes at Sand Creek, Colorado, in 1864, was the most dramatic result of this attitude, put into effect by Colorado volunteer troops. As so often, the immediate result was to aggravate the interracial hostility.

The end of the Civil War left a war-weary nation confronted with greatly intensified Indian-white conflict on the Plains and elsewhere. In 1865 and 1866 the government made a concerted effort to negotiate treaties with the Plains peoples, in hopes of avoiding further conflict and expense. These efforts failed because, as before, neither side could really understand what the other wanted or how the others viewed the situation. The Indians wanted to continue their accustomed way of life, dependent on space and abundant game; certain of the white man's material goods appealed to them as an enhancement of this life, but there was no appeal in the white way of life as a whole.

The whites persisted in making treaties with Indian chiefs, who could generally be induced to sign by distribution of goods to their people, because no other way of dealing with semiindependent tribes was conceivable. But the intention was always to increase control of the tribes, until the time arrived when decisions could be made by white authorities without consulting the Indians' desires. The underlying philosophy was always that the whites knew better than the Indians what was good for them. Thus, even the most honorable white negotiator was in some sense engaged in deception—and in self-deception.

A dramatic example of such confusions was the treaty council at Fort Laramie with the Sioux in 1866. The government had promised to guarantee the Sioux extensive hunting grounds in the Dakotas, Montana, and Wyoming. While the council was in progress, troops passed through Laramie headed for the Powder River country to build forts to protect the Bozeman Trail leading to the Montana goldfields. Remembering the destruction of the natural environment along the Platte River road, the Sioux leaders could not look on this development calmly; a few chiefs signed the treaty, but others prepared to resist the establishment of the garrisons. Apparently it had occurred to no one in authority that the forts would be, to the Indians, incompatible with the promises of the treaty makers.

For the next decade the federal government would follow a carrot-and-stick policy, alternating military operations and attempts at peacemaking in a pattern that confused the Indians and satisfied almost no whites. The end result, of course, was the confinement of the Plains people on reservations, deprived of their way of life and of the power of decision over their own lives. This, of course, was the official goal all along. The overall tendency is clear, but any examination of details produced confusion, as it did for contemporaries.

The Plains tribes varied in their political organization, but none had the type of unitary state, able to compel the obedience of all, that whites considered normal and desirable. Much that seemed inconsistent or "treacherous" in their conduct stemmed from this fact and the related fact that the strongest, overriding loyalties were always to the most immediate group, dwindling as the group grew larger. Family, warrior society, band, division, then tribe, drew attachment—virtually never "the Indians" as a whole.

One clear illustration of this point is the regular appearance of Indian scouts acting in alliance with the army. Often they belonged to tribes who were established enemies of the people the army was fighting. The Sioux, having acquired their dominant position on the Northern Plains at the expense of various weaker tribes, now found the Crows, Shoshonis, Arikaras, and Pawnees ready to provide needed expert assistance to the whites to defeat them. The Comanches on the Southern Plains found themselves in a similar situation. It was the dominant, stronger tribes who had the most to lose by submission to the whites; the weaker, seeing in the whites an ally against their immediate enemy, believed they had something to gain by joining the newcomers.

Other Indian allies of the white military, however, were of what whites considered to be the same tribe as the hostiles. They found various reasons for undertaking to serve the army, generally without disloyalty to the group to which they owed their strongest allegiance. Economic benefits, expected advantages for their people to be gained from the whites, or the simple desire to get away from a reservation and engage in activities proper to warriors were among their motives. Some were bitterly disappointed, while others later judged that they had made the best bargain they could under the circumstances. They were present in most plains campaigns, sometimes a few, sometimes composing a substantial portion of the military force. Their importance was out of proportion to their numbers, because they greatly extended the capabilities of white and black regular troops.

That the U.S. Army had to secure the services of Indians to fight Indians emphasizes some peculiar features of these conflicts. The United States, after all, had a population advantage over the Indians, as separate tribes or all together, that was ridiculously disproportionate. In technology, too, there was no comparison; the whites had railroads, telegraph, and mass production industry, while the Indians could not even make a steel knife. The result of any conflict would seem a foregone conclusion, and in the long run, of course, it was. In the course of the conflict, however, the army encountered innumerable frustrations and a number of tactical defeats. Both the abilities of the Indians and the weaknesses of the army made the conquest less smooth than might have been expected.

The country itself was commonly the Indians' ally and the army's enemy. Sheer distance imposed enormous logistical burdens on an army whose transport was based on animals and wagons. The railroad made a significant difference, of course; Harney's army, campaigning against the Sioux in 1855, had to carry its supplies by wagon all the way from Fort Leavenworth. After the Civil War, the railroad moved the supply bases much nearer the campaigning areas. General William T. Sherman not unreasonably regarded the railroad as the answer to the "Indian Problem." Even so, supplies might have to be carried hundreds of miles from the nearest railroad into remote areas where the hostiles might be found.

The Indians did not share this disability; they lived off the country all their lives. The buffalo was their "commissary," and the decline of the herds may have had as much to do with the defeat of the Plains tribes as any military activity. Nomadic peoples had no such difficulties in traveling rapidly across the country as did the soldiers, for their whole way of life and their material possessions were designed for movement. Indian women and children with their household goods readily crossed streams that the army regarded as impassable.

White men generally did not admire the appearance of the Indian pony, but this scrubby beast had one great advantage over the big "American" horse used by the cavalry; he had lived on prairie grass all his life. The army horse was used to grain, and his performance fell off rapidly without it. Army officers acknowledged that, with any sort of head start, the Indians could stay ahead of the cavalry in a straight chase indefinitely. Since each trooper had only one horse and most Plains warriors had several, a "stern chase" was generally a losing proposition for the military. Some reckless attacks against Indians, like Custer's at the Little Bighorn, were the result of a fear that the hostiles would get away if opportunity was not seized, regardless of odds.

The Plains were not, strictly speaking, a desert, but parts of them, at certain times, were exceedingly short of water. The Indians, of course, knew where the water was better than the army could hope to. Likewise, the Indians almost invariably knew the country in general much better than their enemies, unless the latter had an unusually well-qualified guide, white or Indian. The history of the Plains wars is full of military columns defeated as much by the country and its hardships as by the human enemy. The commands of Nelson Cole and Samuel Walker, marching into the Powder River country in 1865, lost most of their animals to the hardships of the march, were forced, therefore, to burn most of their wagons and supplies, and were near starvation, besides being harassed by the enemy, when rescued by other troops. Eleven years later General George Crook, far more knowledgeable about frontier logistics and Indian campaigning than Cole and Walker, nonetheless found himself making what was called the "Horsemeat March" because his men had to slaughter their mounts as they broke down to keep from starving themselves.

There was no complete answer to the Plains Indians' superior mobility. The army used mule pack trains instead of wagons, and some commanders mounted their infantry on mules and captured ponies, but they could not really hope to overtake a running enemy. They found that to get a fight out of the hostiles they must catch them off guard; if the Indians themselves offered to do battle, it generally meant that they had the advantage or were assured of an escape route.

The sheer immensity of the country also made it hard to locate the Indians. There was, of course, no aerial reconnaissance or electronic communications; the scouts of both sides rode horseback and carried their reports at the horse's speed. No one could deny the Indians their superiority in scouting and trailing; their training started in boyhood, and few white scouts could equal them. Whites preferred to imagine that these "Indian" skills were inherent and hereditary, having nothing to do with intelligence or reasoning, rather than the result of long, intensive training. In any case, the best answer was the recruitment of Indian scouts.

In many ways Indian warfare was still the warfare of preindustrial times, dependent on the skills and hardihood of men, not on the superiority of one side's technological complex. It was not altogether surprising, then, that preindustrial warriors, trained since boyhood to war, hunting, horsemanship, and endurance, fighting in their own country, should enjoy certain immediate advantages over men more dependent on their industrial base and its products, first introduced to military training and Plains conditions as adults.

The disparity in numbers was also not immediately apparent, since it was precisely at the points of contact on the frontier that the whites were thinnest. Many Indians persisted in believing that the few whites they saw in the West were all there were. Those who traveled to the East and saw cities were stunned by the sheer numbers of people. But they found it impossible to make their fellow tribesmen believe them. Numbers of human beings so far beyond experience could not exist; besides, if the reports were true, the implications would be intolerable.

Away from the railroad and the telegraph line, the principal sign of the white man's allegedly superior civilization was his weapon; the point was emphasized by the Kiowa chief Satanta's famous remark that the only parts of the white man's road that appealed to him were guns and whiskey. Chief Washakie of the Shoshonis discouraged certain of his tribesmen who wanted to resist the whites by showing them a revolver and reminding them that, while the whites could make such a weapon, the Shoshonis could make only bows and arrows.

Indian fighting men frequently obtained firearms, either through trade or as prizes of war, but both the numbers and quality of these arms remain subjects of debate. Some army officers insisted that every hostile Indian had a Winchester and an ample supply of ammunition, thoughtfully furnished by the Bureau of Indian Affairs. Some historians contend, on the contrary, that most Indian weapons were muzzle-loading rifles. The safest conclusion is that there must have been great variation over time and place. Plains Indians developed the technique of reloading metallic cartridges before the whites realized this was possible. This coup is a tribute to their ingenuity, but it also points out both their ammunition supply problems and the fact that they were nonetheless familiar with this latest form of ammunition and the weapons that used it.

To point out the preindustrial nature of Plains warfare is not to say that it was not subject to historical change or that the combatants did not adapt to technological innovations. The smoothbore musketry seems to have forced the Plains tribes to abandon the leather armor and massed charges they had developed with the introduction of the horse. They fought stripped to the breechcloth, not because they were "naked savages" but because a bullet could drive bits of clothing into a wound and increase the danger of infection. When the Anglo-Americans first encountered the Plains warriors in Texas, they found that their long rifles were not well-suited to fighting horsemen who could cover several hundred yards and fire twenty arrows in the time it took to reload a muzzle-loading rifle. The Colt revolver, in the hands of the Texas Rangers, made horseback combat possible and shifted the balance in the white man's favor. The revolver-wielding horseman could take on several Indians armed with muskets, bows, or lances, and both Rangers and regular cavalry developed a certain conviction of superiority and a readiness to attack when opportunity offered. A deep-seated conviction of cultural and racial superiority seemed confirmed, and the situation persisted more or less through the Civil War years.

The Civil War brought the first widespread use of new weapons developments, breechloading and repeating rifles. The rifle made previous notions of tactics obsolete, as witnessed by Civil War casualty lists. The breech-loader accentuated the change by making it possible for a soldier to fire from a prone position, with nearly all of his body behind cover. The repeater only enhanced the possibilities.

Over the years after 1865 the Indians seem to have acquired increasing numbers of breechloading firearms. There is no reason to doubt that they fully appreciated the advantage of a weapon allowing the maximum use of cover and firing much faster than the familiar muzzle loader, with far greater range and accuracy than the revolver. The repeater was desirable, but the greatest need was the breechloader, especially when the army gave up the repeating Spencer cavalry carbine in the early 1870s.

We think of the Plains warrior as preeminently the "horse Indian," the "finest light cavalry in the world," in the opinion of some of their more admiring opponents. They could indeed fight on horseback, generally better than the regular cavalry, and they took full advantage of the mobility the horse gave them, but they were by no means incapable of fighting on foot and very often did so, especially on the defensive. In fact, some tribes showed considerable ability in building field fortifications or digging rifle pits. They were as much aware as any Civil War infantryman of the immense advantage held by a man in a hole or behind a rock over a man advancing toward him in the open.

There was a significant difference in military philosophy between the Plains tribes and the United States Army. We know that the Plains people placed a great value on courage and martial achievement; glory was the natural and legitimate desire of young men, a necessity for status. But this philosophy was perfectly compatible with the desire to live to enjoy one's triumph. There was nothing glorious about a high casualty list; war leaders who lost many men soon ceased to have followers, for their "medicine" was obviously deficient. The goal was to inflict the maximum damage on the enemy, perform brave deeds, and come home alive. Therefore the underlying tendency was to minimize loss and to be ready to make an escape if things were going badly.

To be sure, suicidal displays of bravery sometimes occurred when a man wanted to prove his courage, recover a wounded or dead comrade, or literally commit suicide. But the decision was that of the individual warrior, except in cases where a village with its women and children had to be defended. Ordinarily a war chief did not order his men to perform a maneuver which was sure to result in the loss of many of them. The idea that a leader would deliberately order men to attack knowing that heavy losses would occur in order to take some objective deemed worth the certain deaths of many men, was an alien concept.

Military men were ambivalent about this aspect of plains culture. Their prime definition of courage was the willingness to go when ordered into a situation where there was a high risk of death or injury. For some two hundred years the basis of tactics had been the close-order formation, armed with the smoothbore musket, trained to move shoulder to shoulder toward the enemy, taking losses without flinching. The musket was so inaccurate that the best results came from volley firing, not from individual marksmanship. The Civil War, fought with the more accurate rifle, demonstrated the obsolesence of such tactics, but it was hard to escape the philosophical heritage. To most soldiers it seemed that the Indians were deficient in courage.

The real difference was apparent to a few officers. The Indians were highly skilled individual fighting men, trained from boyhood, each relying to a great extent on his own judgment, alert to preserve his own life. The U.S. soldier of the period was sketchily trained, required to rely on his leaders to think for him, and to act in unison with his fellows without considering danger. But weapons technology had reached a point where the old military philosophy was no longer functional. Men had to disperse and make use of cover in order to avoid being slaughtered uselessly by more accurate, faster-firing weapons. An officer could no longer keep all his men within sound of his voice, dictating their every move.

Ironically, the military philosophy of the "primitive" Indians was in some ways better adapted to the new weapons than the outlook of the armies representing industrial civilization. The Indians took full advantage of cover and camouflage, tried every expedient to avoid personal harm, let each man pick his own spot and dictate his own moves within loose battle plans or none at all, and never sacrificed lives to take ground, of which there was plenty on the Plains. Concealment, ambush, and surprise were vital elements in their tactics, and they vastly preferred to have the odds on their side. Battling superior numbers might be glorious, but it was not practical. The chance to kill a number of the enemy at little or no loss to one's own side was highly desirable. The apparent flatness of the plains is deceptive, and its native inhabitants knew well how to use every dip and rise to their advantage.

That the difference was inherent in the cultures and the country is suggested by the North West Rebellion of 1885, the Canadian Army's sole campaign against Plains Indians. In spite of their great difference in tradition and experience from the U.S. Army, the Canadians encountered many of the same difficulties and frustrations, suffered several tactical defeats, and at least once were near a disaster comparable to Custer's. Indeed, some of the Canadian commanders were haunted by the American defeat at Little Bighorn.

The most experienced and perceptive U.S. army officers came to appreciate these points. Increasingly in the years after 1865 the soldiers fought an enemy they seldom saw, except at a distance. They saw rather the puff of smoke from his rifle. Contempt for Indian "cowardice" was small compensation for the frustration of being unable to close with the enemy and defeat him in a pitched battle, to say nothing of the occasional bloody defeat brought about by just such contempt and bad judgment.

Nothing said here should imply that the leaders of the frontier army were stupid or incapable of learning. Some, to be sure, proved incapable of adjusting from the mass battlefields of the Civil War to the elusive skirmishing on the Plains. But the real handicaps of the army were those inherent in its organization and doctrine and in the society it represented. An army organized on conventional, European lines, intended to fight similar enemies, was charged with police duties and with combating foes with a talent for guerrilla warfare in country giving them ample room to take full advantage of their mobility.

A country facing little immediate foreign danger reduced its regular forces to some 25,000 men. The traditional American reliance on wartime volunteers did not apply in Indian wars. In conjunction with the overall tendency toward governmental centralization, the federal forces in the post–Civil War period largely took over the role that had once been shared by frontier riflemen, rangers, and other local volunteers and militia. Frontier whites frequently expressed contempt for the regulars and opined that the government should call on the services of hardy westerners who knew how to use guns and loved to fight. Perhaps there were at least a few such characters outside the pages of fiction, but after 1865 even the Texas Rangers had only a modest role in Indian-white conflicts. The backwoodsmen had given way to the bluecoat.

The postwar reduction of the army moved General Philip Sheridan to complain that no other nation would have tried to control the Plains with an army of less than 50,000. Probably no general in history has ever had enough men, but Sheridan had a point. Distance made concentration slow, and greater numbers of troops might have made it possible to have enough men at a trouble spot to contain hostilities or to prevent them by over-awing the Indians. Sheridan seems temporarily to have overlooked the difficulties experienced in supplying even the number of troops that he had in the field during campaigns.

The army never seems to have developed any official, formal doctrine on fighting Indians, nor on conducting relations with them. At any rate, there were no handbooks or textbooks on the subject. Randolph B. Marcy's *The Prairie Traveler,* published "by authority of the War Department" in 1859, was primarily a survival manual, useful for both military and civilian travelers on the Plains, although some space was devoted to a description of the Plains tribes and some six pages to Indian fighting. Marcy fully appreciated the importance of trailing and the value of Indian scouts; a few years later he did indeed give more detailed prescriptions for coping with the military problems of the Plains in his memoirs, rather than in an official publication. His suggestions were virtually the same as those actually followed by those commanding on the Plains, but no one was required to study his ideas.

What Marcy had learned was also apparent to other experienced frontier soldiers who had open minds and were flexible. Lacking any formal doctrine, it was the judgment of these men that served as the basis of the army's military effort against the Plains tribes. The more sensible men realized that, regrettable as it might be, they would not win these wars in some great prairie Gettysburg. Soldiers had to increase their mobility as much as possible, but they must also acknowledge the enemy's superiority in this area. They could not expect him to cooperate by fighting at a disadvantage. There was no way to avoid fighting in the enemy's country, but troops could campaign in winter, when the Indian horses were in their poorest condition and the hardships of flight and loss of property would fall the hardest on women and children. Above all, they could turn against the enemy his own weapon of surprise.

In the East the Anglo-Americans had generally fought sedentary Indians with permanent villages and fields. They were fine guerrilla fighters, but if a white army could reach the villages it could destroy the enemy's dwellings, crops, and household goods. In the West, however, the farming peoples were generally friendly or at least neutral; the hostiles were nomads with portable homes and no crops to burn. There was no geographical point to label as the objective. Elusive as they were, the enemy villages themselves must be the target.

It is often stated that the great weakness of the Plains tribes was the failure to post sentries. However, the hunting parties that were usually out from their camps often served the same purpose, and their great mobility gave them an excellent chance of getting away, given any warning. The villages had to be taken by surprise, and surprise meant a night attack.

Indian scouts increased the chances of locating Indian camps without alerting them to the presence of soldiers. The scouts were also the guides who led columns of troops to a spot from which they could attack, a task that had to be accomplished in darkness. It was the scouts who often ran off the horses of the hostiles, destroying their mobility.

The best time to attack was just before dawn, catching the victims asleep and bewildered. When dawn came the soldiers could see to fight, in case of a counterattack. Even when truly surprised, the Plains warriors were likely to prove formidable in defense of their families, and some surprises almost proved disastrous for the soldiers. Writing of a march through the Big Horn Mountains to attack the Cheyennes, John G. Bourke commented that if the hostiles received any warning, in the rugged terrain the army's casualties would only be limited by the amount of ammunition the Cheyennes had to expend. Even though surprise was achieved, the Cheyennes quickly retired to the rocks and turned the action into a stalemate, although they lost most of their household goods and horses. General John Gibbon surprised the Nez Perces in their camp at the Big Hole in Montana, having more men than the Nez Perces, chiefly infantry with rifles of greater range and power than cavalry carbines. In spite of all advantages, he was defeated and narrowly avoided a massacre.

An inescapable part of these attacks was that women and children were in the line of fire, at least in the first minutes of the attack. Poor visibility and turmoil insured that some would be hit, even if the soldiers made a conscious effort to avoid this. Such a clear violation of nineteenth-century ideals of chivalry created moral problems, which the army never really resolved and which laid it open to attack by humanitarians. Few were willing to say outright that Indian women and children did not qualify as human beings, though some tried to imply it, for instance, by claiming that the "squaws" were foremost in the torture of captives. Generally speaking, "Indian warfare" was conceived as having different rules from "civilized" warfare, largely due to the fact that the enemy did not follow the rules as laid down by the white man. General George Crook exposed the inconsistency of such thinking by pointing out that the killing of women and children in attacks on Indian camps was similar to what happened when besieged cities were bombarded with artillery; Crook concluded that the whites had not given the Indians many examples of the chivalry they were condemned for failing to emulate.

At any rate, the army had worked out a rough-and-ready strategy for coping with Plains Indian hostility. Converging columns, operating in winter if possible, entered the hunting grounds of the designated enemy, its wagon transport minimized for mobility. Indian scouts sought out the hostile camps and guided a striking force for a dawn attack. Whenever casualties were inflicted, success was in the destruction of the victims' tepees and household goods, the loss of their supplies of dried meat, and the loss of at least part of their horse herd. Above all, the effect on morale was of highest significance. If the enemy managed to evade such an attack, constant harassment in bad weather might eventually discourage them enough to bring them in to surrender.

The formula was not foolproof, as Custer's defeat and the other repeated frustrations of the Sioux campaign of 1876 proved. Winter campaigning on the Northern Plains proved more arduous than in the south, where the pattern was first worked out. Columns could not really support each other because of distance and because communication was still by couriers on horseback, often subject to considerable danger in traversing hostile territory. That the troops managed to function at all on the high Plains of Montana, Dakota, and Wyoming in winter is a tribute to their adaptability. It was when the army adopted a strategy that pushed the Indians into something approximating a war of attrition—a total war against the entire population and its resources—that the Indians realized that they could not win. They had neither the population nor the social organization to sustain such a conflict, and they regarded the loss of even a few men as a disaster. Total war forced proud warriors to consider the welfare of their families and chiefs to think of their bands, however crushing the blow to their pride.

The Indians waged what we might wish to call guerrilla warfare, with some of the success that method has often enjoyed against regular armies operating in difficult terrain to which the guerrillas were well-adapted. But if their tactics were a classic example of guerrilla warfare, there was nothing of the ideological commitment, long-range goals, or centralized leadership we associate with twentieth-century guerrillas. Their goal was simply to be allowed to continue their accustomed way of life; they fought because that way of life was threatened, or for revenge, or because the whites attacked them—reasons for which people have fought throughout history. Considering the imbalance of forces, it is likely that no amount of centralization or elaborate ideology would have given the Indians what they would have considered a victory.

The whites' adoption of a policy of total war—not genocide in any strict sense of the term—might be considered an outgrowth of the Civil War. But as we have seen, the same strategy of attacking Indian camps was practiced by General Harney against the Sioux in 1855 and probably owed much to the experience of Harney and other senior officers in the bitter Seminole War of 1835–1842, when the army fought an elusive guerrilla enemy. Indian war had seldom been a matter of decisive battle between fighting men; it had commonly been necessary to attack the people and resources behind the warriors. Old frontier officers from the days before Fort Sumter, like Randolph Marcy and George Crook, understood the military requirements quite well; it was the men trained on the Civil War battlefields who had to adjust their thinking to the new situation.

The whole concept of "Indian resistance," on the Plains and elsewhere, is in some ways of white man's idea—not because Indians did not resist, weapons in hand, but because the whites in a sense created the situation in which such resistance occurred. They persisted in categorizing and finding unity in the diverse peoples they encountered in the West, and especially so in "war." Since the approach of apprehending and punishing individual Indians for misdeeds proved unsatisfactory, even disastrous in the case of the "Grattan Massacre," then the concept of war against an enemy became mentally necessary. Since one could only be at war with some unified body of people, then the Sioux "nation" or Comanche "nation" had to be designated as the enemy. Some military men and civil officials were sophisticated enough to realize that this concept did not represent reality very well, but for those preferring an unambiguous situation, simple categories like friend and enemy, good and bad, remained powerfully appealing.

Both the civil government and the army were burdened with two divergent concepts of their role in Indian-white relations. One was the concept of the federal government as the mediator and regulator of contacts between whites and Indians, trying to prevent violence and injustice in the interests of both. The other concept was of the government, particularly its military arm, as the instrument for clearing the way for white expansion and settlement—"winning the West" in a campaign of conquest for the sole benefit of white people. Officially there was never any clear-cut decision for one concept over the other, but the latter obviously tended to prevail. Individual officials and army officers wavered as much as the government, though some made unequivocal statements of one view or the other.

Symbolic of this internal struggle is an exchange between Generals Crook and Sheridan in 1879. Reporting on the tragic consequences of the flight of the Northern Cheyennes from Indian Territory and the attempt to make them return, Crook asserted that the military men involved, including himself, were only obeying orders, but that the government itself had been guilty of serious injustice. The Cheyennes had been forced to go to an unfamiliar, unhealthy place, had not received proper care, and had been left with no alternative but resistance. A number of them had served as scouts for Crook earlier, and the general charged the government with ingratitude for forgetting their services. Sheridan, Crook's superior, declared that he could not pass this report on without comment. The "system," as applied to Indian affairs, was certainly faulty, but Sheridan saw no hope of changing it. Besides, said Sheridan, the Cheyennes had committed atrocities in their northward flight and were not deserving of sympathy. In any case, the soldiers could only obey orders.

On other occasions Sheridan was ready to admit that Indians fought because of the pressure of white expansion. Many other soldiers acknowledged as much, and some even said that they would probably have done the same under like circumstances. Military men were quick to blame the civil government, the Bureau of Indian Affairs, Indian agents, and the division of authority between civil and military authorities, not to mention frontier civilians. There was much truth in such indictments, and in some cases there was even truth in the soldiers' assertion that they were the Indians' best friends. But ultimately the army was the arm of white society and necessarily enforced the will of that society on the Indians.

Although it seems almost a cliché, it bears repeating that the two societies confronting each other on the Great Plains in the nineteenth century did not know or understand each other throughout their period of armed conflict. They knew neither each other's strengths nor weaknesses. The whites never imagined that Indian culture was not simply a lack of what white culture possessed—law, religion, morality, among other things—that it had depth, complexity, and vitality, and that in clinging to it the Indians were not simply being obstinate, bloody-minded, or suicidally inflexible. Nor did whites realize that the unitary view of tribal society that they tried to impose on the Indians was hopelessly out of line with the facts, and so rendered their efforts to deal with such tribal units failures from the start.

The Indians did not know that they were up against the modern state, with its ability to control the actions of great numbers of people and to call on the resources of a continent. They could understand territorial expansion, for the stronger tribes regularly engaged in it, but how could they understand or even imagine the implacable purpose that demanded their total subjugation?

## SUGGESTED READING

For an overview of the Plains wars, see Ralph K. Andrist, *The Long Death: The Last Days of the Plains Indians* (New York, 1964). Indispensable military studies are Robert M. Utley's two works: *Frontiersmen in Blue: The United States Army and the Indian, 1848–1865* (New York, 1967) and *Frontier Regulars: The United States Army and the Indian, 1866–1890* (New York, 1973). Another view of the frontier army is Neil B. Thompson, *Crazy Horse Called Them Walk-a-Heaps* (St. Cloud, Minn., 1979). The background of Plains Indian tactics is found in Frank R. Secoy, *Changing Military Patterns on the Great Plains* (Seattle, 1953), showing the effects of horses and firearms to the early nineteenth century.

Among the various accounts of specific campaigns, perhaps the best are James L. Haley, *The Buffalo War: The History of the Red River Indian Uprising of 1874* (New York, 1976); William H. Leckie, *The Military Conquest of the Southern Plains* (Norman, Okla., 1963); Edgar I. Stewart, *Custer's Luck* (Norman, 1955); and John S. Gray, *Centennial Campaign: The Sioux War of 1876* (Fort Collins, Colo., 1976). For the Canadians' sole essay in Plains warfare, see Desmond Morton, *The Last War Drum* (Toronto, 1972). Stan Hoig, *The Sand Creek Massacre* (Norman, 1961) is the standard account of this notorious episode.

For the background of U.S. Indian policy on the Plains, see Robert A. Trennert, *Alternative to Extinction: Federal Indian Policy and the Beginnings of the Reservation System, 1846–51*. For the beginnings of Indian-white conflict on the Plains, see Walter Prescott Webb, *The Texas Rangers* (Austin, 1965).

There are many fine tribal histories; see particularly George Bird Grinnell, *The Fighting Cheyennes* (Norman, 1956); T. R. Fehrenbach, *Comanches: The Destruction of a People* (New York, 1974); George E. Hyde,

*Spotted Tail's Folk: A History of the Brulé Sioux* (Norman, 1961); Donald J. Berthrong, *The Southern Cheyennes* (Norman, 1963); and Ernest Wallace and E. Adamson Hoebel, *The Comanches: Lords of the South Plains* (Norman, 1952), an interesting blend of historical and anthropological technique. W. W. Newcombe, *The Indians of Texas* (Austin, 1961) studies the culture of each tribe and gives a good historical survey of the region.

Personal memoirs have their limitations but are indispensable all the same. One can sample a variety of viewpoints on Indians and analyses of the wars from a military standpoint by reading John G. Bourke, *On the Border With Crook* (New York, 1895); Robert G. Carter, *On the Border With Mackenzie* (Washington, 1935); Richard I. Dodge, *Our Wild Indians: Thirty-three Years Personal Experiences* (Hartford, 1883); Randolph B. Marcy, *Thirty Years of Army Life on the Border* (New York, 1866); and Marcy's *The Prairie Traveler* (New York, 1859).

Luther North, *Man of the Plains: Recollections of Luther H. North, 1856– 1882*, Donald F. Danker, ed. (Lincoln, 1961) is the leading source on the Pawnee scouts and their campaigns. Hyde, *Life of George Bent* (Norman, 1967) is a remarkable account by a mixed-blood who chose to be a Cheyenne. George F. Schmitt, ed., *General George Crook: His Autobiography* (Norman, 1946) is worth reading for the general's pungent opinions, but he did not live to complete the account of his Plains campaigns.

The only published study of the Indian scouts is Thomas W. Dunlay, *Wolves for the Blue Soldiers: Indian Scouts and Auxiliaries with the U.S. Army, 1860–90* (Lincoln, 1982).

On the background of northern Plains warfare, see Richard White, "The Winning of the West: The Expansion of the Western Sioux in the Eighteenth and Nineteenth Centuries." *Journal of American History* 65 (September 1978): 319–343.

Donald J. Berthrong

# 9. The Bitter Years

## Western Indian Reservation Life

In 1878 Washakie, a perceptive and eloquent Shoshoni chief, described the plight of his people. Within his lifetime Washakie remembered when Indians roamed free, enjoying abundant food provided by Mother Earth and her creatures. But the white man came with superior tools and terrible weapons better for war than bow and arrows, driving Indians from their vast hunting and gathering ranges on to confining reservations. The Shoshoni and other tribes, Washakie said, were only "sorry remnants once mighty, [who] are cornered in little spots of the earth all ours by right—cornered like guilty prisoners, and watched by men with guns, who are more than anxious to kill us off." United States government representatives promised the Shoshoni a "comfortable living" and protection from white intruders. Those promises were not honored. In Washakie's later life, he asked is it any wonder the Shoshoni, "nearly starved and . . . half naked . . . have fits of desperation" and think of revenge?

Washakie's remonstrance could have been echoed by numerous other Indian leaders as the U.S. government, after the Civil War, implemented its reservation policy. The Comanches once ranged from north of the Arkansas to south of the Rio Grande. Their population grew to about 14,000 people before warfare, disease, and reduced buffalo ranges began to diminish their numbers. In 1865 they still hunted over 30,000,000 acres, although their population had declined to about 5,000 people. Two years later, the Comanches were forced to cede all but 3,000,000 acres in southwestern Oklahoma where they would live with two other tribes. The confederated Cheyenne and Arapaho tribes shared the central Great Plains until the 1859 Pikes Peak gold rushers carved Colorado Territory out of much of their domain. After three treaties and a presidential executive order, the southern division of the two tribes was pushed aside to a 5,000,000 acre reservation in western Oklahoma. Hardly settled, more than 300,000 acres were sheared off from the Cheyenne and Arapaho reservation without the tribes' consent to provide lands for the Wichita and affiliated tribes. The northern Cheyenne and Arapaho divisions were even less fortunate. The Northern Arapahos rather than submit to Oglala dominance at the Pine Ridge agency in 1878 joined the Shoshonis in the Wind River Valley. Until 1884 the Northern Cheyennes drifted between the Pine Ridge agency and the Tongue River in Montana when they were finally settled on a tract in eastern Montana, which was enlarged in 1900 to include some 440,000 acres of valley and mountain land.

After the Civil War, only the Navajo escaped devastating land losses. In 1868, after suffering through four years at Bosque Redondo on the Pecos River in eastern New Mexico, an estimated 8,000 Navajos were resettled on nearly 4,000,000 acres in northwestern New Mexico and northeastern Arizona. Abandoning marauding raids, the Navajo resumed planting corn, beans, squash, and melons in arroyos and around natural springs for food and carefully tended the 15,000 sheep and goats purchased for them in 1869 by the government. By 1892 their flocks increased to 1,700,000 animals, which became the key element in the Navajo economy. Rations paid for from treaty annuities fended off starvation when crops failed; only at last resort was the natural increase of sheep and goat flocks used to feed families. More dry, plateau land was needed for the Navajos' hardy sheep. Beginning in 1878 and continuing into the 1930s, the Navajo domain was enlarged by an additional 10,500,000 acres. By 1900, while other tribal populations decreased, the Navajos' population increased to 22,000 people. Fortunately too, the 1887 General Allotment Act, which conventionally marks the end of reservation policy, was never used to dismantle the Navajo reservation as it was for the communal lands of scores of other Indian tribes.

The objectives of the reservation policy are easily discernible. Tribes were placed on reserves with fixed boundaries designated by treaties, statutes, or presidential executive orders. After 1871 when the U.S. Congress decided treaties were no longer an appropriate means of negotiating Indian land cessions, the will of Congress or an executive order determined a reservation's size and conditions under which native Americans held land tenure. With plenary power derived from the U.S. constitution Congress enacted laws which most frequently reduced the Indians' land base and intruded on the lives of Indians. Whenever tribal warriors were not subdued, the U.S. Army maintained garrisons to drive war parties back to their reservations. From Forts Reno, Richardson, Sill, and Supply on the southern plains, Forts Ellis, Keogh, Randall, Robinson, and Stevenson on the northern plains, and Forts Bowie, Craig, Huachuca, McDowell, and Thomas in the Southwest, post commanders cooperated with Indian agents to keep warriors and their leaders within their reservations' boundaries.

Once Indian tribes were restricted to reservations, tribal customs and beliefs would be destroyed and replaced by a life-style practiced by Euro-Americans. Every trait, skill, and belief deemed un-American would be suppressed by Indian service personnel and missionaries dispatched to reservations by American churches. Individual property would replace communal holdings, extended families would become nuclear families, traditional ceremonies and religion would be superseded by Christianity, and power of chiefs and elders would be eradicated. Males trained to war, hunt, and fish would learn to be farmers, stockmen, and artisans, while females accustomed to life in camps and lodges would be taught domestic crafts used in white homes. Through schooling English would be substituted for tribal languages. The herbs and incantations of medicine men would give way to the prescriptions and scalpel of agency physicians.

Reservations, whether one hundred-acre rancheros in California or reserves with millions of acres on the plains or mountains, became virtual open-air prisons from which tribesmen could not wander unless passes were obtained from Indian agents. Cavalry and infantry from western forts assisted by Indian scouts and agency police pursued, killed, captured, and imprisoned those who dared to flee the pestilence and hunger of a reservation. The flights of Chief Joseph and the Nez Percés, Standing Bear and his Ponca band, Morning Star, known as Dull Knife to whites, and Northern Cheyennes, and Geronimo and the Chiricahua Apaches between 1877 and 1885 are evidence of the debilitating conditions on Indian reservations. For his audacity Geronimo and five hundred Apaches were incarcerated in Fort Pickens, Florida, Mount Vernon Barracks, Alabama, and finally shifted to near Fort Sill, Oklahoma, where some of them remained until 1913 as prisoners of war.

Why were western Indians penned on desolate, mountainous, and infertile reserves? White farmers, ranchers, miners, lumbermen, railroad promoters, and land speculators coveted Indian land and resources. Edward McCook, territorial governor of Colorado, eager to please his constituents, claimed: "God gave us the earth and the fullness thereof. . . . I do not believe in donating to these indolent savages the best part of my territory, and I do not believe in placing Indians on an equality with the white man as landholder." Indians were deemed inferior to whites in social and economic organization. Their natural inclinations led to continuous warfare, intensive slaughter of large game, and long periods of indolence. Most

Americans, except a few such as Protestant Episcopal Bishop Henry B. Whipple or the novelist Helen H. Jackson, did not disagree with Lieutenant Colonel George A. Custer who viewed an Indian as a "savage in every sense of the word; not worse perhaps, than his white brother would be similarly born and bred, but one whose cruel and ferocious nature far exceeds that of any wild beast of the desert." Only after Indians were driven to reservations, stripped of arms, and rendered incapable of resistance would white farmers, ranchers, miners, and travelers be safe to carry out their civilized enterprises.

Commissioners of Indian Affairs echoed regional and national attitudes calling for alterations of Indian life and culture. In 1871, H. R. Clum, acting commissioner of Indian Affairs, called for Indians rapidly to assume "the relation of citizenship," educate their youths, undertake "industrial pursuits" through labor, develop a "sense of ownership in property, adapt to allotments in severalty and accept the benign and elevating influences of Christian teachings." Otherwise 350,000 Indians in the United States and natives of Alaska faced "utter extinction." Even if Indians managed to survive without change they would, in the opinion of Commissioner of Indian Affairs Francis A. Walker in 1872, become "vagabonds in the midst of civilization . . . [and] festering sores on the communities near which they are located." Industrial instruction and manual labor, Walker believed, would counterbalance the "evil influences" of tribal life and the Indians "strong, animal appetites."

During the reservation era, governmental policymakers considered Indians "barbarous men" who must be taught to live in a "civilized way." It was necessary for the federal government to provide funds "to carry the untaught barbarian through the period of his childhood into civilization." As Indians were led to live by manual labor, agency personnel, Christian teachers, and missionaries would "reclaim them from a debasing paganism, and win them to a purer and more enabling faith." Governmental officials realized Indians' acceptance of a new way of life would be gradual at best. "There is little hope," Indian Commissioner E. A. Hayt concluded in 1877, "of the civilization of the older wild Indian, and the only question is how to control and govern him, so that his savage instincts shall be kept from violent outbreaks." It was more feasible to focus governmental programs on "partial civilized" adult Indians, and especially on children. Educational and missionary efforts among Indian youth eventually would reclaim the Indian population from "barbarism, idolatry and savage life." Until the effect of Christianity and education was appreciable, the goals of reservation policy were not attainable. Traditional tribal organization meant "individual responsibility and welfare . . . [was] swallowed up in that of the whole, and the weaker, less aspiring, and more ignorant of the tribe will be the victims of the more designing, shrewd, selfish and ambitious head-men."

Native Americans had developed appropriate methods to correct or punish transgressors of tribal laws or customs. Behavioral codes were enforced by tribal opinion, by religious beliefs, and among the Five Civilized Tribes by written statutes to maintain order and security. On the plains, warrior societies carried out the decisions of the tribal or chiefs' councils. If possible, shedding of blood was avoided and horses and goods were presented to the offended individual or family to "cover up" a serious misdeed. A strong-willed and influential man could defy law enforcers, accept exile for a period of years, and return to the tribal camp circle without fear of additional punishment.

With reservation life, however, difficulties emerged with traditional tribal law enforcement procedures. New legal procedures were imposed on Indians to bring American justice to the tribes. Indian agents began to undercut the authority of chiefs and warriors, trying to replace those who resisted government regulations and programs with more compliant leaders. Rations and annuity goods formerly distributed through chiefs and headmen in recognition of their positions within tribes were issued to "ration bands" headed by men selected by Indian agents. On many reservations, Indian service personnel also attempted to break up large camps and place smaller groups on land where crops and vegetable gardens could be planted. When schools became available either on or off reservations, parents were expected to send children to them under threats of withholding rations. Men were expected to abandon living with more than one wife, but the injunction was not universally enforced, especially among the older, well-established families. Despite laws prohibiting sale of liquor in "Indian Country," whiskey flooded onto reservations or was readily available in towns bordering Indian reserves. Maddened by liquor men and women brawled and committed acts of violence. Indian agents needed police to control violations of laws and regulations and to maintain order and security on reservations as tribal legal and political institutions were crumbling.

John P. Clum, a young Indian agent, arrived in 1874 at the San Carlos Apache agency. Faced with turbulent conditions and dependence on troops to maintain order, Clum recruited four trustworthy Indian men to act as policemen, and as the police force grew the Indian agent appointed a white man as chief of police. In 1875 Disalin, a Tonto Apache chief, experiencing domestic problems with his wives that he blamed on Clum, strode into the agency office, drew a pistol, and shot without effect at a clerk and the police chief. Hearing the shots, the Indian police rushed to the agency office, prevented Disalin's escape, and killed the chief. One of the policemen was Disalin's brother who quietly related, "I have killed my own chief, my own brother; he tried to kill a white man, so we had to kill him." Clum's police, expanded to several companies, hunted down "renegade" Apaches, killing more than 150 in an effort to end Apache raiding in the Southwest. Other agents confronted with similar if less deadly conditions asked the Indian Office to authorize Indian police forces. In May 1878 Congress appropriated funds to pay small salaries for 430 privates and 50 officers, allowing Indian agents to recruit men whom they trusted for sometimes dangerous duty in "maintaining order and prohibiting illegal traffic in liquor" on Indian reservations.

Indian police were usually warriors led by older men from tribes or from agency employees. As the Indian police proved loyal to the agent, white men were no longer needed as Indian police captains and were replaced by tribal men. Occasionally an Indian agent encountered resistance from chiefs who understood the new police would supplant warrior societies that carried out decisions of the chiefs' councils. At Pine Ridge, Red Cloud fought Agent V. T. McGillycuddy over establishing an agency police force. Yet McGillycuddy and other Sioux agents prevailed by playing on intratribal factionalism to foil chiefs' opposition. Indian police became more than law enforcers as they slaughtered issue beefs, returned truants to boarding schools, carried messages for agents, took tribal censuses, and built roads and agency buildings. When young men began returning in the late 1880s from off-reservation boarding schools such as Carlisle and Haskell, they gradually were incorporated into agency police forces.

Five years after Indian police were organized, Secretary of the Interior Henry M. Teller decreed Courts of Indian Offenses. Except for some nine tribes or nations with recognized tribal governments, about two-thirds of all agencies possessed their own courts whose officers were deemed to be men of undoubted intelligence, honesty, and integrity. Inadequate congressional appropriations shackled the effectiveness of the courts, and agents dissolved courts of some jurisdictions because judges would not act against wrongdoers who belonged to their families or were influential tribal members or friends. Nevertheless Secretary Teller, distressed by the persistence of polygamy and "heathenish dances" such as the sun dance "which perpetuated a war spirit and demoralized the young," believed the courts would reduce the influence of medicine men and adherence to tribalism. Assisted by Indian police, judges would help eliminate "heathenish customs" based on tribal practices "repugnant to common decency and morality." Indian judges were empowered to jail those found guilty of participating in Indian ceremonies, of having more than one wife, and of gambling or drunkenness. An Indian who failed "to adopt the habits of industry, or to engage in civilized pursuits or employments but habitually spends his time in idleness and loafing" could be jailed or fined for the misdemeanor of vagrancy. While acting as Indian police and courts, tribesmen could mitigate Indian Office regulations by their understanding of tribal customs and practices. The next challenge to Indian law, however, stripped tribes of power to sit in judgment over certain crimes as specified by Congress.

In 1881, Spotted Tail, the astute Brulé chief of the Rosebud agency, was murdered by a fellow tribesman, Crow Dog, who resented Spotted Tail's dominance over the agency, the chief's retention of rents collected from cattlemen for rangeland, and, perhaps, Spotted Tail's role in his dismissal as police chief. Knowing Spotted Tail's habits Crow Dog waited for the chief on a road between the agency offices and the chief's home and shot down his supposed adversary. Crow Dog's family hastily assembled ponies and goods, which were given to Spotted Tail's family; by Sioux custom the matter was settled. Shocked by the perceived casualness of the settlement, the U.S. Attorney for Dakota Territory charged Crow Dog with murder. The Brulé headman was convicted in the Deadwood territorial court and sentenced to be hanged for his crime. An appeal of Crow Dog's conviction in 1883 reached the U.S. Supreme Court; the trial court's judgment was reversed in *ex parte Crow Dog* on the ground that the 1868 Treaty of Fort Laramie preserved the right of Sioux to punish their tribal members for serious crimes. The Supreme Court ordered Crow Dog's immediate release from prison because the U.S. courts were without jurisdiction over crimes committed by Indians against Indians, including murder.

Reformers demanded Congress enact a law bringing Indians under federal law for serious crimes. In March 1885 Congress enacted a major crimes statute which made seven crimes—murder, manslaughter, rape, assault with intent to kill, arson, burglary, and larceny—punishable in federal courts when committed on reservations by an Indian against another Indian, excluding members of the Five Civilized Tribes. The latter nations with written penal codes, an organized court system, and provision for appeals of decisions to a federal district court in Arkansas were considered capable of dealing with crimes committed within their lands. A year later, the Supreme Court in *United States v. Kagama* confirmed the major crimes statute in a murder case involving a Hoopa Valley reservation Indian. The law and its approval by the Supreme Court were the initial extension of federal jurisdiction into the internal control exercised by tribes over relations between tribal members. The passage of the major crimes law, "coupled with a new aggression attitude on the part of Indian agents . . . quickly eroded the social cement that tribal custom had provided to tribal societies."

Reservation policy was never an unchanging set of statutes and administrative regulations. And Indians modified their life-styles and institutions to meet their new environment. When federal power began to challenge tribal cohesion, tribes maintained continuity by religious beliefs and ceremonies. Yet the reservation era which continued far beyond the 1887 Dawes Act for many tribes was a time of mounting governmental pressure on tribes to conform to Indian policy goals. When federal officials and Indian reformers found their objectives—conversion to Christianity, education for youths, acceptance of manual labor for self-support, use of fixed tracts of land, accumulation of private property, rejection of medicine men, and destruction of chiefs' authority—were being attained too slowly, governmental pressure increased. Modification of material culture, religion, political systems, and social customs, known as acculturation, was slow and halting, especially on the more isolated western reservations. Absorption into the dominant white population, known as assimilation, during this era was statistically insignificant among many western tribes. Congress never appropriated sufficient funds to implement effectively reservation policy, and Indians clung tenaciously to their separate identity, never completely abandoning ancestoral beliefs and customs. The failure of reservation policy becomes clearer as implementation of and native American reaction to components of the federal programs are examined.

Until the last quarter of the nineteenth century western Indian population was virtually untouched by white education. Only mixed-blood and a handful of full-blood youth supported by philanthropists ever received education in a white schoolroom. Again the Five Civilized Tribes were an exception as their leaders supported schools and academies from national funds and cooperated with missionary societies to educate their children. Yet full-blood children from eastern Oklahoma hill country frequently never attended schools filled with offspring of tribal leaders, most of whom were fully acculturated. After the Indian wars ended, Indian policy planners decided education of children offered the greatest opportunity to implant white traits among tribal people. It was anticipated that churches would also expand their educational activities on western reservations, but most of the cost would be borne by congressional appropriations. Soon after reservation personnel were in place, money was made available to Indian agents to build boarding and day schools and to bring teachers from eastern states. Initially school capacities were limited to fifty pupils or less so that not more than 5 percent of school-age youths were provided places in school rooms and dormitories. On a few remote reservations, into the twentieth century, as few as 10 percent of the children were able to attend reservation or missionary schools because of limited facilities. Educational statistics compiled by the government in the mid-1880s appeared more favorable than actual conditions warranted when there were reportedly accommodations for 48 percent of the total Indian school population. The quality of education received was largely ignored.

Girls and boys fresh from freedom and play of camp life were slowly taught to speak, read, and write the English language. One Hopi man remembered he learned "little at school the first year except 'bright boy,' 'smart boy,' 'yes' and 'no,' 'nail,' and 'candy'." Basic arithmetic and vocational activities were added as the Indian pupils' learning skills increased. At first Indian children knew no English and their teachers knew no tribal language. Reservation boarding school teachers, many of limited competence, frequently quit because of isolation, meager amenities, and low salaries. Lonesome for parents and friends, bored by the rote lessons of the classroom, or frightened by threats of harsh discipline, pupils fled back to camps with such frequency that Indian policemen and school disciplinarians routinely searched out and returned them to the hard boards of school desks and ill-constructed dormitories. For years concerned parents from outlying settlements frequently camped near reservation boarding schools and expected to eat with their children in the schools' dining halls.

Late in the 1870s, two off-reservation boarding schools were added to the Indian educational system. Hampton Normal and Agricultural Institute in Virginia and Carlisle Indian Industrial School in Pennsylvania became models for later vocational training schools scattered throughout the West. Captain Richard H. Pratt, founder of Carlisle, assembled in 1879 young prisoners of war from southern plains tribes and sons and daughters of Indian chiefs, headmen, and prominent warriors, hoping that they after returning to reservations would become a leavening influence among their tribes. As the Indian education system matured, Carlisle and other off-reservation schools restricted their enrollments to students who had completed six grades in reservation schools. Indian youths at Carlisle for as long as eight years were instructed in basic educational and vocational skills. Young males spent one-half of their school days learning to grow crops, care for farm stock, and become carpenters, printers, plumbers, wheelwrights, wagon makers, blacksmiths, painters, and tinsmiths. Female students were taught to cook and preserve food, to sew, and to care for a home. Discipline throughout the Indian schools was harsh. Infractions of school regulations, even speaking a tribal language, were punished by whippings or solitary confinement with a diet of bread and water. Military-style uniforms for boys and starched dresses for girls replaced comfortable camp clothing. The flowing hair of boys was closely cropped when they entered any Indian school. Every Indian custom and trait was discouraged by teachers, disciplinarians, and school officials. Captain Pratt provided Carlisle students with a special experience by sending them to white farm homes where they lived and worked for periods up to three years. One former Cheyenne Carlisle student recalled that he received one dollar per month and his room and board for his work as a farm laborer. Female students assisted the mistress with kitchen and household chores. Pratt believed his "outing system" contributed to the acculturation of Carlisle students.

The returned students were influenced by their education. Designated as "school boys and girls" by tribal members throughout most of their lives, some found employment in agency offices and schools. Their progress to positions of administrative responsibility was minimal. Young women from Carlisle, Hampton, or Haskell became seamstresses, cooks, and matrons for dormitories and dining halls. Men worked as assistant agency farmers, school disciplinarians, interpreters for Indian agents, and a few became Christian ministers or clerks in stores. Indian agents employed men as agency policemen but, failing to find uses for skills learned at off-reservation schools, scores enlisted in Indian scout companies garrisoned at army posts near their reservations. A few Carlisle, Hampton, and Haskell graduating classes easily filled available Indian service appointments for years. Rarely during the reservation era could a returned student expect to enjoy an agency or school appointment for more than a few years so that other former students could be employed. Most simply returned to camp life, much to the displeasure of Indian agents and school officials. On many undeveloped western reservations for perhaps as many as nine of ten returned students there was little opportunity to use the education and skills acquired in Indian schools.

Economically, Indians possessed only the right to use and occupy reservation land. They did not have fee simple, or permanent, titles to land as did white farmers, and even farm or range stock issued by the government could not be sold without permission from the Indian Office. Reservation land was communal property, unavailable as a form of capital or security to finance individual enterprises. On the plains, the government constructed two-story, wood-frame houses for leaders considered principal chiefs such as Quanah Parker of the Comanches, Red Cloud of the Oglalas, and Spotted Tail of the Brulés. Otherwise families lived in canvas tepees or poorly constructed log cabins. For decades after the reservation life began there were no farms to work, no houses to live in, no stoves on which to cook, and no sewing machines to make white-style clothing. With some exaggeration in the early twentieth century Rena Flying Coyote, a Cheyenne who attended Carlisle for six years and lived with white families on six "outings," claimed: "I have tried to show them [my people] that my kind of living (that is like a good citizen) is better than the old Indian way. I am the only full blood Cheyenne girl to return from Carlisle, who did not revert to the Indian custom." After returning to the Cheyenne and Arapho agency, she married a non-Indian. Their resources at marriage were "just one horse and $40 with which we bought a stock of edibles and other necessary things to start housekeeping, and we [five years later] get prasie on every side, we are said to have the best furnished house at Darlington." Among her six sons, several were college graduates, one was a lawyer, and another was a nationally known artist.

Categorizing returned student lives is more complex than Rena Flying Coyote indicated. Early graduates, especially full-blood young women, of reservation and off-reservation schools were pressured by families to marry noneducated tribal members. Indian agents adopted security measures at reservation boarding schools to prevent female students of marriageable age from being whisked off by suitors or family members. Sometimes young women, when enjoying a vacation with relatives, yielded to family desires, married, and ended their education. The number of students who completed courses of study grew in the late 1880s and 1890s, and these were the young men and women who were employed at agencies and schools. No statistical summaries exist to give a comprehensive overview of the postschool lives of former Indian school students. Off-reservation school records and journals, however, provide some insight into the way they worked and lived. Mixed-blood and full-blood former students married their classmates generally at first from their own tribes but later from other tribes. These people frequently provided the next generation of off-reservation school students and worried when their children failed to complete courses of study in government schools. A small number were employed successfully throughout off-reservation schools, others, after passage of the Dawes Act, farmed their allotment, or became small ranchers and at least nominal Christians. Less fortunately, most returned students after the reservation era were, as a group, the first to sell their allotments so they could buy consumer goods enjoyed by white neighbors. When their money was gone, they drifted about, living with older relatives who had not sold their land.

Primarily economic and social improvement was minimal because sufficient resources were unavailable to develop new tribal economies. Tribes began reservation life with only their lodges, some weapons, camp equipment, clothing, pony herds, and an inadequate food supply. By any reasonable standard, parents did not have enough food; their children, when first enrolled in schools, were often malnourished. Soon families became dependent on rations which infrequently lasted until the next issue day. Tough beef and rancid bacon replaced the meat of buffalo and large game. Small amounts of flour, corn, coffee, sugar, and baking powder supplemented beef issues, and, as Congress reduced appropriations, food available for an adult varied from one-third to one-half of an army ration. With large game becoming scarce, women were unable to dress and tan hides for sale to reservation-based traders for food, cloth, and other family needs. Hunger and privation became a familiar condition in lodges of formerly successful hunters.

Where agriculture was considered feasible, Indian agents distributed garden seeds and hand tools for Indian use. Beginnings of agricultural activities were limited to small gardens and acreages for field crops. Because reservation Indians rarely owned work stock or breaking plows to turn over tough prairie sod, agents contracted with white men to break a few acres and paid the cost eked out from surplus agency funds. Men and women with knives and axes tried to plant and cultivate "sod corn" with little success. Many reservations were in regions of limited rainfall, and irrigation, because of cost, was a later development in the arid West. Agency personnel usually from the East or Middle West tried unsuccessfully to replicate the planting, cultivating, and harvesting crop cycles where climate and rainfall made possible decent yields of vegetables and grains. Patiently Indians planted seeds in early spring as instructed. Before crops matured, hot summer winds and droughts withered vegetable gardens and field crops. If one growing season in five produced an appreciable harvest, an Indian farmer or gardener was fortunate. Undaunted by crop failures, agents urged men to use scythes to cut wild hay and axes to cut firewood for winter use. Any expedient, however inefficient, was practiced to force Indians toward self-support by manual labor. After a decade of coaxing and threats by Indian agents, Cheyennes and Arapahos grew enough wheat, a crop well-adapted to Oklahoma's climate, to warrant purchase of a steam-driven threshing machine. Their agent requested authorization to buy a thresher and other appliances at a cost of eight hundred dollars. The commissioner of Indian Affairs rejected the agent's proposal but added that estimates for flails would receive favorable consideration. Without assurance of reasonable returns from agricultural labor it is not surprising that farming, normally scorned by former warriors and hunters as woman's work, was avoided if possible by men during the reservation era.

Because agricultural production contributed little to tribal economies, Indian agents looked to other reservation resources to supplement congressional appropriations. Timber and particularly millions of acres of rangeland could possibly be leased at attractive prices to lumber corporations or ranching syndicates. Informally, chiefs like Quanah Parker of the Comanches and Spotted Tail of the Brulés struck bargains with ranchers while Indian agents looked away. As a group, ranchers preferred to see reservations maintained as a source for inexpensive cattle ranges. Range rental agreements negotiated by Indian agents were less costly to cattlemen than ranges leased from white owners after the vast public domain had been occupied. Syndicates of eastern and foreign investors together with western cattle barons obtained exclusive use of prime reservation rangeland. Indian agents planned to use rental or lease proceeds to buy food and foundation herds to be tended by Indian men. Before the experiment could be fully tested President Grover Cleveland intervened because of sporadic conflicts between cowboys and warriors and because of a ruling by his attorney general, which held that no statutory authority existed to lease reservation land that would give property rights to ranching enterprises on land reserved for Indian use and occupancy.

Indians agents also used Indians as freighters to bring agency supplies from distant railroads. Transportation companies employed scores of Indian men who bought wagons and horses on credit to bring supplies from railroads to agency headquarters. Goods entrusted to Indian freighters arrived intact and undamaged despite weeks enroute over deeply rutted roads and numerous river crossings. From wages the men paid off their debts and earned enough momey to support their families. Freighting jobs were avidly sought and circulated among male relatives. Whole families accompanied freighters, camping along roads, alleviating the tedium and stagnation of reservation life.

Expedients available to even the most resourceful Indian agents were insufficient to care for all the reservations' inhabitants. As early as 1875 Congress enacted a law requiring all able-bodied men to contribute by labor to self-support. Details of how preindustrial Indian societies would be converted into a rural, self-supporting population on the fringe of an increasingly industrializing national economy were never fully considered. Employment was grossly inadequate for even better-educated men and women; for the less skilled, the disabled, and the young no alternative existed other than to rely on rations and annuity payments. The ration system, not terminated until the early twentieth century, was the only feasible way to prevent death by starvation. Toward the end of the reservation era, rations came to be viewed by Indian policy planners and reformers as a cause rather than a by-product of the enervating environment of Indian reservations. The hunting and gathering economies were destroyed, but no viable, economic system evolved to replace what nature had provided to western Indians.

White Indian policy planners hoped to transform Indian society by reducing the chiefs' power to lead their people. White observers attributed more influence to chiefs than they actually possessed. Mistakenly governmental officials believed chiefs were the fonts of authority rather than the spokesmen reflecting tribal consensus arrived at in councils. During times of crises chiefs among the Lakota deferred to the wishes of warrior societies. When cattlemen controlled vast expanses of the Oklahoma Cheyenne and Arapaho reservations, warrior societies led an effort to remove cowboys who harassed Indians in their camps. Warriors were not dissuaded from their objectives when shown rental or lease agreements signed by many of their chiefs. Indian office personnel and reformers believed a "head chief" or a small group of chiefs could replace councils composed of band and warrior society leaders who were keenly attuned to tribal opinion and traditions. In some tribes chiefs were intermediaries guided by elders, invested with religious prerogatives, who shaped tribal consensus. Followings of band chiefs surged upward or ebbed away to immediate family when their counsel proved inappropriate. Black Kettle of the Cheyennes was pushed aside after the 1864 Sand Creek massacre, Red Cloud of the Oglalas maintained his role of agency spokesman, in many instances against his tribal critics, and Manuelito of the Navajos, though revered as a fierce war leader, commanded less influence as his bouts with liquor became more frequent and he became little more than the agents' mouthpiece. If Indian service officials had understood the fluidity of political power within Indian society perhaps they would have worried less about supporting a permanent group of chiefs or a head chief completely amenable to federal Indian policy.

What happened on many reservations was the evolution of three factions. Some of the factionalism was a residue of interband disagreements from the prereservation times. The smallest faction centered about intermarried whites, their spouses' families, and returned students beholden to agents for jobs. When the Dawes Act was applied to reservations, this faction was manipulated and bribed by cession agreement commissioners to acquire "surplus land" for white occupation. A second faction followed chiefs who early believed further warfare against whites was futile. Essentially pragmatic, this faction was willing, however reluctantly, to travel the white man's road, send their children to school, plant gardens and field crops, listen to missionaries' preachings, leave large camps for smaller settlements where more individualized labor was possible, if young, take no more than one wife, wear "citizens dress," and heed the agents' advice. The third faction coalesced about leaders who deeply resented confinement on reservations and were fundamentally opposed to remaking the Indian into the image of a white man. Red Moon of the Cheyennes in Oklahoma led his band as far away from agency headquarters as possible, even refusing to sign an 1890 cession agreement. Sitting Bull after returning from Canada built his cabin forty miles from the Standing Rock headquarters. Lone Wolf of the Kiowas distanced life at the agency, remaining aloof as much as possible from whites although his son, Delos, graduated from Carlisle. When the pragmatists found reservation policy did not lead to a suitable life they too became suspicious of and resistant to the white mans' policies.

Although divided by factions, chiefs shared common characteristics. As young men they had earned redoubtable reputations as warriors and hunters. Many of their fathers, uncles, or grandfathers had been chiefs before them. A fewer number of charismatic men rose to prominence without the support of influential families. If Crazy Horse, son of an Oglala shaman, had chosen life instead of death after surrendering in 1877, his presence would have added strength to those resisting reservation life. Perhaps Crazy Horse despaired that white troops were too numerous for him and his fellow warriors. An Oglala chief commented: "It is good. He has looked for death and it has come."

As a chief's son or nephew matured, he was closely observed to see whether he possessed patience, wisdom, generosity toward less fortunate persons, and knowledge of tribal customs. During the reservation era chances were he never attended a white man's school and needed an interpreter to converse with an Indian agent or commissioner sent to buy reservation land. He was expected, regardless of factionalism, to make wise decisions helpful to all of the tribe's people. If his judgments were contrary to Indian policy as construed by an Indian agent, the chief was moved aside and not invited to subsequent meetings and was not included among those chosen to visit the Great Father in Washington. Agents preferred to deal with chiefs willing to follow regulations flowing from Washington rather than with those resisting government policy. Knowing they would be ignored or ridiculed, some chiefs avoided meetings with agents unless it was vitally necessary. Throughout the West, however, chiefs who lived according to tribal customs maintained their roles as spokesmen and leaders during and beyond the reservation era despite governmental efforts to diminish their influence.

Indian policy planners hoped to use returned students from off-reservation schools to modify reservation politics. While the student population of those schools contained a cross section of tribal youths, a disproportionate percentage of the students were offspring of mixed-blood or parents intermarried with whites. There were, of course, a sprinkling of children whose fathers were chiefs and former warrior leaders. Regardless of parentage Indian policy administrators wanted returned students to become acculturated role models for their tribes. Noneducated persons, however, viewed them with continuing suspicion, fearing the young men and women had been too deeply influenced by white ideas. Further, in the 1880s and 1890s the male students were far too young to be selected as chiefs. Those judged to be the most promising were employed at the agency and issue stations where they were subordinate to Indian service employees. They were expected to live in houses and not in the band camps with older family members. Fairly fluent in English, young men became interpreters whenever agents and land cession commissioners needed to explain policy and documents to chiefs. The chiefs for their part expected their young men to translate faithfully their speeches into English. The young interpreters' status was always inferior to white officials and their tribal leaders and were not expected to speak in their own behalf.

If western Indians did not put aside their leaders neither did they discard traditional beliefs and ceremonies. However, the ceremonies and even the sacred tribal totems changed over time. New ceremonies were borrowed from neighboring tribes and became more complex or differed as priests incorporated their touches into older ceremonies. When woodland tribes took up life on the plains, culture heroes taught new religious ceremonies, reorganized tribal bands and warrior societies, and designated different political structures to govern tribes. Life was controlled by the spirits of nature; people shared the world with spirits whose power for good and evil directly affected human life. Maheo, the All Father of Cheyennes, was part of all life. Through visions and dreams, supernatural spirits directed the actions and lives of humans. If a youth did not understand his vision a holy man explained its meaning and directed him in the use of his personal medicine bundle. The offerings and physical sacrifices to Maheo at a Sun Dance assured Cheyennes of health and well-being as did proper veneration of the sacred medicine arrows and buffalo hat. Other than the Comanches, plains tribes adopted the Sun Dance, varying the ceremony in length and detail to suit tribal needs and the teachings of Sun Dance priests. White observers became so enamored with the spectacle of the Sun Dance that they failed to report the multitude of other tribal ceremonies and invididual religious observances.

Toward the end of the reservation era, Christian teachings found acceptance among a minority of western Indians. Tribal members became ordained clergy and native lay preachers who labored alongside white missionaries to convert people to Christianity. For many, however, Christianity never dominated their religious beliefs. When death approached, men and women, counted as Christian congregation members, asked for the prayers of both Christian clergy and a holy man of their tribe. Uniquely, one former plains warrior was ordained as a deacon in the Protestant Episcopal Church, preached for nearly forty years among his people and was canonized as a saint about one-half century after his death. More usually, Indians simply accepted Christianity as another religious experience in addition to a Sun Dance or the nightlong peyote ceremony.

The visions and teachings of Tavibo and Wovoka, Paiutes of Nevada, spread throughout the western Indians. Beset by pressures from the whites who surged into western states and territories, tribes witnessed an erosion of their freedom and ways of life. For several centuries prophets had arisen when tribes encountered the challenges of Euro-American frontiersmen. Popé of the Pueblos, the Delaware Prophet, Handsome Lake of the Senecas, Tenskwatawa of the Shawnees, and Smohalla of the Columbia River Shahaptans all led earlier revitalization movements among their people. Like the preceding prophets, Tavibo and Wovoka promised that if their teachings were properly observed Indians would be restored to control of their lives and lands. Tavibo, after vigils, received visions in 1870 foretelling destruction of whites, but his teachings attracted followers only among neighboring tribes. Wovoka, his son, known to whites as Jack Wilson, expanded Tavibo's message into a comprehensive set of religious doctrines. From the plateaus, mountains, and finally the plains, tribal delegates visited Wovoka, carrying back to their tribes practices, ceremonies, and prayers which would assure peace and plenty after a cataclysm destroyed white oppressors.

Wovoka's doctrines forbade war and violence. All Indians were to live peacefully as brothers and sisters. They should live simply, reject use of alcohol, purify themselves by ceremonial cleansing, and worship by meditation, prayers, songs, and dances. The dead would rejoin the living, and all Indians would live in a world abounding in game, "free from misery, death and disease." During the five day- and nightlong ceremonies, people danced until they fell unconscious and after reviving reported they had talked to deceased family members and friends—thus Wovoka's teaching became known as the Ghost Dance. Acceptance of the Ghost Dance rituals varied among different tribes. On the southern plains the Kiowas, Comanches, and Cheyennes remained doubtful, while Wovoka's doctrines gained many adherents among the Arapahos and Wichitas. On the northern plains, the Ghost Dance flourished as the western Sioux were beset by drought, starvation, and substantial land losses. The Sioux added a Ghost Dance shirt which, when blessed, would protect a wearer from enemy bullets. Militancy and resistance appealed to distraught Sioux warriors who gathered together in secrecy awaiting an opportunity to rise up against white oppression. How imminent a Sioux uprising was in 1890 depends on interpretation of contemporary reports written by Indian agents and army officers.

After Sitting Bull's return from Canada, agents at Standing Rock kept a wary eye on the Hunkpapa leader. Sioux Indian agents banned the Ghost Dance, which only strengthened the participants' determination to prevail. Requests for additional troops were sent by agents, one of whom claimed "Indians are dancing in the snow and are wild and crazy." James McLaughlin, agent at Standing Rock, ordered the arrest of Sitting Bull, considered the most likely leader of any concerted Sioux uprising. In a violent melee, Sitting Bull was killed, triggering a series of tragic blunders. Ghost dancers from the Sioux agencies fled to camps in the Black Hills, pursued by army units. Pinned down by troops, one group led by Big Foot, a Miniconjou from the Cheyenne River agency, surrendered at Wounded Knee Creek. On December 29, 1890, when the band was being disarmed, a warrior overcome by tension seized his rifle, which discharged. Other men dropped their blankets and aimed their weapons at the surrounding troops. Simultaneously Indians and soldiers began firing at each other, and artillery shells raked Big Foot's people. Panic-stricken men, women, and children bolted from the camp only to be slaughtered by troopers of the Seventh Cavalry. Nearly 150 of Big Foots' band were killed; corpses, including those of women and children, were scattered out for three miles from where the fighting erupted. Perhaps another 100 Sioux died of wounds or froze to death. Dr. Charles A. Eastman, a Santee Sioux physician assigned to Pine Ridge agency where the massacre occurred, worked frantically to save the wounded as they were carried into the agency. The army did not escape without casualties; 25 were dead and 39 were wounded. When the Ghost Dance millennium did not occur as promised by Wovoka, the rituals faded away.

Another longer-lasting ritual filtered into the southern plains as Tavibo received his first visions. Through Apaches, Comanches learned of peyote, the dried fruit of a cactus, which when ingested produced hallucinations and euphoria. Rituals passed by the mid-1880s to the Kiowas, Cheyennes, and Arapahos went unnoticed by Indian agents. For more than a decade after peyote spread to other tribes, agency personnel confused consumption of peyote with mescal. Indian agents visited camps infrequently and few enjoyed enough confidence among Indians to learn all that transpired in settlements remote from agency headquarters. Quanah Parker lent his powerful support early, and, as young men returned from Carlisle, Delos Lone Wolf of the Kiowas, Leonard Tyler of the Cheyennes, and Cleaver Warden of the Arapahos became "road priests" of peyotism, spreading the rituals throughout the plains, and teaching peyote rites to former classmates. The "Peyote Road" was denounced occasionally as "the half-breeds" religion by persons who preferred to practice traditional ceremonies. Combining Christian and native American concepts, peyote became a communion for peyotists who were required to be truthful, abstain from alcohol, be devoted to family, and lead an upright life. Peyote was believed to restore health as its euphoric effects afforded at least temporary relief to many wracked by tuberculosis.

Even though condemned by federal officials, state legislatures, and missionaries, the peyote movement survived. Opponents of peyote urged its suppression, arguing the rite hindered conversion of Indians to Christianity and consumption of peyote buttons was as dangerous as the use of opium. After a series of intertribal conferences, Oklahoma peyotists in 1918 received a state charter incorporating the movement as the Native American Church, which was amended twenty-six years later creating the Native American Church of the United States. The rites varied widely depending on the meetings' leaders, but accompanying the sacramental use of peyote were prayers, songs, meditation, drumming rites, and individual and group dedication to the Holy Spirit above, symbolized by a beautiful, brilliant-colored Peyote Bird. So pervasive was the Peyote Road that perhaps 50 percent of the Indian population by 1930 were participants in the Native American Church. This ritual was credited with bringing health to the sick and success and prosperity to individuals, family, and the larger Indian community. It was a response to the stagnation and despondency experienced by western Indians during the reservation and early agency era. With other older ceremonials, the Peyote Road helped maintain Indian spiritualism, which provided a cohesive force with tribal society.

Substantial modifications of Indian culture occurred during the reservation era. Parents sent their children in increasing numbers to reservation and off-reservation schools where youths learned white man's ways. Older people received instruction in agriculture and stock raising, leading in instances to self-support. Cabins and frame homes began slowly to replace lodges. The expanding white population in western states and territories increased social and economic relations between whites and Indians. More Indians began to wear white-style clothing, and wagons and buggies were purchased. There was less polygamy, and Anglicized names began to dot agency census roles, especially as students returned from schools. While far from complete acculturation, Indian people were forced, cajoled, or persuaded to make some adjustments to their way of life. Indians were selective in their adaptations to white culture, accepting those parts necessary to survive on reservations.

Much of tribal society and institutions remained intact despite intrusion of federal Indian policies into reservation life. Tribal councils gathered to discuss issues affecting the lives and welfare of people. Influential chiefs, headmen, and elders were still entrusted with placing the wishes of their people before Indian agents or the Great Father in Washington. Men and women chose their spouses outside their band or clan, and marriages occasioned feasts and exchanges of presents between families. Possessions, food, and shelter were shared generously with relatives, friends, and visitors. Herbs and incantations of medicine men were preferred to the pills and ministrations of agency physicians. Respectful deference was accorded to holy men and keepers of tribal totems. Among the Cheyennes, for example, an unbroken succession of priests and keepers of the sacred arrows and buffalo hat taught their successors the ceremonies and prayers to supplicate Maheo, their All Father and Mother Earth. Tribal languages predominated in camps and homes; English learned in schools was spoken when dealing with whites. As with any human society, Indian cultural and social change was not sudden. Abundant customs, beliefs, and rituals accompanied Indians into the twentieth century, which provided tribes with means to maintain their separate identity as native Americans.


## SUGGESTED READING

For background information on Indian-white relations in the latter half of the nineteenth century, consult Robert M. Utley, *The Indian Frontier of the American West, 1846–1890* (Albuquerque, 1984). Excellent general studies containing information about the reservation era are Arrell Morgan Gibson, *The American Indian: Prehistory to the Present* (Lexington, 1980), chapters 14–19, and Francis Paul Prucha, *The Great Father: The United States Government and the American Indians* (Lincoln, 1984), chapters 12–25. Robert A. Trennert, Jr., *Alternative to Extinction: Federal Indian Policy and the Reservation System, 1846–1851* (Philadelphia, 1975) examines the origins of the reservation policy and system. There are a number of informative studies detailing conditions for Indians during the reservation period and specific tribal responses: Donald J. Berthrong, *The Southern Cheyennes* (Norman, 1963) and *The Cheyenne and Arapaho Ordeal: Reservation and Agency Life in the Indian Territory, 1875–1907* (Norman, 1976); Angie Debo, *Geronimo: The Man, His Time, His Place* (Norman, 1976); William T. Hagan, *United States-Comanche Relations: The Reservation Years* (New Haven, 1980, Reprint); George E. Hyde, *A Sioux Chronicle* (Norman, ca. 1956); James C. Olson, *Red Cloud and the Sioux Problem* (Lincoln, 1965); Ruth M. Underhill, *The Navajos* (Norman, 1956), especially chapters 9–16; and Donald E. Worcester, *The Apaches: Eagles of the Southwest* (Norman, 1979). Thomas Wildcat Alford, as told to Florence Drake, *Civilization* (Norman, 1936), Hagan, *Indian Police and Judges: Experiments in Acculturation and Control* (Lincoln, 1980, Reprint), and David Humphreys Miller, *Ghost Dance* (New York, 1959) are also important in gaining a better understanding of this subject.

| Philip | **10.** | Indian Policy |
| Weeks | **Humanity** | and the |
| | **and** | Hayes |
| | **Reform** | Presidency |

Two tumultuous episodes were nearing an end when Rutherford B. Hayes commenced his duties in March 1877 as nineteenth president of the United States. "We are in a period when old questions are settled," the new chief executive assessed accurately, "and the new are not yet brought forward." One of the sagas had engaged Americans for the better part of the previous two decades. Almost sixteen years had passed, as Hayes took his oath of office, since the bombardment of Fort Sumter in the harbor of Charleston, South Carolina, touched off a long and bloody Civil War. The problems of peace in the war's aftermath proved equally difficult as the federal government veered from one controversial agenda to another attempting to reconstruct the states of the defeated Southern Confederacy. One of President Hayes's first official acts was to end Reconstruction, thus closing the books, at least officially, on the Civil War era.

The second saga—the wars between the United States and the American Indians—was of older vintage. With roots stretching back to earliest colonial settlement, the struggle with America's native population had embroiled the republic since its inception. The Indians' armed resistance to westward expansion, and the government's response, produced periods of desperate violence. Throughout much of this century-long conflict the government sought to realize three goals: promoting westward expansion and settlement, protecting American settlers, and guaranteeing Indians' land and rights. The goals, however, were inherently conflicting. The government in Washington, faced with intense pressure to support and defend its own citizens, settlers, entrepreneurs, and manifest destiny, found it impossible to pursue all three goals impartially. The American Indians, without question, were marked as the eventual losers. A Wyoming newspaper in 1870 coldly reflected the attitude of most Americans: "The same inscrutable Arbiter that decreed the downfall of Rome, has pronounced the doom of extinction upon the red-men of America. To attempt to defer this result by mawkish sentimentalism . . . is unworthy of the age." The only remaining question was when complete military defeat would come.

Forces stimulating further American westward expansion were never long dormant, and by the middle of the nineteenth century the edge of the frontier had pushed relentlessly into the Trans-Mississippi West, as we have seen. If government or settlers expected western Indians to accept their presence with quiescence, the expectation proved illusory. Much of the 1860s and 1870s witnessed some of the bitterest warfare in the history of Indian relations, as the prairies and plains of the Far West provided the setting for the climactic Indian struggle. Western Indians put up a titanic struggle to prevent seizure of their homelands and to resist relocation on federal reservations. But far too many forces worked against them. The incessant flood of more and more settlers, the growing interest of American investment capital in the West, the construction of an increasingly vast network of railroads, the army's relentless pursuit, and the precipitous decline of the buffalo all combined to hasten the final defeat of the American Indians.

The disappearance of the buffalo was perhaps most distressing to the natives. Buffalo, besides serving as the chief source of food, were also used for many other things. The hides were used for clothing, robes, rawhide ropes, and even bedding for the winter months. The hooves were made into glue, horns were carved into spoons, and muscle tendon was made into bowstrings. Every advancement of settlement came at the expense of resources, especially the buffalo, crucial to the continuance of the western Indians' way of life. With complete realization that loss of the buffalo would relegate them to permanent residence on reservations, General William Tecumseh Sherman jested with deadly earnestness, that "it would be wise to invite all the sportsmen of England and America . . . for a Grand Buffalo hunt, and make one grand sweep of them all." In fact, Washington, during the early 1870s, pursued a policy not dissimilar to Sherman's idea. Hunters, rather than sportsmen, were permitted to dispatch the remaining buffalo herds on the southern plains.

The end of Indian military power—if the Apache campaigns of the 1880s are designated as mopping-up actions—came just prior to Hayes's inauguration. The Sioux War, the last great conflict, and absolute defeat of George Armstrong Custer at the Little Bighorn, lay less than a year in the past. By 1877, as Hayes entered the White House, the American Indians had been completely humbled by the United States. Their lands were drastically reduced, the last armed tribal resistance was all but crushed, many

Indian leaders were confined in federal prison, and the tribal remnants of a once proud, formidable, and fiercely independent people were reduced to grinding poverty and miserable despair on reservations. No less were the psychic costs, the result of loss of freedom, loss of family and tribal members, and loss of a cherished way of life. President Hayes notified Congress in his First Annual Message in December 1877, that "after a series of most deplorable conflicts . . . we are now at peace with all Indian tribes within our borders." He also concluded that "many, if not most, of our Indian wars have had their origin in broken promises and acts of injustice upon our part."

The end of the Indian wars concluded one long chapter of American history and began another. President Hayes realized that the resolution of one issue opened another of equal, perhaps greater magnitude. "How best can we aid them?" "How to deal with them," he reflected, "is a problem which for nearly three centuries has remained almost unsolved." The challenge facing the Hayes administration in 1877 was as formidable as it was clear: what policy should now govern relations between the United States and the American Indians in this period of transition between war and peace? The answer proved elusive and difficult, as Hayes fully anticipated. He did offer a hopeful outline of the answer shortly after taking office: "To preserve . . . peace by a just and humane policy will be the object of my earnest endeavors. Whatever may be said . . . of the difficulties of introducing among them the habits of civilized life, . . . the Indians are certainly entitled to our sympathy and to a conscientious respect on our part for their claim upon our sense of justice." However, some close to the federal Indian bureaucracy, aware of the state of Indian life—the terrible conditions on reservations, the distressing sense of dislocation, the near nonexistent means for them to provide for their needs with traditional methods—feared for the survival of the race. "If they cannot be taught, and taught very soon to accept the necessities of their situation and begin in earnest to provide for their own wants by labor in civilized pursuits," predicted Commissioner of Indian Affairs John Q. Smith, "they are destined to speedy extinction."

President Hayes's concern for the Indians' welfare was reflected, in part, in his appointment of Carl Schurz of Missouri as secretary of the interior. While the detailed administration of Indian affairs is under the direction of the commissioner of Indian affairs, supervisory responsibility of the commissioner and the Bureau of Indian Affairs rests with the secretary of the interior. Schurz, an outspoken critic of the corruption found in the administration of Hayes's predecessor, Ulysses S. Grant, and a long-time champion of civil service reform, came to know Hayes well in 1875. It was Hayes's call for civil service reform and merit employment while running for an unprecedented third term as governor of Ohio that attracted Schurz's attention and support. Schurz campaigned for Governor Hayes, who once reelected did not disappoint the Missourian when he placed merit over patronage in filling state posts. A year later Schurz supported Hayes in his bid for the presidency, remarking hopefully that "this could mean the real start of federal civil service reform, but only if we get our man in the White House." The victory of Hayes guaranteed a new day, not just in the administration of Indian affairs, but in honest government.

Schurz's appointment to the Hayes cabinet provided him the long-anticipated chance to implement federal civil service reform. The advances that he and the president made to reduce the power of political machines and to eliminate officeholders found guilty of corruption, while infuriating party leaders, heartened many Americans. "We think Mr. Hayes has done more for the reform of civil service," declared *Harper's Weekly*, "than any President in our history." President Hayes's insistence on clean government prompted former President Grant to remark bitterly that Hayes seemed influenced by "two great humbugs . . . reform and reformers." The president's insistence on clean government also demanded that the Indian Bureau be scrutinized.

Of all federal departments and bureaus, perhaps the one needing greatest attention and housecleaning was the Indian Bureau. Since its establishment in 1849 it was notorious for fraud, corruption, and inefficiency. Businessmen who contracted with the government to supply Indians on their reservations were guilty, as one Congressional investigation charged, of "the most outrageous and systematic swindling and robbery." And Indian agents were in no better position to be absolved. A job in the Indian service, almost always obtained through political patronage, proved a cornucopia of opportunity for graft. Too many agents, earning an annual salary of $1,500, banked outrageous sums of money during their service. One Indian recalled: "When he [the Indian agent] come he bring everything in a little bag, when he leaves it take two steamboats to carry away his things." General Henry Heth, who had been an inspector in the Indian service, commented about agents: "The Indian Bureau has been made the dumping ground for the sweepings of the political party that is in power." Secretary Schurz exaggerated only slightly in lamenting that "a thoroughly competent, honest, and devoted Indian agent is . . . so rare a jewel that . . . nothing could induce me to part with him."

Obviously something needed to be done, and shortly after taking office

Hayes ordered Schurz to "do what you can . . . to tidy up the Bureau." Schurz took two actions. To get a firsthand look at the Indian Bureau in action he made a six-week tour of Indian Territory (present-day Oklahoma). The tour convinced him that the situation was even worse than expected. The secretary, in June 1877, also ordered a full investigation of the Bureau, Indian agencies, and the agent's methods of doing business. Commissioner Smith assured Schurz that "I know of no custom in the Bureau which can properly be termed an abuse." The report of the investigating team disagreed absolutely, concluding that the Indian Bureau was "simply a license to cheat and swindle the Indians in the name of the United States." The worst suspicions of President Hayes and Secretary Schurz were confirmed. Commissioner Smith was dismissed and was replaced by Ezra A. Hayt of New York. The chief clerk and the worst subordinates were likewise discharged. Schurz also removed any agent convicted of fraud or graft. The practice of nepotism in hiring practices, long a common Indian service practice, was ordered to an end. All agents who continued to practice nepotism were removed. President Hayes proudly reported in his First Annual Message to Congress that "earnest efforts are being made to purify the Indian service, so that every dollar appropriated by Congress shall redound to the benefit of the Indians, as intended. Those efforts . . . have my firm support." General Philip Sheridan was so impressed with the reforms ordered by President Hayes that he fairly crowed: "the service of Indian affairs was finally lifted out of the mire of corruption that had long made it a discredit to our civilization."

Efforts to reform the Indian service soon brought Schurz into conflict with religious reformers. Concern during the Grant presidency over political patronage and rampant corruption in the Bureau spurred philanthropic attempts to gain control over the Indian service and Indian policy. A Board of Indian Commissioners was established by Congress in 1869. Representing the Protestant churches, it consisted of persons "eminent for their intelligence and philanthropy," appointed by the president. The Board advised the secretary of the interior and the commissioner of Indian affairs regarding reform and policy, served as a watchdog over the disbursement of funds appropriated by Congress for the Indians, and supervised the appointment of all agency personnel by Protestant denominations. Trouble soon arose when no Catholics were appointed to the Board, although that church had been more active in the Indian mission field than any other denomination. Already once victimized by nativist sentiment when the Board was constituted, the Catholic Church was further penalized by the low number of agencies assigned it relative to those awarded to Protestant denominations, even though President Grant's guidelines suggested that an agency should be assigned to the missionary group that already worked there among the Indians. The Church pointed out, to little avail, that in over thirty cases Protestant denominations were given preference. A central Catholic agency was established in Washington in 1874, and five years later the Bureau of Catholic Indian Missions emerged to monitor Catholic missions and to act as an agent with the federal government. Once Schurz became secretary of the interior, the Catholic Church pressed its demands with him for religious freedom on the reservations.

"The present system which permits religious societies to nominate candidates for Indian agencies is, in some respects, undoubtedly an improvement upon the former practice of making appointments . . . on political grounds," declared Schurz. Yet he was personally opposed to the heavy denominational influence in the Indian service. In part he felt that denominationally appointed agents lacked appropriate business experience, but he also saw this matter as an impingement on his jurisdiction. Schurz determined to strengthen the authority of the Interior Department over Indian matters, while at the same time undercutting the principle of religious appointment. Because the policy of denominational appointments lacked statutory force, it provided Schurz and Hayt the necessary latitude to undermine it. Early in the Hayes administration the Indian Office began appointing agency clerks and physicians. Before the end of the president's first year in office, thirty-five of the seventy-four Indian agents were replaced. The new policy of widespread replacements and central control struck a heavy blow to the churches, one from which they never recovered. When the controversy between Protestants and Catholics over the exclusive religious jurisdiction on the reservations did not subside, Schurz, in February 1881, ruled that all reservations would be equally open to missionaries of all denominations. Late in the Hayes presidency the churches increased their efforts to regain control of agent appointments, but it was too late. The shift of appointments from religious to governmental nominations ironically had played into the hands of politicians, who also hoped to regain some of their lost influence in the Indian service. And by 1883 and the passage of the Civil Service or Pendleton Act, they had very nearly regained control of appointments to the Indian service. The conflict between Protestants and Catholics did not end here, and, in fact, the period of severest tension was between 1888 and 1912 as the two sides battled over control and apportionment of Indian mission schools.

The evolution of the administration's conduct toward Indians themselves passed through two stages: the first, characterized by a policy of resettlement and concentration, was gradually replaced by one emphasizing various measures to acculturate and assimilate them. Since the mid-1860s, one important aspect of the government's Indian policy called for the resettlement and concentration of all Indians in Indian Territory and a comparable area on the northern plains. Over sixty tribes were resettled in Indian Territory by the time Hayes became president, while many more were shifted from their homeland to new locales. Sioux chief Spotted Tail suggested with mock sincerity: "Why does not the Great Father put his red children on wheels, so he can move them as he will?" This policy evolved because the government slowly came to the realization that it could no longer push Indians westward to minimize contact with settlers, and it was not humane to conduct wars of extermination to "solve" the "Indian problem." Resettlement thus seemed a workable and positive solution. At the beginning of the Hayes presidency, Schurz concurred with this policy and continued to effect it. However, the decision fell hard on the Indians. That the Hayes administration eventually came to realize that the policy of resettlement and concentration was ill-suited is to its credit, but it took two tragic episodes to demonstrate this. One episode involved a portion of the Nez Perce tribe which objected to being relocated and restricted to a smaller and less desirable reservation. The other concerned the Northern Cheyennes, whose relocation in Indian Territory proved such a wretched experience that flight back to their homeland on the northern plains seemed their only salvation.

By all accounts the Chopunnish or Nez Perce were a warm, peaceful, and harmonious people who had always been friendly and helpful to the whites. Their boast was that they had never killed a white man. Their traditional domain was the valley of the Clearwater River, which flows through the three northwestern states of Oregon, Washington, and Idaho. However, they, like all the other western Indian nations, lost most of their land in the 1850s when the newly initiated reservation system was forced on them. The Treaty of the Wallowa River of 1855 obliged the Nez Perce to surrender half of their lands to the United States. The remaining half was organized into a reservation where they were expected to live and where, by treaty, whites were forbidden to enter. There was no doubt about the clauses of the treaty; indeed it was very like most treaties of its time. It was typical too in that, like most of the others, its violation by whites was followed virtually immediately on its creation. Soon, the Americans who had moved illegally onto the reservation made more and more requests to

Washington to have the Nez Perce removed from the best land of the reservation. A subsequent treaty in 1863 took away three-quarters of the reservation to give it to white homesteaders. Most of the chiefs refused to sign, seeing in it nothing but futility. The government would no more honor its terms than those of the earlier treaty of 1855. As a result, some Nez Perce, about six hundred, no longer in possession of any treaty at all, remained on the land of their former reservation.

By the early 1870s, pressure from whites was building to force the non-treaty Nez Perce onto the new, sharply constricted reservation. A federal peace commission came west in 1875 for the specific purpose of talking these Nez Perce into moving to the new reservation. The chief with whom they negotiated was a man named Joseph. Joseph had a calm, self-assured, commanding personality, which was easily a match for the commissioners who tried by reason to persuade his people to leave their traditional lands. He angered several of the commissioners by his gentle but egalitarian behavior toward the Americans and equally by superior intellect. The commissioners returned to Washington without reaching an agreement with Joseph and his followers. Meanwhile, settlers continued to come and to take more of the land of the Nez Perce. In May 1877, the United States, represented now by the new secretary of the interior, Schurz, at last decided to settle the issue and did so by rejecting any further consideration of the issue. All of the non-treaty Nez Perce were to be forced onto the new reservation. General Oliver Otis Howard, the former head of the Freedmen's Bureau who had lost an arm at the Battle of Fair Oaks during the Civil War, was given the responsibility of enforcing the government's orders. Howard gave Chief Joseph one month to bring his people into the reservation and warned him that if they were late, he would order the army out after them. Joseph tried to reason with Howard. He pointed out that the deadline would be difficult to meet because his tribe's horses and cattle were birthing at the time. Even nature failed to move Howard to extend his deadline. Some of the cattle and horses had to be left behind, while the rest were rounded up by the Nez Perce for the journey to the reservation.

Along the way there was a serious outbreak of trouble when a few of the young men whose fathers had been murdered in the past by settlers sought revenge on the whites before they were confined to a reservation. General Howard immediately sent the army to punish the Nez Perce. The guilty and the innocent alike were targets. For Joseph's band, their only chance for freedom or even simple toleration was flight. Two attacks by the army—one in June, the other in July of 1877—were repulsed. After a counsel, the Nez Perce decided to avoid further conflict, quit the area, and seek haven across the Rocky Mountains either in Montana or Canada. Thus in late July 1877, 650 Nez Perce—young, healthy, sick, aged, infants, and wounded—embarked on the dangerous and arduous journey over the Rockies.

Joseph expected that once outside of Howard's jurisdiction the general would find no further reason to chase the fleeing Nez Perce. The error of this assumption became clear quickly as the army relentlessly pursued. Throughout the summer of 1877, Joseph and his followers fought and traveled over the northern Rockies in an incredible effort to escape the army. And throughout the summer, public interest was also generated by stories of the Nez Perce's epic odyssey. Chief Joseph became something of a folk hero to Americans. His legend grew rapidly. The American public became aware that an outstanding Indian tactician was eluding and, when necessary, defeating a much larger force. In late September, exhausted but happy, they made camp just above Bear Paw Mountain in northern Montana. Men, women, and children had traveled 1,700 miles since June over mountainous terrain and now they were only some thirty miles from Canada—a long day's ride. Had they stopped briefly and then pushed on, they might have made it. Instead, yielding to near total exhaustion, they rested. The decision proved fatal; the army caught up with them on September 30, blocking the way to Canada. On October 4, 1877, Joseph surrendered, not wanting to sacrifice the lives of the surviving Nez Perce.

General Howard and General Nelson A. Miles, the man to whom Joseph surrendered, both promised to return the Nez Perce to their homeland. However, General Sherman, general in chief of the army, ruthlessly overrode the promise and ordered Joseph and his followers transported to Indian Territory where over a quarter of them quickly died due to malaria and the totally foreign climate. Schurz, unwilling to compromise the policy of resettlement and concentration, and disregarding public outcry, refused to overrule Sherman's decision. However, it seems that Schurz's complete faith in this policy was shaken by the episode with Joseph and certainly by the one to come shortly with the Northern Cheyenne.

Following the Sioux War of the mid-1870s, many Northern Cheyenne, allies of the Sioux in the recent conflict, were relocated in Indian Territory. While a minimal security of life had taken the place of violence, life was immeasurably degraded and shameful for them on their new reservation. Desperately homesick for their northern plains and increasingly harried and distraught by living conditions in their exile, two bodies of that tribe risked everything to leave their captivity and return to their homelands. In

September 1878 nearly three hundred fled northward, led by Chiefs Dull Knife (Morning Star) and Little Wolf. These fugitives should not be called "warriors." They were in the main old men, women, and children. Only about seventy-five could be considered in or near their prime, nor had the wretched conditions of their captivity given them the strength of earlier times. This operation was not combat but flight.

In their circumstances caution was more appropriate than grandeur. The Cheyennes crossed the plains with the utmost circumspection, always trying to skirt the army patrols that searched for them and the settlers who were always ready to turn them in to the authorities. In this way they reached central Nebraska, where they split into two bands. Little Wolf's band continued their journey northward. Wintering in northern Nebraska, they pressed onward in the spring only to be captured in southeastern Montana by the army. Little Wolf and his followers were taken prisoner to Fort Keogh; but not for long, however. Their fates quickly became mixed-up in the public outcry over the treatment of the Nez Perce and of Dull Knife's Cheyennes.

After the two bands separated, Dull Knife's traveled into northwest Nebraska before running into an army patrol in a heavy snow storm. They were immediately taken captive and removed to Fort Robinson where they were imprisoned. While federal authorities debated whether to permit them to remain in the north or to return them to Indian Territory, the Cheyennes were kept in unheated barracks and given only minimal food and water. Outside the temperature was close to zero. On January 3, 1879, their fate was decided. Schurz had agreed with the advice of General Sheridan that "unless [the Indians] are sent back to where they came from, the whole reservation system will receive a shock which will endanger its stability." Consequently the Northern Cheyennes were to be sent back to Indian Territory. Dull Knife and his people were anguished and bluntly told the fort's officers to kill them all at once, for they would never go back to a slow and agonizing death in the south.

When the report of what happened next later reached President Hayes, he was overwhelmed with anger and shame. The Cheyennes' refusal to be resettled again in Indian Territory prompted the fort's commander to attempt to break their will. Rations of food and water were cut off on January 3. The freezing cold of the plains added to the Cheyennes' torture of hunger, while the prospect of again being forced south was unbearable to them. On January 10 they broke out, sustaining heavy casualties in the process. They did not get far. Soldiers from the fort tracked them down and on January 21 captured them after a bloody fight. Their unsuccessful flight for freedom had cost Dull Knife's Northern Cheyennes dearly. Almost half were killed, only seventy-eight being returned to Fort Robinson.

The Northern Cheyennes' unsuccessful flight to their homeland did serve to help them, although they could not have immediately realized it. The widespread public indignation against the government and the army generated by this incident, especially when compounded by public awareness of the recent flight of the Nez Perce, forced the Hayes administration into a critical reassessment of the policy of resettlement and concentration. Indian Commissioner Hayt wrote Schurz commenting on the "impolicy of sending northern Indians to Indian Territory." General Miles, who continued to press for the return of Joseph and his Nez Perce to their homeland, published a stinging indictment: "The forcing of strong, hardy mountain Indians from the extreme North to the warmer malarial districts of the South was cruel, and the experiment should never be repeated." Schurz now concurred, conceding that "it was believed that [the policy of resettlement] would be apt to keep the Indians out of hostile collision with their neighbors," and concluding that it was "a mistaken policy." The Hayes administration pressed for quick approval for the creation of a Northern Cheyenne reservation in Montana, where Little Wolf's and Dull Knife's people, among others, were soon permitted to reside.

A turning point was reached in the administration of Indian affairs by 1879. President Hayes turned away from the long-standing policy of confinement on reservations and military coercion to keep the Indians in residence there. Instead he sought the means to bring them into the mainstream of the American family. While advocating Indian citizenship, his new policy came to rest on two tenets: allotment of land in severalty and education. Hayes was convinced that only when the Indians were assimilated into the American family would their physical safety and legal and property rights be fully protected from further encroachment. The president's disdain of injustice and his sensitivity to the plight of the Indians decreed an obligation to assist them actively. "We can not expect them to improve . . . unless we keep faith with them in respecting the rights they possess," Hayes stressed, "and unless, instead of depriving them of their opportunities, we lend them a helping hand."

Private or individual ownership of land was a concept foreign to most tribes, and up until the mid-1870s, except where laws had made special exceptions, Indian lands were held in common. Reformers during the late 1870s, led by Senator Henry L. Dawes of Massachusetts and others, hoped to move Indians in the direction of personal, private property. They found willing and influential allies in President Hayes and Secretary Schurz, who stated that "the enjoyment and pride of the individual ownership of property is one of the most effective civilizing agencies." To encourage Indians to end tribal association and take up agriculture or herding as a private enterprise, Congress in 1875 had passed general legislation which extended the land benefits of the 1862 Homestead Act to Indians willing to surrender tribal status. Few Indians availed themselves, however. Each succeeding year advocates of Indian welfare argued that Indians would be "civilized" more quickly if the concept of private property was introduced among them. They stressed that this would remove them from wretched living conditions on reservations, from the "contaminating" influence of tribal affiliation and activities, and from near absolute dependence on the government for subsistence. Increasingly they called for legislation permitting allotment in severalty of Indian land, which, they anticipated, would also result in the break up of the reservations. Many persons, like President Hayes, Secretary Schurz, and Senator Dawes, embraced allotment as a valuable and viable means of promoting the Indians' welfare. As one agent commented, "As long as Indians live in [communal] villages they will retain many of their old and injurious habits. . . . I trust that before another year is ended they will generally be located upon individual land or farms. From that date will begin their real and permanent progress."

It was equally clear that many other Americans who supported allotment legislation were little more than frustrated land grabbers. The Hayes administration was under enormous and steady pressure to liquidate most, if not all, of the some 155,000,000 acres of reservation land. It is to President Hayes's credit that he stood firm against this pressure, stressing that land allotted to Indians must be protected from alienation for a period long enough for them to learn how to use and to hold onto their property.

In 1879 President Hayes recommended passage of a general allotment act, and twice during his term in office allotment legislation was introduced in Congress with the support of the administration. Both times the proposed legislation failed, in part out of fear that Indians were ill-prepared to hold and maintain private property and because allotment seemed to stand little chance of achieving its intended results to advance the Indians' welfare. The minority report issued by the House Committee on Indian Affairs, typifying much of the opposition, stated, "However much we may differ from the humanitarians who are riding this hobby, we are certain that they will agree with us . . . that it does not make a farmer out of an Indian to give him a quarter section of land." Senator Henry M. Teller of Colorado predicted accurately that forty years after the passage of allotment legislation, when the Indians had been alienated from their private allotments, they would "curse the hand that was raised professedly in their defense." While failing to achieve allotment legislation, the movement for it continued and ultimately succeeded with the passage of the Dawes Severalty Act in 1887.

The Hayes administration enjoyed greater success with its second agenda—expanding the government's educational programs for Indians. Education was not a new idea. As early as 1780 the Continental Congress made appropriations of $5,000 for the education of Indian students at Dartmouth College. From 1819 onward an annual appropriation for Indian education by missionary groups was authorized by Congress. By the end of the Indian wars in the 1870s, it was widely agreed by Americans that the Indian could not continue to exist as an Indian and survive. The way to save them from extinction seemed to be through education. One Indian commissioner remarked: "To educate the Indian in the ways of civilized . . . life is to preserve him from extinction." Survival, however, would come at the steep price of their Indianness.

Reformers and personnel associated with the Indian Bureau were in general agreement that a complete separation from the aboriginal home environment was important in educating Indian youths in "civilized" ways and skills. The solution appeared in 1879 with the introduction of a new concept in Indian education—the off-reservation boarding school. The first such school was Carlisle Indian School at Carlisle Barracks, Pennsylvania, founded by Army Captain Richard H. Pratt. Pratt's two principal goals were to civilize Indians through education and to demonstrate to the American public that the Indian was educable. Carlisle, the model for subsequent off-reservation boarding schools, was modeled on manual labor institutions. While the curriculum included academic subjects like reading, writing, arithmetic, and spelling, the greatest emphasis was on pragmatic training in domestic skills for females and agricultural and manual arts for males. Congress was so impressed by the efforts at Carlisle that it annually increased appropriations for Indian education. Congress, throughout the rest of the century, also established off-reservation boarding schools throughout western states and territories where there was a large Indian population.

President Hayes, a staunch advocate of free public education, strongly supported the expansion of educational opportunities for Indian youths. On September 1, 1880, Hayes, while addressing his army reunion in Canton, Ohio, asserted that "the solution of the Indian question will speedily be either the extinction of the Indians or their absorption into American citizenship by means of the civilizing influences of education." Later that month the president embarked on an extensive western trip which took him to the Pacific coast. While in Forest Grove, Oregon, Hayes made a point to visit the government Indian school there. "I think it is the wish and prayer of every good citizen that these Indian boys and girls should become wise, useful, and good citizens," declared Hayes while at the school. "Some people seem to think that God has decreed that Indians should die off like wild animals. With this we have nothing to do. If they are to become extinct we ought to leave that to Providence. . . . If it turns out that their destiny is to be different, we shall have at least done our duty . . . to improve their physical, mental, and moral condition . . . [and] prepare them to become part of the great American family." And this was the legacy which Hayes left on retiring from the presidency. He had fashioned a new direction in the administration of Indian affairs, a direction which the government would follow for the next half century.

In March 1881, Hayes was replaced in the White House by his friend from Ohio, James A. Garfield. President Hayes retired to his estate, Spiegal Grove, at Fremont, Ohio. After leaving office he worked actively as an advocate of the American Indians, becoming one of his generation's most sympathetic champions of their cause. Senator Dawes, like most reformers, grateful for the work done by President Hayes in the area of Indian affairs, offered a memorial at the Lake Mohonk Indian conference of 1893: "His administration was marked by a purity that, without disparagement of any others, has hardly been found in the history of the country. . . . Rich as is the example which he has left us of his public service, . . . the noble work of his private life shine out to cheer and bless, and, I trust, to improve the life of those who knew him as I did."

## SUGGESTED READING

Good treatments of Rutherford B. Hayes are Harry Barnard, *Rutherford B. Hayes and His America* (New York, 1930) and Kennith E. Davison, *The Presidency of Rutherford B. Hayes* (Westport, 1972). T. Harry William's *Hayes: The Diary of a President, 1875–1881* (New York, 1964) provides useful insights into Hayes's career and thinking. Appropriate sections of Robert M. Utley, *The Indian Frontier of the American West, 1846–1890* (Albuquerque, 1984) provide an excellent overview to many of the topics of this chapter.

For Carl Schurz, and especially his role as Hayes's secretary of the interior, see Claude M. Fuess, *Carl Schurz: Reformer* (New York, 1952), especially chapters IXX and XX, and Hans L. Trefousse, *Carl Schurz: A Biography* (Knoxville, 1982), especially chapter XV.

An excellent account of the Indian service and its bureaucracy is Paul Stuart, *The Indian Office: Growth and Development of an American Institution* (Ann Arbor, 1979). Among the various accounts of reform activities in the late nineteenth century, three of the best are Francis Paul Prucha, *American Indian Policy in Crisis: Christian Reformers and the Indians, 1865–1900* (Norman, 1976), Henry E. Fritz, *The Movement for Indian Assimilation, 1860–1890* (Philadelphia, 1963), and Loring B. Priest, *Uncle Sam's Stepchildren: The Reformation of United States Indian Policy, 1865–1887* (New Brunswick, 1942). For background on the peace policy and the role of religious sects therein see Robert H. Keller, Jr., *American Protestantism and United States Indian Policy, 1869–1882* (Lincoln, 1983).

Arrell **11.** Liquidation
Morgan **To** of the
Gibson **Kill a** Five Indian
**Nation** Republics

**P**resident Theodore Roosevelt's action in signing the Oklahoma Statehood Proclamation on November 16, 1907, produced joy in the western half of the new state, the old Oklahoma Territory, but gloom in its eastern half, the old Indian Territory. The governments of the Choctaw, Cherokee, Creek, Seminole, and Chickasaw nations, the so-called Five Civilized Tribes, ceased to function, and the tribal territories were absorbed into the new state.

Liquidation of the five Indian nations had been a part of the federal government's long-standing, calculated program of exiling native Americans into the Western wilderness, appropriating tribal estates, and eventually eradicating their Indianness and absorbing them into the national population. After the United States succeeded Spain, France, and Great Britain as the presumptive imperial master of the Eastern Indians, many tribes violently resisted the expansive Anglo-Americans, suffered shattering defeats, and became easy marks for American agents who forced tribal leaders to cede their homelands and remove to reservations in the less attractive "Great American Desert," as the land west of Missouri and Arkansas was known in the early nineteenth century.

The Five Civilized Tribes occupied large territories in Alabama, Georgia, Florida, Mississippi, and Tennessee. They took a different stance, developing various strategies to protect their lands and their right to remain in the East. One tactic was cooperation with federal officials and support of the national interest. They studiously supported the United States in achieving its international goals. Thus during the War of 1812 these Indian nations politely rejected Tecumseh's plea for Indian brotherhood and war on the Americans, and they remained loyal to the United States. In addition, the Cherokee, Choctaw, Creek, and Chickasaw governments each raised a regiment which joined Major General Andrew Jackson's army to guard the southwestern frontier against British invasion. One Creek faction, the Red Sticks (Baton Rouges), did accept Tecumseh's gospel and made war on American settlements in the Southwest. However, loyal Creek, Cherokee,

Chickasaw, and Choctaw troops in Jackson's army smashed the Red Sticks at the Battle of Horseshoe Bend.

Another tribal strategy was coexistence—the hope held by leaders of the southern tribes that they could so order the lives of their people that Anglo-Americans would be willing to accept them as worthy neighbors. Thus they urged great changes in their nations. Many Indians adopted white customs in dress and industry, established successful farms, plantations, and businesses in their nations, and several became prosperous slave-owners. In addition, they changed their traditional political systems to governments based on written constitutions with elected officials, courts, and other elements of enlightened polity.

Tribal leaders welcomed missionaries to their nations, not necessarily because they found tribal deities inadequate, but rather because missionaries, besides being ministers of the gospel, also were teachers. Missionaries established schools where many Indian youths completed basic studies and then continued their educations in colleges in the Northeast. Soon, in each Indian nation, there was formed a corps of elitist leaders, most of whom were better educated than Anglos in neighboring settlements and were able to work with white counterparts in the professions, business, and politics.

Advancement among the Cherokee illustrates those substantive changes occurring among the southern Indian nations. Tribesmen studiously emulated their white neighbors; several became prominent and wealthy as slaveowners and operators of grain and lumber mills, plantations, and stock farms in the Cherokee nation. A northern visitor during the 1820s observed that Cherokees lived "in comfort and abundance, in good houses of brick, stone, and wood. We saw several houses built of hewn stone, superior to any we had ever seen before. The people seemed to have more money than the whites in our own settlements; they were better clothed. The women were weaving, the men cultivating corn, and raising beef and pork in abundance; butter and milk everywhere. We were at an election for delegates among the Cherokees to form a constitution. They were orderly, and well behaved."

Schools, most of them operated by Congregationalist, Presbyterian, Dutch Reformed (American Board), and Moravian missionaries, instructed Cherokee children in the rudiments of learning. Sequoyah, the Cherokee genius, had invented his syllabary, an eighty-six character alphabet that reduced the Cherokee language to written form. A tribal newspaper, the *Cherokee Phoenix* edited by Elias Boudinot, a Cherokee mixed blood, appeared for the first time in 1828; its columns were printed both in Sequoyah's syllabary and in English. Sequoyah's syllabary was so well received, it stirred such intense pride among Cherokees, that it is said that the nation achieved near total literacy in less than five years.

Cherokees abolished their tribal government in 1827 and formed a constitutional republic. Pathkiller, last of the full-blood traditional chiefs, was replaced by Charles Hicks, a brilliant mixed blood and leading author of the constitution. Shortly he was succeeded by John Ross, a one-eighth Cherokee, who served his nation as elected principal chief until his death in 1866.

Leaders of the Cherokees and other southern Indian nations, in their desperate hope to coexist and adapt to the rapid changes swirling about their nations, could not comprehend that altering tribal lifeways and progressing in education, business, and polity only aroused envy and antagonism among their Anglo-American neighbors. Indian success was regarded as a threat. What leaders of these Indian republics did not understand was that most nineteenth-century Anglo-Americans feared, scorned, and rejected peoples unlike themselves in culture and physical characteristics. A continuum of these virulent ethnocentric attitudes fed into the national bloodstream and poisoned chances for the tribes to survive in their ancient homelands.

Anglo-Americans fashioned counterstrategies to achieve eradication of Indian presence. Citizens of Alabama, Georgia, Mississippi, and Tennessee regarded Indians as barriers to furthering their material goals. In an era of rapid agricultural expansion, particularly cotton culture, Indians occupied fertile lands which settlers coveted. Thus Georgians, Alabamans, Mississippians, and Tennesseans inventively strove to force the Indians into exile, including callous resort to the state and federal political apparatus to accomplish their objectives. Whites were voters in state and federal elections while Indians were not.

Citizen will was reflected in southern legislatures, which, between 1828 and 1830, adopted laws which abolished functioning tribal governments in each state, stipulating arrest and imprisonment for tribal leaders who attempted to exercise the duties of their offices. Under these repressive state laws the only purpose for which tribal councils could meet was to discuss surrender of tribal lands and emigration to the West. Indian testimony was declared inadmissible in state judicial proceedings. Thus settlers could prey with impunity on Indians, their households, and property, and tribesmen had no remedy in state courts. The clear intent of these laws was to make life so miserable for Indians that, in self-defense, they would surrender their tribal estates and move west of the Mississippi River.

The national government was bound by solemn constitutional pledge and treaties with these tribes to protect Indians in their person, property, and territory from trespass. Indian leaders, well aware of the treaty protection guarantees the federal government had pledged to them, petitioned national officials to fulfill the treaty commitments and guard them from state and citizen tyranny. Failure of ballot-sensitive politicians to respond to native American entreaties for protection was another manifestation of the strategic political advantage Anglo-Americans held over Indians. They elected U.S. senators and representatives committed to fulfilling their goal of removing Indians from their home states and opening their lands to settlement. Southern senators and representatives pushed for adoption of laws by Congress which would legalize appropriation of tribal lands and exile the Indians; the classic example was, of course, the Indian Removal Act of 1830. Southern voters also supported presidential candidates who were committed to support this policy. Their counterstrategies triumphed over the pathetic survival attempts of the Five Civilized Tribes.

Government agents braced by the Indian Removal Act moved with dispatch to erase all signs of Indians from the Old Southwest. They connived with malleable tribal factions and extracted minority-approved treaties which committed in each case the entire nation to surrender territory and either emigrate or remain on allotments and abjure tribal status. Native leaders challenged these peremptory actions by state and federal officials, the most noteworthy instance was the Cherokee challenge in *Worcester v. Georgia* (1832) which questioned the state jurisdiction over the Cherokee nation and the responsibility of the federal government to guard Indian interests. The Worcester decision answered the question of Indian tribal status within state jurisdiction in that it declared null and void those state laws seeking to regulate internal affairs of Indian nations and reiterated the national obligation to guard Indian interests. Leaders of the Cherokees and other southern tribes were elated. At last they believed they would receive the justice they merited and the protection they were guaranteed by treaties against repressive state action.

Their hopes were dashed by President Jackson's refusal to enforce the court's decision. When tribal leaders reminded Jackson of his constitutional responsibility he answered, incorrectly, that he was powerless in the matter and that their only hope was to accept their fate, cede their eastern territory, and emigrate.

The president's failure to fulfill his constitutional duty destroyed the will of many Indians to resist state repression and settler harassment; they capitulated and prepared to move to the Indian Territory. The "Trail of Tears" of the Five Civilized Tribes, ruthlessly uprooted to make way for Anglo-American settlers, ranks among the tragedies of the ages. The chief executive who presided over the most sordid phase of this exile stated on March 4, 1837, in his Farewell Address: "The States which had so long been retarded in their improvement by the Indian tribes residing in the midst of them are at length relieved from the evil . . . and this unhappy race—the original dwellers in our land—are now placed in a situation where we may well hope that they will share in the blessings of civilization and be saved from degradation and destruction."

Years of callous pressure from state and federal officials, punishing harassment from settlers, the trauma of being uprooted from ancestral domains, and, in many cases, being driven at the point of a bayonet over their Trail of Tears, certainly fed the erosive forces which, combined with subsequent tribal disasters, produced ultimate liquidation of these Indian nations. However, momentarily, these native American communities experienced a merciful respite. Once relocated in their new western territories the surviving tribesmen—each nation had lost about one-fourth of its population by the ordeal of exile to the Trans-Mississippi wilderness—courageously applied themselves to the demanding task of making a phoenix-like recovery. They cleared forests and established farms, plantations, ranches, towns, transportation systems, newspapers, schools, businesses, and constitutional governments.

One serious threat to their continued existence as self-governing entities occurred during the 1850s. Anglo-American settlers found the Great American Desert, at least its eastern margins, adequate for their needs and demanded access to it. Thus in 1854 the northern half of Indian Territory succumbed to their demands. Congress created Kansas and Nebraska Territories from that portion of the reserved Indian colonization zone, and the remnants of tribesmen, most of them resettled from the Old Northwest, were again displaced. At the same time there was a strong move to open the southern half of Indian Territory, now partitioned into the domains of the Five Civilized Tribes, by the so-called Neosho Statehood Movement. Senator Robert W. Johnson of Arkansas introduced a bill in Congress to organize three territories from the lands of these tribes—Cherokee (capital at Tahlequah), Muskogee (capital at Creek Agency near Fort Gibson), and Chahtah (capital at Doaksville). The land of each Indian republic was to be surveyed, allotments in severalty were to be assigned to tribal citizens, and surplus lands were to be opened to settlers. The plan called for fusion of the three territories into the state of Neosho. Johnson's bill failed at final consideration due largely to the eloquent opposition of tribal leaders supported by powerful church and civic friends in New England. But the proposal is significant in that it marked the beginning of a series of attempts to open the surviving portion of Indian Territory to homeseekers.

Federal officials needed a strong excuse to drive the Five Civilized Tribes to accept dissolution of their quasi-independent republics. It came rather soon as a result of the commitment of these Indian nations to alliances with the Confederate States of America in 1861. The agony of war, its destructive force and eventual defeat, shattered native American morale and made Indians easier marks for the Anglo-American goal of dissolving the five Indian republics. Reconstruction, drastic Indian policy changes inflicted on native Americans after the war, and the imperative adjustments to new ways required by the expansive pressures of the postbellum world exacerbated the tribal ordeal. In less than twenty-five years a network of rail lines laced the Indian Territory and brought cattlemen, boomers, nesters, and displacement of Indians, consummating the process of tribal dissolution begun in the 1820s.

The Reconstruction Treaties imposed by the victorious Union government on the defeated Confederate Indian nations in 1866 stripped them of substantial territories amounting virtually to the western half of present Oklahoma. Federal negotiators appropriated these lands as a sort of reparations of war for the purpose of creating a maze of reservations on which to concentrate tribes from other parts. The Reconstruction Treaties required the Indian nations to grant rights-of-way to railway companies building lines across the Southwest. Also tribal leaders were forced to pledge to work toward formation of a single government for Indian Territory, thus eventually surrendering tribal status and dominion. And like the states of the defeated Confederacy, the Indian nations were expected to alter their constitutions, providing for abolition of slavery and extending tribal citizenship to former bondsmen. But beyond Reconstruction stipulations imposed on other former slaveholding communities, federal officials demanded that the Five Civilized Tribes share their tribal estates, including lands, with these freedmen.

Initially federal officials pressed tribal leaders to meet the Reconstruction Treaty requirement that they take steps to establish a single, integrated government for Indian Territory. However, Indian politicians showed a reluctance to act on this obligation, aware of its effect on tribal sovereignty and prerogative. General tribal opposition to this change braced Indian spokesmen in this regard. During 1867 Congress went so far as to appropriate money to pay the expenses to a convention at Okmulgee in the

Creek Nation to discuss the matter, thus removing at least one excuse for noncompliance. The council convened but was attended only by Creek and Cherokee delegations and representatives from the small tribes residing in northeastern Indian Territory. Little was accomplished. A strong deterrent to the tribes moving toward development of an inclusive territorial government was awareness that creating such a government would assure that railroads building through Indian Territory would be granted much larger right-of-way land grants from tribal domains than Indians were prepared to share. It was common knowledge among tribal leaders that railway officials were strong advocates of the organization of a territorial government for Indian Territory. Under strong pressure from federal agents a second intertribal council met at Okmulgee in 1869. Delegations from all five major tribes were in attendance. Although the delegates did little to achieve the expected organization of territorial government, they did gain valuable experience from working toward the common goal of attempting to preserve the integrity of their respective nations.

An impatient Congress went to work on the matter. Senator Benjamin F. Rice of Arkansas introduced a bill providing for organizing "the Territory of Oklahoma." Alarmed Indian leaders forwarded strong resolutions against the Rice bill to the Congress, but it became clear that either the Indians would act or action would be taken for them, perhaps on terms not to their liking. As a result, the intertribal council was summoned to meet at Okmulgee in emergency session on September 27, 1870. Forty delegates attended. A committee headed by Cherokee William P. Ross, editor of the *Cherokee Advocate*, former principal chief, and Princeton graduate, was assigned the task of drafting a constitution for the proposed unified Indian Territory and future Indian state. The council recessed until December 6. When it reconvened, Ross's committee presented the Okmulgee constitution, which was submitted to the Congress. Members of Congress refused to approve the Okmulgee convention's work on the grounds that the Five Civilized Tribes, in their proposed constitution for a unified territory, were unduly insisting on the honoring of treaty rights due them from the federal government. As one observer put it, "Congress was unwilling to concede the measure of independence for Indians set in the terms" of the Okmulgee constitution.

The U.S. Supreme Court worked with the Congress in abetting the dissolution of the Indian nations. Several postwar decisions by that tribunal inflicted telling blows on tribal prerogative and status. A principal instance is the so-called Cherokee Tobacco Case. The Cherokee Reconstruction Treaty of 1866 included a "sleeper" clause which permitted tribal citizens to produce, manufacture, ship, and market any product throughout the United States without restraint, exempt from federal tax. During 1868, Elias C. Boudinot and Stand Watie, prominent Cherokee mixed bloods, purchased a tobacco factory at Hannibal, Missouri, and moved it to the Cherokee nation. At their settlement, called Boudiville, near the Arkansas state line, Boudinot and Watie produced chewing tobacco, snuff, treated leaf, and pipe tobacco. Their principal market, besides the Indian Territory, was in the adjoining southwestern states.

Tobacco dealers in Missouri, Arkansas, and Texas complained that their market was threatened by the untaxed and thus cheaper tobacco produced at Boudiville. Congress responded by adopting revenue laws annulling this treaty-endowed privilege. A posse of federal deputy marshals, responding to a complaint from the commissioner of internal revenue, seized the Boudinot-Watie tobacco works, arrested the Cherokee owners, and confiscated and dismantled their plant. The Indian defendants lost in the lower federal courts but received a hearing in the U.S. Supreme Court on a writ of error. Attorneys for the Cherokees claimed an invasion of rights under the historic principle that the U.S. Constitution and treaties comprised the supreme law of the land, superior to laws of Congress. The high court rendered its decision in 1870. In effect the justices drew a distinction between treaties made with foreign nations and treaties made with Indian tribes, declaring that the 1868 revenue laws did supersede the Cherokee Treaty of 1866, thus upholding the lower court's ruling.

One writer observed, "The proposition that an act of Congress could be intended to, and did in fact, supersede and qualify any provision of a treaty made with an Indian tribe was a startling innovation that alarmed the Indians. It emboldened the whites to predict, and the Indians to fear, that the new principle would be used to break down the protection [against white aggression] found in the terms of . . . treaties." And this is precisely what happened. Hardly three months after the Cherokee Tobacco Case decision, Congress passed the famous resolution which provided that the federal government would make no additional treaties with Indian tribes. Thereafter, all tribes were subject to laws of Congress and administrative rulings of the president and the federal bureaucracy.

Armed with the potent administrative license implied by the Cherokee Tobacco Case decision and concomitant legislation, federal agents moved to further reduce the vitality of tribal governments and Indian status. A major step in this direction occurred during 1871 when jurisdiction of federal courts was extended over Indian Territory in what became an ever-enlarging process, gradually displacing functioning courts of the Five Civilized Tribes. The first step in this process was establishment of a federal district court at Fort Smith, Arkansas, on the eastern border of Indian Territory. Its stated purpose was to eradicate lawlessness in the Indian nations. This condition was due largely to an invasion by non-Indians desperadoes, products of chaotic conditions on the southwestern border during the early postwar years. Isaac Parker became presiding judge and appointed an army of over two hundred deputy marshals who ranged over the Indian nations singly and in squads in a massive outlaw roundup. Parker became internationally notorious as the "hanging judge" of Fort Smith court.

The federal court at Fort Smith and its army of deputy marshals eventually purged crime from Indian Territory, but Indian citizens came to fear and hate this law enforcement agency. Many tribal leaders charged that the court and deputy marshals had become instruments of tyranny. Most of the conflict grew out of questions of jurisdiction. The federal court at Fort Smith had jurisdiction in criminal matters where one or both parties were non-Indian and in cases where non-Indians and Indians were charged with violation of federal laws. An example of conflict beween federal and Indian jurisdiction was the Going Snake Courthouse affair, and it dramatically illustrates an enlarging context of federal intrusion into local affairs of the Five Civilized Tribes. On April 15, 1872, the Cherokee court at Going Snake Courthouse was in session to try a tribal citizen, Ezekial Proctor, for murder of a fellow Cherokee. During the proceedings a posse of deputy marshals from Fort Smith rode up. The federal officers entered the log courthouse and attempted to take Proctor with them to Fort Smith for trial on another charge. Cherokee officials resisted, and, following a lively gun battle, eleven men were killed, seven marshals and four Cherokees. The exchange wounded the trial judge, a juror, and several spectators. In declaring their resentment of the Fort Smith court and its army of deputy marshals, Indian leaders charged that tribal rights were invaded and that federal officials contrived charges in order to drag innocent Indians to Fort Smith, enabling the marshals to collect their mileage and per diem costs.

Between 1866 and 1906 the non-Indian population of Indian Territory increased in a near phenomenal fashion—by 1906, on the eve of Oklahoma statehood, the Indian Territory portion of the proposed state had a population of over 750,000 and only about 100,000 were Indians. To provide a more convenient and effective means for protecting the rights of non-Indians in the territory, Congress in 1889 authorized establishment of a federal court at Muskogee in the Creek nation. Its criminal jurisdiction was limited to such offenses as were not punishable by death or imprisonment. Felony cases involving non-Indians were tried at federal courts in

Fort Smith, Arkansas, Paris, Texas, and Fort Scott, Kansas. The laws of Arkansas were to be applied to Indian Territory insofar as non-Indians were concerned.

Additional reductions in authority of Indian law and jurisdiction of tribal courts occurred between 1890 and 1895. Reflecting the increase in non-Indian population and the concomitant increase in judicial business for this period, federal law divided Indian Territory into three judicial districts. Courts were established at South McAlester (with jurisdiction over the Choctaw nation), at Ardmore (with jurisdiction over the Chickasaw and Seminole nations), and at Muskogee (with jurisdiction over the Cherokee and Creek nations and the Quapaw agency). The three Indian Territory federal judges sat twice each year at South McAlester as a court of appeals to review decisions of the trial courts. Under this arrangement, the three federal courts for Indian Territory tried all cases formerly going to Fort Smith, Paris, or Fort Scott.

In the process of liquidation of the Indian nations as functioning socio-economic-political communities, a prime factor was the startling increase in power of the federal bureaucracy over the tribes and individual Indians. Originally, agents representing the federal government in the Indian nations were similar to resident quasi-diplomatic officials, maintaining the treaty-defined relationships with the tribes. Through the years as the power of the tribes diminished militarily and politically, these agents increasingly directed tribal activity. Defeat in the Civil War was a milestone in collective tribal power decline. The Five Civilized Tribes, as a part of their Reconstruction settlement, were required to undergo military occupation, much like the defeated Confederacy. For several years federal agents assigned to these tribes were military officers. A major move toward reducing the sense of tribal importance occurred in 1874 when federal officials consolidated the individual agencies of the Five Civilized Tribes into the single Union agency under an official designated superintendent of the Five Civilized Tribes, with headquarters at Muskogee.

Native American governments and individuals also contributed to the demise of the Five Civilized Tribes. During the near-phenomenal surge of economic growth that occurred across the United States in the postbellum age great pressure was applied to the Indian nations to open to exploitation their lands which abounded in coal, minerals, timber, and grazing and agricultural resources. Indian leaders, pressed for funds to maintain tribal governments, schools, and other public functions, became increasingly cooperative with non-Indian investors and developers, eventually concluding lease and royalty agreements which did open their territories to mining, lumbering, and farming and grazing enterprises. These commitments generated sustaining annual revenues to tribal treasuries. Railway companies constructed a grid of lines across Indian Territory to support these emerging industries.

Laborers, mechanics, professional persons, farmers, and cattlemen were attracted to Indian Territory by development prospects. Federal law (rarely enforced) and tribal law forbade non-Indians to enter any tribal nation or reservation without proper authority. To meet the requirements of federal and tribal laws, or to evade them, the rapidly increasing population of intruders and Indian politicians worked out complex arrangements. Marriage was one approach. By wedding an Indian woman, a non-Indian gained the privileges and benefits of tribal citizenship, including exemption from taxes and free use of tribal land. To hasten economic development tribal governments adopted "permit laws," which allowed non-Indian mechanics and laborers and their families to settle in the Indian nations. The permit system was an important source of revenue for tribal governments. The annual license or permit cost $2.50 for laborers and $5.00 for mechanics and farmers. Graduated fees were applied to immigrant lawyers, bankers, coal and timber operators, and railroad promoters.

This "silent migration" became an increasingly powerful force in Indian Territory politics and played a strategic role in achieving the ultimate demise of the Five Civilized Tribes as functioning political entities. By about 1900 non-Indians outnumbered Indians in the territory nearly ten to one. But despite their minority status, Indians retained all political authority and their tribal governments owned all the land. Also, tribal schools were open only to Indian children. Even in the towns, non-Indian business and professional men could not own the land occupied by their stores, banks, and office buildings. Their ever-enlarging presence and escalating pressure on federal officials for resolution of their political and economic limitations became the final precipitant for drastic change in the status of the Five Civilized Tribes.

These conditions meshed well with a substantive change in Indian policy which was aborning. A group of eastern reformers, self-styled "Friends of the Indian," concluded that for the good of native Americans, their system of common (tribal) ownership of land should be terminated. "Friends of the Indian" argued that an Indian's ownership of a patch of land would accomplish that much-desired transformation to a mainstream American, an alternating goal of certain federal officials since Jefferson's time with his hopes for ultimate assimilation of the American Indian. Their ideas were put into practice in the form of allotment in severalty, the ultimate in the reduction and appropriation of the tribal estate. It was carried out under the General Allotment Act, popularly called the Dawes Act, adopted in 1887. This statute authorized the president to direct the survey of each nation and reservation, the preparation of tribal rolls, and the assignment of an allotment, generally 160 acres, to each tribal member. Intense lobbying by leaders of the Five Civilized Tribes resulted initially in their exemption from the Dawes Act; however, in 1893 Congress applied the full force of this measure to them. A federal administrative tribunal, the Dawes Commission, headed by Senator Henry L. Dawes, was directed to manage the liquidation of the landed estates of the Five Civilized Tribes. Tribal leaders adamantly refused to meet with the Dawes Commission to discuss allotment of their communally owned lands. Therefore Congress in 1896 delegated to the Dawes Commission authority unilaterally to prepare rolls and proceed with allotment. Thereupon tribal resistance began to cave.

In 1897 the Choctaws and Chickasaws concluded the Atoka Agreement with the Dawes Commission, a contract providing for total allocation of their lands to tribal citizens. The other tribes persisted in delay so Congress in 1898 passed the Curtis Act, which abolished tribal governments, required tribal citizens to submit to allotment, instituted civil government for Indian Territory, and provided a guide for statehood. The Curtis Act forced the other tribes to capitulate; the Seminoles signed their allotment contract in 1898, the Creeks in 1901, and the Cherokees in 1902. The tribes' allotment contracts stipulated allotments to their former slaves. Thousands of blacks from Texas, Louisiana, Arkansas, and Mississippi swarmed across Indian Territory claiming descent from former slaves of the Indians, joining additional thousands of whites claiming a sufficient tincture of Indian blood to merit enrollment. The Dawes Commission prepared to enroll nearly a half million persons claiming to be of Chickasaw, Choctaw, Seminole, Creek, or Cherokee descent, or former slaves of these tribesmen. Indian leaders refused to permit wholesale, unchallenged enrollment. They formed tribal citizenship commissions which examined all applicants' qualifications and rejected 75 percent of the claimants. The Dawes Commission finally enrolled 101,000 persons deemed eligible for allotments on the domains of the Five Civilized Tribes.

Allotments varied in size. Each Choctaw and Chickasaw received about 320 acres; Creeks, 160 acres each; Seminoles, 120 acres each; and each Cherokee, about 110 acres. The Reconstruction Treaties' requirements that Indians share their tribal estates with freedmen applied in the distribution of tribal lands. Cherokee, Creek, and Seminole former slaves and descendants shared equally with Indians in size of allotment, while Choctaw-

Chickasaw freedmen and descendants each received an allotment of 40 acres.

Through Dawes Commission negotiations with the Five Civilized Tribes, it was agreed that all tribal governments were to cease operation in 1906. Since the Curtis Act preempted their judicial functions, the Indian governments operated until statehood only on a caretaker basis, with most of their activities devoted to disposing of public property.

The trauma of changing from the ancient common ownership of the tribal estate to private ownership of property, the inevitability of statehood, and the dreadful prospects of being attached to Oklahoma Territory to form the new state of Oklahoma fired Indian nationalists to resist. Revolt against allotment appeared in each of the Five Civilized Tribes, primarily among the full bloods, who believed that the Great Holy Force Above had ordained certain things for Indians, including their land system; to them, taking an allotment was violation of a sacred ordinance. The full-blood Keetoowah society among the Cherokees demonstrated, and 5,000 refused to be enrolled for allotments. Finally, the Dawes Commission assigned federal marshals to carry out the full-blood allotment assignments. The most deadly resistance to allotment occurred among the Creeks, where Chitto Harjo led a protest movement known as the Crazy Snake Rebellion. Harjo presumed to establish a new Creek government based on traditional tribal law and custom. His followers arrested tribesmen who accepted allotments and whipped them in public. Chief Pleasant Porter called on the United States for help, and cavalry from Fort Reno rounded up ninety-four Creek rebels. They were tried at Muskogee in federal court and finally accepted allotments as a condition of being set free.

Indian politicians also met regularly, seeking ways to obstruct fusion with Oklahoma Territory. Principal Chiefs W. C. Rogers of the Cherokees, Pleasant Porter of the Creeks, and Green McCurtain of the Choctaws issued a call during 1905 for a statehood convention, scheduled to meet at Muskogee on August 21, 1905. Its purpose was to prepare a constitution for an Indian state to be called Sequoyah. The 182 delegates elected Porter president of the convention; Alexander Posey, popular Creek poet and political essayist, was elected secretary.

The work of the Sequoyah Convention resulted in a well-written document which fairly well followed the traditional pattern of American constitutional government. A referendum for adoption of the Sequoyah constitution by the voters of Indian Territory yielded an overwhelming vote of approval. However, Congress rejected that document and adopted the Oklahoma Enabling Act, directing the fusion of Oklahoma and Indian Territories into the new state of Oklahoma. The melancholy destiny of the Five Civilized Tribes, initiated in the 1820s, had been reached.


## SUGGESTED READING

The demise of the Southern Indian nations (Cherokee, Creek, Choctaw, Seminole, and Chickasaw) can be traced from about 1500–1803 in the records and literature generated by European imperial intruders. Their successor, the United States, shares this melancholy legacy in documents covering the period from colonial times to 1871 when the Congress acknowledged the desperate and near complete erosion of red power by adopting the statute which brought the Indian nations under the direct dominion of federal law and the rulings of the president and his subalterns. Principal records documenting United States/Southern Indian relations, particularly as to national intent, euphemistically called "policy," includes *American State Papers* and records of the Department of War, Department of Interior (Bureau of Indian Affairs), and General Land Office; *United States Statutes at Large*; and Charles J. Kappler (comp. and ed.), *Indian Affairs: Laws and Treaties* (Washington, 1904), 3 vols. Archives of the states of Florida, Alabama, Georgia, Tennessee, and Mississippi yield published legislative histories revealing public intent vis-à-vis the resident Indian nations and their lands which was expressed in repressive laws that coerced these nations to vacate their ancestral estates in the Old Southwest and to emigrate to the Western wilderness. Several volumes of *Territorial Papers of the United States*, edited by Clarence E. Carter, enlarge the record of calculated repression and permissive violence and intimidation inflicted by state militia and citizens to induce leaders of tribal governments to assent to removal. *Redskins, Ruffleshirts, and Rednecks: Indian Allotments in Alabama and Mississippi, 1830–1860* (Norman, 1962), by Mary Elizabeth Young, is the prime study on this collective outrage. Gloria Jahoda, *The Trail of Tears* (New York, 1975), is the most recent study of the tribal ordeal. The writings of Grant Foreman, *The Five Civilized Tribes* (Norman, 1934), *Indian Removal* (Norman, 1932), *Indians and Pioneers* (New Haven, 1930), and *Pioneer Days in the Early Southwest* (Cleveland, 1926) show the shattering impact of relocation from the Old Southwest to Indian Territory on these ethnic Americans. The Cherokee ordeal has received major literary attention. Principal studies include James Mooney *Myths of the Cherokees* (Washington, 1900); Grace Steele Woodward, *The Cherokees* (Norman, 1963);

Thurman Wilkins, *Cherokee Tragedy* (New York, 1970); and Ralph Gabriel, *Elias Boudinot and His America* (Norman, 1941). The Choctaw uprooting and subsequent Western experience is the subject of Arthur H. DeRosier's *The Removal of the Choctaw Indians* (Knoxville, 1970) and Angie Debo's *Rise and Fall of the Choctaw Republic* (Norman, 1931). The Creek removal and adjustment experience in Indian Territory is discussed in Debo's *The Road to Disappearance: A History of the Creek Indians* (Norman, 1941). Edwin D. McReynolds traces the reluctant Seminole Nation from a decade of bloody resistance to forced emigration to Indian Territory under military guard in *The Seminoles* (Norman, 1957). And the Chickasaw removal experience and adjustment to life in Indian Territory is the subject of Arrell Morgan Gibson's *The Chickasaws* (Norman, 1971). Callous handling of the removal by government contractors which contributed to population declines in each of the emigrating nations up to one-fourth by death due to poisoned rations and malnutrition is the subject of Ethan Allen Hitchcock's *A Traveler in Indian Territory* (Cedar Rapids, 1930). Muriel H. Wright's *A Guide to the Indian Tribes of Oklahoma* (Norman, 1951) supplies essential settlement and adjustment information on the five Indian nations as well as an illuminating bibliography. Lester Hargrett's *Bibliography of the Constitutions and Laws of the American Indians* (Cambridge, 1947) illustrates efforts by the Southern tribe to maintain their political integrity with enlightened organic law.

# Part III  Visions of a New Order

William T. Hagan

# 12. Reformers' Images of the Native Americans

## The Late Nineteenth Century

**F**orty years after the founding of the Indian Rights Association, Herbert Welsh, a founder of the association and its guiding force during its first twenty years, characterized its members. "They are," stated Welsh proudly, "the elite of New England, New York, and Philadelphia, sober old society." The same could have been said of most of the members of the other organizations of reformers, or "friends of the Indians," as they liked to describe themselves. As a group they shared another quality: they were devout Christians, members of the Protestant denominations and the Friends (Quaker) societies. Until very late in the nineteenth century, Roman Catholics, although quite active in Indian work, labored almost exclusively through the church's Bureau of Catholic Indian Missions, which was not a part of the coalition of reformers.

The reformers discussed in this chapter belonged to the many organizations that sprang up in the twenty years following the Civil War. With one exception, the Board of Indian Commissioners, they were private organizations with no official status. In contrast, the Board of Indian Commissioners was authorized by Congress in 1869. However, its members were private citizens of a philanthropic bent who served without pay and shared their concern for, and views of, Indians.

The Indian Rights Association was just the most prominent of the reformer's organizations that proliferated in the late 1870s and early 1880s— "proliferated" because the list is long, although most had an ephemeral existence. Besides the Indian Rights Association and the Board of Indian Commissioners, at least three others should be mentioned. Two of them, the Women's National Indian Association and the Boston Indian Citizenship Committee, had their origins in 1879, the former in Philadelphia. The fifth group, the one least inclined to pull in the traces with the others, was the National Indian Defense Association. Although it did not appear until 1885, its founder, Dr. T. A. Bland, had been associated with A. B. Meacham who, in 1878, founded a monthly, *The Council Fire*, to publicize his views of the Indian cause.

There were differences among the reformers, however, the remarkable thing is the degree to which they were in agreement on the potential of the Indian and the policies to be pursued to realize this potential. Dr. Bland and his National Indian Defense Association were even less inclined than Meacham, who died in 1882, to coerce the Indians. Nevertheless, they agreed with the other groups that ultimately the Indian could and should be absorbed into American society.

The Indian policy consensus, as indeed it was, was arrived at through two annual meetings. The first to begin was that of the Board of Indian Commissioners with representatives of missionary societies, later expanded to include Indian rights associations. It was a logical development because President Grant not only had sought the advice and counsel of the Board of Indian Commissioners, he also brought the churches into the Indian Service by permitting them to nominate agency employees. This meeting was held in Washington, usually in January, the first one in 1870. In attendance would be not only the members of the board, and the representatives of the missionary societies and the Indian rights associations, but also heads of boarding schools, such as General S. C. Armstrong and Captain Richard H. Pratt, as well as officials of the Indian Service. Journals of the January meetings, complete with speeches made and recommendations agreed upon, were included in the annual reports of the Board of Indian Commissioners. Thus not only did the meeting facilitate agreement among friends of the Indians who attended, the printed report enabled others to discover the "party line," the strategy for dealing with Indians and federal Indian policy as advocated by many reformers.

An even more celebrated opportunity for consensus was provided by the Lake Mohonk Conferences, which began in 1883 and continued throughout the late nineteenth century. Although they attracted more participants than the January meeting hosted by the Board of Indian Commissioners, the Mohonk Conferences drew from the same group. Every year several who had gathered in Washington in January for that meeting would see one another again in October or late September at Lake Mohonk. The Lake Mohonk Conference also published an annual report, which helped to keep everyone interested in the Indian question aware of what was being discussed and agreed upon among the friends of the Indian.

The images of the Indian held by the reformers naturally reflected the status of Indians in the United States at the time. When the Board of Indian Commissioners was founded, and the churches were invited to participate in the administration of the Indian Service, the Plains tribes and the Apaches were still unconquered. There still remained large areas of the West which were unorganized territories, closed to white settlement. Within the next thirty years the population of the United States nearly doubled, jumping from less than forty million in 1870 to over seventy-five million in 1900. As a result, the pressure on Indian land intensified, and new states and territories were organized. This pressure helped account for the last wave of bloody Indian wars and the restriction of the tribesmen to the reservation.

Reformers were in general agreement that Indian civilization, as contrasted with that of the whites, was at a lower evolutionary stage, many generations behind. At the 1890 Mohonk Conference, the Reverend James McCosh, a former president of Princeton University, compared the Indians with the ancient Britons. The Britons, McCosh pointed out, had also painted their bodies, worn animal skins, and been pagan. However, as McCosh phrased it:

> From this race, or a like race, the great body of the people of that country have sprung, and most of those present at this convention.

> I am sure that by the grace of God and the same means the Indians may be raised to a like belief and civilization.

Five years later at Lake Mohonk, the Reverend M. E. Strieby of the Presbyterian missionary society made a similar comparison, this time with Highland Scots. Strieby declared that like the native Americans, the Highlanders, "before their sudden transformation into a civilized people," consisted of idle men and toiling women, the men's energies being reserved for revenge, robbery, and murder. But like the ancient Britons, the Highlanders had passed rapidly from barbarism to civilization by breaking the power of the clan chiefs and by introducing education and the church. Reverend Strieby was confident the same might be done for the Indians.

Reverend Strieby's reference to idle men was a common criticism of Indian society by the reformers. *City and State*, the weekly newspaper of which Herbert Welsh was editor and publisher, explained it as "the indolence of barbarism lacking civilization's incentives to work." Even Dr. Bland portrayed the Indian as living a life of "careless indolence," as contrasted with the civilized life of "careful industry."

Dr. Bland, like other reformers, believed Indians must demonstrate proper industry by farming. He acknowledged that tribes like the Cherokees had been agriculturalists before the arrival of the white man, but Bland said they had "farmed in a very small way, and in a very primitive fashion." If most tribes had been agriculturalists in the fashion of white settlers, said the good doctor, the white man would not "have felt at liberty to kill them . . . and take their lands from them."

Welsh also viewed the conversion to farming as "in every instance . . . the first step which the Indian takes toward civilization." Raising cattle, in contrast, would not get the job done: "From its nomadic character," the life of a herdsman, said Welsh, " . . . is hostile to settled home life, while its loneliness and isolation are equally so."

But not only the Indian economy must be transformed, so must his social and political organization. Polygamy must be banned and as *Council Fire*, the organ of Meacham and Bland, put it: "Not until Indian women are recognized as women, and the men taught by precept and example to honor and respect womanhood, and that marriage is lawful and honorable, and to be honored, will the Indian race advance." The transitory quality of the marriage relationship in most Indian societies clearly, and understandably, shocked these Victorians.

*Council Fire* also advised the native American, if he hoped to be civilized, to "abandon many of his old superstitions in religious matters." On that subject the 1895 Lake Mohonk platform likewise spoke for the reformers: "Our American civilization is founded upon Christianity. A pagan people can not be fitted for citizenship without learning the principles and acquiring something of the spirit of a Christian people."

For a religious people themselves, the reformers seemed incapable of comprehending the value to Indians of their religions. Welsh dismissed a Navajo medicine dance he observed in 1885 as "neither a very interesting nor edifying performance." However, that was a relatively sophisticated reaction compared with a proposal he had made three years earlier on his first exposure to Indians. Visiting the Rosebud Sioux Reservation shortly after the annual Sun Dance, the most important ceremonial of the Plains Indian, Welsh suggested the government "turn this heathen festival into a Fourth of July Picnic. . . ." Nearly twenty years later he was still railing against "Indian dances which are the nursery and citadel of the superstitious and vicious elements of Indian life."

The reformers also were unanimous in viewing Indian communal ownership of property as incompatible with civilization. What was missing was the "selfishness" which drove the white man, as two people as disparate as

Dr. Bland and Senator H. L. Dawes agreed. It was this consensus that ultimately led to the Dawes Land in Severalty Act of 1887 and a rash of special
agreements negotiated in the 1890s to provide allotment in severalty for
most of the large reservations.

The theory, of course, had developed a large following among government officials and private citizens well before the late nineteenth century.
The Board of Indian Commissioners included it as one of its recommendations in its very first report in 1869 and every year reiterated the recommendation. It also was routinely endorsed by the Mohonk conferences and
the joint meetings of the Board of Indian Commissioners and the representatives of the missionary societies. The Indian Rights Association made it
one of the recommendations of its first annual report. Furthermore, Mrs.
Amelia Quinton, the leading light of the Women's National Indian Association reminded an audience in 1896 that as early as 1881 her organization had petitioned the government to invoke severalty.

Helen Hunt Jackson's celebrated *A Century of Dishonor* was devoted almost entirely to a scathing indictment of U.S. Indian policy. However, in
the brief space she reserved for policy recommendation was an endorsement of severalty: "The utter absence of invididual title to particular lands
deprives every [Indian] . . . of the chief incentive to labor and exertion—
the very mainspring on which the prosperity of a people depends."

Dr. Bland, although unwilling to push the Indian into it, believed that:
"Land in severalty and citizenship must come and will come to the Indians. It is the ultimate solution to the Indian problem."

Welsh and the Indian Rights Association strongly favored allotment in
severalty. Urging the passage of the Dawes Bill, Welsh said it was needed,
"To break down the walls which separate the Indian today from our own
world of thought and action. . . ." After its passage he defended it as
"the bridge over which the Indian may be led from barbarism to civilization. . . ." "The Indian," Welsh continued, "must become in all respects
like ourselves, or else become extinct under the action of those unrestrain-
able forces of civilization which will not tolerate savage and tribal life."

It was recognized by the reformers that the transition from "barbarism
to civilization" would be a traumatic experience for the Indian. Again
Welsh provides the illustration. After visiting the Omahas and Winneba-
goes in 1892, he described them as being in

> the middle of that swift and treacherous stream which divides civiliza-
> tion from barbarism and which all Indians must cross. Doubtless its
> current will carry some away and its quicksands will engulf others,

while those who succeed in getting safely over into the promised land will be both stronger and cleaner than they would have been were they not forced to cross it.

The reformers pointed with pride to those who had made the transition. Those examples of what an Indian could become were invited to the annual meetings and were always singled out for praise when visited on their reservations.

It should be noted also, that the reformers, many of whom were also interested in the plight of American blacks, insisted there was a difference between the races. And in this comparison the Indians usually emerged the winner. One reformer, for example, attributed to them unspecified "noble traits" not shared by the blacks.

Captain Pratt, founder of Carlisle Institute, was an educator who was very concerned about not placing Indians in situations where they would be lumped with blacks for fear that the Indians would suffer from guilt by association. Indeed, Pratt was reluctant to even send Indians out in groups because immediately, whether in churches or public schools, they would be segregated as a group and treated differently.

In general, the reformers were not disturbed by the intermarriage of Indians and whites. There was criticism of the "squawman," the contemporary term for the white man who married an Indian woman, but this was based on the assumption that the man's motivation usually was to get at the property of the woman's tribe. What might have been expected to be the more sensitive subject of the marriage of Indian men to white women actually was approved, if the Indian were a representative of the progressive wing of his tribe. For example, the union of Elaine Goodale, a young white woman active in Indian work, and Dr. Charles Eastman, an educated Sioux, inspired no critical comment.

There was even one class of white man whom the reformers constantly compared unfavorably with the native Americans. This was the Board of Indian Commissioners referred to in 1899 as "The fringe of lawless and dissolute men who too often hung about its borders, taught Indians the white man's vices and prevented true ideals of civilized Christian life from reaching the Indians." In the earlier years when reformers were on the defensive about Indian raids, they retaliated by blaming white frontiersmen. William Nicholson, the Quaker presiding over the Central Superintendency in 1871, illustrates this tactic. Kiowas under his supervision were raiding into Texas. Nicholson's image of the Kiowas had them simply retaliating for having been "engaged in stockraising and doing well." The villains were white men, "worse than Indians" in Nicholson's phrase, who took Kiowa land in Texas and then invaded their reservation in Oklahoma to steal their horses. The "demoralizing influence of the class of white persons always found upon frontier settlements" was a major argument offered for the reservation system by the Board of Indian Commissioners in 1874.

This tendency to form an image of frontiersmen as worse than Indians is further illustrated by statements of Henry S. Pancoast and Philip C. Garrett. Pancoast was Welsh's companion on a trip made to the Sioux reservations in 1882, their first real exposure to Indians. Pancoast described his first native Americans in glowing terms: "tall fine looking men, the faces of many showing great character and intelligence." The Indian women he found to have "generally pleasant and gentle faces." Contrast that with his comments on western whites whom he encountered on the train that took him into Dakota territory. They were "the Falstaff's army of discontented, unsuccessful men—the gamblers, emigrants, and convicts—that go out as representatives of our dominant race to conquer the wilderness. . . ." Even an attractive young German girl who caught his attention was dismissed as having "meaningless blue eyes."

However, it was the gentle Philadelphia Quaker, Garrett, president for several years of the Indian Rights Association and a member of the Board of Indian Commissioners, the very embodiment of the reformer, who delivered the most damning indictment of white frontiersman. He identified hate and avarice as the "two deadly foes to Indian civilization," both of them embodied by white men:

> The more than savage, the satanic, hate of the fiends in human shape, whose thirst for adventure and blood allures them to the wild life on the border, and the equally satanic avarice, whose selfish clutch tolerates no bar of humanity nor morality between it and the gratification of its cupidity.

Although, in general, reformers agreed on the Indian's potential and how to best move him toward civilization, some dissent was inevitable. Meacham and Bland, as already noted, were inclined to see the Indian as less desperately in need of civilization. George Bird Grinnell, an ethnologist and author of some excellent studies on Plains Indians, opposed premature allotment of tribes such as the Pawnee and Cheyenne whom he did not believe were ready for it. But, it was another ethnologist and reformer, Alice Fletcher, who made the best defense of the native American and his way of life.

In a magazine article in 1883, Fletcher presented an image of the native American far removed from the savage sorely in need of civilization, which was usually envisioned by the reformers. She dismissed the idea of Indian anarchy by sketching a closely knit tribal society based on clans and phratries, with tribes united in some instances in confederacies. Fletcher also defended the Indian against the charge of indolence and sloth, heard so often at Lake Mohonk and elsewhere, stressing the "grave responsibility" of the hunter in a society "dependent upon the precariousness of game." After giving him high marks for honesty and faithfulness, she still concluded the Indian would have to change because the "peculiar environment" that had shaped him no longer existed. Fletcher was that unusual reformer who turned her energies to the practical problems. She served as an allotting agent for the government, bringing the severalty, in which she so firmly believed, to the Omahas and other tribes.

What kept Alice Fletcher in the good graces of the reformers was her wholehearted support of the thesis that the tribesmen must abandon his native life-style, regardless of how appropriate it may once have been. Other ethnologists were suspected of opposing integration. At Lake Mohonk in 1886, Garrett first deplored the romanticization of the Indian, criticizing "pandering, on the part of historians, to the popular craving for the picturesque." But he saved his heaviest fire for the ethnologists—specifically exempting Fletcher, whose philanthropy "swallowed up her anthropology." Other ethnologists, he feared, desired "to preserve these utensils for the study of his specialty." As Garrett acknowledged:

> Every tribe converted to civilized ways removes one more living illustration of ethnology, and remands to the past crystallization of written records and museum collections all search into those customs and manners and implements so much easily read in the living tribe.

In June 1893, John Wesley Powell, the director of the Smithsonian's Bureau of Ethnology, made a request of the commissioner of Indian Affairs that illustrates why the reformers disapproved of ethnologists. Powell asked the commissioner to permit the holding of the Kiowa Medicine Dance, which had been prohibited by the Kiowa agent, as "it seems probable that the approaching date for the Medicine Dance will afford one of the last opportunities for studying the ceremonial." This was essential, claimed Powell, because observation of such ceremonials "give exceptional facilities for the study of legendary lore from which the prehistoric origin and development of customs and beliefs may sometimes be ascertained." This is the sort of thing that Welsh denounced as:

the natural conflict between a spirit that would use these Indians for ethnological purposes and, therefore seeks to keep them much as they are, and the Christian spirit which would seek to develop them into a higher manhood and womanhood.

Although they had their differences, Welsh and Captain Pratt saw eye-to-eye on the baneful influence of ethnologists. Pratt accused Powell of "a deep fear that our work would destroy the Indian in the Indian before the Science of Ethnology had developed all the hidden and conjectural history of the Indians." Captain Pratt was not a member of the reformers. However, he depended on them for support, attended their meetings in Washington and Lake Mohonk, and espoused their view that the salvation of the Indian was through integration into American society.

Where Pratt could be distinguished from the reformers was in the way he would implement the change. Pratt was a radical, advocating extreme measures. He had no patience with the reservation system for preparing the Indian for civilization and assimilation, condemning reservations as "prisons." Pratt believed the Indian had to be "individualized." "Christ's mission was to save individuals," he said, "and our efforts must take the same direction else they fail." He opposed granting the Indians allotments in severalty because the allotments "anchored" them to the reservation, forcing them to remain in a "mass of ignorance." By 1900 Captain Pratt found himself increasingly isolated as a result of his abrasive comments on the reformers.

Although he could not agree with most of Pratt's radical program, Senator Dawes did share with Pratt a growing contempt for the reformers. Like Pratt, Senator Dawes frequently attended the reformers' meetings in Washington and at Lake Mohonk, and he welcomed their support when their views coincided. Like Pratt, however, the Senator was inclined to dismiss them as visionaries. To his wife, who had attended the 1888 Lake Mohonk Conference when he did not, Dawes confided his dismay at the conferences' "airing and endorsement of the impracticable schemes of theorists." When Harvard Law School Professor James Bradley Thayer, a member of both the Boston Indian Citizenship Committee and the Indian Rights Association, proposed legislation designed to bring law to the reservation, Dawes was particularly annoyed. Sometime later, describing Thayer to Pratt as one of the Boston "doctrinaires," the Senator deprecated the professor's proposal as a bill drafted in a library by a man who had never "seen an Indian on a reservation." Dawes even disagreed with the reformers about the implementation of the severalty law that carried his name, arguing that they were urging it on Indians not ready for it. "Severalty must follow, not precede the transition from a wild blanket Indian to one having some aspirations for a better life," stated the Senator.

Between 1865 and 1900 reformer's images of the Indian had changed very little. The easy optimism of the 1880s, after the Plains wars had ended and the reservation programs had begun to function, had disappeared. By the 1890s the reformers were disputing with each other about details of the civilization policies. Were rations and annuities pauperizing the Indian, and therefore should be abolished? Should Indian landholdings be further reduced to provide them capital to develop the land they retained? Were day schools or boarding schools best, and should students attending them be supplied government rations and have their tuition paid from tribal funds? Should the funds themselves be distributed per capita to eliminate another crutch for tribalism?

But what was not debatable was the basic image of the native American held throughout this period by the reformers. He was their fellow human being and child of God, endowed with the potential to take his place in American society as a full-fledged citizen. And in this they never wavered. Today, cultural pluralism has achieved an acceptance that causes hypersensitivity to the reformers' ethnocentrism. One flinches at their casual talk of savages and barbarism. But, placed in the context of their times, the reformers' evaluation of the Indian and their willingness to work for his acceptance as a full-fledged fellow citizen deserve recognition and commendation.

## SUGGESTED READING

There is a substantial literature on the reformers. The pioneering work, and one still valuable, was Loring Benson Priest, *Uncle Sam's Stepchildren* (New Brunswick, 1942). Henry E. Fritz, *The Movement for Indian Assimilation, 1860–1890* (Philadelphia, 1963) and Robert Lewis Merdock, *The Reformers and the American Indian* (Columbia, 1971) have expanded on some of Priest's themes. Larry E. Burgess, *The Lake Mohonk Conferences on the Indian, 1883–1916* (Ann Arbor, 1979) traces their history. Important too is Everett Arthur Gilcreast, *Richard Henry Pratt and American Indian Policy, 1877–1906* (Ann Arbor, 1968). *Americanizing the American Indian* (Cambridge, 1973), edited by F. Paul Prucha, contains statements by many of the leading figures on aspects of Indian policy. Prucha, *American Indian Policy in Crisis: Christian Reformers and the Indian, 1865– 1900* (Norman, 1976) is the most recent and best survey of the subject. Robert F. Berkhofer, Jr., *The White Man's Indian: Images of the American Indian from Columbus to the Present* (New York, 1978) has one chapter particularly pertinent for this essay, and other chapters provide valuable background.

David Wallace Adams

# 13. From Bullets to Boarding Schools

The Educational Assault on the American Indian Identity

**E**ven after the military battles had all been fought and the Indian was at last confined within the boundaries of the reservation, his subjugation was still not complete. The process merely shifted to new ground, where a more subtle, but no less fateful chapter in the history of Indian-white relations was about to unfold. If "civilization" was to defeat "savagism"—this was how the confrontation between the two races was defined—then civilization must ultimately win a victory over the Indian that was both psychological and intellectual. In the end, it required that the Indian come to accept the idea that his defeat at the hands of whites was not only in the interests of a higher good—civilization—but in his own best interests as well. It was a matter of common sense to policymakers that the best hope for accomplishing their assimilative aims was to concentrate their efforts on the younger generation of Indians, those not fully confirmed in the old tribal ways of their ancestors. In a word, what was required was an aggressive educational program. The next campaign against the Indian, then, was to be waged in the classroom. The issue at hand was no longer the dispossession of the Indian's land, but rather the possession of his mind, heart, and soul. It was to be a gentle war, but a war just the same.

To understand this next phase of federal Indian policy, it is necessary to understand the mind frame from which policymakers operated. The program they came to erect followed naturally from a series of beliefs which they held as to the Indian's past and future and the power of education as a social and elevating force. The first of these beliefs related to the idea of civilization and its opposite, savagism. The idea here was that some peoples on the globe were more civilized than others. Portrayed as a ladder, the upper rung representing civilization, the lower rung representing savagism, it was believed that some societies such as the nations of Europe and the United States had climbed the ladder of civilization to its highest rung, while other less fortunate peoples were still positioned near the bottom. The Indian, it was held, was still largely a savage. The reasons for this classification stemmed from several factors: his paganism; his lack of appreciation for the values of hard work and private property; his distain for sedentary farming; his entanglement in a weblike network of clans, kinship systems, and religious societies; his casual, even hostile, attitude toward monogamous marriage; and finally, his blind loyalty to hereditary tribal chiefs. It was a long list. And while those who spoke about such matters often possessed little accurate information on the actual nature of Indian lifeways, they remained confident they knew what they were talking about. Whites were civilized; Indians were savages. It was that simple.

A second belief of policymakers stemmed from their view of history as one vast moral tale infused with symbolic meaning. History, in short, was the story of man's progressive evolution from savagism to civilization. Indeed, because civilization was morally superior to savagism, it was virtually an immutable law of history that the former would triumph over the latter. All of this had profound implications for the Indian. For as a relic of an earlier primitive social order, the Indian could no longer continue to exist as an Indian—that is to say, as a savage. To survive, he must choose the path of civilized progress; to reject that path was to invite a well-deserved extinction. The price of the Indian's survival, then, was his cultural suicide. As Henry Price, commissioner of Indian Affairs, expressed it in 1881:

> There is no one who has been a close observer of Indian history and the effect of contact of Indians with civilizations, who is not well satisfied that one of two things must eventually take place, to wit, either civilization or extermination of the Indian. Savage and civilized life cannot live and prosper on the same ground. One of the two must die. If the Indians are to be civilized and become a happy and prosperous people, which is certainly the object and intention of our government, they must learn our language and adopt our modes of life. We are fifty millions of people, and they are only one-fourth of one million. The few must yield to the many.

It was when policymakers addressed the question of how to go about accomplishing the Indian's assimilation that the discussion turned to education. Whereas under normal circumstances it might take the Indian several hundred years to climb to the upper rungs on the ladder of civilization, reformers believed that an aggressive educational campaign could accomplish the Indian's civilization in a single generation. The power of education, then, was that it could speed up the historical evolutionary process. The trick was to gain access to the Indian's mind while it was still malleable, still open to the civilized teachings of whites. If this could be accomplished, if Indian youth could be taught the skills and ideas of white civilization, then the rising generation of Indians could be provided with the necessary means to survive in the white man's world. If after all this the Indian still chose to reject the ways of civilization, then he must face the consequence—extinction. And if it should turn out like this, then at least policymakers could find comfort in the thought that they had fulfilled their Christian responsibility toward the nation's aboriginal wards. But reformers remained optimistic that the Indian could be saved. The answer lay in education. What was needed was schools.

The subsequent rise of the Indian school system represents a dramatic shift in late nineteenth-century federal Indian policy. One need only look at the increase in annual congressional appropriations to see the change. In 1877, Congress appropriated $20,000 for Indian education; by 1880, $75,000; by 1885, $992,800; and by 1890, $1,364,368. Similarly, as the number of schools multiplied during this same period, Indian school attendance increased from a mere 3,598 in 1877 to 12,232 in 1890. While these figures are impressive, they belie the fact that the growth of the Indian school service was in many ways a fitful and chaotic story. For behind the consensus on the power of education as an instrument of assimilation, there was deep disagreement over the most efficacious means of carrying out the educational campaign. More specifically, policymakers differed as to which type of school was best suited to accomplish their aims: the reservation day school, the reservation boarding school, or the off-reservation boarding school.

Some favored the reservation day school. The day school usually took the form of the familiar one room schoolhouse, but, in this case, it was often attached to a modest residence for the teacher and perhaps a small kitchen to provide for the pupils' noontime meals. On larger reservations, there were often several such schools scattered across the landscape, built conveniently near Indian villages. The day school had several advantages. A significant argument in its favor was that it engendered the least amount of resistance from parents. Another advantage was that it held out the possibility of enabling teachers to influence Indian parents through their children, the children, in a sense, becoming messengers of civilization. And finally, of the three approaches it was the least expensive to operate. But in spite of these merits, the day school suffered from one major defect: as an instrument designed to assimilate Indians it was simply ineffective. While it might introduce the Indian child to the mysteries of reading, writing, and arithmetic, it was ill-prepared to accomplish the task at hand; it failed to turn Indian children into whitemen.

The rise of the second type of school—the reservation boarding school—resulted from two weaknesses in the day school approach. First, since many Indians still lived a seminomadic life-style, even behind reservation walls, the day school simply failed to reach large numbers of children. Second, the day school's influence over the child was limited to only those hours of school attendance. Teachers often complained of the fact that their efforts to teach children the ways of whites were undermined by the omnipresent realities of camp life to which the child returned at night and on weekends. What was needed, it was argued, was to place the child in a totally civilized environment, an environment so controlled that the child's every act could be observed, monitored, and altered. The reservation boarding school promised to do just this.

By the 1870s most Indian reservations could claim a boarding school. In what would become an annual fall ritual, Indian children were rounded up by the agency police force, often at gunpoint, and carted off to school. Once in school students not only received instruction in academic subjects but in the manual trades as well, with most attention being given to teaching the Indian child how to farm. Some schools even had some cattle and a few sheep so students might try their hand at raising stock. But just as important as the boarding school's program in the practical arts was the fact that now, under the continuing watchful eye of school officials, the Indian student could be taught to walk, eat, sleep, pray, dress, and think like whites. While deluded old Indians might harbor thoughts of still teaching tribal youth the old ways of life and belief, all this could be more difficult when Indian youth were sequestered behind the school's barbed wire fence for nine months out of the year, their entire range of experiences limited to the world of the boarding school.

But as school and government officials soon learned, the reservation boarding school was not without its problems. While it was indeed more effective than the day school, in its own way it suffered from the same old problem. Put simply, by being located on the reservation, it was still too close to the source of savagism. While students were prevented from having daily contact with their parents, school life was still effected by the pulse of reservation affairs beyond the school gate. While institutionalized, students would still intuitively sense when their relatives were moving out for the fall hunt; they could still steal a glimpse of family members as they gathered at the agency for the semimonthly distribution of annuity goods; and they could still hear, or at least imagined that they could hear, the echo of ceremonial drums in the surrounding hills. Then too, there was the familiar problem of relapse, although now it took on an altogether different form. Whereas before it happened on a daily basis, now it took the more dramatic form of students shedding almost completely in the summer months their newly acquired civilized habits for the old ways of camp life. As one agent observed: "How soon they seem to forget all they have been taught, after they return to camp."

The solution to this problem was to be found in the third type of institution, the off-reservation boarding school. The rise of the off-reservation boarding school can largely be credited to the remarkable and controversial figure of Lieutenant Richard Henry Pratt. To impress upon the southern plains' tribes the government's impatience with Indian harassment of white settlers, the army decided in 1875 to transport seventy-two Arapaho, Cheyenne, Kiowa, and Commanche warriors from Fort Sill, Oklahoma, to St. Augustine, Florida, where they were to be incarcerated for an indefinite period in the city's old Spanish fortress. As an old Indian fighter, Pratt was assigned the task of overseeing the whole venture. But once Pratt had his prisoners under lock and key, he inaugurated an experiment that clearly went beyond his designated orders.

For years Pratt had privately been formulating his own views as to what was needed to solve the Indian problem. Now he had an opportunity to put his plan into operation. Step by step, he turned his Florida prison into a school for civilization. First, the prisoners were issued uniforms and put through a rigorous program of marching and drilling. Then he turned the prison's chapel into a classroom where, aided by a few retired school teachers, he taught his prisoners some English and arithmetic. Next, he involved his Indians in a number of projects, such as performing odd jobs in the community and making Indian curios for local shopowners. All this began to have a profound effect on his Indian pupils. Within a year's time, prisoners could be seen on the streets of St. Augustine speaking a little English and purchasing store items with money they had earned from their own labor. Meanwhile, Pratt's experiment was attracting considerable public attention. Influential visitors began to visit the prison and all were unanimous in their belief that Pratt had made remarkable progress in transforming hardened warriors into civilized red men.

Pratt, meanwhile, was convinced that he had discovered the solution to the Indian problem. When the prisoners were released in 1879, a group of younger Indians expressed their desire to learn more of "the white man's road." Pratt was then allowed to follow seventeen of this group to Hampton Institute, a prominent institution in Virginia hitherto devoted exclusively to the education of blacks. Remaining at Hampton nearly a year, Pratt soon began lobbying with Washington for his own school where his Indian work might be carried on in a grander scale. Finally, he was given some unused military barracks in Carlisle, Pennsylvania, and detailed to carry on his experiment. Pratt was soon roaming across the Dakotas collecting students for his new school. In October 1879, Carlisle Indian School opened its doors with 136 students.

At Carlisle Indian School students were offered an expanded version of Pratt's Florida prison program, a combination of academic study and industrial training in a highly regimented environment. If students could be subjected to such a program for five years, thoroughly isolated from reservation influences, Pratt argued, then the problem of how to civilize the Indian would be solved. Again, visitors flocked to Carlisle to see Pratt's school in operation. And once again, they were impressed with what they saw. Within a few year's time Congress had authorized the construction of several more off-reservation schools in the Far West. A third model for Indian education—the off-reservation boarding school—was now in existence.

In the last two decades of the century a major effort was made to create a true "system" of education. By 1892 Congress had passed a compulsory attendance law for Indian children. As it turned out, the day school, the reservation boarding school, and the off-reservation boarding school were all to have a part to play in the emerging system. Indian children, it was determined, should begin their education of the day school, move on to the reservation boarding school, and then finally complete their education in a Carlisle-type institution. But this was the "ideal" method of sorting. The fact of the matter is that for years countless numbers of Indian children were taken directly from their villages and thrown into the nearest boarding school. But regardless of where children entered the system, government officials were adamant in their belief that the boarding school exerience, whether of the reservation or off-reservation variety, was crucial to accomplishing the Indian's assimilation. It was here that the assault on traditional Indian identity was waged most fiercely.

As soon as the Indian child entered boarding school the war for his mind, heart, and soul began. For those children unfamiliar with whites the first few days at school were particularly harrowing. Almost immediately the new arrival was subjected to a series of ordeals which, taken together, were designed to strip him of all outward signs of his cultural heritage. After a thorough scrubbing, where he was introduced to the "gospel of soap," the child discovered that his camp clothes and moccasins had been taken away to be replaced by the standard wool uniform and a pair of stiff-soled shoes. Next, if his family had not already been assigned an English-speaking name at the agency, the new recruit received one at school. This was done partly because the teacher was often simply unable to pronounce the child's name in his native language. But the name change was also motivated by the fact that traditional Indian-naming practices did not provide for surnames. In the eyes of school officials, this was simply further evidence of the Indian's primitive cultural ways; it revealed the little value that Indian societies placed on lines of inheritance and their disdain for private property. From this perspective, giving the Indian child a new name was a significant step in the civilization process.

The next assault on the new arrival came in the form of a haircut. While cutting the Indian boy's long hair may have appeared to school officials to be a modest alteration on behalf of civilization, to the child it signified much more. How much more is suggested by this description of what transpired in the late 1880s when school officials attempted to give haircuts to some Sioux boys at Pine Ridge Boarding School. As J. C. McGillycuddy described the scene in *McGillycuddy, Agent*:

> In each bathroom a teacher armed with shears was prepared to begin operations. Curious peepers stood close to the windows on the ground floor, deeply regretful of the drawn shades which barred their observation of the activities carried on behind them. There the matron seated a small boy and taking a lousy braid in one hand, raised the shears hanging by a chain from her waist. A single clip and the filthy braid would be severed. But unfortunately, at that moment a breeze blew back the shade from the window. The previously baffled effort of a youngster plastered against the casing on the outside of the window was now rewarded by a fleeing glimpse of his playmate seated in the chair and a tall lean woman with a pair of shears in her hand prepared to divest the boy of his hair—a Delilah bring calamity upon an embryo Samson.
>
> Like a war whoop rang out the cry: *"Pahin Kaksa, Pahin Kaksa!"* The enclosure rang with alarm, it invaded every room in the building and floated out on the prairie. No warning of fire or flood or tornado or hurricane, not even the approach of an enemy could have more effec-

tively emptied the building as well as the grounds of the new school as did the ominous cry. "They were cutting the hair!" Through doors and windows the children flew, down the steps, through the gates and over fences in a mad flight toward the Indian villages, followed by a mob of bucks and squaws as though all were pursued by a bad spirit. They had been suspicious of the school from the beginning; now they knew it was intended to bring disgrace upon them.

Once the student had been stripped of the outward signs of his tribal past, he attempted to adjust as best he could to the realities of school life. What he soon found was that every minute of the day was regulated and scheduled, from the early morning dawn when he was awakened by a bugle call until he fell asleep at day's end when the order came for "lights out." The time in between, when not attending class or performing chores, the student spent marching and drilling in military fashion. For those who went through the experience, some of their most vivid memories of boarding school would be the military atmosphere which pervaded its day-to-day routine. Remembers one Hopi: "When I entered school it was just like entering the school for Army or soldiering. Every morning we were rolled out of bed and the biggest part of the time we would have to line up and put guns in our hands. . . . When a man gave a command we had to stand at attention, another command grab our guns, and then march off at another command." All of this was to instill in the student what was presumed to be lacking in his native upbringing—a sense of self-discipline, habits of orderliness, and a respect for punctuality. The school now took it upon itself to impose from without what the child lacked from within.

Students were expected to respond to the regimentation of boarding school life with absolute obedience. As one school reminded its students: "The moment a student is instructed to do a certain thing, no matter how small or how great, immediate action on his part is a duty and should be a pleasure. . . . Obedience means marching right on whether you feel like it or not." Should students resist the institutional demands for complete compliance, school officials had at their disposal a host of methods for whipping the noncompliant back into line. While the Indian office officially announced in 1895 that corporal punishment was no longer to be used in Indian schools, the fact of the matter is that it was resorted to for many years to come. "Sometimes I would see the teacher or principal whip a boy with a good-sized willow," recalls one Klamath man. "Sometimes they would make the boy take off his shirt and then the boy would never get over it." One of the most commonly reported methods was to have the guilty party run the gauntlet between two lines of students armed with straps. But there were many other forms of punishment in the school superintendent's arsenal, most of which appear to have been designed to induce psychological pain in the student. Realizing that Indian youth dreaded public humiliation even more than physical punishment, school officials readily employed such measures as shaving heads, forcing the guilty to wear signs on their backs, or sentencing boys to the awful fate of wearing dresses. At one school a student recalls that the superintendent utilized an especially cruel method of shaming students who wet the bed, the punishment being to carry the urine-soaked mattress on his back around the school grounds. As one Kiowa woman would remember of her boarding school experience in Oklahoma: 'You get punished. Everything you do you get punished."

Regimentation and stiff discipline alone would not transform the Indian child. In the last analysis, the Indian child had to learn all the knowledge and values associated with civilized living. Furthermore, he must be taught the manual skills that would enable him to support himself without government assistance. These notions translated into a standardized instructional program wherein students divided their time between academic subjects and the "practical arts." Most educators agreed with the boarding school superintendent who had worked among the Sioux that "a string of textbooks piled up in the storehouse high enough to surround a reservation if laid side by side will never educate a being with centuries of laziness instilled in his race." It was commonly agreed, then, that the Indian must be taught to think in the white man's way, but he must also be taught to work.

The first years of academic instruction were given over to teaching the Indian child the basic skills associated with reading, writing, and arithmetic. English, not surprisingly, assumed a position of immense importance in the first few years of the child's education. The reason for this was as much political as pedagogical. If the Indian was to be thoroughly absorbed into the mainstream of American life, it was deemed a matter of common sense that he should acquire the national language. "This language, which is good enough for a white man and a black man," the commissioner of Indian Affairs explained in 1887, "ought to be good enough for the red man." It followed that the rule "English only" was rigidly enforced both in and out of the classroom and that its violation was sure to meet with stiff punishment. Many students found the process of learning the white man's language a painful and frustrating ordeal. Charles Eastman, a Sioux, would never forget the first time the teacher called on the class to recite. "For a whole week, we youthful warriors were held up and harassed with words of three letters," he recalls. "Like raspberry bushes in the path, they tore, bled, and sweated us those little words rat, eat, and so forth—until not a semblance of our native dignity and self-respect was left."

Once the words began to come, the student was introduced to other subjects. Two subjects which assumed particular importance were U.S. history and geography. The study of the nation's history promised to engender patriotic sympathies, develop an appreciation for the duties and rights of citizenship, and, perhaps most important of all, convince the child that his colonial status was both inevitable, and, in the end, justified. This latter lesson was to be reinforced in geography class where teachers not only taught the physical features of the earth but carried on a comparative evaluation of the cultural contributions made by the different races. It was here that the Indian student first encountered directly the ladder of civilization as an idea. It was here that he could come to accept his own degradation as an objective fact, a necessary step, it was argued, if he was to begin the climb to civilization. Operating from this perspective, one school chose to publish some examinations marked "excellent" in geography class. Among those published was this one:

Question: To what race do we all belong?
Answer: The Human race

Question: How many classes belong to this race?
Answer: There are five large classes belonging to the Human race.

Question: Which are the first?
Answer: The white people are the strongest.

Question: Which are the next?
Answer: The Mongolians or yellows

Question: The next?
Answer: The Ethiopeans or blacks

Question: Next?
Answer: The Americans or reds

Question: Tell me something of the white people.
Answer: The Caucasian is away ahead of all of the other races—he thought more than any other race, he thought that some-

body must made the earth, and if the white people did not find that out, nobody would never know it—it is God who made the world.

In this class the students appeared to be learning their lessons well. On another paper one student commented: "The red people they big savages; they don't know anything."

Given the content of their academic subjects, many students no doubt welcomed the fact that half of the school day was devoted to manual and industrial training. At reservation boarding schools this meant that Indian boys spent a good deal of the day working with saws and hammers and hoeing in the school garden. For girls the emphasis was on cooking, cleaning, and sewing. The off-reservation school offered a more varied and advanced curriculum, with boys having the opportunity to master a specific trade such as masonry, harness making, or tailoring and girls getting a chance to pursue coursework in secretarial training. For the most part, however, the thrust of the curriculum was to turn the sons of warriors into productive farmers and the daughters of "squaws" into nineteenth-century Victorian housewives. The tranformation sought was thought to be not only consistent with the dictates of civilization, but, once accomplished, it would relieve the government of its moral responsibility to feed and clothe a people once proud and independent but now reduced to indolence and dependency.

While industrial training unquestionably taught students many valuable skills, all too often the effectiveness of such programs was undermined by institutional realities at odds with stated educational aims. The problem was that boarding school officials were under great pressure from Washington to make their institution as self-sufficient and efficient as possible. The consequence of this was that students were expected to grow much of their own food, make their own uniforms and dresses, clean the school buildings and grounds, and build new additions to the school complex. This push for self-sufficiency, carried out in an environment where the concern for orderliness took on paranoic proportions, had the effect of transforming a potentially meaningful industrial training program into a prisonlike labor camp. The aim of students acquiring new skills frequently gave way to concerns with student productivity. In 1890, for instance, the superintendent at Albuquerque pointed with pride to the fact that sixteen girls in the sewing department had turned out in a single year 238 aprons, 33 bedspreads, 73 chemises, 170 dresses, 261 pairs of trousers, 194 pillow cases, 224 sheets, 107 skirts, and 85 towels. The sacrifice of educational aims to institutional efficiency is also reflected in the manner in which chores were assigned. Students often found themselves consigned for several months at a time to such jobs as laundering, scrubbing floors, or cleaning the school stable. As one Winnebago complained: "I worked two years in turning a washing machine in a Government school to reduce the running expenses of the institution." If this was the white man's idea of education, many students concluded, they wanted nothing of it.

But as school officials saw it, this very attitude was part of the Indian's problem. The Indian not only needed to be taught *how* to work, he needed to be taught to *want* to work. This was in turned linked to the problem that the Indian child came from a culture that placed little value on individual competition in the form of property accumulation. In a word, the Indian lacked in his approach to life a firm appreciation for the most important ideal in the entire American belief system—rugged individualism. It followed that the student should be bombarded throughout the school day with references to the virtues of work, competition, and individual accomplishment. This message was in fact transmitted in the workplace, classroom primers, sermons, and school assemblies. And in the following instance the theme even received poetic expression in the school newspaper under the title "The Man Who Wins."

> The man who wins is the man who works
> The man who toils while the next man shirks . . .
> And the man who wins is the man who hears
> The curse of the envious in his ears
> But who goes his way with head held high
> And passes the wrecks of the failures by—
> For he is the man who wins.

To students who came from cultures where individual status was attained through cooperative sharing, often ritualized in the form of elaborate gift-giving ceremonies, the message was a strange one.

In many ways the most pronounced assault on the Indian's identity came from the school's effort to convert him to Christianity. For many educators, the Indian's "heathenish superstition" was at the very heart of his backwardness. As one government official observed, it was quite impossible to construct a "superstructure of enlightened civilization" on a "foundation of savage superstition." Operating on this assumption it made sense that the missionary spirit should pervade every aspect of the child's education. And so it did. In the dining hall and the classroom, at Sunday church services and periodic prayer meetings, the message was the same: the gods, rituals, and ceremonies of the Indian, while often picturesque, must be sacrificed upon the alter of the white man's more civilized religion.

For those students who had been instructed to the sacred ways of their grandfathers or who had experienced firsthand the great religious ceremonies of their people, the message was a disquieting one to say the least. Many students, before leaving for school, had been warned by their elders about this very subject. Thomas Wildcat Alford, a Shawnee, would always remember clearly the instructions that he and others had received from village chiefs on the eve of their departure. The young braves were to learn all that the white teachers tried to teach them, it was explained, with one exception.

> Very solemnly the chiefs spoke to us. They reminded us of the responsibility we had assumed for our people when we consented to undertake the mission. We were not to go as individuals, but as representatives of the Shawnee tribe. The honor, the dignity, and the integrity of the tribe was placed in our hands. They told us of their desire that we should learn the white man's wisdom. . . . We should learn all this in order that when we came back we would be able to direct the affairs of our tribe and to assume the duties and position of chiefs at the death of the present chiefs. . . . But there was a proviso attached to the promise that we would be chiefs—*a positive demand that we should not accept the white man's religion; we must remain true to the Shawnee faith*.

"But as time passed," Alford goes on to explain, "and the interests of my teachers became stronger, their pleas more insistent, I could not ignore the subject." In the end he would come to know "deep in my soul that Jesus Christ was my Savior." Other students would make other choices.

All of this leads us to the question: How did the Indian student respond to the boarding school experience? Many students simply resisted the whole educational process. The reasons are not difficult to discern. Many perceived the efforts of school officials as little more than a self-serving attempt to dispossess the Indian of his last possession—his culture and identity. Viewing the experience from this cultural, even political perspective, these students viewed the classroom and drill field as but another setting for the historic confrontation between whites and Indians. But there were other reasons as well, some of which younger children may have scarcely been able to articulate. These reasons had not so much to do with the content of the school curriculum as with the manner in which it was transmitted. The school's heavy reliance on corporal punishment and public shaming techniques, as well as the teacher's total insensitivity to the child's cultural background, clearly fall into this category. And then too, there was the pain and loneliness that came with being separated from parents and relatives. All in all, it is little wonder that the Indian child, especially if he was taken directly from the Indian camp, should experience a full range of emotions, beginning with fright and confusion and culminating in resentment. This attitude was all the more likely if he had been taken by the reservation police against the wishes of his parents. Imagine, for example, how receptive the Mescalero Apache children rounded up for school in the fall of 1887 would be to the white man's school. As the agent described it, when the police appeared on the scene on the morning of the roundup, the parents "hurried their children off to the mountains or hid them away in camp, and the police had to chase and capture them like so many wild rabbits." When it was all over, we are told, "the men were sullen and muttering, the women loud in their lamentations, and the children almost out of their wits with fright." It is difficult to imagine that these children, once in school, would easily be converted to the ways of whites.

The response of resistance took several forms. Some students chose the path of escape. They simply ran away. While the distant location of the off-reservation school often ruled out this option, the reservation boarding school was a different matter. To some superintendents it seemed to make little difference how many bars they placed on the dormitory windows, how closely students were watched, or how stiff the punishment for running away might be, the discontented still seemed to find a way to slip beyond the school fence. Sometimes as individuals, sometimes in small groups, they set out on foot for the open prairie, picked their way along wooded river banks, and ran like the wind across desolate mesas in search of a friendly campfire. Neither the threat of a sudden desert storm, a prairie blizzard, or the inevitability that a policeman would soon be on their tracks was sufficient to dissuade the determined runaway. As one superintendent in Sioux country complained: "An Indian child will runaway whenever the roving disposition seizes it." This official, like many others, had come to the conclusion that only "a wall surrounding the school, with iron gates, sentinels posted, could prevent escape."

A more dramatic form of resistance was to burn down the school. It is difficult to judge how many students actually turned to arson as a form of protest. What is clear is that the school reports sent back to Washington make frequent reference to the outbreak of unexplained fires. "The burning of the boarding school and laundry buildings the past spring was a serious loss to the reservation," one superintendent reported. "It still is a mystery how the fire originated in the school room proper." Some of these fires can of course be explained away by the all too shabby construction of some school structures and the outright negligence on the part of employees, but it is also evident from the tone of many of these reports that student conspiracy was strongly suspected. A simple scolding, a public thrashing, or a denied request to visit relatives might be enough to provoke an embittered student to plot the school's destruction. But many no doubt acted out of a much deeper dissatisfaction with boarding school life and thought out carefully the beneficial consequences that would flow from an arson plot successfully executed. Thus, many Winnebago students got what they wanted when a "mysterious" fire swept away the school in 1891. The agent was forced to announce: "The children were all sent home." Whatever their motivation, to the consternation of government officials, students continued to express their displeasure with the white man's schools by setting them ablaze. By the first decade of the twentieth century, the problem had grown to epidemic proportions. As commissioner of Indian Affairs, Francis E. Leupp, would later recall: "Remonstrances, explanations of the perils as well as the wickedness of such actions, and even the ordinary penalties which lay within the power of the teachers to impose, were alike powerless to break up this wanton fancy for the firebrand as a panacea."

A third manner of resistance took on the form of passive resistance. When teachers came West to raise up the "savage," most assumed that they would find their new pupils eager to learn the teachings of civilization. To their unpleasant surprise, what they frequently encountered were suspicious captives consciously determined to maintain their cultural identity, regardless of the teacher's remonstrances to the contrary. Most frustrating from the teacher's standpoint was the uncanny ability of the Indian student to dutifully go through the motions of boarding school routine, outwardly compliant with all its rules and regulations, but inwardly resistant to the substance of the school's teachings. In the classroom this attitude manifested itself in the form of the student responding to the teacher's lesson with earthshaking silence. Needless to say, most teachers found this attitude both ungrateful and unnerving, and it may go a long way toward explaining why teacher turnover posed such a problem for the Indian school service. In any case, teachers could only wonder day in and day out what thoughts were running through the minds that lay behind the expressionless eyes that stared back at them. The answer to this question may be provided in part by a poem written by a group of Navajo students in the 1930s titled "My Thinking":

If I do not believe you
The things you say,
Maybe I will not tell you
That is my way.

Maybe you think I believe you
That thing you say,
But always my thoughts stay with me
My own way.

If many students resisted the boarding school, many others cooperated with it. The question here is why? Answering this question is especially difficult for the simple reason that students left behind only the sketchiest of testimony as to the reasons for their compliance. While there is some evidence of this sort, a more profitable approach would seem to be to analyze what tribal leaders were saying on the school issue. This discussion must in turn be prefaced by the understanding that Indian communities were deeply divided on how to respond to their status as subjugated wards of the nation. While some chose to resist all efforts of the government to teach them the "new way," others came to the conclusion that the Indian must seek to accommodate himself to the new realities of his present situation. For those adopting the latter position, the value of learning the white man's way took on a different light.

That some tribal leaders looked favorably on the boarding school there is little doubt. When one old Sioux chief visited some of his people's children away at boarding school, he compared their presence in school to putting "seeds in the ground." "If I don't see them growing after a time I feel uneasy," he explained. "Then I look again, and if I see them sprouting, I feel glad. So I feel about our children. I see that seed is growing here now, and by and by it will do good among my people." Occasionally, Indian parents, with the aid of an interpreter and the reservation agent, wrote letters to their offspring in school urging them to be diligent scholars. Thus, one Sioux father wrote his son: "I am glad that you are trying to learn. Don't run away from school. It will be your own good if you learn. . . . Learn to talk English; don't be ashamed to talk it." Similarly, an Indian mother wrote to her child: "I am sorry you are not coming home next summer, dear child, but if you like to learn something it is a good place for you. Learn all you can; it will be for your own benefit."

While responses such as these do not appear to have represented the sentiments of most Indian parents, they still raise the question of why even small tribal factions should favor cooperation with an institution whose major purpose was to forcibly assimilate Indian children to the ways of whites. One reason for this response is that some Indian parents as well as students came to accept and internalize the white man's definition of the basis of Indian-white conflict. As previously shown, school officials went to great lengths to convince students that the historic conflict between Indians and whites was in fact one great moral tale, that it could only be understood if viewed in the deeper context of savagism versus civilization. It appears that some Indian elders, in the wake of their race's near destruction at the hands of whites, and confronted with the immense technological power and material wealth of their conquerers, were beginning to accept as truth white pronouncements on the limited worth of native cultures. Thus, when a group of Navajo headmen, long opposed to white schooling, returned from a government-sponsored visit to the World Columbian Exposition held in Chicago in 1893, one description of what the group had witnessed sounded strangely similar to the doctrine of civilized progress. It all started with Columbus.

> The boats were there like which men had when they discovered this country. White man said there might be more land. That ship went back across the ocean and told the people more land here, and more came across. Mexicans at first came over. 'Way back the ships used to go by sail and wind; now they go by steam. We saw lots of white people's guns. 'Way back they did not have good guns; now they have good ones. Light used to be from lard or grease, and then oil; now it's electric lights. We saw different kinds of hoes and plows and shovels— all things to work with. To know how to read and write does good, for they can think more; they can see more; they see better with eyes.

The speaker ended his account with the line: "It is time to let up now." The meaning to the assembled Navajos was eminently clear. They should turn their children over to the agent for education.

Further evidence that changing parental attitudes on the comparative worth of Indian and white ways could affect attitudes on the education question is illustrated by a letter written by a Sioux father, Brave Bull, to his daughter at Carlisle:

> Ever since you told me I have worked hard, and put up a good house, and am trying to be civilized like the whites, so you will never hear anything bad from me. When Captain Pratt was here he came to my house, and asked me to let you go to school. I want you to be a good

girl and study. I have dropped all the Indian ways, and am getting like a white man, and don't do anything but what the agent tells me. I listen to him. I have always loved you, and it makes me very happy to know that you are learning.

The letter ends with Brave Bull's answer to a request from his daughter: "Why do you ask for moccasins? I sent you there to be like a white girl, and wear shoes." Needless to say, while the denial of the desired moccasins was surely a disappointment, her father's conversion to white ways must have considerably lessened any guilt the girl might have felt in abandoning the ways of her people.

A second reason for cooperating with the school program sprang from a very different motivation: the desire to survive as a people. It will be remembered that policymakers in Washington constantly stressed the point that the only alternative to the Indian's civilization was his extinction. Indeed, the entire Indian school system had been created out of the philanthropic desire to acculturate the Indian child to the ways of whites, thereby saving him from the tragic fate that awaited the unassimilated. As the Indian reflected on his current status and on his past fortunes, there was considerable evidence to justify the conclusion that the choice facing the Indian was exactly as policymakers had framed it: civilization or extinction. Thus, it appears that a major reason why some Indian leaders cooperated with government efforts to educate their children was not out of the belief that white ways were superior to Indian ways but out of the conclusion that education was the only road to survival as a people. Perhaps this was the meaning behind Geronimo's remarks to Carlisle students in 1904. "You are here to study, to learn the ways of the white man. Do it well," he said. And then in reference to Pratt, the old warrior added: "Your father is here. Do as he tells you. Obey him as you would your own father. . . . Obey all orders. Do as you are told all the time and you won't get hungry."

And this leads us to still another aspect of the cooperative response, and one that is markedly similar to the earlier discussion of passive resistance. Here again the student demonstrated outward compliance, but, rather than throwing up a general wall of opposition to white instruction, in this case the student listened to what his white teachers taught him, accepted some things, rejected others, integrated some teachings into his own system of beliefs, but in all cases retained a sense of who he was—Navajo, Sioux, or Hopi. Under this form of cooperation, then, students consciously, or perhaps even unconsciously, sorted out and accepted knowledge which was essential to individual and tribal survival and discarded that which posed a threat to their cultural identity. Some students may have, for instance, regarded it as a matter of tribal self-defense that they should learn to read and write the white man's language but out of the same motivation concluded that they should spurn the words of the white preacher. Hopi anthropologist Emory Sekaquaptewa has termed this response "compartmentalization." "The nature of compartmentalization," he writes, "argues that one need not reject his cultural values to make an adjustment to an alien situation." Sekaquaptewa suggests that Hopi children over the past century have become very adept at this. The concept of compartmentalization suggests, then, that boarding schools were a place where Indian students began to learn ways of reaching an accommodation with the larger white world, but not at the price of surrendering their distinctive Indian identity.

The process whereby students attempted to define the terms on which they would reach an accommodation with the white world extended beyond the years spent at boarding school. And this leads us to the question: What happened to students when they returned home? The answer to this question was an immensely important one to the Indian Bureau. The rationale for the boarding school had always been that it provided the ultimate solution to the problem of how to assimilate the Indian. Boarding school graduates, it was argued, would return to their reservations as emissaries of Christian civilization, dedicated to uplift and transform their fellow tribesmen. This was the plan. But as it turned out, the Indian Bureau was soon confronted with what it chose to call "the returned student problem." Numerous reports observed that many returned students who appeared to be thoroughly made over by their school experience, once back on the reservation almost immediately began to "backslide" down the ladder of civilization, in some cases slipping all the way to their original lowly position—savagism. Boarding school officials countered these pessimistic reports with studies of their own, suggesting that the vast majority of students did indeed live up to school expectations. As to which assessment was really correct, it is difficult to say. It does appear, however, that a significant number of boarding school graduates, when confronted with the option of returning to the lifeways of their ancestors, willingly abandoned many of their white teachings.

Typical was the case of Don Talayesva. Talayesva, a Hopi, had attended both a reservation and an off-reservation boarding school before returning to his village in 1909. Freed from the restraints of institutional life, he spent the first night home sleeping on the roof of a pueblo dwelling where he gazed at the star-speckled Arizona sky and contemplated the meaning of his boarding school experience. As he later recalled this moment in his autobiography, *Sun Chief*:

> As I lay on my blanket I thought about my school days and all that I had learned. I could talk like a gentleman, read, write, and cipher. I could name all the states in the Union with their capitals, repeat the names of all the books in the Bible, quote a hundred verses of Scripture, sing more than two dozen Christian hymns and patriotic songs, debate, shout football yells, swing my partners in square dances, bake bread, sew well enough to make a pair of trousers, and tell "dirty" Dutchman stories by the hour.

But as for the future, Talayesva now "wanted to become a real Hopi again, to sing the good old Katcina songs, and to feel free to make love without fear of sin or rawhide."

If the case of Talayesva had been an isolated story of a returned student having gone astray, it would have been of little concern to policymakers. But such was not the case. Federal officials were more and more coming to learn what missionaries over the past two and a half centuries had learned before them, namely, that the process of turning Indians into whites was not an easy business.

By the 1920s, a new generation of reformers was calling for a wholesale revampment of Indian education. Their views soon found forceful expression in a government-sponsored but independent investigation of the nation's entire Indian policy. Carried out under the direction of Lewis Meriam, this landmark study resulted in a series of findings and recommendations which were published in 1928 under the title *The Problem of Indian Administration*. The so-called Meriam report offered a blistering indictment of boarding school conditions, arguing that instead of educators attempting to eradicate all vestiges of Indian culture, they ought to attempt "to develop it and build on it rather than crush out all that is Indian." And while both the reservation and off-reservation boarding school were to remain permanent fixtures in the Indian school system, the Meriam report set in motion a gradual decline in their numbers, with the reservation day school and the local public school assuming an increased importance in the structure of Indian schooling. But the most important legacy of the Meriam report was that it prompted a long overdue reexamination of those fundamental principles which had historically governed the nation's Indian policy. Policymakers were now asked to consider the possibility that Indian ways were not necessarily savage ways, that education was not synonymous with civilization. Indian education would never again be quite the same.

## SUGGESTED READING

For an overview of the issues surrounding federal Indian educational policy during the period treated in this chapter, see Henry E. Fritz, *The Movement for Indian Assimilation, 1860–1890* (Philadelphia, 1963); Loring Benson Priest, *Uncle Sam's Stepchildren: The Reformation of United States Policy, 1865–1887* (New Brunswick, 1942); Francis Paul Prucha, *American Indian Policy in Crisis: Christian Reformers and the Indian, 1865–1900* (Norman, 1976); Prucha, *The Churches and the Indian Schools, 1888–1912* (Lincoln, 1979); Brian W. Dippie, *The Vanishing American: White Attitudes and U.S. Indian Policy* (Middletown, 1982); Frederick E. Hoxie, *A Final Promise: The Campaign to Assimilate the Indians, 1880–1920* (Lincoln, 1984); Wilbert H. Ahern, "Assimilationist Racism: The Case of the 'Friends of the Indian,'" *Journal of Ethnic Studies* 4 (Summer 1976): 23–32; and Irving G. Hendrick, "The Federal Campaign for the Admission of Indian Children into Public Schools, 1890–1934," *American Indian Culture and Research Journal* 5 (1981): 13–32.

For the role of Pratt and Carlisle Indian School in the history of Indian education, see Richard Henry Pratt, *Battlefield and Classroom*, edited by Robert M. Utley (New Haven, 1964); Elaine Goodale Eastman, *Pratt, the Red Man's Moses* (Norman, 1935); and Everett Arthur Gilcreast, "Richard Henry Pratt and American Indian Policy, 1877–1906" (Ph.D. dissertation, Yale University, 1967).

For selected aspects of the boarding school story, see David Wallace Adams, "Education in Hues: Red and Black at Hampton Institute, 1878–1893," *South Atlantic Quarterly* 76 (Spring 1977): 159–176; Adams, "Schooling the Hopi: Federal Indian Policy Writ Small, 1887–1917," *Pacific Historical Review* 48 (August 1979): 335–356; Ahern, "The Returned Indians: Hampton Institute and Its Indian Alumni, 1879–1893," *Journal of Ethnic Studies* 10 (Winter 1983): 101–124; Robert A. Trennert, "From Carlisle to Phoenix: The Rise and Fall of the Indian Outing System, 1878–1930," *Pacific Historical Review* 52 (August 1983): 267–291; Trennert, "Educating Indian Girls at Nonreservation Boarding Schools, 1878–1920," *Western Historical Quarterly* 13 (July 1982): 271–290; Margaret Connell Szasz, "Federal Boarding Schools and the Indian Child: 1920–1960," *South Dakota History* 7 (Fall 1977): 371–384; and Sally J.

McBeth, *Ethnic Identity and the Boarding School Experience of West-Central Oklahoma America Indians* (Washington, D.C., 1983).

Several native American autobiographical accounts include descriptions of boarding school life. Notable among these are Luther Standing Bear, *My People, the Sioux* (Boston, 1928); Standing Bear, *Land of the Spotted Eagle* (Boston, 1933); Leo W. Simmons, ed., *Sun Chief: The Autobiography of a Hopi Indian* (New Haven, 1942); Jim Whitewolf, *The Life of a Kiowa Apache Indian*, edited by Charles S. Brant (New York, 1969); Louise Udall, *Me and Mine: The Life Story of Helen Sekaquaptewa* (Tucson, 1969); and Charlotte J. Frisbe and David P. McAllester, eds., *Navajo Blessingway Singer: The Autobiography of Frank Mitchell, 1881–1967* (Tucson, 1978).

Graham **14.** The
D. **The** Indian
Taylor **Divided** New
**Heart** Deal

In the summer of 1928, the Brookings Institute for
Government Research released a report of more than
eight hundred pages entitled *The Problem of Indian Administration*. Based
on two years' investigation by a team of social scientists under the direction
of Lewis Meriam, the report was objective and moderate in tone, in striking contrast to the polemics that characterized much of the debate over
the conditions of native Americans in that era. Nevertheless, the Meriam
study's conclusions were bleak and pessimistic. Provisions for welfare,
health, and education of the people on the reservations were "grossly inadequate," and the administration of allotment had "resulted in much loss of
land . . . without a compensating advance in the economic ability of the
Indians." As a result, native Americans were among the most impoverished
people in the United States. Less than 2 percent of native Americans had
incomes of more than $500 a year, and more than half had incomes well
below $200 a year, derived primarily from leasing or selling of their inade-
quate parcels of lands to neighboring white farmers or ranchers. The policy of assimilation, deliberately intended to "crush out all that is Indian"
had further demoralized these people, destroying their family and community life, producing a mixture of mistrust and indifference toward even
genuine efforts to improve their conditions.

The understatement typical of the Meriam report made it all the more
devastating an indictment of government policies dating back to the Dawes
Act of 1887. For forty years these policies had been imposed virtually without opposition. Now they were demonstrably and categorically judged to
have failed. Through its quiet but unqualified condemnation of the results
of allotment, and its proposals for reform, the Meriam study represented a
watershed in the history of government relations with native Americans.

The Meriam report, however, also marked the culmination of a movement for reform that had begun earlier in the 1920s. Initially that reform
movement had focused on the perennial problems of corruption and mismanagement in the administration of the Bureau of Indian Affairs. Within a

short time, criticism expanded to encompass a wide-ranging attack not simply on the administration but on the underlying premises of government policies toward native Americans. This challenge to the fundamental principle of assimilation was ultimately incorporated in the programs of the Indian New Deal in the 1930s. At the same time, it created divisions between the "old" missionary-based reformers, who remained committed to assimilation and the "new" reform movement of the 1920s. These divisions extended into the native American communities and ultimately would undermine the achievements of the New Deal era.

By 1920 the full impact of the allotment policy was becoming apparent on the western reservations. Under the Dawes Act, allotments were to be held in trust by the government for a minimum of twenty-five years, but by the First World War the trust period was coming to an end for many native Americans. The Burke Act of 1906 provided for an acceleration of the process of transferring title to allotments to those deemed "competent" to manage their own affairs. Commissioners of Indian Affairs between 1909 and 1928, including Charles Burke himself, sponsor of the 1906 act, sought to extend the trust period as they witnessed the results of the policy. But western spokesmen in Congress pushed effectively for rapid implementation of allotment to achieve the ultimate goals of the Dawes Act— the establishment of the native American as individual property owner and U.S. citizen. In 1924 an Indian Citizenship Act was passed to hasten this process, and legislators looked forward to the day when the Bureau of Indian Affairs could be terminated completely. In fact, the process resulted in the rapid dispossession of much of what remained of native Americans' lands as the newly entitled proprietors were forced to sell their meager estates to pay local taxes or simply to survive. By the 1930s the land base of native Americans had diminished to less than fifty million acres, one-third its size in 1887.

The devastating results of allotment were most dramatic in Oklahoma, where the Five Civilized Tribes (subjected to measures similar to those of the Dawes Act in the 1890s) had lost 40 percent of their lands, and in the plains and Great Lakes regions, where the Sioux had alienated one-third of their allotted acreage. Some groups such as the Chippewa of Minnesota and the Winnebago of Wisconsin had lost more than 80 percent of their lands. Their reservations were characterized by "checkerboarding" of allotted and alienated lands, which provided an insurmountable obstacle to later efforts to consolidate native American resources to promote economic development.

Ironically, however, the new reform movement of the 1920s initially directed its attention toward the problems of native American communities in the Southwest who had escaped the full implementation of allotment and resisted pressures for assimilation. The Pueblos of New Mexico became the focal point for a revival of public concern over the government's Indian policies. At the same time, the various controversies that surrounded the Pueblos revealed the fissures that would ultimately separate the traditional reformers from their new allies.

The Pueblos confronted challenges from two directions in 1921. The first threat involved their traditional lands. Although the Pueblo lands had not been allotted, about 10 percent of their grants had been alienated between 1848 and 1912, including valuable irrigated acreage. The question of title to these lands was a subject of considerable historical controversy and was further confused by a 1913 Supreme Court decision that implied that the Pueblos did not have the authority to alienate their lands as they were in effect wards of the U.S. government. At the instigation of Interior Secretary Albert Fall, in 1921 Senator Holm Bursum of New Mexico introduced a bill that would confirm the transfer of title to the disputed claims out of the hands of the Pueblos, who now took the position that the land continued to be theirs, although they disputed the Supreme Court ruling that they lacked the competence to dispose of their resources as they saw fit.

The Indian Rights Association, a Philadelphia-based organization that represented the traditional white reform movement, opposed the Bursum bill and was joined by two new groups, the Eastern Association of Indian Affairs, led by anthropologists interested in preserving Pueblo society and culture, and the New Mexico Association on Indian Affairs, comprising white artists and intellectuals living around Taos, New Mexico. The New Mexico group was most active in generating national interest in the Pueblo land issue, promoting an All-Pueblo Council among the villages, and using their contacts in the media to publicize the plight of these people. Their efforts were enhanced by the sudden resignation of Secretary Fall amidst emerging scandals in the Interior Department in 1923. The Bursum bill was defeated, and, after considerable legislative maneuvering, a Pueblo Lands Act was passed in 1924 that established procedures for an equitable settlement of the disputed claims.

The alliance of old and new reformers to block the Bursum bill dissolved, however, over a concurrent issue, the proclamations of Indian Commissioner Burke in 1921 and 1923 that prohibited or limited traditional ceremonies such as the Sun Dance among the Pueblos and other native Americans. This "Dance Order" had been an objective of the Indian Rights Association and missionary reformers for many years. The Taos-based group, which had broadened into a national organization, the American Indian Defense Association, opposed the Dance Order, regarding these measures as attempts to suppress native American culture and attacks on religious freedom. They encouraged the Pueblos to openly defy the Bureau of Indian Affairs and vigorously lobbied to repeal the orders. By 1926 the Indian Defense Association had stymied the Dance Orders and blocked passage of a bill that would have enabled Burke to prosecute native Americans in federal courts or before reservation tribunals that had no due process procedures.

Throughout the remainder of the decade the reform groups expanded their activities to address the broad range of problems of native Americans. The Indian Rights Association and Indian Defense Association worked in tandem to successfully resist another of Fall's schemes that would have opened up some of the reservations to mining and oil drilling without compensating the native American communities residing on them but made an unsuccessful attempt to block construction of a bridge at Lee's Ferry on the Navajo reservation in Arizona. But the underlying divisions among the reformers that had emerged in the Dance Order debate were never far from the surface. Both groups agreed that native American communities must be protected from despoliation by white landowners and business interests and that the Bureau of Indian Affairs was underfunded and inefficient. Their differences became apparent when they addressed the question of changing basic government policies toward the native American.

At the center of this debate was John Collier. The emerging leader of the Indian Defense Association, Collier was the virtual embodiment of the new reform movement, a vigorous lobbyist, organizer, and publicist, and a man of strong, abrasive views and overwhelming energy. To a certain extent, Collier's ideas about native Americans were uniquely personal, but they reflected as well a general shift in intellectual attitudes toward race, culture, and material achievement as a measure of social value.

John Collier brought to the problems of native Americans in the 1920s an unconventional and wide-ranging intellectual background. A "reform Darwinist and self-made sociologist," Collier admired the ideas of critics of industrial society such as Peter Kropotkin and William Morris. He devoted much of his life to preserving traditional communities against what he perceived to be the onslaught of western industrialization with its emphasis on individual self-interest and unlimited technological change. During the period of the First World War, Collier was drawn into the community organization movement among immigrant groups in New York City.

Throughout his career, Collier alternated periods of energetic reform activity with periods of withdrawal into wilderness solitude. After the demise of the community organization movement at the end of the war and a brief, frustrating experience as director of adult education in California, Collier retreated to Taos, New Mexico, where he encountered the Pueblos. Here at last he believed he had found a genuinely cohesive cultural group that had successfully resisted the encroachments of white civilization with its attendant social ills. He quickly embraced their cause as his own.

Collier was attracted to native American communities in the Southwest precisely because they so clearly rejected assimilation. To him the pressures to assimilate represented a far more insidious and fundamental threat to native Americans than the crass and open exploitation denounced by traditional white reformers. Collier's ideas on this subject reflected his own basic rejection of the values of industrial society. At the same time, his respect for native American cultures was shared by a growing number of intellectuals and social scientists in the 1920s. Novelists and poets such as Oliver La Farge, Mary Austin, and John Niehardt began to undermine the literary stereotypes of native Americans, while anthropologists such as Franz Boas, Robert Lowie, and Ruth Benedict argued that cultural differences among groups did not demonstrate their relative position on a single evolutionary scale and that each culture must be viewed on its own terms rather than in comparison with the values of white Anglo-American society. These views were not widely accepted in the 1920s, but by the middle of that decade they had emerged to challenge the conventional evolutionist arguments that had been used to justify the assimilation of native Americans.

Total rejection of assimilation, however, remained a minority view even among supporters of Collier's Indian Defense Association. Even the Meriam report, commissioned by Interior Secretary Hubert Work in 1926 after the reformers rejected an in-house investigation of the Bureau of Indian Affairs, circled gingerly around this subject. While documenting the results of existing policies and deploring them, the Brookings study concluded that the "fundamental requirement" of government programs should be "the social and economic advancement of the Indians so that they may be absorbed into the prevailing civilization or be fitted to live in the presence of that civilization at least in accordance with a minimum standard of health and decency."

The Hoover administration endorsed the findings of the Meriam report, and in 1929 Charles Rhoads, a former president of the Indian Rights Association, was appointed Indian commissioner by Interior Secretary Ray L. Wilbur, also a supporter of the Philadelphia-based reform group. Rhoads moved quickly to introduce improvements in the Bureau along the lines proposed by the Meriam study. W. Carson Ryan, his director of Indian education, began closing down the unpopular boarding schools and replacing them with day schools located near the reservations, established a placement service and student loan program, and generally upgraded the quality of teaching. Health services were also improved through enlargement of medical and nursing facilities and staff and an emphasis on preventive medicine. Rhoads even joined with Collier in 1929 in drafting proposals for legislation to encourage tribal councils, to establish a special federal court to review treaty claims, and to settle outstanding debts incurred by native Americans under a misconceived loan program set up in the First World War to expand tribal livestock herds.

But Rhoads remained committed to the ultimate goal of assimilation and refused to halt the allotment process. The Meriam report had suggested that the Bureau permit the consolidation of allotted lands under tribal management on a trial basis on several reservations, but Rhoads and Wilbur declined to undertake even this limited experiment. Consequently, by 1930 Collier and the antiassimilationist reformers had parted ways with Rhoads. Collier lobbied with the Senate Indian Affairs Committee that had initiated its own study of the problems of native Americans in 1928, urging it to repudiate the new commissioner's policies. The committee, dominated by western Democrats such as Senator Burton Wheeler of Montana and Senator Elmer Thomas of Oklahoma, supported Collier's position, partly in order to discredit the Republican administration.

By 1932 the Rhoads reform program was in shambles, assaulted by Collier and Congressmen, and undermined by the Depression that reduced appropriations to the Bureau of Indian Affairs to a point where native Americans, badly off at the best of times, were reduced to desperate circumstances. Rhoad's failure to improve conditions for native Americans relying on moderate and conventional reform measures set the stage for a more far-reaching change in policy following the election of Franklin Roosevelt.

President Roosevelt's appointment of Collier as commissioner of Indian Affairs in 1933, after considerable political maneuvering by interested parties, came as a shock to the old reformers, but even the Indian Rights Association gamely offered "support and cooperation," noting that Collier, "an outstanding critic," was "being told in effect, 'Show us how it should be done.'" While moving quickly to acquire relief funds for native Americans through the various emergency programs set up by the Roosevelt administration, Collier began to work on a major policy initiative, with the assurance of support from Interior Secretary Harold Ickes, who had been one of the founding members of the Indian Defense Association.

In keeping with the spirit of reconciliation that temporarily prevailed among reform groups, Collier solicited advice on policy changes from a wide variety of sources. In January 1934 a conference of reform groups chaired by Meriam met at the Cosmos Club in Washington, D.C. The conference recommended an end to allotment, the settlement of all treaty claims, the establishment of tribal organizations that would gradually take over the administrative powers of the Bureau of Indian Affairs and would assume control of tribal resources, including allotted lands which should be consolidated into economically viable units, and the establishment of a substantial loan fund to promote economic development. Collier also circulated questionnaires to anthropologists and reservation superintendents, and subsequently presented his proposals to a series of assemblies of native Americans around the country. Although some critics charged that these meetings were little more than "window dressing," intended to present the appearance of widespread support for Collier's program, the process of consultation was unusual, reflecting the new commissioner's conviction that policies should not be unilaterally imposed by the government, as had been the case in the past, as well as his desire to preempt potential opposition to the reforms.

The bill drafted by Collier and two Interior Department lawyers, Nathan Margold and Felix Cohen, was introduced in Congress by Senator Wheeler and Representative Edgar Howard of Nebraska in February 1934. It was a long and extremely complex piece of legislation, encompassing virtually the entire range of policies affecting native Americans. In addition to the proposals of the Cosmos Club conference, the bill included provisions for the establishment of a special federal court for Indian affairs and measures that would not only expand educational opportunities for native Americans but would "promote the study of Indian civilization and preserve and develop the special cultural contributions and achievements of such civilization, including Indian arts, crafts, and traditions." Various loan funds were proposed to encourage tribal organization, to improve health and educational facilities, and to contribute to the consolidation and development of tribal economic resources.

The unity among reform groups eroded quickly, however, following the introduction of the Wheeler-Howard bill. By the end of March 1934 the Indian Rights Association began openly criticizing the provisions for an Indian court and tribal organization, charging that these measures would perpetuate the segregation of native American communities from the mainstream of American society and would retard progress toward the ultimate goal of assimilation. Harsher critics argued that tribal organization and land consolidation would make the program a "communist experiment," a claim that extremist groups among the native Americans, such as Joseph Bruner's American Indian Federation, would later resurrect. Meanwhile, white interests in the west and their representatives in Congress were suspicious of the proposals relating to consolidation of reservation resources, not because this step would transfer ownership of allotments to tribes but because in practice it would extend the control of the federal government over these resources since the Interior secretary would have ultimate power over the classification, leasing, sale, or development of tribal lands, timber, and subsurface minerals. Native American leaders also noted the ambiguity of these provisions. Those who held allotments in trust feared the loss of their property to community control, while tribes that already had councils such as the Navajos in the Southwest and the Iroquois in New York believed that the program would dilute the authority they now possessed and would undermine their historic claims to sovereignty.

Collier was inclined to dismiss the arguments of white westerners as self-serving, but he was troubled by opposition from native American groups and still wanted to accommodate the views of the assimilationist reformers, particularly since Senator Wheeler began to share their doubts about the bill, proclaiming that his aim was to help native Americans "adopt the white man's ways and laws." In April 1934 Collier proposed a series of amendments that would ensure that individual property would not be arbitrarily transferred to tribal ownership and—a crucial concession—that would allow tribes to decide by referenda whether to come under the provisions of the bill.

Even these concessions were not satisfactory to critics of the plan, and in May 1934 the House Committee on Indian Affairs redrafted the entire bill, eliminating the proposal for a federal Indian court, substantially limiting the powers of tribal organizations over economic resources, and requiring a series of tribal plebiscites to determine whether native American communities would come under the Act, to organize tribal governments, and to establish tribal corporations to manage resources. Those groups that rejected any or all of these steps would remain under the existing regulations of the Bureau of Indian Affairs.

Collier would later maintain that the changes in the bill were "a major disaster to the Indians," and other historians of the Indian New Deal have concurred that the final measure, signed into law as the Indian Reorganization Act on June 18, 1934, "bore little resemblance to Collier's original proposal." The point is well taken, although the act did bring an end to allotment, established the legal groundwork for protecting native American culture, and initiated local self-government in place of the bureaucratic absolutism that had prevailed over most of these communities in the preceding fifty years. The limitations imposed by Congress on the original proposal, however, reflected the divisions and uncertainties that characterized not only the reform movement but also native American communities at the time. Despite the bad effects of earlier policies, allotment and assimilation had produced changes that could not be reversed or ignored. Some native Americans actively favored assimilation. Others, tempered by experience with wildly fluctuating government policies in the past, simply wanted to hang on to what little property they still possessed. Still others, reflecting traditions of independence or motivated by less admirable aims of personal aggrandizement or enrichment, simply rejected any measures that left native Americans under the control of a government agency.

Among white reformers as well there were divisions over the purpose of the act that extended beyond, or, more accurately, intermeshed with differences over the desirability of assimilation to create a confusing pattern. In testimony before Congress on the Wheeler-Howard bill, Collier offered ambiguous views on the subject of assimilation. At one point he flatly stated that the bill was not intended to reverse that trend or to substitute "collective" for "individual enterprise." Later, he predicted that the transition from the present condition of trusteeship to full self-determination would be a matter of generations at least. At another point he suggested that the Mexican communal village would provide a model for native American tribal organizations. Some critics have cynically concluded that "Collier gave every faction . . . what it wanted, stood firm on nothing but the need to pass the bill, and was purposely vague throughout."

Yet Collier and those who shared his aspirations faced dilemmas that they believed required a tempering of their commitment to full self-determination for native Americans and their rejection of assimilation. They recognized that native American groups varied widely in terms of cultural cohesion and economic circumstances, and they wanted a program that would be flexible enough to accommodate assimilated groups while protecting others, like the Pueblos, from future attempts to force assimilation upon them. The reformers also feared that too rapid a devolution of government control over tribal resources to native American communities would result in the permanent loss of these resources, duplicating the experience of individual allottees under the Dawes Act. During the drafting of the original Wheeler-Howard bill, Allan Harper and La Farge, two of Collier's closest allies in the reform movement, warned that "if we advance too fast or fail to safeguard the exercise of [tribal self government] in a manner that ensures that . . . they will be really educational and beneficial to the Indians . . . the result will be only a reaction which will set back the whole process of freedom among our Indians."

Neither assimilation as an end nor paternalism as a means to improve native American economic conditions was completely abandoned, despite Collier's own predilections. These ambiguities—on the question of assimilation as opposed to preservation of culturally unique groups and on the question of guardianship as opposed to full self-determination—lay at the heart of the Indian New Deal. The inability of Collier and his administration to resolve these ambiguities to the satisfaction of the reform groups and the native Americans themselves would ultimately weaken and limit the effects of a program that by any standard represented the most enlightened approach ever attempted in the grim history of relations between the U.S. government and the native people of this continent.

Despite his disappointment over the Wheeler-Howard Act, Collier set about implementing the new policies with his customary vigor. Making a virtue of necessity the reformers in the bureau announced that "the principle of self government" would be "carried to a new phase" through the referenda required under the act. During 1934 and 1935, 263 native American tribes and communities participated in the referenda, with 172 agreeing to come under the act and 63 rejecting it. Although the summary statistics of tribal voting on the Indian Reorganization Act are a matter of some controversy, the best estimate is that 70 percent of the 258 groups that held referenda between 1934 and 1935 agreed to accept it, comprising about 60 percent of the native American population of the United States, excluding Oklahoma and Alaska.

To Collier's dismay, some of the largest and most prominent tribes were among those rejecting the act. The Iroquois of New York, who had sought unsuccessfully to be excluded from the act during the debates in Congress, vigorously opposed it, maintaining that it impinged on their claims to sovereignty. The Klamaths of Oregon, who also had a strong tribal organization, rejected the act by a large margin. Perhaps the biggest disappointment to the bureau was the rejection of the act by the Navajos of Arizona and New Mexico, the most populous native American community in the country, by a close vote in a heavily attended referendum in June 1935. Furthermore, many of the tribes that did vote favorably in the initial referenda moved slowly or not at all toward the subsequent phases of tribal council organization and establishment of tribal corporations. Between 1936 and 1945 only about half of the native American groups that had accepted the act set up tribal governments, and 40 percent reached the point of setting up business enterprises, thus qualifying for loans from a $2 million revolving credit fund provided for in the Wheeler-Howard Act.

Meanwhile, however, Collier continued to work for additional legislation to extend the Reorganization program. During the debates over the Wheeler-Howard bill, Senator Thomas of Oklahoma had intervened to exclude native Americans in his state from the key provisions of the proposal, including those relating to organization of tribal corporations. This effectively blocked their access to the revolving credit fund. During October 1934 Thomas and Collier met with assemblies of Oklahoma tribes. Following these sessions, Collier drafted a bill that would protect native Americans there from the kind of swindling that had deprived many of them of their lands and mineral claims while permitting those individuals who were deemed "competent" to manage their property to assume full ownership. The bill also provided a mechanism for establishment of tribal corporations that could acquire land and borrow from a special fund.

This bill also encountered much resistance when introduced by Thomas and Representative Will Rogers of Oklahoma in Congress in April 1935, and a number of objectionable features were removed, although the provisions for tribal incorporation and establishment of a loan fund were retained. A number of native American groups in the western part of the state organized tribal governments under the act and made good use of their loans, but only a small part of the Five Civilized Tribes was able to take full advantage of the measures as their land base had been diminished beyond hope of recovery. Nevertheless, Collier encouraged resurrection of local governments among these groups and provided loans to them through credit associations.

Native people in Alaska had also been excluded from the Wheeler-Howard Act through an oversight in drafting the revised bill, and in 1936 Congress enacted an Alaskan Reoganization Act to enable them to draw on the revolving credit fund. A number of villages were able to tap these funds to develop fishing and canning industries. Meanwhile, the Interior Department attempted to establish six Alaskan reservations in order to secure title to these lands to the native people. But, in this endeavor, the Department encountered resistance from white commercial groups whose arguments that the government did not have the authority to transfer title claims to the lands was upheld by the U.S. Supreme Court in 1949.

One of the problems that Collier recognized from the outset of his tenure as commissioner was that most bureau personnel were not well-informed about the varying cultural traditions of native American groups, due in part to the past commitment of the bureau to assimilation, aggravated by the practice of shifting officials from one reservation to another. Furthermore, as the tribal organization process got underway, it became apparent that many native American groups were equally unfamiliar with the legal intricacies involved in drafting constitutions and charters, and the "models" drafted by the Interior Department lawyers were not always appropriate to particular situations. To bridge the communciations gap, in 1934 Collier established an applied anthropology unit to provide information on traditional tribal organization. This experiment was not entirely successful, although some anthropologists such as La Farge and Morris Opler contributed effectively to organizational efforts among tribes in the Southwest. Collier later concluded that anthropologists were not well-equipped to carry out the kind of specific program-related studies that he needed, while some anthropologists believed that their attempts to provide objective analysis had been undermined by resistance from administrators both at the reservation level and by Collier's own staff, each having equally doctrinaire views about native American culture. The applied anthropology unit was disbanded in 1938. Despite this discouraging experience, Collier continued to seek a role for anthropology in government policy, encouraging an "Indian Administration Research Project" sponsored by the University of Chicago in 1941–1945, and his general attitude toward the value of social science in administration represented a significant break with past practice in the Bureau of Indian Affairs.

Collier had an equally wide-ranging and ambitious view of the value of economic planning of native American resources. He encouraged cooperative efforts between the bureau and other New Deal agencies such as the Civilian Conservation Corps and the Resettlement Administration, culminating with the establishment of the Technical Cooperation-Bureau of Indian Affairs (TC-BIA) project with the Soil Conservation Service in 1936. Under this project the two agencies carried out joint surveys of a number of western reservations and drafted plans to conserve and improve physical resources without disrupting the cultural and social patterns of native American communities on the reservations. Although most of these recommendations were pigeonholed after 1941 when funding for Indian Affairs was sharply curtailed, the surveys provided valuable information on resource needs, particularly in the Southwest, and reflected Collier's commitment to end the isolation of the bureau and to overcome administrators' preoccupation with day to day routines at the expense of long-range development.

Collier's desire to promote cooperative relations with other government agencies was shaped in part by his need to find additional funds to carry out his reform program. While Congress passed the Wheeler-Howard Act and other related measures, opponents of the program in Congress managed to delay appropriations for several months while seeking to impose limits on funding for controversial elements such as tribal organization and land consolidation. Throughout his term as commissioner, Collier had to fend off sniping attacks on his program from hostile Congressmen, including Senator Wheeler who in 1937 introduced a bill to repeal the act bearing his name. Although the process was time-consuming and did little to improve Collier's image as an abrasive and dogmatic spokesman, his appearances before various Indian Affairs committees were effective in turning back these direct challenges, and he was supported in these endeavors by other reformers, including the Indian Rights Association. More insidious was the battle of the budget as both the Bureau of the Budget and Congress chipped away at appropriations for the Bureau of Indian Affairs. Regular operating expenditures increased by only 25 percent between 1935 and 1940. Collier was able to augment funding for his programs by tapping other New Deal agencies, but after 1941 these sources were also cutback at the same time that appropriations for his bureau were being slashed. Funds for specific programs such as tribal organization and promotion of traditional crafts were virtually eliminated.

Collier and his supporters were inclined to assign to Congressional parsimony the major responsibility for the limitations and weaknesses of the Indian New Deal, but there were some serious internal problems as well. While reform groups such as the Indian Rights Association supported Collier against frontal attacks on the Reorganization Act, they were far from uncritical of the program. In 1939 when a second effort to repeal the Wheeler-Howard Act was mounted, the Indian Rights Association supported an alternative proposal that would exempt certain tribes from the organizational provisions of the act while ensuring them access to educational benefits and other financial aid. Throughout the 1930s that association persistently criticized those aspects of the Indian New Deal that they believed would permanently segregate native Americans and retard progress toward assimilation.

These views had a receptive audience among the reservation administrators in the Bureau of Indian Affairs. Many of the veterans of the pre-Collier era had trouble adjusting to the new approach to policy and, as one observer noted, "screened the instructions they got from Washington and their appraisal of the local situation" to fit these preconceptions, in which assimilation and paternalism continued to be the most important elements. A number of bureau officials had loudly opposed the Wheeler-Howard bill in 1934, leading Ickes to impose a controversial "gag order." Some continued to covertly undermine the program, but even the majority who loyally sought to carry out the reforms did not accept or even clearly comprehend the underlying philosophy. This breakdown of communication was particularly notable in the implementation of tribal organization, as reservation officials were reluctant to encourage any serious participation by native Americans. One superintendent, for example, proposed to handpick a committee of "levelheaded men" who "are not too anxious for too much authority" to draft a tribal constitution, and keep out "reactionary Indians who are incompetent." Most reservation officials were less blunt, but there were few who exhibited much interest in encouraging tribal councils to assume a substantial role in the administration of social and economic programs on the reservations.

Collier's most serious problems of communication, however, were with the native Americans themselves. Convinced of the value of direct, face-to-face contact, Collier devoted much of his time to meeting with delegations and assemblies of native Americans to explain his programs and deal with complaints and misconceptions. Nevertheless, many of his listeners remained unconvinced or were perplexed by the intricacies of the array of laws and regulations introduced in the Indian New Deal. In 1934, for example, Collier presented the bureau draft of the Reorganization bill to various native American groups. The differences between this draft and the final Wheeler-Howard Act remained unclear, however, and a number of native Americans opposed tribal organization because they feared that as a result they would lose title to their allotments even though the act specified that consolidation of allotments under tribal control could only be carried out voluntarily. During a later phase of the process, some tribal councils introduced measures that the bureau determined exceeded their authority under the act, contributing to widespread suspicion that tribal self-government was little more than a sham.

A few native American leaders chose to exploit this confusion and mistrust to advance their own political or pecuniary interests. The American Indian Federation, an Oklahoma-based organization established in 1936 by Bruner and O. K. Chandler, started a campaign to repeal the Wheeler-Howard Act and provided a rich source of hostile witnesses for Congressional committees seeking to discredit Collier's program. Collier in turn charged that this group's major aim was to swindle native Americans and that it was associated with Nazi organizations such as the Silver Shirts and the German-American Bund. His vigorous arguments helped to stem growing legislative hostility toward the Indian New Deal on the eve of the Second World War.

But not all the native American critics of the Collier program could be dismissed as cranks or schemers. There were some who sincerely believed that the Indian New Deal, by retarding assimilation, would condemn their poeple to perpetual poverty and subjection. Among these were adherents to the views of Carlos Montezuma, who, before his death in 1923, had maintained that the only solution to the problems of his people would be the abolition of the Bureau of Indian Affairs and that "reform only meant the strengthening, not the diminishing of bureaucratic control in the lives of American Indians." During the New Deal era, Montezuma's ideas were expounded by critics such as the Iroquois Alice Lee Jemison, and various "Montezumist" groups emerged on reservations in the Southwest.

Tribal organization under the Wheeler-Howard Act contributed to discontent among native Americans by exacerbating existing factional rivalries on the reservations, particularly in the Plains region where younger mixed-blood tribesmen educated in white schools were able to acquire control over some of the tribal councils, arousing fears that they would use their positions to deprive full-bloods of their allotments and claims. Even in the southwest where the divisions produced elsewhere by allotment and assimilation were absent, factionalism emerged, as for example among the Pueblos where traditional religious leaders confronted followers of the "Peyote Church."

The frustrations and internal divisions that helped to undermine the Indian New Deal can be traced in microcosm through the experience of the Navajos of New Mexico and Arizona during the Collier era. The political, social, and economic problems that shaped the Navajo response to the New Deal were complex though by no means unique among native Americans. The Navajo reservation had not been allotted, but the prospect of oil discoveries there had led the bureau in 1922 to set up a tribal council to represent the Navajos in leasing drilling rights, required under the 1868 treaty. As was to be the case with tribal organizations in the New Deal period, the formation of the council promptly led to the outbreak of factional disputes between the communities in the southern section of the reservation, led by Chee Dodge, a wealthy rancher, and those in the northern section, whose spokesman was Jacob Morgan, a strong proponent of assimilation who had support from local white Protestant missionary groups. Throughout the 1920s the factions disputed issues involving the disposition of contemplated oil leasing revenues.

Initially Collier had endorsed the creation of the Navajo council as an example of the kind of reform he hoped would extend to all native American communities. By the end of the 1920s, however, Collier had reversed his position, denouncing the council as a puppet government that endorsed the schemes of bureau officials and local white business interests and was unrepresentative of the Navajo people. By the time Collier became commissioner, the problems of the Navajos had become more complicated. Most of them depended on livestock—principally sheep—herding for their livelihood, but by 1930 the bureau had determined that the Navajo range was overgrazed and that the Navajo herds would have to be reduced. The situation worsened over the next two years as the Navajos were unable to sell their stock and the range continued to deteriorate.

Despite his hostility toward the tribal council, Collier concluded that he had to depend on it to carry out a program of herd reduction and conservation of the Navajo range. When he unveiled these plans to the Navajos in 1933, proposing to supplement diminished earnings as a result of herd reduction with emergency relief funds, there were some objections from the Navajos but the council agreed to endorse the program. But the larger herders successfully lobbied for an across-the-board reduction in livestock, enabling them to cull their herds of less-productive animals while poorer Navajos lost most of their traditional source of income. Furthermore, the stock reduction program was inadequate, and further cuts had to be introduced in 1934. Collier's hopes to alleviate the problem by extending the Navajo reservation proved futile when Congress failed to enact a proposed boundary extension bill.

At this inopportune moment, the Indian Reorganization Act was presented to the Navajos for ratification. Although the bureau tried to ensure that the second herd reduction effort was carried out more equitably than the previous one, the large herders continued to resist, and the general mismanagement of the program left a residue of enduring bitterness among the Navajos toward Collier. Morgan's faction, opposed to the Reorganization Act because of what he considered its antiassimilationist bias, exploited this dissatisfaction, and the tribe rejected the program in June 1934. La Farge, who was on the reservation during the ratification campaign, noted that there was "complete confusion in the Indian mind due to treating soil erosion, stock reduction, the boundary bills and the reorganization bills all together," and that "this was a vote of non-confidence in the present administration." Collier did not improve matters by announcing to the Navajos that their rejection of the Wheeler-Howard Act would not have any effect on the stock reduction program.

Subsequently, Collier endeavored to introduce improvements in Navajo economic conditions and to reorganize the council to make it more representative. But many Navajos remained embittered over herd reduction and what they perceived as the commissioner's high-handed methods of administration. In 1938 Morgan's faction took control of the tribal council and, although unable to alter Collier's programs, Morgan used his position as a forum for criticizing the Indian New Deal and demanding Collier's resignation.

The problems of the Navajos were extraordinarily difficult and convoluted, and the failure of the Indian New Deal to take hold among them was due as much to fortuitous circumstances as to midjudgments on the part of Collier and his staff. Nevertheless, the Navajo situation highlighted some of the inherent weaknesses of the Indian New Deal. Tribal organization on many of the reservations succumbed to factionalism that undermined the effectiveness of the councils. Distrustful of tribal governments that seemed unrepresentative and ineffective, many native Americans refused to support New Deal programs. Those with allotments, except on a few reservations, declined to exchange them for shares in tribal corporations, severely limiting the process of land consolidation essential to the success of the program of economic development. The absence of indigenous support for tribal organization opened the way for critics such as Morgan and Jemison and their allies among the missionary organizations and assimilationist reformers who charged that the Indian New Deal perpetuated bureaucratic control of native Americans behind a facade of self-government and threatened to leave their people stranded indefinitely in poverty and backwardness, isolated from American society. Collier's hopes to revive native American communities as self-sufficient and autonomous entities were thwarted by the crushing and complex economic problems of the reservations, the growing hostility of Congress and traditional white reform groups toward his program, and the legacy of bitterness, mistrust, and division that shaped the response of native Americans toward the programs of the New Deal.

The Indian New Deal was by no means a complete failure. Even though the funds allocated by Congress to Collier's programs were inadequate to meet the needs of native Americans in the depression years, there were some significant improvements in conditions for many tribes, particularly in the Plains region where cooperatives were able to draw on the revolving loan fund to build up their livestock herds and conserve their lands. Even among the Navajos, Collier was able to bring in additional income through emergency work relief programs of the New Deal and to reduce the kind of petty graft in the bureau that in the past siphoned government money away from the native American communities for whom it was intended. The renewed emphasis on native American traditions in education and promotion of arts and crafts had a lasting effect; these measures probably represent the major achievements of the Collier era. Even the tribal organization program, for all its defects, encouraged a degree of political activism on the reservations that had been absent before 1934, culminating with the establishment of the National Congress of American Indians in 1944 that lobbied successfully over the next two years for an Indian Claims Commission, a significant measure that had been blocked in Congress when it was introduced in the Indian Reorganization bill.

Despite these achievements, Collier's vision of native American communities as autonomous, self-sufficient, and self-governing entities remained unrealized when he resigned as commissioner in 1945, worn down by the continuing battles over appropriations with Congress and increasingly interested in promoting a Pan-Indian movement throughout the Americas. The limited impact of the New Deal on native Americans weakened their resistance to a renewed drive for assimilation in the aftermath of the Second World War, which took the form of proposals to "terminate" the role of the federal government in Indian affairs and to "relocate" native Americans off the reservations so that they would become part of America's industrial work force. In the long run, Collier's efforts to stimulate a renewed self-consciousness among native Americans laid the foundation for a reversal of these disastrous policies in the 1960s. But the tribal organizations of the New Deal represented at best a first step toward the goal of the reformers of the 1920s to create a genuinely democratic, economically self-sufficient, and culturally independent system for native Americans within the United States.

## SUGGESTED READING

The historiography of the native American in the twentieth century and particularly of the Indian New Deal has experienced explosive growth in the past decade and should continue to expand our knowledge as more specialized works are published. The interested reader might want to consult periodicals such as *The Western Historical Review, Journal of the West, Pacific Historical Review, Ethnohistory, The Indian Historian*, and *The Journal of American History* as well as the various books mentioned here. Included here are only some of the major works in the field.

The effects of the Dawes Act summarized in the Meriam report cited in this essay have also received substantial analysis in three other books. Delos S. Otis, *The Dawes Act and the Allotment of Indian Lands* (Norman, 1973), edited by Francis P. Prucha, is a republication of a study made in 1933 for Congress, with Collier's support, to document his argument for repeal of allotment. Leonard A. Carlson, *Indians, Bureaucrats and Land: The Dawes Act and the Decline of Indian Farming* (Westport, 1981) is a work by an economist. The background to the Dawes Act is traced by Wilcomb Washburn, *The Assault on Indian Tribalism: The General Allotment Law (Dawes Act) of 1887* (Philadelphia, 1975).

John Collier's own account of his career and the Indian New Deal is in *From Every Zenith: A Memoir* (Denver, 1963) and in an earlier version, *Indians of the Americas* (New York, 1947). D'Arcy McNickle, who worked with Collier in the Bureau of Indian Affairs, provides a sympathetic account in McNickle and Harold E. Fey, *Indians and Other Americans: Two Ways of Life Meet* (New York, 1959 and 1970). The most comprehensive study of Collier and the Indian New Deal in general is Kenneth R. Philp, *John Collier's Crusade for Indian Reform, 1920–1954* (Tucson, 1977). The first of a two-volume study of Collier is Lawrence C. Kelly's *The Assault on Assimilation: John Collier and the Origins of Indian Policy Reform* (Albuquerque, 1983), which focuses on the reform movement of the 1920s. Graham D. Taylor, *The New Deal and American Indian Tribalism: The Administration of the Indian Reorganization Act 1934–1945* (Lincoln, 1980) examines tribal organization in the Indian New Deal. Margaret Szasz, *Education and the American Indian: The Road to Self-Determination 1928–1973* (Albuquerque, 1974) reviews educational reforms under Rhoads and Collier. There are some useful unpublished Ph.D. theses in the field, including John L. Freeman, "The New Deal for the Indians: A Study of Bureau-Committee Relations in American Government," (Princeton University, 1952), which traces disputes over the Wheeler-Howard Act in Congress, and Donald L. Parman, "The Indian and the Civilian Conservation Corps," (University of Oklahoma, 1967).

Studies of the impact of the New Deal on particular native American communities are also increasing. The Navajos have been the subject of a number of valuable works, most notably Kelly, *The Navajo Indian and Federal Indian Policy, 1900–1935* (Tucson, 1968); Parman, *The Navajos and the New Deal* (New Haven, 1976); and Peter Iverson, *The Navajo Nation* (Westport, 1981). Laurence M. Hauptman, *The Iroquois and the New Deal* (Syracuse, 1981) analyzes opposition to the Collier policies among the Six Nations. Another valuable study of native Americans that reviews their reactions to the Indian New Deal is Hazel W. Hertzberg, *The Search for an American Indian Identity: Modern Pan-Indian Movements* (Syracuse, 1971).

No study of modern native American history would be complete without reference to Felix Cohen's *Handbook of Federal Indian Law* (Washington, D.C., 1941), which brought together a wide range of sources on the subject. Cohen's analysis has been challenged on the subject of tribal sovereignty by Russell L. Barsh and James Y. Henderson in *The Road: Indian Tribes and Political Liberty* (Berkeley, 1980). Washburn, ed., *The American Indian and the United States: A Documentary History* (New York, 1973) assembles numerous government materials on native Americans, including reports of the commissioners of Indian Affairs, Congressional debates on the Wheeler-Howard Act and other laws, and various court decisions and related legal materials.

Donald **15.**                The Federal Policy
L.       **Dislocated**       of Termination
Fixico                        and Relocation,
                              1945–1960


World War II brought about many changes to the
world, the United States, and the American In-
dians. A myriad of sociocultural experiences emerged among Indian
Americans after approximately 25,000 voluntarily served in the armed services and an estimated 40,000 to 50,000 native men and women worked
in ammunition plants, airplane factories, and other war industries.[1] Their
devoted patriotism was impressive, convincing federal officials and the
American public that Indians were ready to be assimilated into the mainstream society. Within several years a twofold federal Indian policy of termination and relocation was enacted to sever the federal government's pa-
ternalistic, protective "trust" relationship with the tribal groups and to
move the Indians to urban areas.

Termination and relocation were not new concepts conceived during the
years following the war. Since the American founding fathers established
the U.S. government in 1776, federal policy had frequently attempted to
"assimilate" native Americans into the dominant society by terminating
the unique legal rights of Indian people and their properties, despite the
fact that the Constitution recognized the legal status of the tribes (Article 1,
Section 8). Treaties between the United States and tribal groups authorized relocating the people to reservations, especially during the 1800s.
The Dawes Land Allotment Act of 1887 sought to individualize and civilize Indians during the turn of the twentieth century, until Commissioner
of Indian Affairs John Collier implemented "New Deal" programs to re-
structure tribal governments and preserve Indian cultures. The interrup-

---

1. Of the estimated 25,000 Indian men who served in the armed forces, 22,000
enlisted in the United States Army, 2,000 in the Navy, 120 in the Coast Guard, and
730 in the Marines. Their performances in the war netted 71 Air Medals, 51 Silver
Stars, 47 Bronze Stars, and 2 Congressional Medals of Honor (Lieutenant Ernest
Childers, an Oklahoma Creek, and Lieutenant Jack Montgomery, an Oklahoma
Cherokee). An estimated 200 to 300 Indian women joined the nurses' corps, mili-
tary auxiliaries, Red Cross, and the American Women's Voluntary Service. See
William Coffer, *Phoenix Decline and Rebirth of the Indian People* (New York, 1979).

tion of World War II and increasing anti-Collier sentiment spawned a change between 1945–1960 in federal Indian policy, commonly known as termination and relocation, billed by bureaucrats as a sincere policy to alleviate the native Americans' poor living conditions.

Assimilation was the fundamental objective of this Indian policy, and understanding its underlying ideology is a prerequisite for comprehending the concepts of recent termination and relocation. Presumably Indian people would benefit from assimilation and enjoy living as "modern citizens." Reservations could no longer support the people, argued the bureaucrats, and relocating them to urban areas seemed logical since they could find jobs and better housing there. In short, integration into urban society would liberate Indians from the bonds of unemployment, poor housing, malnutrition, and discontentment. Furthermore, federal Indian experts interpreted native American participation in World War II as an important step in desegregating rural Indian communities. To government officials, integrating Indians into society was raison d'être for abrogating federal Indian "trust" relations which held the people captives on the reservations.

The view that American Indians were ready to become members of society was reinforced by two federal reform measures that played major roles in effecting a revision of Indian policy. First, the Hoover Task Force Commission Report in 1947 advised limiting governmental involvement in Indian affairs, concluding that native Americans were ready for assimilation. The Task Force's positive overall evaluation of Indian progress resulted in a recommendation for reducing the superfluous bureaucracy of the Bureau of Indian Affairs. Offices would be consolidated to provide efficient, streamlined services, and selected Indian hospitals and schools would be closed. Decentralizing the Indian Service in Washington was the chief recommendation of the Hoover Report, which included an outline of actions for discontinuing most programs. This was the basis for the second relevant measure—the Zimmerman Plan. Based on their economies, the Bureau of Indian Affairs categorized tribes into three groups: those ready for immediate independence by liquidating the trust relationships, intermediate tribes requiring some assistance before withdrawal of all federal responsibilities, and a large third group needing continued assistance.

The second major reform offered individual tribes millions of dollars as compensation for the past violations of their treaties, if authorized by a review commission. In 1946 Congress passed the Indian Claims Commission Act, establishing a commission "to hear and determine the following claims against the United States on behalf of any Indian tribe, band, or other identifiable group of American Indians of the United States or Alaska." In effect, once and for all, the federal government attempted to settle its debts with the tribes; once payments were made, past federal injustices committed against Indian people would be redeemed. By the end of the 1950s, the Indian Claims Commission had reviewed some 125 cases and had authorized an estimated $42 million to the tribes for past violations. Within several years, the number of claims filed increased faster than the commission could render its decisions. Twice, the Claims Commission asked for and was granted two additional five-year periods to complete its work, but not all of the filed claims were presented. A total of $669 million had been awarded to the tribes by September 1978 when Congress dissolved the commission, leaving 133 of 617 dockets unresolved. These were transferrred to the U.S. Court of Claims.

Indian participation in World War II had nurtured the seeds of termination, which grew into a reform policy when Congress took action under advisement from the Bureau of Indian Affairs. Bureaucrats erroneously interpreted Indian participation in the war as readiness for integration into the mainstream society. Instead, after the war Indian veterans and those who served in the industrial factories experienced disordered, social changes. Many had left reservations and rural allotments for the first time. In the months spent away from their traditional home environments, they practiced the lifeways of the dominant culture. Out of their native element, they compromised their traditional values in order to cope with the outside world and could not help but compare their native life-style with that of the mainstream.

Furthermore, the people waiting for them to return said they had been contaminated by the spirits of the dead enemy soldiers. (Purification ceremonies were customarily held to decontaminate the veterans.) Living again on reservations and rural allotments proved difficult for the returned warriors whose personalities and native perspectives had changed, causing the psychological disharmony of their spiritual balance. While they had changed, life on the reservations and allotted homelands had remained relatively the same.

Sad accounts of maladjustment occurred too frequently among Indian veterans. N. Scott Momaday captured this traumatic experience in his Pulitzer prize-winning novel, *House Made of Dawn*, as did Leslie Silko in a similar account, *Ceremony*, a story about Indian veterans returning to the reservation after fighting in the Pacific theater. These vivid literary works narrate and interpret the drastic social and psychological changes in Indian life-styles. The Pima war hero, Ira Hayes, a private first-class marine who

helped raise the American flag at Iwo Jima, became one of the most celebrated Indians of World War II. Unfortunately, he encountered a series of
personal and social problems. Piecing his life together after returning to
the Pima Reservation in Arizona, the war hero found interacting socially
with his people to be difficult, and he could not successfully cope with the
mainstream society. Feeling alienated from his Pima brethren, Hayes
turned to alcohol. During a cold night in the mountains of Arizona in
January 1955, Hayes died of exposure. He was a broken man.

The immediate postwar years were extremely difficult for native Americans. Scarce jobs on the reservations and in rural communities and an over-
burdened land base could not support the overgrowing Indian population.
To make matters worse, a severe blizzard struck the Southwest during the
winter of 1947–1948; the Navajos were devastated, some to the point of
starvation. The media reported their destitution, thereby arousing national
concern for the hapless Indians. In an effort to help the Navajos and their
Hopi neighbors, Secretary of the Interior Julius Krug, at President Truman's request, proposed a ten-year program to provide vocational training
for both tribes and to develop their reservation's resources. In early December 1947, President Truman summarized federal efforts in succoring
American Indians. "Our basic purpose is to assist the Navajos—and other
Indians—to become healthy, enlightened, and self-supporting citizens,
able to enjoy the full fruits of our democracy and to contribute their share
to the prosperity of our country."

Two years passed before Congress approved the Navajo-Hopi bill in
1950, funding a program to improve the two tribes' livelihoods. The government assisted Navajos by relocating them in Los Angeles, Salt Lake
City, and Denver, and helped them to find jobs. During midsummer 1951,
the Bureau of Indian Affairs began assigning relocation workers to Oklahoma, New Mexico, California, Arizona, Utah, and Colorado with the intention to expand the program. The next year the Bureau officially extended the Relocation Program to all Indians and added more cities that
offered employment and housing. In early February, the first relocatees arrived in Chicago. During 1955 relocation workers processed 442 native
Americans for direct employment in Los Angeles, Denver, and Chicago, at
an average cost per relocation of $450, which increased to $750 five years
later. To help place the increasing number of applicants in cities, the Bureau
of Indian Affairs opened additional offices in Dallas, Cleveland, Minneapolis, Oklahoma City, Seattle, Tulsa, and the San Francisco Bay Area.
In the next several months, offices were established in St. Louis and San
Jose. By late 1954, 6,200 native Americans out of an estimated reservation

population of 245,000 had been resettled in cities. Approximately 54 percent of the relocatees came from three northern areas—Aberdeen, South Dakota, Billings, Montana, and Minneapolis, Minnesota. The remaining 46 percent were from southern areas—Gallup, New Mexico, Phoenix, Arizona, and Anadarko and Muskogee, Oklahoma. Native Americans were relocated to twenty states, with Los Angeles and Chicago being the leading urban relocation centers.

Curiosity and the attraction of city life influenced many Indians to apply for relocation. Veterans, relatives, and friends made reservation Indians envious when they talked about adventurous good times in the cities. Typically, an inquiry made at the Indian agency on a reservation or a regional area office started the paperwork. Both young and old could apply. For the young, one had to be at least 18 years old and in reasonably good health. Officials checked the applicant's job skills and employment records, then contacted the relocation office in the city of the applicant's choice. Relocatees arrived in the designated city, usually via bus or train, where a relocation worker met them. Next, the relocation office issued a check to the relocatee to purchase toiletries, cookware, groceries, bedding, clothes, and an alarm clock to ensure punctual arrival for work. Normally the Bureau of Indian Affairs paid the first month's rent, including travel expenses to work, clothing, and groceries. After the first month, the relocatee and his or her family were financially on their own. Periodically a neighborhood clergyman stopped by to visit them. Relocation officers provided counseling and assistance in job placement and monitored the urban Indian's progress up to nine years.

The most common applicants were young males. Frequently men left families on reservations until they found a job and housing in the city and then sent for them. Generally, relocatees with higher education moved farther from tribal homelands, and they proved more successful in making the transition from reservation to urban life-style.

As more Indians entered the metropolitan mainstream, government officials assumed they would be easily assimilated into the cities. Maintaining quotas for processing relocatees and the false impression of successful Indian urbanization later inspired federal cutbacks of Indian programs. One frugal congressman, who asserted that Indian programs strained the federal budget, emphatically stated that the government's expensive supervision of Indian affairs for the next fifty years would cost between a half billion to two billion dollars. *"They do not need a Federal guardian NOW, nor will they need one for the next 50 years!"*

Truman's "Fair Deal" programs provided social services to all needy citizens, including native Americans and other minorities. The president saw all segments of society as having the same rights. He even supported de-segregation at the risk of losing his popularity. He advocated that equal rights and educational opportunity should not be denied to any citizen. During a conversation, Truman philosophically stated that he looked on all Americans as one nation, "White, black, red, the working man [and] the banker."

Truman's philosophy on desegregation of Indian communities was implemented through the Bureau of Indian Affairs when he appointed Dillon S. Myer, a Republican from Ohio, to be the new commissioner of Indian Affairs. Indians qualified for the commissioner's position were passed over, provoking Indian groups and pro-Indian supporters to criticize Myer's appointment, especially when presiding Indian Commissioner John Nichols had not been notified that he was being replaced. Myer shared the same ideas on Indian affairs as President Truman and was regarded as a hard-line assimilationist. Also a headstrong advocate of dissolving "needless" Indian programs, Myer worked to terminate trust relationships in order to assimilate Indians into the mainstream. Myer had served as the director of the War Relocation Authority, a program that had moved Japanese-Americans from the west coast to concentration camps inland during the war years. At fifty-nine years of age, Myer operated in his customary military-like manner. His stern and forceful personality demanded immediate action in terminating trust relationships and the expedient reduction of federal Indian services.

Myer's actions upset citizens who criticized the Bureau of Indian Affairs for abruptly dissolving its responsibilities to native Americans. Pro-Indian supporters charged the commissioner with expediting termination of federal trust relations with tribes who were not ready and misusing his authority. Myer was derogatorily referred to as "Stalin" and "Mussolini" rolled into one, and labeled a "tin-headed dictator." Complaints calling for Myer's removal quickly followed with Dwight D. Eisenhower's election as president in 1952.

Ike followed the tradition of other incoming presidents by appointing new personnel to top federal positions. He selected Glenn L. Emmons, a banker from Gallup, New Mexico, as his commissioner of Indian Affairs. Again, qualified Indians like Choctaw Harry F. W. Belvin of Oklahoma and New Mexico's Indian Council representative, Alva Adams Smith, were passed over for the position. Frustrated over the matter, Senator William Langer of North Dakota objected to Emmons's appointment, charging that one commissioner after another came from New Mexico (referring to

William Brophy and John Nichols). The Senator had the support of the National Congress of American Indians and rumor had the two collaborating to overturn Emmons's appointment.

Like Myer, Emmons advocated termination of federal Indian trust relations, although he enjoyed a friendly relationship with Indian people in the Southwest. Having spent much of his life in New Mexico, he was familiar with their cultures and had learned about their ways. And, as a banker he personally knew many Indians and sometimes arranged loans for those who were poor financial risks. Emmons sincerely believed that termination was best for Indian Americans, if in the long run they were to improve their livelihoods. Gradual withdrawal of federal trust responsibilities, he believed, would allow Indians an opportunity to exercise economic independence without federal restrictions hindering them. Unlike Commissioner Myer and Senator Arthur Watkins, who publicly opposed Indians frequently, Emmons was a liberal terminationist who possessed a humanitarian sensitivity for his constituents. He particularly worked to prevent exploitation of Indian groups and to provide relocation services for succoring them.

The presidential change from Democrat to Republican during the early 1950s saw relocation gain momentum as a moving force behind the termination policy. Throughout the Eisenhower years, increasing migration from reservations and allotments to cities, plus termination of trust relations, complemented the Eisenhower ideology of conforming all Americans, including ethnic groups, into one society. Eisenhowerism promoted a nationalistic attempt to involve everyone in building a patriotic, strong, but conservative society to protect American principles for a free democracy. As a result, Americans in general experienced an improved standard of living through their own achievements.

Astronomically high debts left from the war made the Eisenhower administration conscious of excessive spending, urging retrenchment in federal budgeting. An acute difference in philosophies of the Truman and Eisenhower administrations on federal Indian spending is noteworthy. Under the Truman administration, the Indian Claims Commission authorized large settlements to pay off Indian groups, and the Hoover Task Force surveyed Indian conditions, resulting in large expenditures and additional bureaucratic paperwork. Although the Truman administration laid the groundwork for termination, the Eisenhower administration actively prepared tribal groups for the end of government trusteeship and services. Under Eisenhower retrenchment of the national budget ominously warned the tribes of dangerous realities that lay ahead; expensive federal programs like theirs would likely be cut.

During this period, terminationists such as Senator Patrick McCarran of Nevada, Senator Watkins of Utah, and Representative Henry M. Jackson of Washington were the leading policymakers for federal Indian affairs in Congress. They wanted to end the trust relationship and federal Indian programs for two important reasons. They deemed native Americans were capable of supporting themselves without governmental assistance and funding Indian programs was too costly.

Economy-minded administrators and insensitive actions worried native Americans who operated on a different system of ingrained cultural values which terminationists failed to understand. Powerful political figures who controlled congressional Indian affairs such as Senator Watkins were convinced that Indians had life too easy, and they wanted Indians placed on a competitive basis with everyone else. To compound the situation, racial prejudices and discrimination hindered Indian progress, thereby preventing native Americans from obtaining well-paying professional jobs and attaining respectable social status in the "white man's world."

Another influential group in Congress consisted of sincere protectionists such as Senators Reva Beck Bosone of Utah, Richard Neuberger of Oregon, and James Murray of Montana. Familiar with Indian people and reservation conditions, they only introduced legislation to end trust status at the requests of tribal groups. (Certain tribes and individuals were quite capable of running their own business affairs without trust restrictions, although this number was small.) Some congressmen, such as Senator George Smathers of Florida, originally advocated dissolving federal/Indian relations but, after learning more about native American conditions, they joined the antitermination ranks. On the other side of the termination issue, the proterminationists swelled in numbers, especially when uninformed and neutral congressmen were easily convinced to vote for termination legislation.

Termination reached its peak in 1953 and 1954 during the Eighty-third congressional session. In all, Congress entertained 288 public bills and resolutions affecting Indians, 46 of which were enacted into law. The Bureau of Indian Affairs submitted 162 reports to the Senate and House of Representatives as part of the legislative studies on Indians. Finally in early June, the fate of Indian people was sealed when Congress approved a general resolution that established the termination policy affecting all tribal groups. Senator Jackson introduced House Concurrent Resolution 108 in the Senate and Representative William Harrison of Wyoming sponsored the legislation in the House of Representatives. The essence of this landmark resolution reads as follows.

> Whereas it is the policy of Congress, as rapidly as possible, to make the Indians within the territorial limits of the United States subject to the same laws and entitled to the same privileges and responsibilities as are applicable to other citizens of the United States, to end their status as wards of the United States and to grant them all of the rights and prerogatives, pertaining to American citizenship; and
>
> Whereas the Indians within the territorial limits of the United States should assume their full responsibilities as American citizens.

Within several weeks, H.C.R. 108 had initiated other legislative efforts to liquidate applications implemented under the Indian Reorganization Act of 1934. This largely involved dissolving tribal corporations based on the act. More important, H.C.R. 108 singled out thirteen tribes for withdrawal of trust status, and Congress started immediate termination procedures for six groups. Protermination bureaucrats in Washington were convinced that tribalism and federal trust paternalism hindered Indians from improving their livelihoods. The following year, Congress approved termination legislation for the six groups—the Menominee of Wisconsin, Klamath of Oregon, Western Indian groups of Oregon, Alabama-Coushatta of Texas, Ouray and Ute of Utah, and mixed-blood Paiute of Nevada. The move to end federal-Indian relations caused tense feelings among the tribes as the momentum for termination increased. One Indian Bureau official asserted that the Indian Service knew well that H.C.R. 108 would shock Indians across the nation, and he hoped Congress would not consider any similar legislation until it studied the effects of termination on the six groups.

Reports to Congress described the members of these tribes as fairly educated, economically self-sufficient, and already assimilated into nearby towns composed mainly of whites. The Eighty-third Congress terminated the federal trust relationship with the Menominees, who were to serve as a role model for other groups. Considered as one of the largest and wealthiest tribes, the tribe numbered 3,059 members who owned 233,902 acres of bountiful timberland. The Menominees seemed ready for termination, but a disagreement occurred between some tribal members and federal officials over the terms negotiated for dissolving the tribe's trust relationship. A pending per capita payment of $1,500 was partially to blame when Assistant Secretary of the Interior Orme Lewis opposed the payment. He claimed the tribal members were already economically independent and had no need for the payment. Approximately two-thirds of the Menominees were employed in the tribal forest or the sawmill and the remaining one-third worked in nearby communities. Besides the per capita issue, a faction of Menominees vehemently protested the elimination of the government trust relationship. In fact, Gordon Keshena charged the Bureau of Indian Affairs with meddlesome paternalism, stating it had been in business 125 years and had controlled everything his tribe did. "Everything we wanted to do, we had to go to the Bureau and ask them," said Keshena, "Can we do this? Can we do that? You cannot ask the people to go on their own and govern themselves now, when for all those years they have not been permitted to do anything for themselves."

Without delay, the Bureau of Indian Affairs carried out the provisions of termination legislation for the Menominee and began procedures to withdraw trust relations from other tribes. On June 30, 1953, the Muskogee Area Office reported withdrawal programs would be implemented for the Five Civilized Tribes, certain Indians of the Quapaw Agency, and the Mississippi Choctaws. In addition, withdrawal programs for the Coushatta and Chitmacha groups in Louisiana, Cherokees on the Kenwood Reservation, and the Thlothlocco Creek Tribal Town were being studied. On the same day, the Interior Department reported that the Prairie Island Band of Minnesota had approved a proposal to abolish federal supervision over half of their affairs. Meanwhile, the bureau initiated programs to prepare the Osages of Oklahoma and the Flatheads of Montana for termination. Three Bureau hospitals were closed, and local public school authorities took over operations of sixteen bureau day schools and assumed the academic work at three boarding schools, affecting 1,100 Indian students.

The movement to free Indians from federal trust restrictions continued during the rest of the decade. From 1954 to 1960, Congress terminated the trust relationships of fifty-four tribes, Indian groups, communities, and allotments. Although this figure is high, some persons owning allotted lands desired abolition of their trust status. These self-confident abolitionists had sufficient education and adequate business experience to succeed without governmental trust protection. Unfortunately, the Bureau of Indian Affairs had convinced Congress that most native Americans could supervise their own affairs. The truth was the majority of Indian Americans needed more time before they could achieve satisfactory livelihoods.

Emmons and his administration soon realized possible dangers of terminating tribes too quickly, especially the native groups who claimed they were ready. This caused federal Indian affairs to focus on economic progress as a means of "preparation" for terminating tribes. Unlike the earlier years of the decade when congressional action concentrated on passing termination legislation, the remainder of the 1950s stressed preparing tribal groups economically for the ultimate end of federal trust supervision. The bureau made loans to tribes, enabling them to invest in enterprises, develop programs, and arrange loans to its members. In addition, the Bureau of Indian Affairs began educational programs designed to make Indians self-sufficient and to convince them they no longer required federal assistance.

Some tribes were pressured into accepting final termination deadlines; others experienced reduction of federal services. Whether tribes were ready for full independence was not a primary consideration. Federal officials were intent on fulfilling quotas to ensure that termination deadlines were met. Unfortuntately, over the years the tribes had become too dependent on federal assistance, and only a few appeared ready for total independence. But the fact is those few, like the Menominees and the Klamaths, who owned rich timberlands and possessed large deposits of natural resources on their reservations, proved unable to manage their business affairs effectively for competing as corporations in the business world.

After approving H.C.R. 108, Congress entertained another important measure, House Resolution 1063, in an attempt to reduce federal involvement in Indian affairs. This resolution proposed to extend state jurisdiction over Indian reservations in Wisconsin, Nebraska, California, Oregon (except Warm Springs Reservation), and Minnesota (except Red Lake Reservation). President Eisenhower approved the resolution as Public Law 280 without consulting the tribes or obtaining their consent for authorizing state jurisdiction over their reservations. Public Law 280 expedited decentralization of the Indian Service in Washington and shifted government responsibilities to the states; the transfer burdened state governments. In addition to assuming civil and criminal jurisdiction over Indian country, the states contracted with the federal government for providing services to native Americans. State officials criticized P.L. 280 for the increased responsibilities that it transferred to state governments, claiming the services for Indian citizens strained state budgets.

Indian health service was another responsibility that the federal government wanted to relinquish. Congressional approval of P.L. 568 authorized transferring Indian health facilities and services to another federal department, Public Health Service. Commissioner Emmons and Minnesota Senator Hubert Humphrey claimed the move would provide better health care to native Americans. Many Indians felt uncomfortable applying for health services with non-Indian citizens. Red tape and excessive paperwork compounded their uneasiness. For treatment, they turned to native cures as an alternative or they did without professional health treatment. Still, statistics for the next ten years indicated a dire need for health care. Disease and fatality rates were extraordinarily high among the native American population. Indians were three times more likely to die of pneumonia and influenza than Anglo-Americans. Hepatitis ranked eight times greater among Indians than any other ethnic group, and Indian infant mortality, tuberculosis, and alcoholism rates were the highest in the nation. Overall, native Americans had a life expectancy of forty-four years, compared to seventy years for white Americans.

Federal policymakers hypothesized that by dissolving Indian health services, native Americans would start relying on public services such as the Public Health Service or even private health care centers. In actuality, they avoided public health services. Many Indians believed that they were socially unacceptable to the mainstream population, for even among financially, independent Indians, many individuals experienced social maladjustments, feelings of discomfort living in non-Indian neighborhoods, and uneasiness working with strangers. The cities were so different, with their tall buildings, strange noises, and crowds of people, that a large number of relocatees elected to return to their quiet, less populated reservations to escape the tension and anxiety of urban adjustment.

In spite of the foreign, urban environment of metropolitan areas, an increasing number of Indians applied for relocation to leave impoverished reservations and rural allotments behind and to try their luck in the cities. In an effort to meet the needs of the increasing number of relocatees, Congress passed P.L. 959 in August 1956. The act provided vocational adult training for Indians, which became a part of the Relocation Program. Three types of general services were offered. First, on-the-job training provided twenty-four-month apprenticeships for training and gaining occupational experience for working on or near reservations. Relocatees needed work experience, and acquiring job skills increased their chances for better employment in urban areas. Second, the adult training proram focused on adults only, particularly those with families. Training was available in specific occupational areas such as carpentry and plumbing, stressing manual job skills. Applicants had to be eighteen to thirty-five years old, but older persons were accepted, if they were promising candidates. The third vocational service provided information about jobs and found work for native

Americans near reservations. To improve the general situation, the Bureau of Indian Affairs urged industries to locate near reservations, and program officers negotiated with employers in urban areas to hire relocatees.

During 1957 the bureau's relocation services assisted 7,000 native Americans, costing $3.5 million, more than twice the sum appropriated for the previous year. Overall, Indian progress seemed to be on the upswing. An estimated 132,000 Indian children attended schools of all types throughout the country. Financially, the total income for oil, gas, and other minerals leased on reservation lands nearly doubled from $41 million in 1956 to more than $75 million in 1957.

Relocation offered a fresh start for native Americans who wanted to begin new lives. Bureau officials encouraged urban relocation on a voluntary basis, although some people reported that they were cajoled into relocating. Brochures and pamphlets were circulated throughout reservations and communities to convince Indians that a better life awaited them in cities. Pictures of executives dressed in white shirts wearing ties and sitting behind desks insinuated that relocatees could obtain similar positions. Photographs of surburban homes with white picket fences were included to entice women to think that relocation was best for their families. Still, these propagated efforts were not enough if federal policy was to be successful in relocating the reservation and rural Indian population. Continual pressure was applied on nonurban Indians as long as a significant portion of native Americans remained on reservations and allotments.

Promises of successful livelihoods in urban areas did not materialize most of the time; rather relocation disillusioned the relocatees, especially those who had never left reservations or traveled long distances before. The reality confronting them was a cultural shock. Getting off a bus in a strange, large city for the first time was traumatic for most relocatees. The newcomers knew very little about modern gadgets and street life in big cities. Stoplights, traffic, sirens, clocks, elevators, telephones, and other mechanical contrivances were alien to Indians fresh off the reservations. Confused, they became frustrated with their ignorance of modernization. Learning to live in the "white man's world" was a difficult challenge and often overwhelmed the neophytes. One individual was "lost" in his hotel room for twenty-four hours. Having misplaced the Bureau of Indian Affairs' address, he was perplexed and did not know what to do. Although he had the Bureau of Indian Affairs' telephone number, he was ashamed to ask anyone how to dial.

Psychological self-doubt typically afflicted urban Indians who had foregone native traditions for assimilation into white society to learn the ways of the dominant culture. Relocatees, once a people proud of their heritage, lost confidence and felt they had no control over their lives. Loneliness engulfed them, while thoughts of relatives back home occupied their minds. Even more damaging, loss of traditional family roles occurred when fathers could not support their loved ones and left, thereby creating an absence of the traditional father-figure and extra burdens for mothers who were forced to raise their children alone. Lacking sufficient training and education to find decent jobs, such Indian mothers were at a loss. Marital problems and broken families fostered deliquency among children who were absent from school or dropped out. All too often relocatees turned to alcoholism to escape the harsh reality of urbanization. Demoralized and not knowing what to do, they lived a "drifting" existence in the cities' ghettos. Need for food and shelter sometimes compelled them to commit petty crimes—others contemplated self-destruction, a frequent occurrence that contradicted many tribes' traditional values of cherishing life.

In response to the pressures of forced assimilation into metropolitan areas, Indian youths expressed their dissatisfaction with federel policy and the Bureau of Indian Affairs. The newly founded National Indian Youth Council became the Indian voice of unhappiness, and the National Congress of American Indians, founded in 1944, also criticized the Bureau of Indian Affairs. Instead of solving Indian problems through termination and relocation, the National Congress of American Indians claimed the government had created more problems for Indians. Now they had to contend with the bureau's bureaucracy, "withdrawal of trust" policy, and urbanization.

In addition to rising Indian protest, organizations led by non-Indians and former bureau officials spoke out against the Eisenhower administration's supervision of Indian affairs. Oliver La Farge, president of the Association on American Indian Affairs in New York, blasted the Bureau of Indian Affairs, alleging that the federal government broke its trust relations and did not act in the best interests of Indians. In one instance, La Farge stated that desire for oil and other minerals under Paiute land was the real motive for terminating the trust with the Paiutes. Former Commissioner John Collier pointed out that 177 full-blooded Paiutes, who possessed 45,000 acres of land in Utah, would lose land because abundant subsurface minerals were believed to exist there. Shrewd opportunists, Collier claimed, would manipulate the Indians out of their lands. He concurred with La Farge that greed was the real motive behind termination and charged that Commissioner Myer had acted "to atomize and suffocate the group life of the tribes—that group life which is their vitality, motivism, and hope."

Rumors circulated that Commissioner Emmons and other government officials harassed tribal leaders into ending federal trust relations. Emmons became the focus of an attack when critics accused him of being a tool of "big business" that would exploit Indians to control their natural resources. During a meeting with a delegation of Standing Rock Sioux, the commissioner rose to his own defense, insisting that "We have to face the day when the Government is going to get out of the Indian business." The concerned commissioner asserted that he had "a solemn obligation to raise the standards of the Indian people so when that times does come they will have such a level of income that they can afford to be relieved of the Government restrictions." Emmons said it plainly, "darn it I will fight to the last ditch to see that doesn't come over night, of course."

Undoubtedly Emmons strove to assist native Americans, and with other government officials he worked for Indian independence, but harming Indian people was unavoidable. Varying degrees of Indian socioeconomic progress toward assimilation created a paradox for the government. Frequently, federal officials were led to believe that Indian residents of a particular area were socially and economically ready for termination, when actually they were not. This resulted in confusion and opposition from tribal members as well as criticism from concerned persons. Whether they were ready, Emmons planned to give all American Indians full rights as well as freedom from discriminatory restrictions by July 4, 1976—the celebration of America's bicentennial.

Concerned citizens wrote President Eisenhower about the government's inept termination policy and the destructive effects of relocation on Indian Americans. The President explained that the central aim of federal policy was working constructively and cooperatively with Indians on programs to prepare them for full independence. He clarified the government's position by assuring the public that both the secretary of the Interior and the commissioner of Indian Affairs explicitly opposed "wholesale" or "overnight" termination of federal trust responsibilities in Indian affairs.

In spite of additional legislation and efforts of the Indian Service to help Indian people, attacks on the federal government persisted. Unfortunately, the inability of bureaucrats to understand the complex socioeconomic conditions of Indian maladjustment to urbanization fueled the criticism. Undoubtedly, Secretary of Interior Douglas McKay and Commissioner Emmons wanted what was best for Indians, but, as most bureaucrats, they lacked perception of the social and psychological consequences that termination and relocation programs caused. It was imperative to understand that American Indians had surrendered much of their native identity as they strove to fulfill their potentials as middle-class citizens. In short, native Americans were deindianized and forced to assume roles as non-Indians in a foreign environment—something many lacked the ability to do.

Following World War II, the decade of the 1950s was an embroiled period of drastic change in federal-Indian relations. During the latter half of the 1950s Congress was committed to protecting Indian rights, whereas the Eighty-third Congress in the earlier years had stressed termination of trust responsibilities. The shortsightedness of members in the Eighty-third Congress on Indian affairs is evident with the optimistic approval of H.C.R. 108, which had been blindly promoted without sufficient discussion or consideration of possible negative repercussions on the Indian population. Incredibly, a small body of federal officials exercised tremendous power over Indian affairs, while congressional attention focused mainly on foreign relations in Indochina, McCarthyism, and civil rights. Moreover, Indian affairs seemed far less important after the nation slipped into an economic slump during the fall of 1957 and early 1958.

While the nation suffered financially, increased monies were appropriated for Indian programs, which contradicted the retrenchment guidelines of the early 1950s. The Eighty-fifth Congress, for instance, appropriated a record $109,410,000 for Indian programs, and Bureau of Indian Affairs' operations in 1957 amounted to 25 percent, or $21 million, more than the previous year. Improving the overall economy of native American groups forced the cost of administering Indian affairs to spiral upwards. Meanwhile, developing tribal programs became a distinguishing characteristic of federal Indian policy in the late 1950s. Emmons's leadership exemplified a more patient and humanitarian attitude toward Indian affairs than preceding administrations in the Indian Service. In contrast to the tough "get out of the Indian business" approach of the Eighty-third Congress, the later congresses exhibited a concerned "prepare the Indians" policy. This change in federal attitude toward Indian affairs predominated throughout the remaining years of the second Eisenhower administration. Fewer new tribes were named for termination, and the essence of federal-Indian relations focused on seeking solutions to federal "trust withdrawal" problems. A prime example is the Klamath controversy over the procedure to sell timberlands. With the final withdrawal of trust status set for 1961, 250 to 275 members would receive $43,000 each in per capita payments from the timberland sales. When the termination deadline arrived, 78 percent of the

Klamaths voted to receive revenue from the sales. Thus, the government distributed $68 million to the tribe.

The end of the 1950s did not represent the end to termination and relocation. Throughout the early and mid-1960s, tribes and allotments were still being terminated of trust status. In fact, between World War II to the origin of the Indian self-determination policy in the late 1960s, the government processed 109 cases of termination, affecting 1,369 acres of Indian land and an estimated 12,000 native Americans. Relocation of reservation and rural Indian populations to cities continued, and a noticeable demographic trend emerged, indicating that an increasing number of native Americans were urbanized. (Today, just over one-half of the total Indian population resides in urban areas.) As native Americans entered the 1960s, the federal government's attitude toward Indian affairs changed to a federal commitment of preserving indigenous American cultures and supporting Indian self-determination. Relocated Indians became accustomed to a new life-style in cities. And, out of the terminated tribal communities and urban ghettos sprang forth a new generation of urban Indians.

## SUGGESTED READING

There are few major studies on termination. They are Larry W. Burt, *Tribalism and Crisis, Federal Indian Policy, 1953–1961* (Albuquerque, 1982) and Donald L. Fixico, *Termination and Relocation: Federal Indian Policy, 1945–1960* (Albuquerque, 1986).

Earlier studies include Gary Orfield, *A Study of the Termination Policy* (Denver, n.d.); Oliver La Farge, "Termination of Federal Supervision: Disintegration and the American Indians," *Annals of the American Academy of Political and Social Science* 1 (May 1957): 41–46; and Arthur V. Watkins, "Termination of Federal Supervision: The Removal of Restrictions over Indian Property and Person," *Annals of the American Academy of Political and Social Science* 311 (May 1957): 47–55.

Overviews about termination are Charles F. Wilkinson and Eric R. Briggs, "The Evolution of the Termination Policy," *American Indian Law Review* 5 (1977): 139–184 and Frederick J. Stefon, "The Irony of Termination, 1943–1958," *Indian Historian* 11 (September 1978): 3–14. See also Debra R. Boender, "Termination and the Administration of Glenn L. Emmons as Commissioner of Indian Affairs, 1953–1961," *New Mexico Historical Review* 54 (October 1979): 287–304. Other studies include S. Lyman Tyler, *Indian Affairs: A Work Paper on Termination, with an At-*

*tempt to Show Its Antecedents* (Provo, 1964) and Larry Hasse, "Termination and Assimilation: Federal Indian Policy, 1943–1961," Ph.D. diss., Washington State University, 1974.

The first terminated tribe, Menominee, is the focus of Stephen H. Herzberg, "The Menominee Indians: From Treaty to Termination," *Wisconsin Magazine of History* 60 (1977): 266–329 and "The Menominee Indians: Termination to Restoration," *American Indian Law Review* 6 (1978): 143–204. Refer also to Nancy O. Lurie, "Menominee Termination: From Reservation to Colony," *Human Organization* 31 (Fall 1972): 257–270. The most thorough study is Nicholas Peroff, *Menominee Drums, Tribal Termination and Restoration, 1954–1974* (Norman, 1982).

Literature on other tribal groups are Susan Hood, "Termination of the Klamath Indian Tribe of Oregon," *Ethnohistory* 19 (Fall 1972): 379–392; Angie Debo, "Termination of the Oklahoma Indians," *American Indian* 7 (Spring 1955): 17–23; Stanley Underdal, "On the Road Toward Termination: The Pyramid Lake Paiutes and the Indian Attorney Controversy of the 1950s," Ph.D. diss., Columbia University, 1977; and Faun Dixon, "Native American Property Rights: The Pyramid Lake Reservation Land Controversy," Ph.D. diss., University of Nevada, 1980. Retribalism after termination is in William T. Hagan, "Tribalism Rejuvenated: The Native American Since the Era of Termination," *Western History Quarterly* 12 (1981): 4–16.

The Relocation Program and Indians in urban areas is covered in James Gundlach, "Native American Indian Migration and Relocation: Success or Failure," *Pacific Sociological Review* 21 (January 1978): 117–127. See also Lawrence Clinton, Bruce A. Chadwick, and Howard Bahr, "Urban Relocation Reconsidered: Antecedents of Employment Among Indian Males," *Rural Sociology* 40 (1975): 117–133. A major study is Elaine Neils, *The Urbanization of the American Indian and the Federal Program of Relocation and Assistance* (Chicago, 1971).

Relocation to certain cities are in Theodore Graves and Minor Van Arsdale, "Values, Expectations and Relocation: The Navajo Migrant to Denver," *Human Organization* 25 (Winter 1966): 300–307; and Joan Ablon, "Relocated American Indians in the San Francisco Bay Area: Social Interaction and Indian Identity," *Human Organization* 23 (Winter 1964): 296–304, "America Indian Relocation Problems of Dependency and Management in the City," *Phylon* 66 (Winter 1965): 362–371, and "Relocated American Indians in the San Francisco Bay Area: Concepts of Acculturation, Success, and Identity in the City," Ph.D. diss., University of Chicago, 1963.

Blue
Clark

# 16. Bury My Heart in Smog

Urban Indians

Their lives were a circle.
The American Indian husband and wife were born on a reservation or in a rural Indian community. Indian grandparents helped raise the youngsters, and Indian aunts and uncles assisted the transition of the children to adulthood. Once married, the Indian couple moved to a town to obtain money. There they brought up their own children.

The curve of their circle began with frequent visits to their reservation kinfolk to maintain cultural ties. The circle was completed when the couple retired with a little money to live out their lives in the land of their ancestors' birth. The big city provided hardly more than a street with a house number. Home was not their urban residence. Home was where traditions were rooted.

### HISTORY

Before the turn of the twentieth century, official U.S. government policy encouraged the placement of boarding school Indian youth in Anglo-American homes during the summers and holidays. Called the outing system, the policy fostered assimilation and prevented the Indian student from returning to "the blanket" on the reservation. Many of the outing system Indians joined an urbanizing America and remained in or near cities. Using their newly acquired training and skills, they found jobs which allowed them to send some extra money back to their reservation family.[1]

1. Although the term "urban Indian" is widely used, and the practice is continued in the present chapter because of the ease of the phrase, it is wrong. A more correct phrasing is Indians in an urban setting. Indians are not really urban; they

The decision to remain away from the tribe in adult life was economically remunerative but it was often costly in unforeseen ways. In 1884 the Supreme Court of the United States ruled that a Sioux Indian man named Elk was not able to vote in a municipal election in Omaha, Nebraska, where he lived, because he was a member of an Indian tribe. Elk had ended his tribal membership when he moved into the city. He was left without the safety of the tribe and without the rights of the voting citizen in the city of his residence. He was caught between tribal identification and uncompromising assimilation.

To discourage the alleged idleness of the dole, the Indian Service in 1903 began make-work projects on Indian reservations to replace government rations. Officials hoped that in the process of turning hunters into laborers the government would spend far less money on Indians. Two years later, Charles E. Dagenett of the Bureau of Indian Affairs (BIA) opened a small office to find off-reservation employment for Indians in the Southwest. Dagenett, a Peoria Indian, provided Indian gang labor to railroads, seasonal agricultural workers, and outing employment for Indian girls to work as domestics in towns.

The Dagenett plan grew modestly but steadily. The idea spread slowly from the Denver office into the northern plains region and into Southern California. Dagenett contacted potential employers who had a railroad project or irrigation channel, made arrangements for Indian workers, persuaded the area superintendent of Indians to deliver the laborers, and then encouraged the Indians in the nearest agency to go to work. Congress appropriated small sums of money in 1907 and 1911 to increase on-reservation economic development and off-reservation employment. Dagenett's efforts assisted the urban transition of the first generation of city Indians in recent history. These few city workers and their families became the nucleus of the large numbers of urban Indians in the United States today.

The railroad and farm laborers lived on the outskirts of cities in squatter camps. In the 1920s, the Meriam survey staff discovered deplorable conditions in the migrants' tent settlements. The Indians lived either in tents or in shacks without running water and sanitary facilities. Still, the workers made more money than their reservation relatives. Towns near concentrations of Indians received the largest numbers of Indian migrants from the 1920s onward.

---

reside in cities, then return to their reservation or rural homes. Many Indians do not display the characteristics of an urban resident, as for instance, aggressiveness, materialism, and white and middle-class values.

America's foreign involvement offered other avenues for employment experience. Over 10,000 American Indian males served in the U.S. armed forces during World War I. Some Indian females held factory jobs to replace men in the service. Families of Indians moved under government sponsorship to work in defense-related industries.

For some of the nation's Indians, the wartime exposure to the nonreservation world served as a bridge between cultures. The agent for the Southern Cheyenne reported with obvious satisfaction after the war:

> One Cheyenne, typical, no account, reservation Indian with long hair went to France, was wounded, gassed, and shell shocked. Was returned, honorably discharged. He reported to the agency office square shouldered, level eyed, courteous, self-reliant, and talked intelligently. A wonderful transformation, and caused by contact with the outside world. He is at work.

The skills that many Indians learned in the employment sector or overseas benefited them in the nation's cities. However, their overall numbers were small compared with the vast majority of Indians on reservations and in other rural enclaves. Between the two world wars, Indians traveled to Oklahoma cities in the largest numbers as the trend in urbanization of Indians increased.

The Great Depression brought further urbanization pressures to bear on Indians. When Indians faced starvation during the earliest years of the Depression, they received a small share of the federal funds of the New Deal. With part of the funds, the BIA expanded its off-reservation employment program for Indians. The plan established in 1930 focused on boarding school graduates who had skills and the important sponsorship of their school and agency superintendents for finding jobs. The bureau opened ten centers near reservations in the Southwest for locating urban employment for the native worker. In addition, the Indian Division of the New Deal's Civilian Conservation Corps employed some 20,000 Indians each year from 1933–1943. Unfortunately, as the Depression worsened so did the placement record of the revitalized Guidance and Placement Division of the Indian Service. Job opportunities dried up for Indians and non-Indians. Finally, in 1940 the employment section of the bureau closed.

America's entry into World War II provided another boost to Indian urbanization. Between 1941 and 1945 an estimated 150,000 Indians participated directly in the agricultural, industrial, and armed services aspects of the nation's war effort. For the first time they left reservations in large numbers for cities where they worked in defense-related factories. With that push, New York City, followed closely by Chicago, took the lead in 1940 for Indian urban population. Among the Navajo, located in the Southwest, over 3,600 saw direct military service, while over 15,000 Navajos moved into urban defense industry jobs.

Navajo and other GIs and urban workers who returned to Indian reservations after the war faced hard times that grew more harsh as the years passed. New Deal programs were gone. Knowledge learned in the Pacific war campaigns or in the factories had no outlet on the reservation. Veterans trained for civilian careers could find no jobs. When nearby towns failed to offer employment opportunities, idleness turned to restlessness in the postwar recession.

Building on a special program for placing selected Navajo youth in off-reservation jobs, the federal government opened job-placement offices in Denver, Salt Lake City, and Los Angeles in 1948. Congress responded with a labor recruitment and relief measure (Public Law 390) and then with the Navajo-Hopi rehabilitation act in 1950 (Public Law 474) to encourage on-reservation relief and development and additional off-reservation employment. It was another removal effort. The object was partly to move the overcrowded Indian reservation population to cities. In this case, instead of a "Long Walk," the Navajos took a long ride on a bus. The following year one of the most famous Indians of the era, Ira Hayes, arrived in Chicago aboard a bus for relocation. He did not like the city and resented the coercion used to gain his transfer from his Pima family in Arizona to the loneliness of Chicago streets. It was a complaint heard over and over from others who were relocated.

In 1954 the BIA changed the name of relocation to the Voluntary Relocation Program to sweeten the image of the operation as well as to mute the sting of what opponents termed pressured relocation.

The cold-blooded image of the relocation program arose in part from the application of the controversial federal policy of termination. Termination meant an end of the federal trust protection over Indian lands and the "transfer of Bureau functions to the Indians themselves or to appropriate agencies of local, State, or Federal government." Just as in the earlier allotment policy, the role of relocation was to terminate the Indians' relationship with the land and sever their relationship with the federal government. The government would "get out of the Indian business" even if the cost was the loss of Indian lives and lands. The chief of the relocation division of the BIA stated at the inception of the program that, "The sooner we can get out, the better it will be. . . ."

Indian urbanization changed in both pace and direction. From 1930 to

1960 Indian urban population increased fourfold, and a demographic movement evolved from East to West, from Oklahoma to California. During these years, Indians moved outward, in a circular pattern at times, from their reservation or rural homes to nearby towns and then to more distant cities. Indians of all groups demonstrated the greatest and most rapid increases in urban population in the United States for that time period. Indians favored New York City as the terminus for their move in the East. In the Midwest, Chicago served as the end of their journey.

Since 1960 Indians in growing numbers have moved farther away from their reservations. The trend continues. Nearly one-fourth of all Indians moving to another state moved to California. The great majority of those settled in urban centers. California cities were the favorite destinations for Indians in the West once they decided to leave home.

New forces and individuals gathered in cities to confront Indian policymakers in the 1960s. Some of the Indian youth by the early years of the decade had attended urban colleges. Though they were more articulate and more aggressive than their elders, they retained a strong link to their reservations. The more educated Indian youth had seen the problems of their people in the cities and felt the anguish of governmental neglect of native lives. They had also been exposed to the materialism of towns and to the organizational activities of the civil rights and antiwar groups that were beginning to stir on campuses.

American Indians in various communities also began to air their concerns in conferences and public hearings. Indians had attended the first national Indian conference to consider off-reservation problems in Seattle in early 1968. The President's National Council on Indian Opportunity held public hearings in 1968 and 1969 throughout the West. LaDonna Harris, the Comanche Indian wife of a U.S. senator from Oklahoma, chaired the Committee on Urban Indians. Committee members were appalled to hear testimony about chronic problems in an unceasing stream. To point out only one example, in Dallas, Texas, with an estimated 8,000 Indians in the poorer sections of the city who needed municipal recognition, the director of the community action projects was not even aware that there were Indians in his city. In other urban centers Indians were the most underserved of minorities. They were invisible to municipal agencies.

The Council study concluded that "one-half of the Indian population in the United States is located in urban areas. Yet none of the programs of the Federal government are aimed" at urban Indians. The study requested that Congress move some funding to urban regions, that Indians make decisions affecting Indians, and that Indians be free to choose the life that they wanted to live without government dictation but with some government funding. Urban legal aid offices were recommended to inform urban natives of their rights and to jar municipal officials into recognizing Indian rights.

In his historic message to Congress on American Indians the same year, President Richard Nixon recognized "the severe problems faced by urban Indians." He added that "the time has come to break decisively with the past and to create conditions for a new era in which the Indian future is determined by Indian acts and Indian decisions." Responding to the request of Indian people in the hearings, the president officially halted the policy of termination of tribes. He turned the emphasis of relocation from removal to self-help. President Nixon's special message on Indians also specifically underlined the bureau's obligation to reservation people to the exclusion of urban natives.

Amid the agitation of activism, the press of public hearings, and the relentless drift of Indians into urban areas, the bureau determined to change relocation policy. New offices for employment assistance for Indians opened in 1970, and more services for adjustment were provided. Successful job placement intensified. Even so, vocal opposition continued to mount steadily as more Indians discussed relocation and employment in public forums. Most of those who expressed an opinion supported job training and counseling while at the same time wished an end to the imposition of a move to the city upon an individual unprepared to contend with the bustle of town life.

In 1972, the BIA allowed relocation to end, although it still retained many of the positive aspects of counseling, instruction, and employment assistance training. The basic shell remained, but the official program ended. Government money henceforth was channeled into reservation economic development schemes and industrial plants.

What effect did relocation have? Indians were coerced into an urban life they would have chosen eventually, but at their own, less costly pace. The government successfully transferred the reservation crisis from one area to another. The attention given to relocation took desperately needed resources away from reservations. Government abrogated many responsibilities to Indians in the process. The migration did not bring economic well-being to the people relocated. Neither the reservation nor the individuals materially benefited much.

Government relocation as a policy actually brought only one-third of the

Indians to cities. Most Indians in urban centers came there without government assistance. They visited relatives, left military service, sought a brother or sister who knew of a job, or came to the city seeking economic gain. First Americans stayed in cities in the hopes of earning more money than they could on their reservation. Those who moved suffered physical and psychological cultural shock. Some suffered trauma so severe they dropped out of any future efforts to better their lot in life. The government attempt to force assimilation on the Indian failed in the city as it had failed in the allotment era in an earlier epoch.

The planned movement of large numbers of American Indians to cities was the greatest threat to tribal survival since the end of the Indian wars and the start of the reservation period. For the first time Indian children were born in cities in large numbers and were cut off from their reservation heritage. They were far removed from their tribal languages and totems. A major potential source for help in retribalizing many Indian children passed Congress in 1978. The Indian Child Welfare Act protected the "best interests of Indian children" in ensuring they were placed with the Indian extended family or placed with the consent of their tribe when a foster home was required.

Governmental leaders' hope that the Indian would disappear into the larger population in the cities in part took place. Indians marry non-Indian spouses in far greater numbers in cities than when on reservations. Full-blood distinctiveness diluted in urban centers. Most urban Indian women marry non-Indian mates. In spite of the thinning of bloodlines, the American Indian had not assimilated into the U.S. urban population. The native had not melted into the general American populace. All of the historic policies that forced, pressured, and exploited Indians did not succeed in ending the separateness of Indians. The native spirit, the tribal distinction, the yearning for the past, the bitterness of the present, continued. The spiritual heritage, the ethnic roots, and their tribe remained outside the city for many Indians. Urban centers were places to earn a living, but not a complete way of life.

## CULTURAL CONFLICT

Commissioner Dillon Myer hoped that Indians in cities would melt into the urban populace and cease to be a drain on the federal treasury. Hardliners, among them the termination advocates in the 1950s, viewed with satisfaction the idea of Indians in cities using the bus as the new buffalo, to be chased across concrete prairies, without any bureau involvement.

Early expectations were falsely high. Government officials planned for relocation to improve the economic well-being of native peoples. At the agency office, Indians looked at brochures that portrayed suburban ranch-style houses with picket fences in photographs aimed at enticing wives to town. Pictures circulated in pamphlets showed women beside an electric refrigerator or television set. The pictures, with alluring views of city success, stood in stark contrast to the squalor and desperation on the reservation or in rural communities. What happened to relocated Indians, whether with bureau sponsorship or on their own, was quite different from the plans of government hardliners.

American Indians have been the most rural group of any in the U.S. population. In many aspects the city was the opposite of what the rural Indian was accustomed to seeing. It was as if a resident of the United States had been transported to China and was then expected to fend for himself or herself.

The Indian person new to the city was bewildered, alone, and frightened. He was far from people and objects of tribal familiarity, from tribal language, from elders, from longed for valleys, and from the coyote, the bear, and the turtle.

City noise contrasted with the solitude and expanse of the reservation. The congestion of town was alien to a person from an extended family in a rural area where strangers were rarely encountered. The coldness of the city dweller hurt the Indian accustomed to the camaraderie of relatives.

The aggressiveness and materialism of city residents appeared rude and crass to a person accustomed to propriety and poverty. Loneliness screamed out in a person safe in communal quarters at home. Among Indians, outspoken individuality and acquisitiveness stood in glaring contrast to identification with the group. Strict punctuality as opposed to a good-natured and tolerant sense of time confused many natives.

The great chasm of language was never bridged by some Indians. Non-Indians characterized the Indian's polite silence as sullenness when the Indian did not respond readily in conversation. In reality, the Indian may have given careful attention to the well-meaning banter the non-Indian person produced in an endless sociable stream.

In an urban classroom the silent Indian child did not receive help because the pupil did not speak up to ask the teacher for help. The children who needed help did not receive it. One Indian mother reported her frustration when she stated that from her children in public school, "I hear a lot of things I get sore about, but then I don't do anything about it because of my poor English and all that."

The Indian woman who needed prenatal care may not have received it because she did not have a telephone and probably had no automobile to travel to a physician. She may have lacked bus fare.

Housing customs in cities did not allow large Indian families under one roof. Municipal ordinances limited extended family dwelling. Children could not obtain the cultural reinforcement from grandparents who were forced to return to the reservation or had to move in with another relative.

Once in the city for job training, the Indian person was instructed in a low-skill job, such as automobile fender repair. The bureau spent only a short time finding a job for the relocated trainee once instruction was completed. The BIA permitted one job change at the start. A standard joke of the time was that the Indian trainee got a choice of a great variety of occupations in the city, as long as it was either as a welder or a beautician.

Once on the job, though, the worker faced more than the usual adjustment problems. The American Indian from the reservation was not from a home that had a father get up in the morning to go to work and return with a weekly paycheck. Wage labor was not a long-standing ancestral trait. Worse, the laborer had to survive the usual round of jibes about his "squaw" and endure derogatory names of "chief" and "buck." He encountered disparaging jokes about the rain: too much rain and the worker was dancing too much; too little dancing brought not enough rain.

As the individual Indian worker struggled through the work week, he realized that grasping at the dream of success could never assure the reality of success. The almost desperate hope of the migrant seemed out of reach. By every measurement, American Indians ranked on the lowest economic and social levels in cities.

Indian people concentrated in service work, domestic, and laborer categories—the lower end of the occupational scale. Urban Indians resided in the most substandard housing, had the least satisfactory sanitary facilities, had the highest rate of illiteracy, commanded the highest rate of diseases per capita, were more often unemployed, and when employed were more often underemployed and received lower wages than all of the other groups in the city. The Indian in the city was among the poorest of poor city dwellers. The urban Indian was only slightly better off economically than his reservation relatives.

Some of the Indian family members fell into an all too familiar pattern of frustration, despair, alienation, apathy, and suicidal behavior. City vices were easier to pick up than city virtues. Many Indians found temporary companionship in the neighborhood tavern. Because most of the Indian drinking was done out of doors or in a few bars known for their rowdy clientele, the image of the "drunken Indian" quickly emerged. Some of those Indians entered the revolving door of alcoholism with its arrests, hospitalization, and release back to skid row. Most arrest rates for American Indians were alcohol-related. Rising absenteeism on his job then resulted in the layoff of the Indian worker and the addition of another relocation "failure" to the statistics.

With so many barriers, both brought with them and provided to them in the city, it is a wonder any Indians at all remained in the cities.

In frustration, desperation, and anxiety, most of the relocated Indians abandoned their tiny apartment along with dreams of city success. Figures on the numbers vary widely but usually hover between 40 to 70 percent. Some Indians left the city after as little as three months. The director of social services for the Minneapolis Native American Center, Dennis His Gun, a Sioux, summed up the defeat that was repeated time and time again:

> But I think everybody who comes to the city has a dream—a dream of making it, a dream about improving their lives. But then prejudice slaps them right in the face and they're worse off. Call it culture shock. When your bubble is burst, there's nothing left but to go back home and start dreaming again.

There were determined ones who remained to strive for betterment for their families. Other workers hesitatingly returned to the city for another try. In all instances, the BIA offered no assistance after the time limit for adjustment ended for those who qualified.

Indians sought assistance in the town from other groups. There were only a few avenues of help available. The forlorn, lost, and confused city dweller could turn to travelers' aid for limited material assistance, but, for cultural reinforcement and support, the weary Indian family turned most often to relatives, if there were any in the city. If not, then the migrants sought assistance from other American Indians whom they might encounter.

Another source of support was an Indian church in the poorer section of the town. American Indian churches sometimes produced American Indian centers. In Chicago, St. Augustine's, and in Sioux City, St. Paul's Episcopal Church, provided the nucleus around which developed an American Indian center to aid other needy Indians. In Los Angeles, the American Friends Service Committee provided monetary and clerical assistance for the fledgling American Indian operation, which began as an Indian social club and expanded into social services to help fill the vacuum.

The urban Indian center served as a focal point for the complex network of intertribal organizations that had informally begun in the city. As relocation pressures continued, the resources of the centers were stretched to the breaking point. Even the BIA had to expand its services to Indian clients as the volume of need rose. In Chicago, the BIA staff helped found the American Indian Center. Gradually, more Indians became involved as new skills were learned and Indian cultural values were successfully used in assisting Indians in cities.

To break the barrier of adjustment to the city, some urban migrants would cluster in a part of the city, creating small versions of a reservation as a cultural enclave. Native language and native customs would predominate and lessen the intrusion of the wider city into the lives of individual Indians.

A myriad of clubs, guilds, societies, and other organizations would spring into existence in the Indian areas of cities. A Saturday night Indian dance club would hold meetings for drummers to practice, for youth to meet, and for elders to gather for conversation about the week's activities. An Indian powow club would meet regularly to perform dances and ceremonies as a link to the past. Sometimes members would perform for money for civic groups, but most often the club carried on cherished traditions for its own members.

Assistance in adjusting came also from the cyclical movement of Indian families to the reservation to maintain kinship ties, attend ceremonies, and share in tribal experiences. Many Indians traveled the summer circuit of reservation powwows and ceremonials. Navajo families commuted from Albuquerque to the Navajo Reservation, while Sioux families journeyed from work in Denver to the Rosebud Reservation, or Mohawks working in high steel returned to their reservations for gatherings. One Onondaga ironworker apprentice gave his explanation of the circular traveling he did yearly. Fortunately, his employer understood and allowed his absences:

> I missed five or six days of school to go home for Midwinters, for the Ceremonies. We have the longest Midwinters at Onondaga, lasts 18 to 21 days, it's our New Year, it's like Thanksgiving for different things,

with a separate day for each. I'm one of the younger singers, that sings the spiritual songs as well as the social songs.

. . . it's more important to me right now that I went home for the Ceremonies than to continue in school.

Natives carried strong cultural ties into the cities, too. Indian community center socials, the all-night "49" or Indian sing that may have used a car hood as an impromptu drum, and the spread of the powwow by the urban phenomenon among Indians continued Indian traditions. Indian culture had not died out in the cities, as was the ardent hope when relocation began. Even Christian Indian churches retained much of the flavor and essence of Indian traditions. The music at the Fifth Sunday Sing at an Indian Christian church incorporated reservation vocables, melodies, and musical style. Other singers in the urban region blended Indian and modern Anglo-American types of music. Paul Ortega entertained audiences with a folk style, while Floyd Westerman utilized country and western arrangements, and Larry Emerson inspired Indian youth with Christian evangelism. The band XIT as well as Billy Thundercloud, Redbone, and Jim Pepper offered American Indian rock music.

A strong plains Indian stream flowed through modern Indian ceremonial patterns, centered on the powwow and Indian art. The city gallery featured Western Indian art of plains and Southwestern sections. The dual role of Indian and urbanite was reinforced through adoption of intertribal art forms and ceremonial costuming. One Indian artist might have painted a scene of another's tribe, while color mixtures representing clan membership may have been mingled into another tribal artist's work on canvas. On the powwow field, a dancer of one tribe might have borrowed the bead work design or feather work of his neighbor from another tribe. An Indian woman from the Pacific Northwest participated in a plains-style powwow, even though that was not her home tradition.

The Pan-Indian movement formed a bridge between tribes and brought marginal mixed-bloods back into full-blood ceremonies. All of the participants shared in the cultural spirituality that set Indians apart from their non-Indian neighbors. What may have appeared to an outsider as a self-indulgent social gathering done to the hypnotic repetition of a drum was in reality a method that built an ethnic identity, broke social isolation, passed on traditions to youth, and reaffirmed religious bonds. In Indian associations, many sought refuge from the terrible loss of identity that marked modern urban existence. In the Pacific Northwest, some workers commuted to an Indian Shaker Church service. On the plains, the Indian individual could have attended a peyote ceremony of the Native American Church. The services blended traditional ritual with Christian symbolism, rural with urban worshippers, and native languages with English.

## CONCLUSION

The limited sociological and anthropological literature that examined urban natives of North America found that women weathered the acculturation of cities better than men. Traditional couples survived, especially those with previous job experience, better than individuals. All underwent profound shock when they entered the alien world of urban centers. Some who had successful experiences in towns bordering reservations fared better than those who came directly from reservations or rural communities and who lacked communication and work skills.

Native peoples have not vanished down concrete sidewalks. Recent policies did not drastically change native attachment to a separate identity. American Indians maintained their customs and lifeways in cities for a very long time. Mission Indians within the San Antonio, Texas, church compounds stubbornly clung to their heritage in spite of Spanish efforts to assimilate them. Indian people of Long Island and Massachusetts continued their links with the past in the face of European-American assimilation. American Indians have been a vital part of urban life in the Americas since the first settlements of Europeans. Natives will continue to play an important role in cities in the United States as part of an enduring legacy.

## SUGGESTED READING

Literary works offer a glimpse into the lives of urban Indians. Byrd Baylor's *Yes Is Better Than No* (New York, 1977) is a delightful tragicomic novel about Arizona Papago Indians in Tucson trying to live with the inscrutable white man. Gerald Vizenor, *Wordarrows: Indians and Whites in the New Fur Trade* (Minneapolis, 1978) is a Chippewa writer who combines autobiography, biography, fantasy, and vision in depiction of realities of urban Indians in Minneapolis. In *The Death of Jim Loney* (New York, 1979), James Welch, a well-known American Indian novelist and poet, offers a dark, somber novel of alienation of a mixed-blood male who finds little sanctuary in white or Indian society. Indian author Janet Campbell Hale, in *The Jailing of Cecelia Capture* (New York, 1985), describes the troubled experiences of an Indian female law student in the San Francisco Bay Area. An uproarious novel about the escapades of an Indian GI on the reservation who commutes to the city, leading his mother often to exclaim *Stay Away, Joe* (New York, 1953), was penned by Dan Cushman. Clair Huffaker wrote *Nobody Loves a Drunken Indian* (New York, 1967); the novel deals with the antics of Flapping Eagle, an alcoholic resident of a fictitious Paiute reservation on the outskirts of Phoenix. He "conquers" the city in a revolution, using an old treaty, a train, an ocean of booze, and a large contingent of friends. Simon Ortiz, "Woman Singing," in John R. Milton, ed., *The American Indian Speaks* (Vermillion, 1969): 34–44, provides one of the finest literary treatments of the cultural "draw" of the reservation and kinfolk. Ortiz is an Ácoma poet and writer. The Kiowa playwright Hanay Geiogamah in the acclaimed "Body Indian," in his *New Native American Drama: Three Plays* (Norman, 1980): 3–44, gives a disturbing, gritty portrayal of an Indian alcoholic's acute needs for rehabilitation, for companionship, for a healing of the misery and stress of modern urban existence.

Scholarly literature abounds on the subject of the urban Indian. Among the more useful is the collection of chapters in Jack Waddell and Michael Watson, eds., *The American Indian in Urban Society* (Boston, 1971). Blending history, social work, law, and Indian viewpoints into an overview is the government document *Urban and Rural Non-Reservation Indians* (Washington, D.C., 1977) by the American Indian Policy Review Commission's Task Force Eight. Elaine Neils in *Reservation to City* (Chicago, 1971) examines the federal relocation program in a heavily statistical account. The noted anthropologist Sol Tax in "The Impact of Urbanization on American Indians," *Annals of the American Academy of Political and Social Science* 436 (March 1978): 121–136, assesses kin groups, numbers, and adjustment issues of urban Indians. In the same issue, Sam Stanley and Robert Thomas look at contemporary changes (pages 111–120). A pioneering modern study that is still pertinent is Joan Ablon's "American Indian Relocation: Problems of Dependency and Management in the City," *Phylon* 26 (Winter 1965): 362–371. Another is John Price, "The Migration and Adaptation of American Indians to Los Angeles," *Human Organization* 27 (December 1968): 168–175. It is reprinted in Howard Bahr, Bruce Chadwick, and Robert Day, eds., *Native Americans Today: Sociological Perspectives* (New York, 1972): 428–439.

Roger **17.** Indians
L. **Something** since
Nichols **Old,** World
  War
**Something** II
**New**

T he Great Depression of the 1930s and World War II,
  which followed on its heels, brought drastic and
permanent changes to American society. For native Americans, however,
neither of these two events had as much impact as did the decades after the
war. From the 1940s to the 1980s the Indian population of the United
States doubled, or perhaps even tripled. During those same years nearly
half of all tribal peoples came to live in cities and towns among the general population rather than on isolated reservations, chiefly in the West.
Whether living on reservations or in towns and cities, native American
young people obtained more education than had their parents. In small
but growing numbers, they attended colleges and universities, receiving
degrees in many fields. For all Indians general levels of health improved,
longevity increased, and standards of living inched upward toward the
position attained by other groups of poor in the nation.

Despite these and other developments for native Americans, in some
ways few major changes occurred. To put it another way, both temporary
and long-term difficulties remained. Relations with the federal government, and, in particular, with the employees of the Bureau of Indian Affairs (BIA) and related federal offices continued unsettled. While Indians
strove for personal independence, those bureaucrats who had made decisions for them endeavored to keep their charges docile and obedient.
Questions about tribal treaty rights and benefits caused repeated debate.
Reformers and Indian-haters alike worked for changes in the treatment
and status of the tribes. The push for assimilation of all native Americans
into the general population, which extended back to the early days of the
Republic, continued as well. Whether because of misdirected efforts to
"help" the tribesmen or because of greed and envy over their special relationship with the government, individuals and groups worked to make Indians disappear.

Not that any responsible persons called for extermination. Rather, many

*292*

Americans hoped and assumed that right-thinking Indians should begin the process of shedding their distinctiveness and then merge with the general population. Existing issues continued to draw attention and energy while new matters arose which brought change and conflict for Indians in American society.

During the 1930s and World War II the federal government had changed its perspective toward Indian affairs. Rather than force assimiliation it turned, under John Collier's administration of the BIA, to policies of self-determination, cultural encouragement, and a much higher level of Indian participation in planning and decision making than had been the case ever before that era. As a result, native Americans enjoyed having some control over their lives and activities. In addition, temporary jobs offered by various New Deal agencies and increased employment during the war brought Indians into contact with other Americans in increasing numbers. Once the war ended, however, cost cutting in government became a national mania. The old hue and cry about getting the government out of the Indian business and of "liberating" tribal people so that they might live as other citizens could be heard in the halls of Congress. Calls for the government to dismantle the reservations, abolish the newly created tribal governments, and stop giving Indians special treatment emanated from both the House and the Senate.

Led by Senator Arthur Watkins of Utah and Congressman E. Y. Berry of South Dakota, congressional critics of New Deal Indian policies launched a broad attack on existing programs. The first result of this was the 1946 creation of the Indian Claims Commission. Hailed as a means to right past wrongs to the tribes, this body was in reality the first new step along the path of ending any special treatment or relationship enjoyed by individual Indians or tribes. It gave Indian groups a vehicle for suing the government for past damages. Forced cessions of land or other resources, unfair or crooked treaty negotiations, underpayment of promised benefits, loss of fishing or hunting rights, and the seizure of timber and mineral rights would all be considered. The commission would hear cases which then might be appealed to the federal courts should its judgments be rejected.

Prior to this time tribes had to persuade Congress to pass special legislation in order to bring suit against the government in the Court of Claims. The Court rejected a high percentage of Indian claims, and the remaining few took years or even decades to inch their way through repeated hearings and delays. Obviously the new procedure was an improvement for the Indians. Yet once the Claims Commission held its hearings and the tribes accepted its judgment or appealed to the federal courts for a settlement, all past claims were held to be satisfied. In trying to reach that point, bands, villages, and tribes often became enmeshed in litigation which lasted for years. The difficulties of the new process and its casual, even slow pace, may be seen in the fact that the commission docket became so filled that Congress extended its life far beyond the original ten years. In fact, some cases are still unresolved, although during the 1970s most claims were settled.

The experience of the tiny Kalispel tribe of Washington State provides a clear example of the difficulties and mixed results of working with the Claims Commission. By 1950 when Kalispel leaders turned to the commission, less than one hundred Indians lived on the reservation in poverty. From the time they filed their first petition in 1951 until they reached a settlement fifteen years passed. Lawyers died, law firms had to be changed, expert witnesses hired, contracts signed, and conflicts with the claims of other tribes all had to be resolved before the issues could be settled. By 1963 the commission approved a judgment for three million dollars from which the law firms deducted their 10 percent fee. That same year Congress appropriated the money, but the funds remained impounded until the tribe submitted plans for spending this sum. Then Congress had to pass a second bill actually releasing the funds to the tribe. During Senate hearings on the Kalispel bill Western senators demanded that the money be withheld until the tribe accepted a termination plan. Bitter disputes erupted within the tribe during the following months, and it took until late 1965 for the tribe to receive its long-awaited funds. Divisions and quarrels which broke out during the fifteen-year process continue to be present. Other than actually getting the extra money, the only other positive result of these proceedings was that some tribesmen learned how to cope with at least some of the federal bureaucracy.

Closely related to long-term efforts to end government programs for Indians and related directly to the Claims Commission procedures, was the policy known as termination. During 1947, as part of the postwar efforts to streamline the size, operations, and cost of the federal government, Herbert Hoover chaired a study commission which bore his name. In its report the Hoover Commission called for the "discontinuance of all specialized Indian activity" by the federal government. It recommended that as soon as possible the native Americans be integrated into the general society, and when that occurred the government should "close out its responsibilities to the Indian people."

The Hoover Commission recommendations found eager listeners in Congress. Senator Watkins spoke for many in the West when he issued calls for an end to special treatment of the Indians. Responding to the Hoover Commission Report, he and other congressmen asked the BIA to examine the situation of each group or tribe. Then the BIA was to indicate which Indians were able to do without federal services. That same year, 1947, acting Commissioner of Indian Affairs William Zimmerman, under pressure from Congressional committees, prepared a list of tribes which might be able to get along without federal assistance. Nevertheless actual termination took shape slowly, and it was not until early 1951 that Commissioner Dillon S. Myer set up a staff committee to begin preparing his charges for the new policy.

Although calls for termination became insistent as early as 1947, it was not until 1952 that the House of Representatives called on the BIA for a report on the Indians' ability to survive without federal programs. Commissioner Myer responded that groups in California, Kansas, Michigan, and New York needed no further help. As a result, in 1953 Congress adopted House Resolution 108 calling for full-fledged termination of all benefits to tribes in ten states and asserting that such an action represented the will of Congress. Within the next year Congress passed other legislation setting termination into rapid motion. What reformers, Indian-haters, and Westerners greedy for tribal lands and resources had demanded for a century had come to pass. The government was actually trying to get out of the Indian business.

Once begun the process went ahead with little careful planning and certainly without any premonition of the social and economic disasters which lay ahead. Sometimes actions counted far more than results. On the other hand, the encouragement of states to be more aggressive in assuming jurisdiction over native Americans under Public Law 280 led to the actual loss of some rights for a time. States began to enforce hunting and fishing laws among Indians who often had treaty rights a century old exempting them from such local laws. The BIA itself worked diligently to carry out the new policy, and within the first decade of termination at least sixty-one tribes, villages, bands, and ranchers lost rights and services they had previously enjoyed.

Although dozens of Indian groups experienced the rigors of termination, none suffered more than the Menominee of Wisconsin. Located on 235,000 acres of good timberland in northcentral Wisconsin, this modest-sized tribe of about 3,200 members had retained its land base by opposing the General Indian Allotment Act of 1887. Alone among the tribes of that state it had not been forced off its land along the Wolf River. By the early twentieth century, the Menominee built and operated their own tribal sawmill, which, in turn, helped them carry out sustained yield lumbering on their reservation. This provided jobs and a modest income for the tribe as well as allowing them to receive the services of a hospital and school run jointly with nearby Roman Catholic missionaries. As a result of a relatively stable population and their local lumbering industry, the tribe remained in better condition than most Indians at the time.

By the 1930s suspicion that inefficient officials from the BIA were not managing their tribal timber resources effectively led Menominee leaders to launch a lawsuit against the federal government. Settled in 1951 in the United States Court of Claims, the suit gave the tribe victory and a judgment of $7,600,000. Indian joy at having won their case against the government proved short-lived. The actual cash languished in the federal treasury and could be paid only with the approval of Congress. In 1951 the disbursement bill had a termination rider attached, and when the tribe opposed that requirement they learned that they could not get their money.

While the Menominee grumbled, Congress moved toward applying complete termination to the tribe. In June 1953, Senator Watkins visited the reservation, urging the tribesmen to accept "the principle of termination" and issued vague threats predicting trouble for the tribe should it vote against termination. By the time Senator Watkins left for Washington the Indians had voted in favor of the new policy. Later the same summer, when they learned what the results of their earlier vote might be, the Indians took a second ballot in which they unanimously chose to forego per capita payments if termination was the only way to get them.

Despite repeated Indian objections termination continued. In 1961 it became fully operative when the reservation became Wisconsin's newest county and a corporation, Menominee Enterprises, Incorporated, took charge of tribal property and funds. From the start the new county experienced major difficulties in financing local services. Its hospital failed to meet state standards and had to be closed. Continuing shortages of funds led the corporation to begin selling tribal land and to work with real estate developers to encourage affluent whites to buy cabin sites on the lakes and rivers of the former reservation. In this way, the new policy of termination produced the same results as had the older policy of allotment, which had occurred some seventy-five years earlier. Indians continued losing land to whites. Individual Indians lost their property through default or inability to pay local taxes. Seeing wealthy whites building on some of the most desirable parts of the reservation eventually angered the Indians. After much difficulty they organized as DRUMS—Determination of Rights and Unity for Menominee Stockholders. Working within the cor-

poration, through the tribal government, and with some Wisconsin political leaders, the Menominee majority succeeded in getting the government
to repeal the act of termination. This effort took more than a decade, however, and during that time untold damage to tribal life and well-being had
been done.

The Menominee example is perhaps the most stark and the policy failure
the most dramatic, but it represents clearly what was meant to happen to
all terminated groups of native Americans. Much of the rhetoric surrounding this policy resembled that offered in support of allotment in the 1880s.
Indians were to be freed from the reservations, were to be treated as other
citizens, and were to be allowed to sink or swim in the general society.
While that occurred the government was to end its special relationship toward the tribal peoples. With these policies few considered that the process
took place in the face of overwhelming Indian opposition—obviously a
sign that something might be amiss. Although many individuals representing groups interested in getting Indian timber, oil, coal, water, or other
resources waited eagerly for their chance, such pressures remained outside
most public discussion of the issues surrounding termination. Apparently
few in or out of government foresaw the grave social and economic problems which arose directly out of the termination efforts.

Although termination was the most spectacular failure of the Eisenhower era approach to native Americans, it certainly was not the only one.
Relocation, another new policy but directly related to termination, arose
during the 1950s too. Based on the assumption that when federal benefits
for reservation dwellers ceased many Indians would leave their homes seeking employment, relocation was to help them move. Its planners wanted to
find jobs in the towns and cities for the former reservation dwellers. While
appearing as something new in white-Indian relations, this policy merely
made formal an unstated goal of long-standing—to break up the reservations. In this case it was to be through encouraging people to move
into the cities rather than by taking tribal land. Clearly the result would be
similar.

In 1952 the BIA established the Voluntary Relocation Program. Later,
perhaps because of negative publicity, this came to be called the Employment Assistance Program. Whatever its name, the program did encourage
Indian migration from reservations and rural areas into the cities. In theory, after local BIA officers interviewed reservation dwellers, those with
the most skills or the best chances for success would be encouraged to
move to a city with a Field Relocation Office. These communities included
Denver, Phoenix, Albuquerque, San Francisco, Seattle, Dallas, Oklahoma

City, Chicago, and Minneapolis. Reservation dwellers got financial help moving to the city, some maintenance and living expenses until getting their first wages, and general help with employment, housing, and counseling.

Between its inception and 1970, some 100,000 native Americans participated in some part of this relocation program. At first the BIA efforts lacked careful planning and coordination, and many of the relocatees left the cities for home after a short time. Statistics for the program are notoriously inaccurate. For example, they give little indication that both families and individuals often returned home frequently but drifted back to the cities in months or even weeks. By 1957 the Adult Vocational Training Program was in full swing. This provided training in marketable skills to Indians aged 18 to 35 on the assumption that once trained, these people would be more likely to get and hold jobs than those without such help.

One significant theme usually overlooked in discussions of relocation is the fact that it did not start the flow of reservation dwellers into the cities. This had begun as early as the 1920s and, except for the Great Depression of the 1930s, continued to the present. In fact, even accepting the figure of 100,000 as the number of Indians who did move to town by 1970, one must remember that had all of these people remained there they would still be less than one-third of all urban Indians in the United States that year. So while the program itself was new or mostly new, it merely added its results to existing social and economic trends then in motion.

The stories of Indians' experiences in the cities vary widely. Those with some adequate job skills managed reasonably well. Those lacking needed skills did not. Clearly for many the move was difficult. They missed home, family, and friends. They had difficulties in adjusting to the impersonal life in large cities. Many, who might have done better, settled for low-paying, but steady jobs which seemed to offer security. Like immigrants of earlier generations, Indians sought each other out in the cities, often living together or in the same neighborhoods. In the cities many Indians experienced some discrimination in housing, jobs, and education. This was particularly true in smaller communities near large reservations. Nevertheless, the urban dwelling native Americans' story includes many things experienced by other immigrants to U.S. cities in the twentieth century. The pattern of returning home either permanently or frequently for short periods of time is a good example. Both Southern blacks and Appalachian whites moving into the northern industrial cites did the same thing. In fact, so did large numbers of Greeks, Lebanese, and Syrians during the decade just before World War I. For many Indian immigrants the city was more hostile than they had expected. Still, large numbers of them have made the transition to urban life successfully, and their growing skills and competence will help ease the way for those who follow.

While both termination and urban relocation strove to dismantle the tribes, other federal actions moved in the direction of self-determination, even if that might strengthen native American communities. For example, in 1961 Congress passed the Area Redevelopment Administration Act. This legislation made the tribes eligible to buy or develop land for commercial or industrial projects as well as to establish public facilities such as motels, ski resorts, and fishing camps. Several years later President Lyndon Johnson announced that administration policy was to achieve a new goal for Indians. He specifically labeled it "self-determination." In 1975 this goal became law when Congress passed the Indian Self-Determination and Educational Assistance Act. Under this law tribes had the option of accepting or rejecting the application of federal programs to their members. Some hailed the law as a major change in Indian-federal relations, but critics noted sourly that it seemed nothing more than a tired rehash of the earlier discredited Indian Reorganization Act of the 1930s.

Trends in education follow the same dichotomy already noted in so many areas of the Indian experience during the past four decades. The centuries-old goal of teaching native Americans to become successful whites has continued. At the same time, however, substantial changes in content, method, and goals of Indian education have occurred both by accident and by design. For much of the twentieth century some native American children attended local reservation day schools staffed by BIA appointees. Others traveled far from home to attend government-operated boarding schools such as the Haskell Institute in Kansas or the Phoenix Indian School in Arizona. Often Indians living near towns and cities had to send their children to public schools in white communities. Regardless of what sort of school they attended, however, few Indian children received good academic or vocational training. Perhaps of equal importance, Indian tribes, villages, or families rarely had anything whatsoever to say about any aspect of their children's schooling.

This certainly was the case as World War II drew to a close. BIA educators considered vocational skills and education for an urban life a must. As early as 1944 they began offering Indian veterans training as carpenters, electricians, machinists, masons, printers, and welders. Thus, if they had not already done so, the BIA boarding schools shifted to a curriculum aimed at producing skilled urban workers.

By the 1950s the BIA boarding schools increasingly received students from broken homes, those whose parents were on welfare, and those adjudged predelinquent. With a growing percentage of emotionally disturbed and often hard-to-teach students, it is little wonder that teachers, staff members, and parents alike became discouraged. The schools lacked the funds, equipment, and staff for such a assignment. The fact is that for several decades the boarding schools had been getting increasing numbers of such students, but despite repeated requests for more money and staff the Congress provided no relief. By 1969 when the Kennedy Report appeared, its authors had little choice but to chronicle the difficulties and denounce the results.

For native American youngsters not attending boarding schools the changes came slowly at first. As early as the 1930s the Johnson-O'Malley Act had begun providing funds for local schools to use in meeting the added costs of educating reservation children. The success of this program after the war is questionable. In fact, by the 1960s federal investigators uncovered many instances of white school boards diverting this money into programs for non-Indian children. In many cases, honest school boards and administrators throughout the West did try to use the Johnson-O'Malley funds effectively, but even then long-time anti-Indian prejudice in communities near reservations limited the success of many public schools. These problems led to growing demands for Indian community-operated day schools, in which the tribe or village had substantial say in all aspects of the curriculum and the methods for teaching it.

A growing clamor for more native American control of their children's education surfaced during the mid-1960s just at the time when the federal civil rights programs and the War on Poverty went into operation. In an abrupt turnaround the government seemed to strip the BIA of much of its ability to thwart Indian desires or to continue its long-standing paternalism toward its charges. In 1966 the Coleman *Report on Equality and Educational Opportunity* appeared. It noted that repeated BIA efforts to use the schools to bring about Indian assimilation had failed. In addition, the report noted that the schools' chief success had been in destroying the cultural pride and self-awareness of Indian young people. Reformers had been saying such things for decades, but to have the federal government acknowledge the problem was a major change.

During the 1960s a host of new federal legislation, agencies, and programs all helped make educational improvements available to Indians. The Manpower Development and Training Act of 1962 set up facilities for giving Indians more vocational skills. The Economic Opportunity Act of 1964 was of more long-range importance, however. It established the Office of Economic Opportunity in order to administer the series of antipoverty programs then coming into operation. Perhaps of most significance was the provision which allowed Indian communities and tribal councils to create their own reservation-based programs. Not only would such activities provide jobs for reservation dwellers, but the Indians themselves would plan, operate, and administer them. This concept was startlingly new, at least for native Americans. From Jamestown to the 1960s whites had always assumed that they knew best. Now, after generations of asking to run their own affairs tribal leaders had the opportunity, at least in some areas of their lives.

Within a short time, communities and tribal governments moved to set up programs such as Head Start to help preschool children and those in the lower elementary school grades improve their language skills. For older students the Upward Bound program offered encouragement to finish high school, and because of it some young people went to college who otherwise might not have done so. Volunteers in Service to America programs brought young whites to reservations as volunteers to assist with many local programs. In each of these efforts, local and tribal authorities demonstrated what they had said for years—that they could manage their own affairs if only the BIA would step out of the way and give them a chance. Now, surprisingly, it had been forced to do just that. The results startled practically everyone except the Indians themselves.

One of the most convincing examples of Indian competence to run their own affairs came in the efforts of a traditional Navajo community at Rough Rock in Arizona. Most of the reservation dwellers there spoke no English and had little formal education themselves. Yet when the Office of Economic Opportunity offered funds to help the Indians take charge of their own schools, the community proved equal to the challenge. Not only did the people at Rough Rock manage the school well, but their example led to a major shift in educational approach. The most obvious change came when English was treated as a second language rather than being used as the center of all instruction. Of equal importance was the idea that the local community people would have a major role in determining both policy and content for their schools. Similar Indian-run school districts developed in Montana, Iowa, and New Mexico within a few years of the Rough Rock success.

Following the host of laws passed during the 1960s, the federal government continued enacting social legislation into the next decade, which helped Indian groups. In 1972 the Indian Education Act continued the federal efforts. This law established new programs to overcome the lack of educational opportunities for Indian children. The broader Indian Self-

Determination Act of 1975 included educational provisions too. It went beyond the practice of giving aid to both Indian students and Indian schools in several ways. The new law required teachers in Indian schools to be bilingual so they could teach the students in their native language as well as in English. It also required that native Americans have more say in the immediate operations of their schools. Clearly these innovations in Indian educational policy varied widely from earlier ideas that the tribal peoples had to be "civilized" through the white man's schools.

The changes in attitudes and actions regarding Indians just discussed did not develop spontaneously but resulted from many causes. Certainly the disaster of termination helped. Beyond that, however, national political and social trends coupled with a growing Indian awareness and cultural pride played an important part in the changes. The civil rights actions of the 1960s caught the enthusiasm of some young Indians. As early as the summer of 1961 the American Indian Charter Convention met in Chicago. Unlike many previous pan-Indian meetings, this gathering agreed on "A Declaration of Indian Purpose," one of the first times native Americans had agreed on any broad set of ideas. Following that meeting many of the younger participants met again to form the National Indian Youth Council (NIYC). This organization probably owed its existence to knowledge of the black participation in the civil rights movement and to a growing split among native Americans. The NIYC represented the poorer, more traditional Indians on the reservations, claiming that nearly assimilated mixed-bloods dominated the other organizations. These young leaders spoke in favor of using native languages, of pride in being Indian, and of using Red Power to achieve their goals.

Clyde Warrior, an Oklahoma Ponca, was the most outspoken early leader of this group. Although he soon died, others followed his ideas. The result was that during the next few years Indian militancy increased. NIYC members demonstrated against the loss of Indian rights and for including tribal groups in newly prepared federal legislation and programs. In the Pacific Northwest, young native Americans sponsored and participated in several "fish-ins" protesting state efforts to curb or even end long-standing guarantees of fishing rights there. Scores of demonstrators, including some Hollywood personalities, took part, bringing national media attention to the issue. Certainly this was a tactic rarely used in earlier decades. Other young Indians objected to nearly any cooperation with BIA-sponsored programs. Organizing on college campuses, they published a newsletter, *Americans before Columbus*, through which they sought to exchange ideas and raise the interest among nonparticipating students.

The thrust for self-determination grew, helped by federal legislation, growing Indian militance, and a gradual public awakening to some of the issues. Few white Americans realized how many native Americans remained at the bottom of society, and even fewer had any idea of what native Americans wanted. When hearing of the fish-ins or similar events, such as the occupation of a lighthouse on Lake Michigan near Milwaukee, Wisconsin, few people gave the incidents much serious thought. For native Americans, however, such efforts indicated their increasing use of protest methods which previously they had shunned. Now they realized that dignified, silent protests brought few results and that those groups which managed to get full media coverage often received more productive hearings than those which did not. However, more traditional Indians objected to confrontation tactics, and the new approaches tended to further divide tribal people.

During the terms of both Presidents Johnson and Richard Nixon, Indian affairs got more attention than usual. President Johnson was the first American president to deliver a special message to Congress solely on Indian matters. In 1968, to help coordinate programs for native Americans, he established the National Council on Indian Opportunity. Although Johnson left office within a year, his successor followed suit. The Republican victory in 1968 had sent chills of fear through many Indian groups. They remembered the discredited termination policy pushed so actively by the Republicans during their preceding term in office and wondered what new disasters were about to come out of Washington. To their surprise, President Nixon announced an enlightened approach on Indian matters. As Johnson had done, he appointed an Indian, this time a Sioux-Mohawk, Louis R. Bruce, as commissioner of Indian Affairs. Then in early 1970, he too sent a special message to Congress in which he called for the repeal of the earlier termination laws, for Indian authority to serve as contractors for federal programs, and for complete Indian control of reservation schools. Some of these things had been started earlier, but Nixon's call helped push them along.

Despite what seems to have been a continuing series of steps giving native Americans more help and opportunity to control their own actions, plenty of anger and disagreement remained. In particular, Nixon's appointment of Walter Hickel, former governor of Alaska and an outspoken opponent of conservationists, as his secretary of the Interior, angered the militants. In late 1969 activists picketed Hickel at the annual meeting of the National Council of American Indians in Albuquerque. A few months later native Americans in the San Francisco region occupied Alcatraz Island, which housed the abandoned federal prison of the same name. Claiming it under a clause in the Sioux Treaty of 1868 which allowed Indians to occupy vacant federal land, the militants demanded that the government build an Indian cultural and educational center there. Public opinion across the country seemed favorable. Why should anyone object to a positive use for the former prison? Trying to appear reasonable, the administration negotiated with the occupiers, but disagreements among the Indians themselves and a certain inability to bend by the administration doomed the talks. They failed, and, after public attention turned to other matters, the government moved in June 1971 to remove the remaining occupiers.

In a more successful manner, the Nixon administration worked to return ownership of Blue Lake to the Indians of Taos Pueblo in New Mexico. The lake had been considered sacred by the Pueblo dwellers for generations and when the U.S. Forest Service opened it for use by tourists, the Indians objected—but to no avail. Taos won a decision giving them a cash settlement from the Indian Claims Commission in 1965, but Pueblo leaders rejected the money. They demanded the return of their sacred lake and the surrounding forest land from the government. Feeling more comfortable dealing with established tribal authorities than with radicals who invaded and occupied government property at Alcatraz, the administration supported legislation which would return Blue Lake to the Pueblo, and in 1971 the Indians regained their land. That same year the Alaska Native Claims Settlement occurred. This agreement, concluded after intense negotiations between the Alaska native people, the State of Alaska, the federal government, and several outspoken conservation groups, awarded 40,000,000 acres of land to the Indians, Aleuts, and Eskimos of Alaska. Despite that decision controversy over who got what land and under what conditions continued. Nevertheless, this agreement was seen as a major achievement in gaining secure title to lands long used and claimed by the native groups.

The Nixon years saw few other successes as far as government-Indian cooperation, however. Native American militancy continued, and the government became more heavy-handed as the decade of the seventies progressed. Bruce's Braves, as the young militants within the BIA called themselves, grew increasingly frustrated at the slow, legalistic approach of the administration. They demanded that the bureau give preference to hiring Indians despite equal opportunity laws then in effect. They criticized older Indians within the government as too hesitant and conservative, and a number of them resigned, hoping to be more effective outside the government. For example, Leon Cook, a Red Lake Ojibawa, became the president of the National Council of American Indians in 1971. In his acceptance speech to what had been one of the most conservative native American organizations, he denounced the federal government as trying to destroy Indian people by forcing them into "the polluted mainstream of American life." Clearly spokesmen of that persuasion still thought that the nation had a long way to go in righting past wrongs for the Indians.

As early as 1968 some militant Indians chose to follow the example set by the Black Panthers and other black civil rights groups. That year Dennis Banks and George Mitchell had founded the American Indian Movement (AIM). It grew out of the problems and despair of Indians huddled in a Minneapolis ghetto often called "the reservation." Objecting to police brutality they sought to focus public attention on the treatment of urban Indians. In addition they launched a series of sit-ins to gain public attention, seizing the *Mayflower II*, a replica of the Pilgrim's ship, and staging an illegal camp out on Mount Rushmore. At a Virginia conference on the problems of urban Indians, they took over the meeting and ruined parts of the conference center. In late 1972, eight native American organizations sponsored a caravan to Washington over what they called the "Trail of Broken Treaties." Supposedly the caravan wanted only to publicize Indian problems and mistreatment, but, in Washington on November 2, some of the travelers occupied the BIA building. AIM leaders issued a list of some twenty demands calling for an end of the BIA, the return of millions of acres of tribal lands, and a return to the treaty system for dealing with the government. While administration negotiators talked with the militants, some of the latter stole documents and artifacts from the offices in the building. Others ruined parts of the tribal files. When the occupation ended, the occupiers had failed to achieve any of their publicly stated goals.

As the Indians struggled back west, some of the federal funds they got for their travel expenses were spent for guns and ammunition. In February 1973, more AIM members occupied the Village of Wounded Knee, South Dakota. Using an intratribal election dispute between traditionalists and mixed-bloods on the Pine Ridge reservation as an excuse, the militants seized the community and demanded that the federal government overturn the tribal government and constitution then in operation on the reservation. By this time most other Americans reacted with little patience or sympathy to the violence. The news media no longer pictured the militants as Indian patriots, but more likely as thugs. AIM spokesmen contradicted each other and seemed unable to get their followers to agree on any single course of action. The Justice Department received orders to end the dispute and surrounded the community with an armed force of U.S. marshalls and others, while simply outwaiting the Indians. As a result, the dispute died quietly.

By the mid-1970s it was clear that all was not going well for the Indians. The creation and operations of the American Indian Policy Review Commission—often referred to by the shorter title of the Abourezk Commission—certainly seemed to demonstrate this. Established in 1975 this body was to review existing federal policies and make recommendations for change. From the start infighting among various native American groups and leaders undermined the commission's effectiveness. It held hearings across the country but the members failed to attend these fact-finding ventures. Instead eleven task forces toured the nation gathering data for nearly two years. At the end of that time the commission staff practically threw together its final report and recommendations. As a result there was little time to assess them with care, so the commission offered over two hundred proposals to Congress. Looking at this list a reader gets no sense of program, purpose, or ideology for positive reform.

Militancy having achieved only modest gains, most Indians turned to continued lobbying and legal efforts to protect themselves and their claims. In most cases the economic gains made in the past fifteen years far outweigh any achievements in social equality or civil rights. Throughout the West Indians work for tribal enterprises quarrying rock, processing lumber, and operating fishing, camping, and ski resorts. Coal and uranium mining also offer long-term employment for some tribes. Efforts by non-Indian businessmen and corporations may offer at least as much future promise. Industries currently operate more than one hundred factories and processing plants on reservations throughout the country. These range from Idaho in the northwest to Florida, and from Wisconsin southwest to Arizona. They give jobs to more than 10,000 native American workers and include such types of industries as electronics, food processing, gear manufacturing, diamond processing, and textile work. During the 1970s the result of efforts by the federal government, the tribes, and private business provided a greatly improved living standard for Indians.

Yet there remain problems in some parts of the country. There is still confusion between tribal, state, and federal courts and law enforcement. Tribes retaining treaty rights still have a "special" relationship with the federal government, which sets them apart from all other American citizens. For example, it was not until 1970 that the federal government allowed members of the so-called Five Civilized Tribes in Oklahoma to elect their own leaders. From 1906 until 1970 tribal executives had been federal appointees. For more than half a century, while other Americans could vote for city councilmen, county supervisors, and state leaders, these Oklahoma tribes had to accept appointed local officials.

Other problems for native Americans appeared in the 1961 findings of the Civil Rights Commission. That body compiled countless examples of unreasonable law enforcement practices aimed at Indians. It and other recent studies of this problem indicate that the arrest rate for Indians in communities near large reservations is nearly thirty times as high as it is for whites in the same cities. This selective law enforcement helped bring about the 1968 complaints that in Minnesota the local police arrested Indians for vagrancy, loitering, and drunkenness while ignoring similar actions by others. Locally AIM established "red patrols" designed to help keep native Americans out of trouble with the police. One of the most blatant examples of selective law enforcement took place in 1972 at Gordon, Nebraska. There, local vigilantes beat Raymond Yellow Thunder to death. When local officials ruled his death a suicide, hundreds of enraged Sioux from the nearby Pine Ridge reservation protested. This brought questions from the national media and others, forcing a sudden change of local attitude. An autopsy revealed that Yellow Thunder had been killed by force. This led to a more thorough investigation, and eventually two men were tried and convicted of manslaughter.

Investigations including the states of South Dakota, North Dakota, Nebraska, Oklahoma, and Arizona indicated similar actions and attitudes were widespread. Frequently local law enforcement officials arrested and jailed Indians under circumstances which would not have resulted in an arrest for whites. Arresting officers routinely used more force when dealing with native Americans than with others, and examples of law enforcement officers publicly voicing negative racial views toward Indians appear frequently. Perhaps none of these findings should surprise a modern reader because similar findings in studies which focused on blacks, Chicanos, and other minorities are common. Indian responses to this treatment appear new or certainly a modification of traditional reactions. Today few people are willing to suffer in silence, and that certainly had become true of many Indian groups.

Related to this increased militancy is a gradual strengthening of tribal bonds. Even among native Americans living in major urban centers, there is more likelihood that they identify themselves with their tribe or band now than there was twenty or thirty years ago. In part this resulted from the federal attack on the tribes through termination and relocation. Some of it came from increasing cultural pride because of educational changes which focused more attention on Indian languages, arts, and customs. In part the federal antipoverty programs which helped Indians economically enabled them to strengthen tribal bonds through employment on the reservations. In fact, one scholar dealing with the increasing Indian tribalism claims that the movement owes most of its success to federal programs and money. Claims of tribal sovereignty abound. The Mohawks are the best example of this. They occupy a 6,000-acre tract in New York State and claim absolute sovereignty from both New York State and the United States. This status they maintain goes back to colonial era treaties with Great Britain and later the United States and Canada.

Other native American groups which had long existed in limbo without any tribal status have worked diligently to be recognized as tribes. Obviously part of such a drive is to become eligible for federal funds, which they cannot receive as individuals, but the growing pride in being Indians surely plays a part in this movement too. In New England, for example, several tribal remnants have launched suits against the states claiming lands taken illegally shortly after Independence. The Penobscots and Passamaquoddies reached a tentative settlement with Maine for a tract of some 300,000 acres and a large trust fund. The settlement awaits Congressional action, however, before the funds to put it into motion become available. The nearby Narragansetts sued Rhode Island in 1980, winning their case and through it ownership of some 1,800 acres of land there. The tract they got is of only modest quality, but it makes them eligible for the numerous federal grants and programs now existing.

Clearly federal actions and laws which encouraged self-determination had a major impact on the lives of native Americans during the past two decades. Not all of the legislation had the desired results, however, and some brought about circumstances which not only failed to provide new rights or opportunities, but did the opposite. For example the Civil Rights Act of 1968 did both. By including an equal protection of the law clause it forced changes in how tribes conducted reservation elections, thus reducing Indian control over some local elections. When questions related to religious freedom arose both the courts and Congress strove to resolve them. For example, in the 1959 case *Native American Church v. Navajo Tribal Council*, a federal court held that the rulings of the tribe did not always fall under the guarantees of the Constitution, and because of that tribal authorities could prevent the use of peyote on the reservation. On the other hand, off the reservation the First Amendment promise of freedom of religion was upheld in *People v. Woody*. That 1964 decision upheld Indians' right to use peyote as a part of their worship ceremony.

The 1968 Indian Civil Rights Act did more than protect Indians or expand their rights, however. It opened the door to suits of many types, which native Americans and lawyers alike failed to anticipate. For example during the 1970s Julia Martinez, a member of the Santa Clara Pueblo in New Mexico, brought suit against the tribal government because of a local law which denied membership to her children. She had married outside the tribe, but men of the pueblo who did that did not face the cut off of tribal membership for their children. In its 1978 decision of *Santa Clara Pueblo v. Martinez*, the U.S. Supreme Court held that the Indian Civil Rights Act of a decade earlier had waived tribal sovereignty and immunity, and thus the court stepped in to settle the matter. Although it decided that the Pueblo could indeed determine its membership, it held that eligibility could be based on traditional values and practices even when those proved at variance with general social practices in the rest of the country. Martinez lost her case, but the important result was the entry of federal courts into areas which they had left to the Indians for decades.

In one other area the federal courts provided protection for Indians as individuals and as tribes too. That was in protecting them from the continuing encroachments of state governments. Beginning with termination during the 1950s, western state governments moved rapidly to control many areas of Indian life. They enforced state fishing and hunting regulations, tried to outlaw the use of peyote in religious services, and tried to impose states taxes, particularly on liquor and tobacco sales. In some cases the federal courts accepted this growing state intervention, but in others they rejected it. For example in 1980 in the *White Mountain Apache Tribe v. Bracker* the Supreme Court ruled that the state of Arizona could not impose taxes on non-Indian logging operations on the reservation because the federal government already regulated such activity. In another 1980 decision the court allowed the State of Washington to levy sales taxes on cigarette sales by the Colville Indians to whites and nonreservation Indians. In this instance the courts protected the Indians but also expanded state jurisdiction at least slightly.

Since 1945 the winds of change have swept through American society, and for Indians this has meant many things. There have been changes—in some cases drastic ones. New trends or major modifications of old ones have been mixed with continuing long-standing policies. Certainly termination and relocation can only be understood as modern versions of nineteenth-century programs to bring about forced assimilation. The continuing "special relationship" experienced by tribes and bands with long-term treaty rights remains to complicate present and future actions of both the government and the Indians. Native Americans still enjoy the mixed blessings of being the subject of social reformers' actions. In the past thirty years, however, most reformers have worked with rather than for the Indians, so that the results have been more nearly what native Americans have desired.

Large amounts of both federal and tribal funds continue to be spent on education. For almost the first time Indians have been able to control much of what their young people are taught. Culture, arts, language, and other parts of the curriculum have been more nearly integrated into something which native Americans want and can use effectively. For the past sixty years reservation people have been leaving home to seek jobs, and, with better education, many now have the vocational skills needed to get good-paying work in the cities. Others have been able to work for corporations building factories on or near the reservations. Thus in education and the related field of employment, existing trends continue, but with some obvious changes.

A few trends seem more new than those mentioned above. The most important is the new federal policy of self-determination. True, something like it was tried under John Collier during the 1930s, but even that put native American desires aside much of the time. Now Indians have a broader range of choices than ever before in American history. They still receive federal aid, support, and even regulation, but most of it is theirs to use or not. For example, federal money has been spent by tribes to repurchase lost land. In a few cases people who lacked tribal status as far as the government was concerned have gained such recognition in the past ten years. Instead of disappearing, Indians are increasing, both as individuals and as groups because of federal efforts to be of help without trying to control. Certainly all of the problems have not been solved. All Indians have not been treated as they like or even deserve. Yet American society in the 1980s offers opportunities for native American people rarely even dreamed of in earlier decades. The most striking difference today is that they have a large measure of say in their own present and future. That certainly is a new phenomenon in American history.

## SUGGESTED READING

Few general studies for the post–1945 era exist, but there are some items which are helpful in whole or in part for the issues considered in this chapter. One of these is Wilcomb E. Washburn, *The Indian in America* (New York, 1975), a general treatment of American Indian relations. D'Arcy McNickle, *Native American Tribalism: Indian Survivals and Renewals* (New York, 1973) gives a moderate Indian point of view. Alan L. Sorkin, *The Government and the Indians* (Washington, 1971) and *American Indians and Federal Aid* (Washington, 1973) give a discussion of policy and government actions. Alvin M. Josephy, "Toward Freedom: The American Indian in the Twentieth Century," *Indian Historical Society Lectures, 1970–1971* (Indianapolis, 1971) and the last six articles in Roger L. Nicols, ed., *The American Indian; Past and Present* (New York, 1981) focus on several of the problems considered in the chapter.

For a discussion of termination, see Gary Orfield, *A Study of the Termination Policy* (Denver, 1965) and Deborah Shames, ed., *Freedom With Reservation* (Madison, 1972). Among numerous articles on this topic, see: Susan Hood, "The Termination of the Klamath Indian Tribe of Oregon," *Ethnohistory* 19 (Fall 1972): 379–392 and Nancy Oestreich Lurie, "Menominee Termination: From Reservation to Colony," *Human Organization* 31 (Fall 1972): 257–270.

The relocation program and some of its results are discussed in two general studies, Elaine M. Neils, *Reservation to City* (Chicago, 1971) and Jack O. Waddell and O. Michael Watson, eds., *American Indians in Urban Society* (Boston, 1971). Studies of individual communities include Prafulla Neog, Richard G. Woods, and Arthur M. Harkins, *Indian Americans in Chicago* (Minneapolis, 1970) and James Goodner, *Indian Americans in Dallas* (Minneapolis, 1969). Articles giving a briefer look at some of the same issues are: Joan Ablon, "American Indian Relocation: Problems of Dependence and Management in the City," *Phylon* 24 (Winter 1965): 362–371, Bruce A. Chadwick and Joseph H. Stauss, "The Assimilation of American Indians into Urban Society: The Seattle Case," *Human Organization* 34 (Winter 1975): 359–369, and Arthur Margon, "Indians and Immigrants: A Comparison of Groups New to the City," *The Journal of Ethnic Studies* 4 (Winter 1977): 17–28.

Despite widespread interest in educational developments, practically the only scholarly study available on the subject is Margaret Connell Szasz, *Education and the American Indian* (Albuquerque, 1974). Among the several government-sponsored reports on the topic the best is probably James S. Coleman, et al., *Equality and Educational Opportunity* (Washington, 1966).

Pan-Indian movements are treated in Hazel Hertzberg, *The Search for an American Indian Identity: Modern Pan-Indian Movements* (Syracuse, 1971), but most of this study ends prior to 1960. Actions since then have received much attention. Among the best items are: Rupert Costo, "Alcatraz," *The Indian Historian* 3 (Winter 1970): 4–12, Donald L. Parman, "American Indians and the Bicentennial," *New Mexico Historical Review* 51 (July 1976): 233–246, and Josephy, *Red Power: The American Indian's Fight for Freedom* (New York, 1971).

For Indian views on some of these issues, see: Vine Deloria, Jr., *Custer Died for Your Sins: An Indian Manifesto* (New York, 1969) and *We Talk, You Listen: New Tribes, New Turf* (New York, 1970).

Several scholars consider civil and legal rights of native Americans, including Ralph A. Barney, "Legal Problems Peculiar to Indian Claims Litigation," *Ethnohistory* 2 (Fall 1955): 314–324 and Warren Weston, "Freedom of Religion and the American Indian," *Rocky Mountain Social Science Journal* 2 (March 1965): 1–6.

# Index

The American Indian Experience, A Profile: 1524 to the Present *was copyedited and proofread by Martha Kreger; Brad Barrett served as production editor; development and editorial management by Maureen Hewitt. The book was typeset by G&S Typesetters, Inc., and printed and bound by Edwards Brothers.*

*Cover and book design by Richard Hendel.*